B A S I C
SOCIAL STATISTICS

David Knoke
University of Minnesota

George W. Bohrnstedt
American Institutes for Research

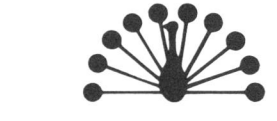

F. E. PEACOCK PUBLISHERS, INC.

To Ted

Cover Painting, *Nineteen*, Laura Ovresat
Proof Positive/Farrowlyne Associates, Inc.

Printing   10   9   8   7   6   5   4

Year   95

Abbreviated Contents

Contents

Preface

And so each venture
Is a new beginning, a raid on the inarticulate
With shabby equipment always deteriorating

T.S. Eliot, *East Coker*

For more than a decade we have been introducing college students to the fundamentals of social statistics. *Basic Social Statistics* is the result of our experiences. Like our earlier book *Statistics for Social Data Analysis* (Bohrnstedt and Knoke, 2nd ed., 1988, F. E. Peacock Publishers), *Basic Social Statistics* covers univariate distributions and bivariate relationships, but unlike that text it does not treat multivariate statistical methods such as multiple regression and path analysis. This book is aimed at the undergraduate taking a first course in social statistics. It should be suitable for anyone having a basic high school algebra background. Mastery of the materials will permit progression to intermediate statistics courses that cover multivariate analysis.

In *Basic Social Statistics* we continue to avoid the usual format of presenting statistics for nominal, ordinal, interval, and ratio levels of measurement. Our focus is on whether a variable is continuous or discrete. We believe our approach is consistent with current practice as exemplified in the major professional journals in social and behavioral sciences.

The nine chapters expose students to the basic principles of social research with statistics. Chapter 1 presents the idea of a social relationship between two variables as a starting point for research. Collecting data on the types of variables is the focus of Chapter 2, which discusses frequency distributions. Chapter 3 presents summary statistics for the central tendencies and variations of univariate distributions for describing, evaluating, and simplifying data. Chapter 4 shows how to evaluate joint outcomes on two variables with two-variable crosstabulations constructed from sample data. This chapter also explains how chi-square tests can be applied to make probabilistic inferences to a population relationship. Chapter 5 describes a variety of measures of association for bivariate crosstabulations. Chapters 6–9 each deal with topics in statistical inference, specifically testing hypotheses about single means, two means, several means, and bivariate correlation and regression.

We treat social statistics as tools for solving research problems that involve the relationships between variables. We continually stress the ways in which statistical tests can help a student decide whether or not an hypothesized relationship exists between two variables and how strong this relationship's covariation is. We avoid excessive proofs and theorems in favor of a hands-on approach to data analysis that uses realistic examples. One strength of this text is that some problems at the end of each chapter are designed to require only pencil-and-paper or hand-held calculators to find a solution, while other problems allow students to work individually with computers using prepared data files of actual social data. We've created two data sets for use as illustrations in the main text and as end-of-chapter problems. The first data set contains 112 variables on 1,466 respondents in the 1987 General Social Survey (GSS), a well-known annual survey of the American adult population. The second data set contains 33 variables on the 50 American states (see Appendix G). Both data sets are available on a floppy diskette from the publisher in the form of SPSS/PC+™ export files.[1] They can be compiled and installed in IBM compatible personal computers or exported to a mainframe computer for students to use on their homework assignments. Further information on these data sets and the use of SPSS to analyze them can be found in our *Instructor's Manual.*

[1]SPSS/PC+ is a trademark of SPSS Inc., of Chicago, Illinois for its proprietary computer software. No materials describing such software may be produced or distributed without the written permission of SPSS Inc.

We are indebted to A. Hald for reprinting the Area Under the Normal Curve and E. S. Pearson and H. O. Hartley for the reprint of the *F* Distribution Table. We are also grateful to the literary executor of the late Sir Ronald A. Fisher, F.R.S., to Dr. Frank Yates, F.R.S., and to the Longman Group Ltd. of London, for permission to reprint Tables III and IV from their book *Statistical Tables for Biological, Agricultural and Medical Research* (6th ed., 1974).

We acknowledge permission from SPSS Inc. to use their software package SPSS/PC+™ throughout the book to illustrate the analysis of survey data with the computer. We also acknowledge cooperation of the National Opinion Research Center and the Roper Opinion Research Center for making available the General Social Surveys.

Any book with technical materials will have some errors. In spite of our best attempt to prevent them, we are certain some will be found. We ask instructors and students to notify us or the publisher if you find errors. We will attempt to correct them in future printings of the book.

We are grateful to Karl Krohn for assistance in data preparation; Gloria DeWolfe for manuscript typing; to Barbara Bessey for unsolicited but invaluable help in proofing; to Kathleen Ermitage and the staff at Proof Positive/Farrowlyne Associates, Inc., for editorial help; and to our publisher F. Edward Peacock for his steadfast support over many years in nurturing our ideas into print. Once again, we thank our wives and children for their forebearance as we wrestled this manuscript into shape.

David Knoke
Minneapolis, Minnesota

George W. Bohrnstedt
Palo Alto, California

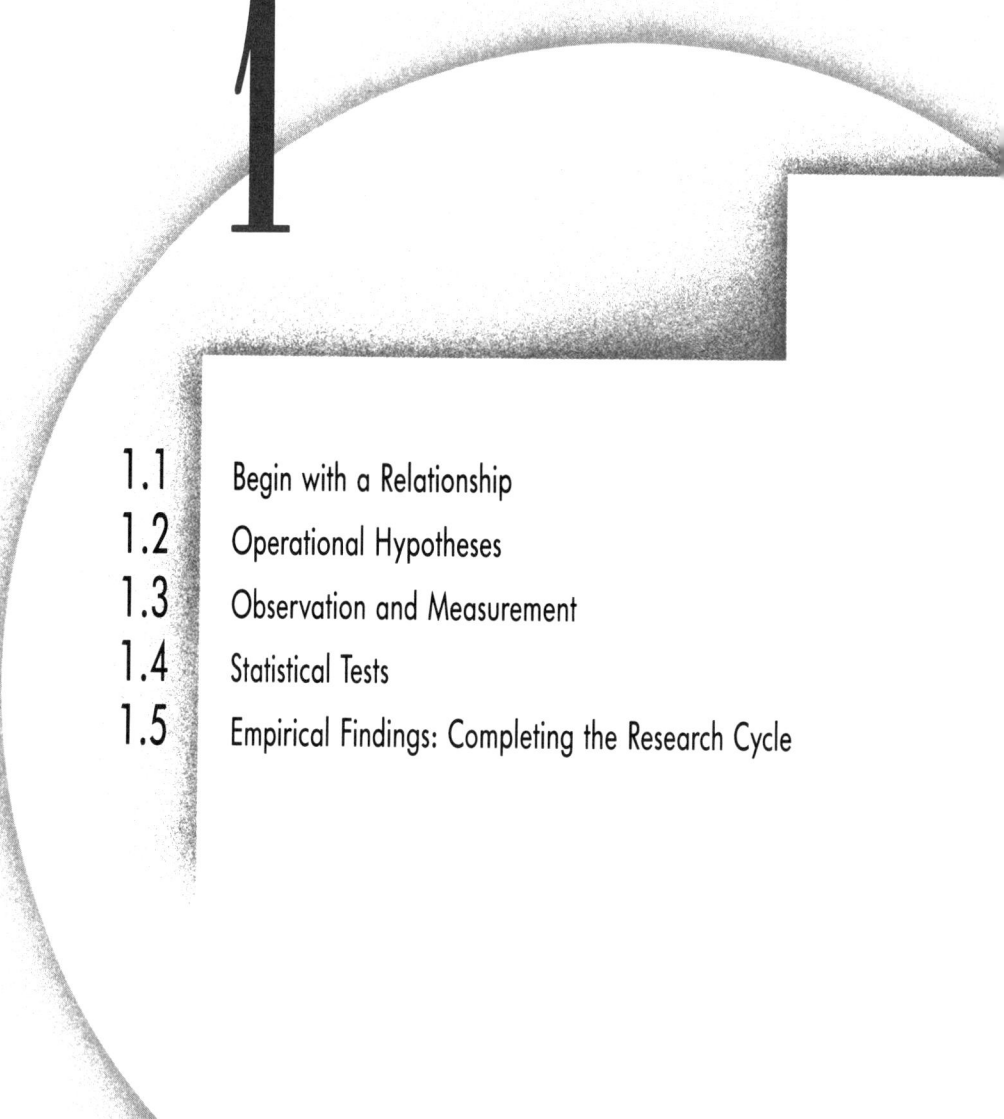

The Social Research Process

Social research is a complex activity that seeks to increase our understanding of human behavior. Whether it is a single observer watching pedestrians in a shopping mall, or the Census Bureau analyzing millions of questionnaires with supercomputers, all researchers collect data to uncover diverse patterns of social thought and action. Some data serve mainly to describe conditions: the number of homes with indoor plumbing, the average time to drive to work, the chances of a home burglary last year. Such "social facts" may be ends in themselves, but more often lead to questions about the relationships between two or more characteristics of persons or groups: Do college graduates earn more in their lifetimes than do high school grads? Do abused children do less well on school tests than those who have not been abused? Who are more productive—Japanese or American auto workers? Answers to these questions require social researchers to make meaningful comparisons among different social variables. In this text, you will learn various methods of analyzing data to reach conclusions about relationships.

To guide our investigations, we follow the idealized research cycle shown in Figure 1.1. Although research can begin at any point, we typically start with a relationship or a set of relationships. A **relationship** may concern current knowledge of or provoke speculation about any aspect of human behavior: the causes of juvenile delinquency, political revolution, voting choice, musical tastes, and so forth. To be used in research, a relationship or a set of relationships must first be translated into

● **relationship**
a connection between two concepts or variables that is the focus of social research

1

precise operational hypotheses. An hypothesis expresses the exact connection that a researcher expects to find among the variables in the data. Hypotheses should be stated in a form that will allow the researcher to reject them as untrue if evidence cannot be found to support the predictions.

Next, a researcher finds suitable subjects or objects, observes the behaviors in question, and records the observations systematically in the form of numerical codes. These records may range from simply counting the number of customers entering a business at different times of the day to elaborate clinical tests for mental illness symptoms. Once the data are recorded, and perhaps stored as electronic codes in a computer, the researcher can use them to test the truth or falsity of the hypotheses. Because data often come from only small samples of all possible observations, methods must be followed that allow meaningful conclusions to be drawn about the larger set of unobserved phenomena. Most of this text deals with the various ways to perform statistical tests to reach conclusions about the operational hypotheses. The research cycle closes when the empirical findings either strengthen or change our knowledge about the original relationship. The process can then begin again with new efforts to extend our understanding. Although the cycle shown in Figure 1.1 is a general image, it fits closely with the order followed by most social researchers. The next sections in this chapter elaborate on each of these features.

1.1   Begin with a Relationship

A relationship that expresses some idea about an event or condition typically serves as the starting point for research. Ideas worthy of serious investigation can come from many sources, including previous research projects, formal theory, conversations with teachers and friends, church sermons, political commentary, newspaper editorials, even casual remarks at the supermarket checkout line. The origin of an idea is less important than the researcher's ability to convert it into a clear proposition about the connection between observable variables; this directs the collection of data that permit a statistical test of the truth about the hypothesized relationship. A **proposition** is a statement asserting a causal connection between two or more concepts. Although all social scientists do not accept this definition, its principles are fairly widely shared, and we will use it in this text. This definition of a proposition has several ele-

● **proposition**
a statement about the causal connection between abstract concepts

The Research Cycle   FIGURE 1.1

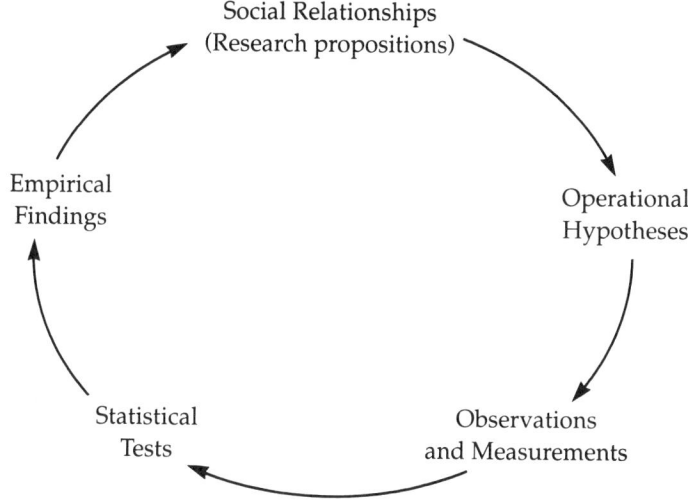

Source: Adapted from Walter Wallace, *The Logic of Science in Sociology* (New York: Aldine de Gruyter). Copyright © 1971 by Walter L. Wallace.

ments. Any proposition can be written in a common language, such as English, or in the more elegant shorthand notations of mathematics or symbolic logic.

A recent Sunday newspaper feature story on cooperative learning in grade schools suggests a testable proposition. Cooperative learning is a technique in which pupils gather, without regard to ability, in groups of three or four at their desks or on the floor. They decide among themselves how to complete a particular assignment, such as solving an arithmetic problem or memorizing a spelling list. The members of each group help one another with little involvement from the teacher. Rather than competing in isolation, the pupils theoretically are not inhibited from expressing their ideas, and they gain self-confidence by working with peers, reinforcing their learning by the need to explain their solutions to others. If this teaching innovation (actually a return to practices of the nineteenth century) does in fact increase pupils' knowledge, then the following proposition should be true:

P1: The more that school children participate in cooperative learning activities, the more they learn about the subject matter.

This book will designate propositions by the initial P and a number, for easy reference. By our own definition, P1 is a proposition because it indicates that a change in one concept — participation in cooperative learning — causes a change in a second concept — subject matter learning. Note that the proposition excludes other causal factors that may affect learning, such as the students' abilities or their parents' encouragement. All other such factors are presumed to have no effect on the relationship that holds true *ceteris paribus* ("everything else equal" — a phrase social scientists often use when stating propositions).

● **concept**
a precise definition of an object, behavior, perception (self or other), or phenomenon that is theoretically relevant

To further elaborate, the concepts in a proposition are the substance of a proposition. A **concept** is a characteristic of an object, behavior, perception of oneself or of others, or any other phenomenon that is relevant to the proposition at hand. Such attributes and actions vary from one object to another (that is, they are not constant). A student can be in a cooperative learning group for a large part of the day, a small part, or not at all. He or she can learn a great deal, a little bit, or nothing at all about the subject matter. Presumably the definition of each concept is known to those social scientists who are reading about or doing research on the proposition. Typically, specialists in some area extensively discuss and argue about concepts, so they arrive at a shared understanding of the terms. Thus social science concepts often have meanings that are not the same as those used in everyday language. For example, *status, power, culture,* and *response* mean quite different things to sociologists, political scientists, anthropologists, and psychologists than they do to persons not involved in the social sciences. To be useful in research, the characteristics that identify a concept must be carefully and rigorously defined. Otherwise two scientists who think they are studying the same social activity may in fact be looking at two quite different things. Obviously such a situation does not favor an orderly increase in knowledge about the social world.

A proposition is more than just a list of concepts. Our definition specifies that a proposition must describe a causal connection between the concepts, either explicitly or implicitly. In P1, participation in a cooperative learning activity is depicted as a *cause* of increased subject matter learning. Presumably, this technique is superior to individualized or competitive studying techniques for raising pupils' knowledge.

A proposition is often meant to apply only under certain conditions or to particular objects. A proposition's **scope conditions** include the specific times and places within which the phenomena supposedly occur. For example, Marx's class struggle theory of historical development was intended to include ancient, medieval, and modern societies. On the other hand, the microeconomic theory of the firm applies only to profitmaking corporations in capitalist societies. In P1, the relationship presumably holds true for all grade-school children anywhere around the world. A proposition's **units of analysis** may be entire societies, nations, complex organizations, communities, small groups, families, individuals, or even personality traits. Each of these objects constitutes a different unit or level of analysis. Propositions that hold true for one unit of analysis may not apply for a different unit. For example, individuals with more education generally turn out to vote in elections more often than people with less education. But, if we shift the unit or level of analysis from the person to the neighborhood, an apparently contradictory pattern emerges: Precincts whose residents have lower average units of education may have higher voting rates than precincts with higher education levels. Perhaps a political party is more active in inner-city areas than in suburban districts, organizing the poorer and less-educated constituents to register and seeing that they show up to vote on election day. No such party machine operates in the better-educated suburbs, so that without active encouragement fewer people bother to vote. In this example, the different relationships between education and voting for different units of analysis become understandable once we take into account a third factor—the activity of a political party organization. Propositions are unfairly tested if research is conducted on the wrong unit of analysis or under improperly defined scope conditions. All may be fair in love and war but not in social research.

- **scope conditions** the times, places, or units of analysis for which a proposition is expected to be valid

- **units of analysis** the general levels of social phenomena that are the objects of observations (e.g., individuals, nations)

1.2   Operational Hypotheses

A proposition does not necessarily contain any directions to researchers about how they should test it. The researcher's first task is to translate a concept's definition into some observable activity or characteristic of the unit of analysis. This observable, or empirical, indicator must faithfully correspond to the intent of the original concept. We could not accept, for example, that an ability to skip rope or shoot a basketball is a good indicator of how much learning took place in a cooperative study group devoted to arithmetic problems! Once each concept in a proposition is matched to a corresponding empirical indicator, we can rewrite the original proposition as an **operational hypothesis** or working hypothesis. Consider P1. In the United States we might decide that a good indicator of cooperative learning participation is the number of minutes per day that a pupil spends working on arithmetic problems in groups with two or three other children. Similarly, the amount of learning could be measured by the scores a child gets on his or her weekly arithmetic quizzes. Of course, other indicators of these two concepts could be found (such as the pupil's homework grades). Clearly, there are many ways to turn an abstract proposition with unobservable concepts into an operational hypothesis that refers to concrete items. But, the process is by no means straightforward and mechanical. Indeed, much argument among social scientists flares up over the best way to state testable hypotheses for a given proposition. However, if there are several indicators of a single concept, and one is presumably as good as another, then hypotheses supported (or rejected) by one set of indicators should also be supported (or rejected) by other sets as well. Hypotheses are strengthened or weakened depending on the use of several indicators of a concept.

By substituting indicators, we can restate P1 as an operational hypothesis. Using the initial *H* instead of *P*, this hypothesis would be stated as follows:

> H1: The more minutes per day that a school child spends working on arithmetic problems in a group of three or four pupils, the higher the score he or she will get on a weekly arithmetic quiz.

The hypothesis tells us what to look for in the research. It indicates not only what specific things to examine, but how these empirical indicators of the concepts relate to one another. To be useful in promoting research on social behavior, propositions must be translated into testable hypotheses; that is, they must be translated into statements about the relationships between *observable* indicators.

● **operational hypothesis**
a proposition restated with observable, concrete referents or terms replacing abstract concepts

A term that is often applied to the indicators in a hypothesis is *variable.* A **variable** is a property or characteristic of persons, objects, or events that differs across persons, objects, or events. Religiosity is a variable: some people are more strongly committed to their church's beliefs, while others have weak or no commitment. Militarization is a variable condition of nations: some have more powerful armies than others. Any property that has only one value cannot be a variable. Instead, it is a **constant,** or a single category of a variable. Female is not a variable but a constant. But, sex (gender) is a variable because there are two categories (male and female) into which cases may be logically sorted. Any time you are in doubt about whether some coding scheme is a variable or a constant, ask yourself, are there two or more other divisions into which I could potentially sort an observation?

● **variable**
a characteristic or attribute of persons, objects, or events that differs in value across persons, objects, or events

● **constant**
a value that does not change

A research scientist is interested in finding social patterns, in particular, regular patterns that are due to causal relationships between variables. A causal relationship assumes that change in one variable creates some predictable change in another variable; one variable precedes the other (its consequent or effect). The prior variable is called the **independent variable,** and the consequent variable is called the **dependent variable.** In its everyday meaning, the term *independent variable* is most suitable to experiments where prior variables can be controlled and manipulated by the researcher. An agricultural experimenter, for example, can freely change the amounts of fertilizer applied to various garden plots (independent variables) and can then observe the growth consequences for plants (dependent variable) for different amounts of fertilizer. In our learning example (H1), the amount of exposure to cooperative learning activity hypothetically causes an increase in subject matter knowledge.

● **independent variable**
a variable that has an antecedent, or causal, role in relation to a dependent variable

● **dependent variable**
a variable that has a consequent, or affected, role in relation to an independent variable

In contrast, many outcomes observed in the social sciences must be assumed to be fixed for a given observation. A person who is chosen for a survey sample has a fixed religious identification, gender, intelligence, education level, and so on. Social scientists cannot change these characteristics in the manner of experimental natural scientists. But, even though many variables thought to exist prior to the observation cannot be manipulated by social science researchers, the term *independent variable* is still used. It points to a factor believed to have a strong connection to the *dependent variable,* that property which is the object of theoretical explanation.

The terms *independent* and *dependent* are widespread in the research literature of the social sciences, and you should be certain to learn the distinction between them. Some examples may help to reinforce the distinction. If we assume that adults' yearly earnings vary by the years of education they had as children and young adults, then earnings is the dependent variable (consequent) and education the independent variable (prior). A causal process operates where more education qualifies people to be selected by employers for higher-paying jobs. But, researchers also apply the terms *independent variables* and *dependent variables* to relationships in which no direct causality is suggested. For example, blacks voting for Democrats and whites voting for Republicans may suggest a connection between a person's race and his or her vote for a presidential candidate. Race does not directly "cause" voting, but the connection arises from a more complicated sequence of history, attitudes and beliefs, socialization, group traditions, and so forth to shape the eventual voting choice. Yet, researchers still refer to race as the independent variable in this relationship, because it occurs prior to the vote and it is a major social condition that affects the other, more proximate, causes of the vote. Our research effort is designed to determine how strong the connection is between an independent and dependent variable, regardless of whether or not we think of that connection in directly causal terms.

1.3   Observation and Measurement

After translating a proposition's concepts into operational hypotheses, the next step in the research cycle is to make observations and measurements. To do this, a social researcher must pick an **operation**—a method for observing and recording those characteristics of persons, objects, or events that are relevant to testing a hypothesis. Researchers have invented and developed a wide variety of operations to meet different research needs. Entire volumes have been written on various forms and methods of data collection: historical records and archival documents, pottery shards and artifacts, participant observations, survey and questionnaire responses, content analyses of verbal exchanges, unobtrusive observations, videotapes, automatic experimental tabulations, brain-wave and galvanic skin responses. The list is potentially endless, limited only by social scientific imagination and boldness. Many operations are rou-

● **operation**
any method for observing and recording those aspects of persons, objects, or events that are relevant to testing a hypothesis

tine, widely shared sets of activities. The forms in which observations are recorded are quite diverse, ranging from rambling raw field notes in participant-observer studies to the highly specialized numerical coding schemes of small-group interactions in laboratory settings.

Observations and measurements are distinct steps, though we show them together in the diagram of the research cycle in Figure 1.1. The researcher first decides how observations are to be made on variables in the hypotheses. Once these observations are made, the researcher must decide how to assign numbers to the information collected so that statistical analyses of that data become possible. Assigning numbers to observations by using specific rules is called **measurement.** Reducing observations to a numerical coding system lets researchers use mathematical methods to test whether the hypothesized relationship between variables is true or false.

● **measurement**
the assignment of numbers to observations according to a set of rules

The types of numbers that can be attached to observations depend on what the researcher believes are the underlying features of the object under study. There are two broad measurement types: discrete and continuous.

Discrete variables classify persons, objects, or events by the kind or quality of their attributes. The simplest discrete measure is the *dichotomy*, in which observations are classified only according to whether the defining attribute is present or absent. Typically one category is coded as "1" for present and the other category as "0" for absent. Examples are dead or not dead, male or not male, black or not black. Other discrete attributes are *multicategorical* (or polychotomous); that is, there are more than two possible outcomes. Examples include the following: hair color is specified as blond, brunette, or redhead; Americans live in 50 states; immigrants come from 150 countries of national origin. Multicategory coding for a classification involving N different categories usually assigns the integer "1" to the first category on the list and concludes with N for the last. We can further sort discrete variables by whether or not their categories are orderable. **Orderable discrete variables** have categories that can be ranked from low to high, or the reverse. An example of an orderable discrete variable is "How well is President Bush doing his job?" The response categories might be excellent, good, fair, or poor. These ordered responses might be coded 4, 3, 2, and 1, respectively, to represent high to low levels of job performance. **Nonorderable discrete variables** cannot be ranked. Examples include race, ethnicity, gender, and national origin.

● **discrete variables**
variables that classify persons, objects, or events according to the kind or quality of their attributes

● **orderable discrete variables**
discrete measures in which the categories are arranged from smallest to largest, or vice versa

● **nonorderable discrete variables**
discrete measures in which the sequence of categories cannot be meaningfully ordered

Here the numbers assigned to categories are arbitrary and do not represent greater or lesser magnitudes. Thus, male and female might be coded 0 and 1, but just as well could be coded 2 and 1.

● **continuous variables**
variables that, in theory, can take on all possible numerical values in a given interval

Continuous variables classify persons, objects, or events by the quantity or amount of their attributes. The numerical codes assigned have precise meanings that designate the magnitude of the characteristic present in the specific case. The main difference between continuous and discrete variables is that continuous measures allow for fractional numeric values, but discrete measures do not. In principle, a continuous variable can be measured to any desired degree of precision, while a discrete variable is always limited to an integer number of categories. In the natural sciences, such as physics and chemistry, continuous variables are common: mass, height, time, velocity, and so on. Social scientists also assume that many of their concepts are continuous, for example, sexual attractiveness, industrialization, and musical ability. Although these concepts are clearly continuous, their operational measures often only approximate this goal. Social researchers must rely on imprecise survey questionnaires, attitude rating scales, and so on. These measurement devices scarcely approach the precision of physicists' beam scales and electron microscopes. As a result, much greater measurement error occurs in the social compared to the physical sciences. Nevertheless, percentages and proportions do serve as continuous measures. Examples are the percentage of 18-year-olds who have smoked marijuana, the annual rate of small business bankruptcies, and the proportion of state residents voting in an election.

● **mutual exclusiveness**
a property of a classification system that places each observation in one and only one category of a variable

● **exhaustiveness**
a property of a classification system that provides sufficient categories so that all observations can be located in some category

For both continuous and discrete measures, observations must be assigned to categories that are *both* mutually exclusive and exhaustive. **Mutual exclusiveness** refers to the need to place each observation in one and only one of the variable's categories. **Exhaustiveness** means that enough categories must exist for every observation to be put into some category. For example, if a measure of religious identification used only Protestant, Catholic, and Baptist categories, the mutual exclusiveness criterion would be violated, because Baptists are also Protestants. If only the Catholic and Protestant categories were used, then the exhaustiveness criterion would be violated, because no categories exist for Jews and Buddhists. A better scheme for this variable might be "Catholic, Protestant, Jew, other, or not ascertained." For some purposes an even better approach might be to break the large Protestant category into several subcategories for major denominations, such as Baptist, Methodist, Lutheran, and so forth.

While "other," "not determined," or "uncertain" are convenient and often necessary categories for recording observations, statistical models assume that objects classified the same way are in fact identical or nearly identical in how they relate to other variables. For this reason, social scientists try to use detailed, well-thought-out measurement categories. As much as possible, they avoid lumping together many dissimilar outcomes into a single "other" category.

1.4   Statistical Tests

After observation and measurement, a researcher's next step in the research cycle is making statistical tests or calculations. We will not say much about statistical analysis in this chapter, because the rest of the book examines various techniques in detail. If you find yourself somewhat confused by the number of terms introduced in this chapter, do not be too concerned. They will be elaborated on in later chapters. As a brief introduction, however, two broad types of statistics can be noted: **descriptive statistics** and **inferential statistics.**

Single variables may be *described* according to their numerical properties. Newspaper and TV accounts use such figures as *averages* (mean rainfall for June, average take-home pay for workers), *rates* (annual unemployment rate, monthly rate of inflation), *proportions* (percentage of blacks earning over $30,000, proportion of first marriages ending in divorce), and *frequency counts* (populations of the largest states, number of intercontinental missiles stockpiled by major powers). Such descriptive statistics form the bedrock for more advanced techniques.

The core of our approach to statistics as tools for data analysis is the analysis of *relationships* between two or more variables. The relationships to be analyzed are indicated by the operational hypotheses. An entire branch of descriptive statistics is concerned with **measures of association** or *covariation* among variables. These methods allow a researcher to decide if the data support such operational hypotheses as, "The more years of formal schooling, the more income people earn," or,

● **descriptive statistics** numbers that describe features of a set of observations; examples are percentages, modes, variances, and correlations

● **inferential statistics** numbers that represent generalizations, or inferences, drawn about some characteristic of a population, based on evidence from a sample of observations from the population

● **measures of association** statistics that show the direction and/or magnitude of a relationship between variables

"The greater the test anxiety, the lower the test performance." Measures of association are intended to reveal the strength of covariation among variables that are discrete, continuous, or both. Many of these statistics are *standardized* to a common scale that ranges between no association (0) and perfect association (1.0). Standardization allows a relationship to be compared when two or more samples involve different sizes and when their variables are measured on different scales. For example, we might hypothesize that years of education better predict the earned incomes of women than of men. On the other hand, we might ask whether attitudes about foreign aid covary by political party identification more strongly among Americans or among Germans. In both these examples, the basic use of a measure of association is to discover how well our knowledge about one variable helps us to predict the value of a second variable.

● **sample**
a subset of cases or elements selected from a population

● **population**
a set of persons, objects, or events having at least one common attribute allowing a researcher to generalize on the basis of a representative sample of observations

● **inference**
the process of making generalizations or drawing conclusions about the attributes of a population from evidence contained in a sample

● **random sample**
a sample whose cases or elements are selected at random from a population

Much social research is conducted with a **sample** or a limited number of observations, rather than with an entire **population** of persons, objects, or events. Typically, a researcher collects data only on some small portion of all the existing units of analysis, but would like to conclude something about the larger group from which the sample data came. Because selecting a sample involves an element of chance—what gets into or gets left out of the sample is a probability process—a researcher cannot simply conclude that the sample findings hold for the population. A different sample drawn from the same population might have resulted in different findings. An entire statistical field studies the problem of **inference**, or making generalizations from a sample's descriptive statistics to a population's parameters. These techniques are based on the laws of probability.

For example, suppose that a researcher wanted to know how well you could spell, or how many of the 500,000 words in the English language you know. Obviously, you could not be asked to try to spell every word or give a definition of each one. The population of words is too large. But it is possible to estimate how many words are in your vocabulary or your spelling skills by testing you with a **random sample** of just a few dozen words selected to represent all the words in an unabridged dictionary. If the sample is random and sufficiently large, the number of correct answers you give on the test lets the researcher make an inference about how you might perform if the impossible test were conducted on the entire word population. Along with descriptive statistics and measures of association, this book will expose you to the variety of useful inferential statistics. These statistics help a social scientist to decide whether sample findings can be generalized to the population from which the sample was taken.

Statistical inference cautions researchers to distrust their results. Consider again proposition P1 and hypothesis H1 about the effect of cooperative learning activities on pupils' arithmetic learning. Suppose a well-designed experiment finds that children involved in cooperative learning do better on arithmetic tests than do students taught the same material with more traditional methods, such as individualized and competitive learning. These results might be found across many replications of the experiment. Still, the researchers should not conclude that the cooperative learning technique has been conclusively proven to be superior. A single experiment in which the cooperative method failed to produce the hypothesized results would cast doubt on its unqualified truth. And, because even very elaborate experimental designs cannot include all possible combinations of pupils, subject matter, instructor experience, and so on, the possibility remains—no matter how remote and improbable—that one day the hypothesis might not be supported.

Later in this book we will show how the probabilities of error are taken into account in statistical tests. Here we consider only the basic strategy of hypothesis testing. Research cannot be conducted under all the relevant conditions for all the relevant populations (it is not possible to do research on the past or the future, for example). Given these limits, researchers would be foolish to base their scientific criterion in the notion that statistical tests *prove* the existence of a hypothesized relationship. A better criterion is to state operational hypotheses in a form capable of *rejection* by statistical tests. The hypothesis that we wish to reject, or to nullify, is called the *null hypothesis*. It is usually stated as the exact opposite of the research hypothesis, which is the one we believe to be more accurate. If we succeed in rejecting the null hypothesis as contrary to the empirical evidence, then we have strengthened the credibility of the research hypothesis. If we can reject the null in favor of the research hypothesis across several repeated investigations, then we have even greater evidence favoring our preferred proposition. A hypothesis that has not been disproved in many studies, under many conditions, has much greater truth value than a relationship that is supported by only a single study. The important point is that rejection is much easier than proof in science, and for this reason the truth of a theory is best found by trying to show that it is false and then failing to do so.

1.5   Empirical Findings: Completing the Research Cycle

Statistical tests show whether or not the operational hypotheses, stated as null hypotheses, should be rejected. If the test results do not permit a research scientist to reject the hypothesis, confidence increases in the proposition's truth value, at least for the population studied. If the findings cause the hypothesis to be rejected, and the scientist has great confidence that the sample results agree with the true population situation, then belief in the truth of the proposition will be severely shaken. Indeed, a researcher may want to modify the proposition to account for the research results. In effect such changes produce a new proposition, although the family resemblance to the now-discredited proposition may still be strong. This feedback of research findings completes the cycle that began with the proposition in Figure 1.1.

The research cycle is a highly idealized simplification of what may be a very complex process in which many researchers work on a single social problem with minimal coordination of their activities. We believe this idealized cycle captures the basic spirit of social research, but the best way for you to find out what research entails is by trying to do some research yourself.

> There is no simple substitute for direct experience in trying to understand what any social activity is all about. We have designed this book to give you hands-on experience by doing research through the analysis of actual data.

If you follow our examples and try to replicate them on topics of your choice, you will gain a greater insight into the research process than you could by merely reading about how others have done their research. Indeed, the research reports in professional journals do not tell very much about the hard work, false starts, raised expectations, shattered hopes, doldrums, and breakthroughs that typically occur on the way to discovering a few gems of social behavior. By applying statistical methods to already collected data, this book exposes you to the heart of the research cycle—that point where we find out whether our beliefs about social reality stated in the hypotheses have any empirical support. From our own experiences in learning to become social scientists (a learning experience that is never completed, as we find out every time we revise this book), *doing* social research can be an exhilarating or a frustrating experience—usually both! Although you may experience neither extreme, you are certain to gain great insight into a very important activity of our society.

Key Concepts

These concepts are listed in the order of appearance in the chapter. Combined with the definitions in the margins, these will help you review the material and can serve as a self-test for mastery of the concepts.

relationship
proposition
concept
scope conditions
units of analysis
operational hypothesis
variable
constant
independent variable
dependent variable
operation
measurement
discrete variables

orderable discrete variables
nonorderable discrete
   variables
continuous variables
mutual exclusiveness
exhaustiveness
descriptive statistics
inferential statistics
measures of association
sample
population
inference
random sample

PROBLEMS

General Problems

1. Are each of the following statements propositions? Why or why not?

   a. The greater the amount of time spent studying, the higher the course grade a college student receives.

    b. Study time includes the number of hours spent reviewing lecture notes, reading assignments, and discussing course content with other students in a class.

    c. The higher a student's average course grades upon graduation, the larger the salary earned in the first job.

2. In each statement of Problem 1, identify the concept(s) and their relationships to one another.

3. Make a simple causal proposition using the following concepts: watching violent TV programs; support for capital punishment.

4. Give three operational definitions of the concept of *social power* that could be used in a research project on public policy influence by groups in American cities.

5. Identify the following as either variables or constants:

    a. Honda Civic   e. box office appeal
    b. annual income   f. Toledo
    c. city size   g. gross national product
    d. Sylvester Stallone   h. engine horsepower

6. Identify the independent and dependent variables in the following hypotheses:

    a. The larger the profits to be made from illegal drug sales, the greater the number of persons who will become smugglers and dealers.

    b. The closer the competition between two candidates for office, the higher the voter turnout on election day.

    c. Church attendance is higher among older than among younger persons.

7. Indicate which of the following variables are continuous, orderable discrete, or nonorderable discrete:

    a. Homework: amount of time spent doing course assignments

    b. Club membership: belonging to a fraternity, sorority, service, or sports club

    c. Olympic medal: gold, silver, bronze

    d. College major: English, chemistry, music, sociology

    e. Minority composition: percentage of city residents who are Asian, Black, and Hispanic

    f. Health status: excellent, good, fair, poor

    g. Unemployment: nearest number of weeks without a job

    h. Winning time: minutes and seconds to cross goal line

8. a. What measurement criteria are violated if only the fol-
        lowing categories are used to record respondents'
        ethnicity?

    (1) English   (4) African
    (2) Italian   (5) Vietnamese
    (3) European   (6) Mexican

    b. What changes would you suggest?

9. Finish the following statements:

    a. Most social research is based on _____ of
        observations, rather than on _____.
    b. The truth of a theory is best found by trying to show
        that it is _____ and failing to do so.
    c. Statistics that measure relationships among variables
        are _____.
    d. The statistical field that studies how one makes gener-
        alizations from descriptive statistics to population
        parameters is _____.

10. How do the results of a statistical analysis of data affect
    a social scientist's theoretical knowledge?

Frequency Distributions

Social scientists usually collect data to test hypothesized relationships between two or more variables. The results of these tests, which are performed with the various statistical procedures that we will introduce to you throughout this text, determine whether the operational hypotheses under study should be rejected or supported, as we noted in Chapter 1.

2.1 Constructing a Frequency Distribution

A preliminary step in data collection is to determine the number of observations in each response category for the variables. Suppose we want to learn how satisfied Americans are with their family's incomes. First, we choose a random sample of 86 adults living in non-southern states. (These cases were actually drawn as a subsample from the 1987 General Social Survey (GSS); see Box 2.1.) Next, we make a **tally** of the number of persons saying that they are "pretty well satisfied," "more or less satisfied," and "not satisfied at all." We use the tally results to construct a **frequency distribution,** which is a table of the **outcomes,** or response categories, of a variable and the number of times each outcome is observed in the sample. For this example, Table 2.1 shows there are 22 pretty well satisfied, 42 more or less satisfied, and 22 not satisfied respondents in the

● **tally**
a count of the frequency of outcomes observed for a variable or the frequency of joint outcomes of several variables

● **frequency distribution**
a table of the outcomes of a variable and the number of times each outcome is observed in a sample

● **outcomes**
response categories of variables

Box 2.1   General Social Survey

The General Social Surveys, begun in 1972 under the guidance of James A. Davis, then director of the National Opinion Research Center, combine a data diffusion project and a social indicator research program. Funded originally on an annual basis from 1972–91 (except for 1979 and 1981) by the National Science Foundation, the GSS conducts interviews with a cross-section sample of about 1,500 adult Americans during the spring season. In interviews lasting about an hour and a half, questions are asked on a variety of topics, including occupational and labor force participation, family situation, social activity, religion, leisure, political behavior, attitudes on race relations, sexual behavior, violence, political institutions, life satisfaction, childrearing, women's roles, and abortion. Some permanent items appear in every survey, while other items rotate: two years on and one year off. The more recent surveys use a complex three-form interview that allows most items to appear every year for two-thirds of the sample.

The data have been compiled into a comprehensive file for the first 18 surveys, having more than 27,000 respondents. They provide a cornucopia of high-quality information that is available at cost (for computer tape and codebook) to the general public and the academic community. The GSS program has resulted in hundreds of scholarly research publications and literally thousands of student classroom projects.

The GSS uses sampling design and interview specifications that are too complex to discuss here. Details may be found in Appendixes A and B of the GSS *Cumulative Codebook*, which advise that "investigators who have applied statistical tests to previous data should continue to apply those tests." Our purpose in using the GSS is mainly illustrative, and we will of course apply various statistical tests to this data.

For many of the text examples and for chapter problems requiring use of the computer, we have created an SPSS/PC+ data file with 112 variables from the 1987 GSS. This data set is available on a floppy diskette from the publisher. It can be compiled and installed in IBM compatible personal computers for classroom or research use.

non-southern sample. On this basis, we conclude that as many non-southern Americans are financially satisfied as unsatisfied, while almost half the sample falls in between these extremes.

While this is a perfectly reasonable conclusion, scientists generally are interested in how the frequencies of a distribution are related, since they want to be able to compare the results from one sample with those of other samples. For purposes of comparison, suppose we also study the South by sampling 33 persons from that region. If we were also to find 22 pretty satisfied respondents, this would be a much larger proportion than 22 respondents in the sample of 86 non-Southerners. To see this difference clearly, we must examine the relative frequency or proportion of cases for each outcome of the variable of interest. **Relative frequencies,** or **proportions,** are formed by dividing the cases associated with each outcome by the total number of cases. In the non-South the proportion of pretty satisfied persons is 22/86 = .256, of somewhat satisfied is 42/86 = .488, and of not satisfied is 22/86 = .256. We can again conclude that non-Southerners have a much higher proportion somewhat satisfied than at either extreme. Now, however, comparisons across different size samples will be easier to make and more meaningful using relative proportions. (As we shall see later, the proportions among Southerners *do* differ from the non-Southerners, with .212 pretty satisfied, .485 somewhat satisfied, and .303 not satisfied among the 33 southern cases.)

● **relative frequencies (proportions)** numbers formed by dividing the cases associated with an outcome of a variable by the total number of cases

2.1.1   Percentage Distributions

Percentages created for the proportion of each outcome provide a more familiar interpretation of these findings. **Percentages** are created by multiplying each proportion by 100. For example, the percentage of non-Southerners who are pretty satisfied is (.256) (100) = 25.6%. By calculating percentages we *standardize* for sample size by indicating the number of observations that would fall into each outcome of a variable if the total number of cases were 100.

● **percentages** numbers created by multiplying proportions by 100

Percentages usually are arrayed in a **percentage distribution.** The frequency data from the tally in Table 2.1, for example, are displayed in a percentage table as shown in Table 2.2.

● **percentage distribution** a distribution of relative frequencies or proportions in which each entry has been multiplied by 100

If we had 100 persons in the non-Southern sample, 25.6 would be pretty satisfied. Since it makes no sense to consider six-tenths of a person, we can do one of two things. First, we could round our results up or down. Convention varies on how

TABLE 2.1   Frequency Distribution: Family Financial Satisfaction of Non-Southern Respondents

Financial satisfaction	Tally	Frequency
Pretty satisfied	⊬⊤ ⊬⊤ ⊬⊤ ⊬⊤ ‖	22
More or less satisfied	⊬⊤ ⊬⊤ ⊬⊤ ⊬⊤ ⊬⊤	
	⊬⊤ ⊬⊤ ⊬⊤ ‖	42
Not satisfied	⊬⊤ ⊬⊤ ⊬⊤ ⊬⊤ ‖	22
Total		86

Source: 1987 General Social Survey.

to do this, but generally values of 0.1 to 0.4 are rounded down to the next whole number, and values of 0.5 to 0.9 are rounded up. (Rules for rounding are given in Section 2.4.2) Thus, we conclude that 26 of every 100 persons in our non-southern sample are pretty satisfied, 49 are more or less satisfied, and 26 are not satisfied. (Note that the total is now 101, due to "rounding error.") Second, we could multiply each percentage by 10 and say that *if* we had observed 1,000 persons, we would expect 256 to be pretty satisfied, 488 more or less satisfied, and 256 not satisfied.

With either procedure, an important point is evident: Whenever data are summarized, some distortion almost always occurs. What we gain in understanding and interpretation, however, usually makes this distortion acceptable. It is easier to comprehend that 25.6% of non-Southerners are pretty satisfied than to make sense of the fact that 22 out of 86 respondents are pretty satisfied. For this reason statisticians and researchers quickly get used to the idea of dealing with rough percentages of persons.

To aid discussions about frequencies and relative frequencies, a shorthand notation is used. In this system, N denotes the total sample size (in the non-southern example, $N = 86$). And f_i denotes the number of cases or the frequency associated with the ith outcome (category) of a variable. The subscript i assumes values from 1 to the number of categories that code the variable.

Percentage Distribution: Family Financial Satisfaction of Non-Southern Respondents

TABLE 2.2

Financial satisfaction	Frequency (f)	Percentage
Pretty satisfied	22	25.6
More or less satisfied	42	48.8
Not satisfied	22	25.6
Total	86	100.0

Source: 1987 General Social Survey.

In our example, if we code pretty satisfied = 1, more or less satisfied = 2, and not satisfied = 3, then f_1 = 22 (there are 22 pretty satisfied in the sample), f_2 = 42, and f_3 = 22. Notice that the second column of Table 2.2 is labeled f, and it gives the number of cases associated with each category of satisfaction. The sum of the frequencies associated with each outcome equals the total sample size.

$$f_1 + f_2 + f_3 = N$$

With the values for the non-southern sample, the equation is as follows:

$$22 + 42 + 22 = 86$$

In the notation system, p_i denotes the *proportion* of cases in the *i*th outcome of a variable. Following is the formula for finding this proportion:

$$p_i = \frac{f_i}{N}$$

In the non-southern sample, as we saw earlier, the proportion pretty satisfied is p_1 = 22/86 = 0.256. Similarly, p_2 = 42/86 = 0.488, and p_3 = 22/86 = 0.256.

The sum of proportions must always equal 1.00 (except for any rounding error). This is easy to show.

$$p_1 + p_2 + p_3$$

$$= \frac{f_1}{N} + \frac{f_2}{N} + \frac{f_3}{N}$$

$$= \frac{(f_1 + f_2 + f_3)}{N}$$

$$= \frac{N}{N} = 1.00$$

Because a percentage is simply a proportion multiplied by 100, it also follows that the sum of the percentages associated with each outcome must total 100%. The last column in Table 2.2 verifies this fact.

Now suppose we want to know if the distribution of financial satisfaction is the same among Southerners as among non-Southerners. To begin, we choose a random subsample of southern respondents. In the 1987 GSS, the sampling procedure that selected the 86 non-southern respondents also selected 33 respondents living in southern states. The different subsample sizes reflect the fact more Americans live outside the South. The results of the GSS question on financial satisfaction in both regions are shown as a frequency distribution in Table 2.3.

TABLE 2.3

Family Financial Satisfaction Frequencies in the Non-South and the South

Financial satisfaction	Non-South	South
Pretty satisfied	22	7
More or less satisfied	42	16
Not satisfied	22	10
Total	86	33

Source: 1987 General Social Survey.

Clearly, the non-southern sample has more pretty satisfied respondents than the southern sample (22 versus 7), but it is not immediately clear just by looking at Table 2.3 whether or not the non-South has *relatively* more satisfaction than the South. To answer this question we need to look at the standardized distributions for the two regions (the *percentages* shown in Table 2.4). The South has *relatively* fewer pretty satisfied (21.2% vs. 25.6%), slightly more not satisfied (30.3% vs. 25.6%), and almost the same percentage more or less satisfied (48.5% vs. 48.8%).

> Whenever one data set is compared to another, the most meaningful comparisons usually can be made by examining the relative frequencies or the percentages of the various outcomes. This principle of data analysis is so basic that social scientists take it for granted: To compare two or more distributions, relative rather than absolute frequencies should be used. This basic principle is underscored by the fact that scientists usually compare two or more distributions; they are rarely interested only in a single distribution. Indeed, science can be thought of as the attempt to explain why two or more distributions differ from one another.

Family Financial Satisfaction Percentages in the Non-South and the South

TABLE 2.4

Financial satisfaction	Non-South	South
Pretty satisfied	25.6%	21.2%
More or less satisfied	48.8	48.5
Not satisfied	25.6	30.3
Total	100.0%	100.0%
(*N*)	(86)	(33)

Source: 1987 General Social Survey.

Note that the two percentage distributions shown in Table 2.4 are calculated within each category of region. We could have reversed the procedure and calculated the percentages of non-South and South within each of the three categories of financial satisfaction, but we did not do so because we felt it would not be meaningful. The reason for our choice lies in the distinction between independent and dependent variables made in Chapter 1. We identify region of residence as a cause or condition affecting financial satisfaction and hence treat it as the independent variable. In other words, it makes more sense to assume that the place where one lives and works influences one's current financial situation (and hence one's satisfaction), than to assume that current financial satisfaction influences the choice of region (although past dissatisfaction might cause migration to another region). Therefore we treat region of current residence as the independent variable and financial satisfaction as the dependent variable. And, when two or more variables are considered together, we always calculate percentages within categories of the independent variable. We discuss this principle again in Chapter 3.

Our finding that GSS respondents living in different regions have different levels of financial satisfaction might present a new starting point for research. Further analyses could examine why Southerners have relatively less satisfaction with their families' financial situations than do people living in other regions. A sociologist or economist might develop propositions involving additional social relationships believed to be connected to region and financial satisfaction. For example, such variables as the extent of industrial unionization, subjective expectations of earnings, racial differences in employment, or patterns of working spouses each could explain some of the regional differences. Before considering such multiple variable approaches, however, you must acquire a solid foundation in basic statistical data analysis techniques.

2.2   Frequency Distributions for Discrete Measures

We are now ready to examine frequency distributions using the entire 1987 GSS sample data. Relative frequency distributions for three variables are shown in Table 2.5. The genders

Percentage Distributions in General Social Survey for Gender, Marital Status, and Church Attendance

TABLE 2.5

Gender		Marital status		Church attendance	
Male	43.7%	Married	54.6%	Never	11.8%
Female	56.3	Widowed	11.4	Less than once a year	6.6
		Divorced	11.6	Once or twice a year	14.0
Total	100.0%	Separated	3.5	Several times a year	15.8
(N = 1,466)		Never married	18.8	About once a month	8.0
				2–3 times a month	10.1
		Total	100.0%	Nearly every week	5.2
		(N = 1,466)		Every week	20.3
				Several times a week	7.4
				Don't know, no answer	0.8
				Total	100.0%
				(N = 1,466)	

Source: 1987 General Social Survey.

of the 1,466 respondents were determined by the interviewer at the beginning of the interview. Marital status was obtained by asking each respondent, "Are you currently married, widowed, divorced, separated, or have you never been married?" To measure church attendance, the respondents were asked, "How often do you attend religious services?" Nine categories of increasing frequency were offered for their responses. They were not explicitly offered "don't know" as a choice. That response was recorded by the interviewer only if it was volunteered by a respondent.

These three measures are *discrete variables*, which classify observations only according to the *quality* or kind of person, event, or object (see Chapter 1). The response categories associated with gender, marital status, and church attendance are clearly *not* continuous, because they do not classify respondents according to magnitude or *quantity* of the response. However, church attendance is an *ordered discrete variable*, in the sense that the rate of participation increases from one category to the next, while both gender and marital status have no intrinsic order to the sequence in which the categories can be displayed. Variables

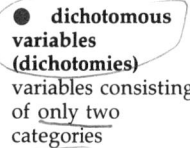

● **dichotomous variables (dichotomies)**
variables consisting of only two categories

with only two categories are called **dichotomous variables,** or **dichotomies.** Gender—male or female—is an example of a dichotomy.

So few responses or outcomes are associated with the gender and marital status measures that you can easily see that in 1987 a majority of GSS respondents classified by gender were women. Also, a majority of those classified by marital status were married. But, the largest category for the church attendance measure is not so obvious, as none contains a majority of the cases. Church attendance is coded in great detail in the GSS, and some categories have fewer than 100 cases in 1987. Variables with large numbers of categories often prove unwieldy for analysis and interpretation. By combining some logically similar groups together and using a residual category for unclassifiable persons ("not codable"), we can reduce the number of categories to a more manageable number. (Rules for deciding how many categories to use when recoding are given in Section 2.4, which describes frequency distributions with continuous data, and in Box 2.2.)

The recoded results for church attendance appear in Table 2.6, which has only five categories. Following the mutually exclusive and exhaustive criteria for assigning categories stated in Chapter 1, we have recoded categories on the basis of presumed similarity (e.g., less than yearly, once per year, and several times per year were recoded into a single "annually" category). Even after recoding, however, none of the new categories contain a majority of the cases. The result clarifies that Americans' church attendance patterns are split into two segments of roughly equal size: those who attend on a weekly basis (32.9%) and those who go only a few times per year (36.4%). Those who never attend and those going to services on a monthly basis are distinct minorities.

2.2.1   Techniques for Displaying Data: Tables and Bar Charts

● **statistical tables**
numerical displays which either summarize data or present the results of data analyses

In this chapter the tables of frequency distribution illustrate one way to display data and present quantitative information in a clear, precise manner. **Statistical tables** are an important means of scientific communication, and some rules for constructing them are given in Box 2.3.

Box 2.2   Rules for Recoding and Rounding

Recoding Rules

1. The more measurement precision, the better; so do not group categories together if only a few exist in the original measure.
2. Choose a measurement interval that is small enough to avoid distortion of the original distribution of observations, but large enough to avoid too many categories that conceal the underlying distribution shape.
3. The number of intervals for presenting data in frequency distributions should be somewhere between 6 and 20; a larger number of categories generally cannot be grasped by the reader.

Rounding Rules

1. Significant digits ending in 1 to 4 are rounded down by leaving the digit to the left unchanged.
2. Digits ending in 6 to 9 are rounded up by increasing the digit to the left by 1.
3. Numbers ending in 5 are allocated alternatively; the first number ending in 5 is rounded down, the second is rounded up, the third is rounded down, and so on.
4. Never round past the original unit of measurement or degree of measurement precision.

Following are several examples of rounding 999.52 and 999.37:

Unit of Measurement	Original Number	Rounded Number
Dollars	999.52	1,000
Dollars	999.37	999
Hundreds of dollars	999.52	10
Hundreds of dollars	999.37	10
Thousands of dollars	999.52	1
Thousands of dollars	999.37	1

Box 2.3   Statistical Tables

Statistical tables are a basic tool of the social scientist's trade. The arts of constructing tables and reading and interpreting them can best be learned, as are all crafts, by much practice. Some basic pointers on how to communicate findings through tables are given here.*

Tables come in two basic forms: those that display raw data and those that present analyses. Raw data tables contain frequencies or counts of observations classified in various ways, such as the number of burglaries reported in each of 50 neighborhoods last year, or the number of homicides classified according to familiarity between murderer and victim in each of eight regions of the United States. Analytic tables display the consequences of some manipulation of the data by a researcher that claims to give an interpretation of the process producing the raw data. Such tables are highly varied and may range from simple percentages of raw data to systems of nonlinear simultaneous equations for complex mathematical models.

Each table begins with a heading, usually the word *Table,* an identifying number, and a brief phrase describing its central contents. Examples from a recent issue of the *American Sociological Review* are the following:

Table 1. Regression Analyses of Cumulative Net Colonization on Long Wave, Imperial, Hegemony, War, Socialist, Population, and Time Trend Variables

Table 2. Zero-Order Correlations among Three Positional Power Variables 1963–77

Table 3. Mean Frequency of Self-Reported Delinquency by Dichotomized Strain Measures

Under the heading, usually below a rule, are subheadings that label the various columns in the main body of the table. These subheadings most often are either variable names and categories or summary statistics such as column marginals (Ns). To save space, short labels are preferred; if further clarification is required, subheadings can be footnoted, with the expanded explanations appearing at the bottom of the table.

Additional information, as in a crosstabulation between two or more variables, appears in the column farthest to the left (sometimes called the *stub*). Each entry in this column describes the content of one of the rows forming the body of the table. For example, if attitude responses are to appear in the rows, the labels or response categories in the first column, from top to bottom, might be: "very strongly agree," "strongly agree," "agree," "neither agree nor disagree," "disagree," "strongly disagree," and "very strongly disagree."

The main body of the table consists of the intersections of the entries under column and row headings. It displays the appropriate data in either raw or analyzed form. If the table contents are percentages, the preferable way to arrange them is so that they total to 100% down each column. A percentage total is usually the next to last row entry. The last row, labeled (N) at the left, gives the base frequencies on which the percentages were calculated. Examples of percentage tables in this chapter are Tables 2.4 and 2.8.

The number of cases with missing data (observations that could not be used in the main body of the table due to lack of information) may be reported directly below the body of the table. Any additional information about the data (such as its source) or about the analyses performed should be included in notes below the table.

*An extended discussion of table construction and interpretation appears in the article by James A. Davis and Ann M. Jacobs, "Tabular Presentation," ed. D. L. Sills *International Encyclopedia of the Social Sciences,* Vol. 15, (New York: Macmillan Co., 1968), 497–509.

Tables are not the only way to display frequency distributions of single variables, however. Striking visual impact can be achieved through a variety of **diagrams** or **graphs,** such as bar charts, pie charts, and histograms. For discrete variables,

● **diagrams (graphs)** visual representations of sets of data

TABLE 2.6   Percentage Distribution for Recoded
                   Categories of Church Attendance

Recoded categories	Original categories	Percentage
Never	Never	11.8
Annually	Less than once a year; once or twice a year; several times a year	36.4
Monthly	About once a month; 2–3 times a month	18.1
Weekly	Nearly every week; every week; several times a week	32.9
Not codable	Don't know, no answer	0.8
Total (N = 1,466)		100.0

Source: 1987 General Social Survey.

● **bar chart**
a type of diagram
for discrete variables
in which the
numbers or
percentages of cases
in each outcome are
displayed

a **bar chart** is one of the most effective visual representations of distributions, as well as one of the easiest to construct. To form a bar chart, categories of the discrete variable are arrayed along the horizontal axis, and equally spaced vertical bars are erected above each category label to heights proportional to the frequency (either actual numbers or percentages) of the observations classified into each category. Frequencies or the percentages are sometimes shown above each bar.

Figure 2.1 is a bar chart illustrating the marital status responses in the 1987 GSS, compiled from data in Table 2.5. An important point to observe in constructing bar charts is that when the discrete variable categories have no inherent order, the bars should not touch one another but should stand alone. Only when the categories are *orderable* should the bars touch, as in the histograms described in Section 2.3.1.

A diagram such as a bar chart does not add any information beyond that given in a table showing the same data. In fact, it communicates less information if the sample sizes on which categories are based are omitted and only the percentages are shown. After all, diagrams can be prepared only after the information has been assembled for a table.

Bar Chart Showing Marital Status   FIGURE 2.1

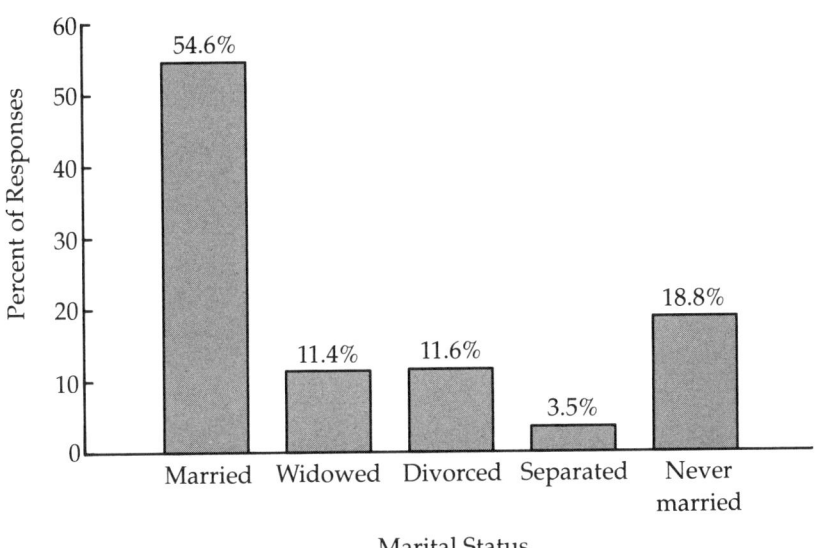

Source: Data derived from Table 2.5.

2.3   Frequency Distributions for Orderable Discrete Variables

Two of the frequency distributions described in the preceding section deal with *nonorderable* discrete variables whose outcomes, as defined in Chapter 1, cannot be ranked from high to low or vice versa. The other type, *orderable* discrete variables, uses measures that classify observations into categories that can be compared by various degrees: two persons or events possess either the same, greater, or lesser amounts of the measured quality. The church attendance measure illustrates an orderable discrete variable. In the most extreme cases, no two observations are equal, and all the persons or events observed can be arranged in order or **ranks,** either ranked from first to last in magnitude or vice versa. American states, for example, can

● **ranks**
positions occupied by observations in distributions when scores on some variables have been ordered from smallest to largest, or vice versa

be ranked from first to fiftieth by total land area, by population size, by number of murders, or by many other characteristics.

More often, however, measures with ordered outcomes contain relatively few categories (perhaps only half a dozen). Many observations are placed into a single category, even though they may differ somewhat in the precise amount of the variable quality they have. For example, if we construct a variable to measure how often people smoke marijuana, we might use the response categories, "regularly, often, seldom, or never." But, what one person means by regularly (every weekend) may not be the same as what another means by that term (twice a day). Even more distressing, two persons who smoke with the same actual frequency may choose different categories for their self-reports of pot smoking. Unfortunately, self-reported measures of behavioral frequency often suffer from this imprecision, although in many cases more careful measurement techniques could easily be designed. In this example, the researcher would do better to ask the subjects to indicate the *number* of marijuana cigarettes they smoke on average each week. While this measure is still imprecise, since it asks for an average rather than an exact number, it is clearly more precise than a measure asking for broad response categories, "regularly, often, seldom, or never."

Table 2.7 displays percentage distributions for two ordered discrete variables, health and health satisfaction, drawn from the 1987 GSS for 825 women. Health was measured in the GSS by responses to the question: "Would you say your health, in general, is excellent, good, fair, or poor?" Health satisfaction was also self-reported, measured as part of a 5-item set of life satisfaction variables: "For each area of life I am going to name, tell me the number (on the card handed to respondent) that shows how much *satisfaction* you get from that area." One of the areas named was "Your health and physical condition," and the responses recorded were: "a very great deal, a great deal, quite a bit, a fair amount, some, a little, or none." The response categories "don't know" and "no answer," that were not on the card, were recoded as "not ascertained." The results show that a majority of American women report they enjoy good or excellent health, and most express a great or very great deal of satisfaction with their health. Later chapters will show methods for examining whether or not health status and health satisfaction are related.

Percentage Distributions for Health and   TABLE 2.7
Health Satisfaction, GSS Women

Health		Health satisfaction	
Excellent	32.0%	A very great deal	27.6%
Good	43.0	A great deal	30.4
Fair	19.5	Quite a bit	16.1
Poor	5.5	A fair amount	15.0
Not ascertained	0.1	Some	5.3
		A little	2.8
Total	100.1%*	None	1.9
(N = 825)		Not ascertained	0.7
		Total	100.0%
		(N = 825)	

Source: 1987 General Social Survey.
* Does not total to 100.0% due to rounding.

2.3.1   Techniques for Displaying Data: Histograms and Polygons

Visual displays for discrete variables were introduced in the preceding section with the bar chart. A similar diagram, called a **histogram,** can be drawn to display distributions of ordered discrete variables.

The distinguishing characteristic of a *histogram* is that the vertical bars touch one another, indicating an underlying order among categories that is absent from unordered discrete variables. Figure 2.2 shows a histogram for the GSS health satisfaction variable.

Instead of drawing bars, as in the bar chart and the histogram, if the midpoints of each category are connected by a line, the resulting diagram is called a **polygon.** Figure 2.3 shows a polygon for the health satisfaction variable, using the data from

● **histogram**
a type of diagram that uses bars to represent the frequency, proportion, or percentage of cases associated with each outcome or interval of outcomes of an ordered discrete variable

● **polygon**
a diagram constructed by connecting the midpoints of a histogram with a straight line

FIGURE 2.2   Histogram Showing Health Satisfaction of Women

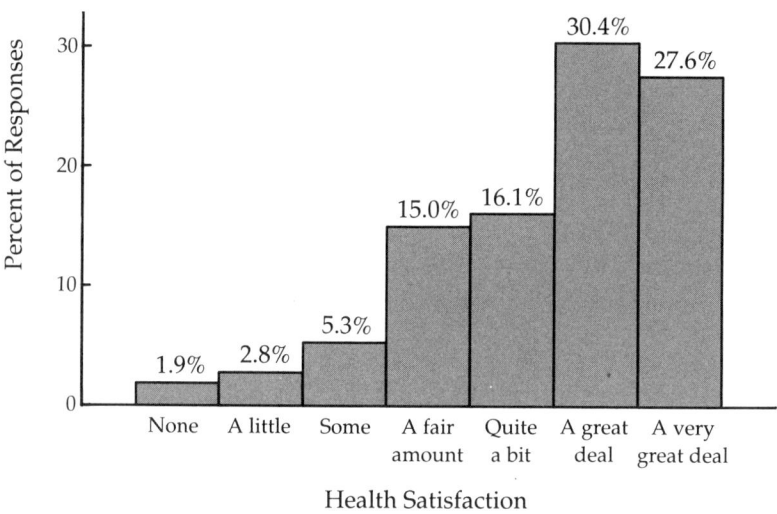

Source: Data derived from Table 2.7.

FIGURE 2.3   Polygon Showing Health Satisfaction of Women

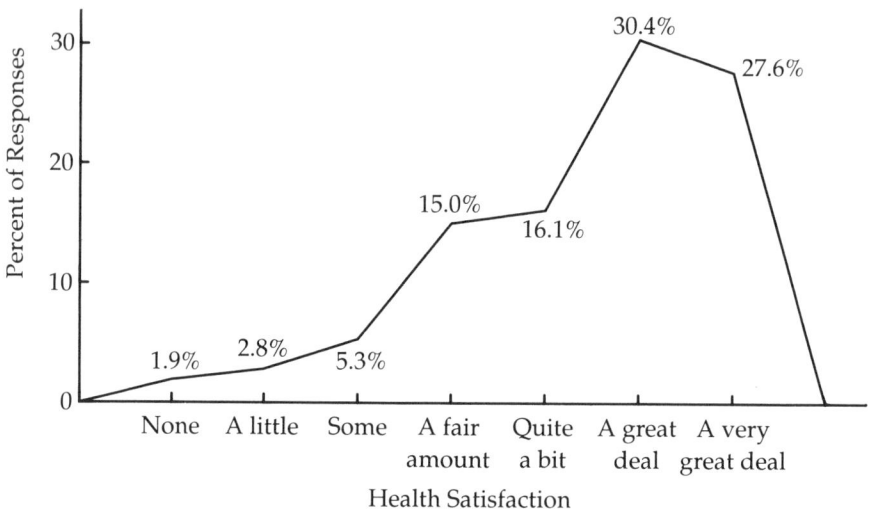

Source: 1987 General Social Survey.

FIGURE 2.4   Polygons Showing Numbers of Own
                   Children and of Siblings

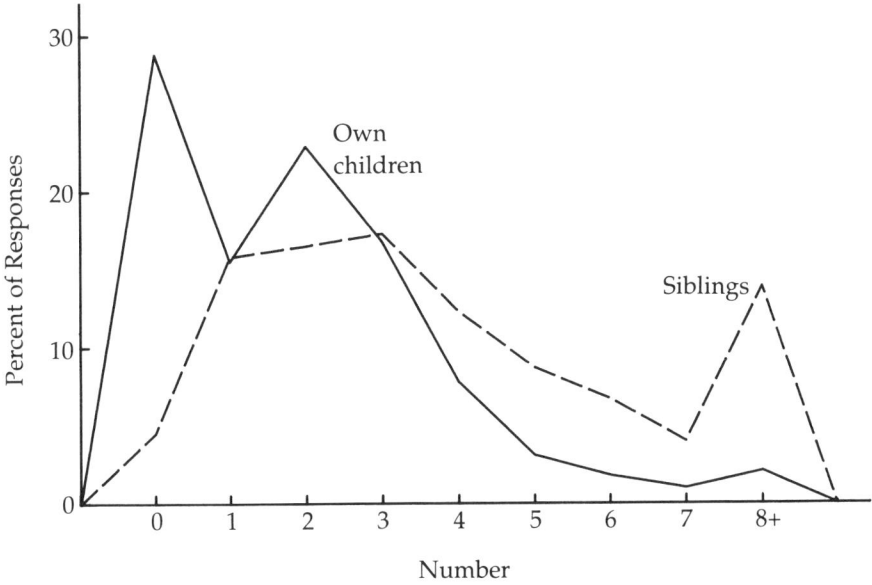

Source: Data drawn from Table 2.8.

Table 2.7. In both cases, the basis for constructing the histogram
or polygon was the frequency or percentage distribution of sample observations across categories of the variable.

Figure 2.4 provides another illustration of graphing or di-
agramming a discrete variable with ordered categories using the
1987 GSS data. Respondents were asked the number of brothers
and sisters they had (whether living at the time of the interview
or not), including step-siblings. They were also asked the number of children they had. These percentage polygons illustrate
the distribution of both the number of siblings and the number
of one's own children for the GSS respondents. The percentage distributions for these variables are shown in Table 2.8. The
distributions suggest that the respondents' families of orientation (those in which they were born) are larger than their families of procreation (the ones in which they currently reside).
However, the brothers-and-sisters variable excludes the respondent from the count, as well as leaving out families that had
no children. Furthermore, since many respondents are still in

TABLE 2.8   Percentage Distributions for Number of
             Siblings and Number of Own Children, GSS
             Respondents

Number	Brothers and sisters	Own children
None	4.5%	28.8%
One	15.8	15.5
Two	16.5	22.9
Three	17.3	16.8
Four	12.3	7.8
Five	8.7	3.1
Six	6.7	1.8
Seven	4.0	1.0
Eight or more	13.9	2.1
Not ascertained	0.3	0.2
Total	100.0%	100.0%
$(N = 1,466)$		

Source: 1987 General Social Survey.

their childbearing years, we would not want to draw this conclusion without additional data and analyses. These polygons
make even clearer the *tentative* inference that respondents' families of orientation are larger than their families of procreation.

2.4   Frequency Distributions for Continuous Measures

Building frequency distributions is little trouble when variables are discrete. Classifying a person as male or female, for
example, and then counting the numbers of each gender is easy.
To count the numbers of children in families and then build a
distribution of family size is also easy. When the variable of interest is *continuous*, however, constructing a frequency distribution first requires **grouped data;** that is, the observations must
be grouped in some way.

● **grouped data**
data that have been
collapsed into a
smaller number of
categories

In theory, any two coded values on the scale of a continuous variable can be subdivided infinitely. Take height as an example. Suppose someone's height is recorded with a mark on a tape measure, as in the illustration below:

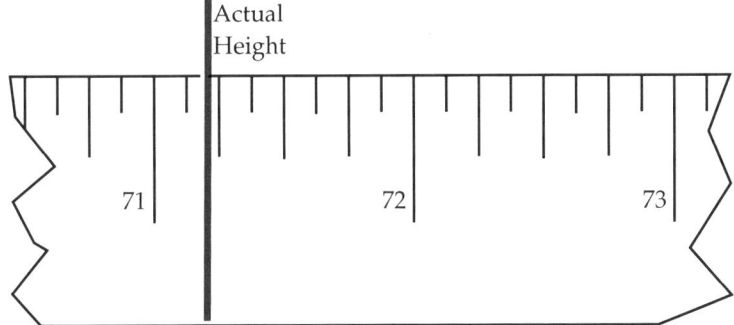

This person's height is 71.203125 inches, to be precise. But usually we do not need this much precision. In everyday conversation we would say the person is 71 inches tall; that is, we would round to the nearest whole number. For some scientific work, this value might be too imprecise. A scientist might decide, however, that measurement in sixteenths of an inch is precise enough, in which case the person's height would be recorded as 71 3/16 of an inch, or 71.1875 inches.

> With continuous variables, measurement can be
> as precise as the measuring instrument will allow.
> At some point, however, a decision on how to
> group observations must be made.

In some instances the unit of measurement for a variable is obvious. For example, if people's ages are to be used in a study of adult voters, the year of birth is probably sufficiently accurate. But, for a study of infants' social learning, the measurement of age to the nearest month is necessary, since changes occur with great frequency in shorter time spans. In a study of economic organizations the scale of operations would dictate the choice of units of measurement. Profits to the nearest $1 million would be adequate for a study of multinational corporations, while measurement to the nearest $100 would be required for local retail stores.

In many analyses, the unit of measurement is less clear because a standard, well-investigated scale has not been developed. For example, a study of job satisfaction might ask workers to agree or disagree with seven statements, such as "This job gives me good opportunities to use my technical skills." Here the unit might be the number of items with which a worker agrees, or it could be the average across the seven questions or responses using a 5-point Likert-type scale from "strongly agree" (5) to "neutral" (3) to "strongly disagree" (1). In this example, either measurement would classify respondents by their levels of agreement, but the actual numerical values would differ according to which units were chosen. Clearly, continuous variables require the researcher to make decisions about the degree of measurement detail.

2.4.1   Grouping Data in Measurement Classes

● **measurement classes (measurement intervals)**
ranges of scores on variables into which observations are grouped

● **recoding**
changing a range of codes or scores of a variable to have equal values

After deciding on the unit of measurement, observations are grouped into **measurement classes** or **measurement intervals** for easier comprehension. The process of grouping data from many original values into fewer categories is often called **recoding.** For example, a report of annual incomes of the hundreds of millions of people in the United States could not display each of the unique reported values, from a few hundred to several millions of dollars. Instead, we might group or recode the original income data into the following categories:

$9,999 or less

$10,000–19,999

$20,000–29,999

$30,000–39,999

$40,000–49,999

$50,000–59,999

$60,000–69,999

$70,000–79,999

$80,000 or more

For a study of the ages of childbearing among women in a developing nation, their ages might be classified into the following categories:

> 10–14 years
> 15–19 years
> 20–24 years
> 25–29 years
> 30–34 years
> 35–39 years
> 40–44 years
> 45 years or older

How does the researcher decide how wide a measurement interval to choose when working with continuous data? The rule of thumb is to choose a measurement interval which is small enough to avoid distortion of the original distribution of observations, but an interval large enough to avoid too many categories that conceal the underlying distribution. Common sense would indicate that $10,000 may be a reasonable interval for the study of Americans' yearly income, but it would not do for a survey of the prices of women's dresses, even if Nancy Reagan were included in the sample. Grouping women into those under 30 years of age and those 30 and over would conceal important variations in childbearing that are revealed by using the five-year intervals above.

For many statistical techniques presented in later chapters, the more measurement precision, the better. But, presenting data in frequency distributions often forces us to violate this rule if the data are to be comprehended at all. On the one hand, 200 income categories in $500 intervals would still be too many codes for easy comprehension of income distribution in the United States. On the other hand, the nine categories of income presented earlier may be too few: the categories may seriously distort large variation in the true income distribution that falls into the upper category ($80,000 or more). Generally, the number of intervals for presenting data in frequency distributions should be somewhere between 6 and 20, but this is only a rule of thumb. Sometimes fewer than six intervals will not significantly distort the shape of the distribution. More than 20 categories are seldom used, however, because a large number of categories makes it difficult for readers to interpret the distribution.

Notice that the intervals above do not permit any overlap between them. That is, when presenting the nine measurement categories for income we did *not* overlap the categories' endpoints in the following way:

$10,000 or less

$10,000–20,000

$20,000–30,000

$30,000–40,000

$40,000–50,000

$50,000–60,000

$60,000–70,000

$70,000–80,000

$80,000 or more

To have done so would have violated the principle of mutual exclusiveness discussed in Chapter 1. A person earning $10,000, $20,000, $30,000, $40,000, $50,000, $60,000, $70,000, or $80,000 could be placed in two categories rather than in a single measurement class. Box 2.2 summarizes the basic principles for grouping or recoding measures.

2.4.2   Rounding

The slight gap that always exists between grouped measurement categories creates another type of problem: Where could someone with a yearly income of $9,999.85, for example, be placed in the nine nonoverlapping income categories? The solution is **rounding;** that is, we would round the income to the nearest dollar—$10,000 in this case—and place that person in the $10,000–19,999 category. The number $9,999.25 would be rounded down to $9,999 and placed in the "$9,999 or less" category. In general, do not round past the original degree of measurement precision. In the example above, income was measured in dollars, and thus we rounded to the nearest dollar. If the income categories had been set up for *hundreds* of dollars earned, then $9,999.75 and $9,999.25 would both have been rounded to $10,000, but $9,948 would have been rounded to $9,900. If the unit of measurement had been *thousands* of dollars earned, then all of the above amounts would have been rounded to

● **rounding**
expressing digits in more convenient and interpretable units, such as tens, hundreds, or thousands, by applying an explicit rule

$10,000, but $9,450 would have been rounded to $9,000. Rules for rounding and examples of rounding digits according to unit of measurement are given in Box 2.2.

2.5   Cumulative Distributions

Often the researcher needs to know the *relative* position of a given outcome in a distribution of scores. If an American state has an unemployment rate of 6.5%, how high is that rate relative to other states? If 45 persons were murdered last year in your city, is that high or low relative to other cities of the same size? Questions like these can be answered by constructing a cumulative frequency distribution or cumulative percentage distribution.

The **cumulative frequency** at a given score is the total number of frequencies at or below that score. In the 1986 GSS, respondents were asked, "What do you think is the ideal number of children for a family to have?" Table 2.9 shows the resulting cumulative distribution. In this example, the **cumulative frequency distribution** is the distribution of responses at or below each number of children desired. The cumulative frequencies are shown in the third column of Table 2.9, denoted by *cf*. To produce a *cf*, simply start with the frequency in the lowest category (*f*), add to it the frequency in the next highest category,

● **cumulative frequency** for a given score or outcome of a variable, the total number of cases in a distribution at or below that value

● **cumulative frequency distribution** a distribution of scores showing the number of cases at or below each outcome of the variable being displayed in the distribution

Cumulative Distribution of Ideal Number of Children, GSS Respondents

TABLE 2.9

Number	f	%	cf	c%
None	15	1.1%	15	1.1%
One	24	1.8	39	2.9
Two	724	53.6	763	56.4
Three	359	26.6	1,122	83.0
Four	185	13.7	1,307	96.7
Five	25	1.8	1,332	98.5
Six	15	1.1	1,347	99.6
Seven or more	5	0.4	1,352	100.0

Source: 1986 General Social Survey.
Note: *N* = 1,352.

then add to that total the frequency in the third highest category, and so forth. The cumulative frequency to one child is 39, to two children is 763, to three children is 1,122, and so on.

● **cumulative percentage**
for a given score or outcome of a variable, the percentage of cases in a distribution at or below that value

More interesting for interpretative purposes is the **cumulative percentage** of responses. The second column of Table 2.9 shows the percentage distribution of responses. In the last column (denoted by $c\%$), these percentages are cumulated to form a **cumulative percentage distribution.** The procedure is similar to calculating the values of the cf, except that the percentages at each category, instead of the frequencies, are totaled. The table shows that only 2.9% of the sample desired one or no children, while 96.7% of the sample thought that four or fewer children were ideal. Like the percentage distribution described at the beginning of the chapter, the cumulative percentage distribution clarifies the *relative* standing of a given observation. You can quickly see that 56.4% of respondents chose 0–2 children as ideal, a fairly small number of desired children compared to earlier times. Cumulative percentage distributions can also be diagrammed. A diagram of the ideal number of children distribution in Table 2.9 is shown in Figure 2.5.

● **cumulative percentage distribution**
a distribution of scores showing the percentage of cases at or below each outcome of the variable being displayed in the distribution

FIGURE 2.5   Cumulative Percentage Distribution of Ideal Number of Children

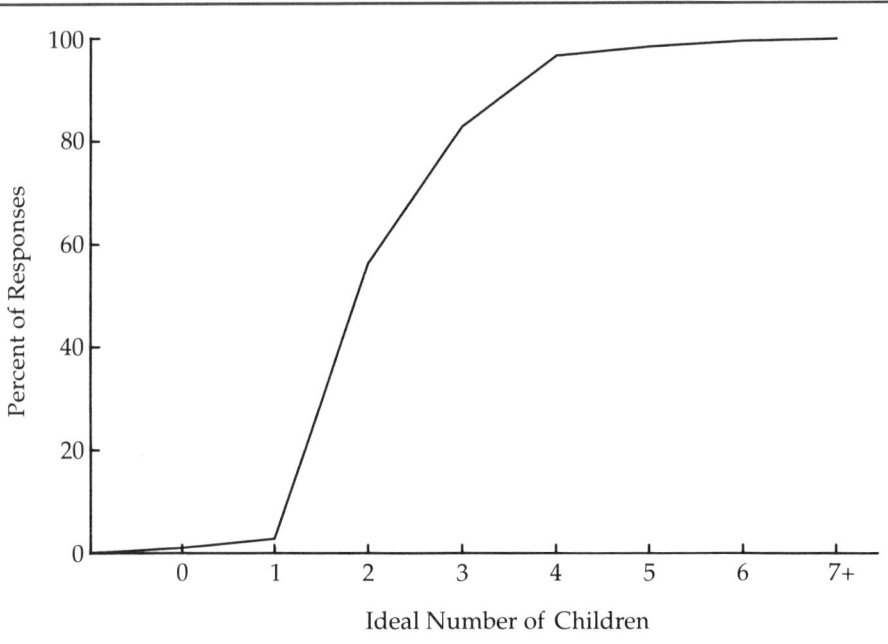

Ideal Number of Children

Source: Data from Table 2.9.

One common application of cumulative percentage distributions is in calculating percentiles, for example, in showing the distribution of achievement test scores for school children. In that case, the distributions of two or more schools can be compared to see whether the test results differ. Although we do not make much use of percentiles in this book, their frequent appearance elsewhere prompted us to include an optional section on them, in Box 2.4.

Box 2.4   Percentiles

A useful statistic that can be derived from cumulative distributions is the **percentile,** which is the outcome or score below which a given percentage of observations falls. With discrete variables, such as the ideal number of children in Table 2.9, percentiles are easy to see. The 83rd percentile is 3, since 83% of the choices lie at or below the category "three children." With continuous variables, where data have been grouped, percentiles are computed using the following formula:

● **percentile**
the outcome or score below which a given percentage of the observations in a distribution falls

$$P_i = L_p + \frac{(p_i)(N) - c_p}{f_p} (W_i)$$

Where:

P_i = The score of the ith percentile

L_p = The true lower limit of the interval containing the ith percentile

p_i = The ith percentile written as a proportion (e.g., the 75th percentile becomes .75 in the formula)

N = The total number of observations

c_p = The cumulative frequency up to but not including the interval containing P_i

f_p = The frequency in the interval containing the ith percentile

W_i = The width of the interval containing P_i; $W_i = U_p - L_p$ where U_p and L_p are the upper and lower true limits of the interval containing P_i

To illustrate the application for grouped data, consider the following table for gross national product per capita for 24 industrial nations:

GNP per capita	f	c_p	L_p
$2,001–4,000	2	2	$2,000.5
$4,001–6,000	4	6	$4,000.5
$6,001–8,000	1	7	$6,000.5
$8,001–10,000	5	12	$8,000.5
$10,001–12,000	6	18	$10,000.5
$12,001–14,000	5	23	$12,000.5
$14,001–16,000	1	24	$14,000.5

The 90th percentile is given by

$$P_{90} = \$12,000.50 + \frac{(.90)(24) - 18}{5} (\$2,000)$$

$$= \$13,440.5$$

since $i = 90$, $L_p = \$12,000.50$, $p_i = .90$, $N = 24$, $c_p = 18$, $f_p = 5$, and $W_i = \$14,000.50 - \$12,000.50 = \$2,000$.

Key Concepts and Symbols

These key concepts and symbols are listed in the order of appearance in the chapter. Combined with the definitions in the margins, these will help you review the material and can serve as a self-test for mastery of the concepts.

tally
frequency distribution
outcomes
relative frequencies
    (proportions)
percentages
percentage distribution
dichotomous variables
    (dichotomies)
statistical tables
diagrams (graphs)
bar chart
ranks
histogram
polygon
grouped data
measurement classes
    (measurement intervals)

recoding
rounding
cumulative frequency
cumulative frequency
    distribution
cumulative percentage
cumulative percentage
    distribution
percentile
%
f_i
p_i
N
cf
$c\%$

Problems

General Problems

1. A field researcher observes fifth-grade pupils at recess. The following symbols were used to record their behaviors during a 10-minute interval: M = playing marbles; H = playing hopscotch; J = jumping rope; T = talking; O = other activity.

Here are the field researcher's raw observations for 24 pupils:

M	J	J	T	M	H
J	T	M	H	M	H
T	J	M	O	H	J
T	H	J	M	T	O

a. Construct a tally to summarize these data.
b. Construct a table of relative frequencies for these data.
c. Transform these data into a percentage table.
d. Display the results of these data in a bar chart.

2. Of the 50 American states, the Census Bureau classifies 9 in the Northeast, 11 in the South, 17 in the North Central, and 13 in the West. Construct a table of relative frequencies, a percentage table, and a bar chart for this variable.

3. In a statistics class there are 14 seniors, 12 juniors, 3 sophomores, and 4 special students. Construct a table of relative frequencies, a percentage table, and a histogram.

4. Every year, the GSS asks respondents how many members over 17 years of age are living in their households. The following are the frequencies for two surveys:

Household Sizes

Number of Members	1972 f	1987 f
1	195	386
2	1,007	809
3	280	206
4	96	51
5	24	9
6	7	4
7	0	1
8 or more	4	0

Source: 1972 and 1982 General Social Surveys.

Superimpose two percentage polygons for these two distributions and decide whether there was any noticeable shift in adult household size over the eight years.

5. In 1987, 0.346 of American adults described their religion as fundamentalist, 0.371 as moderate, 0.250 as liberal, and 0.033 gave no answer. What were the frequencies giving each response, if the total number interviewed was 1,466?

6. Construct a histogram from the following frequencies in response to the 1984 GSS survey item, "In the U.S. there are still great differences between social levels, and what one can achieve in life depends mainly upon one's family background": strongly agree ($N = 133$); somewhat agree ($N = 508$); somewhat disagree ($N = 469$); strongly disagree ($N = 312$).

7. In 1984, GSS respondents were asked how often they had "felt as though you were really in touch with someone who had died." Of those who answered, 834 said "never in my life," 337 said "once or twice," 200 said "several times," and 74 said "often." Show the cumulative percentage distribution and construct a cumulative percentage polygon.

8. For the years 1983–87, the GSS gave the following frequencies on respondents who were asked whether the U.S. was spending too little money, about the right amount, or too much money on the military, armaments, and defense:

Opinions on U.S. Military Spending

	Too little	About right	Too much
1983	385	603	518
1984	84	200	185
1985	107	315	300
1986	118	279	294
1987	71	196	196

Source: 1984 and 1987 General Social Survey.

a. Compute the proportions of persons responding "too much" in each year.

b. Construct a histogram with year on the horizontal axis. What do you observe?

9. Round the following numbers as indicated:

Unit of measure	Original number
Feet	3.62 feet
Feet	14.38 feet
Inches	12.97 inches
Inches	12.50 inches
Miles	10.9 miles
Miles	6.499 miles

10. In 1984, GSS respondents were asked whether they had ever been threatened with a gun or shot at, and how often this had occurred. The following frequency distribution shows these results:

Being Threatened or Shot at by a Gun

Category	f
Never	1,180
Once	170
Two or three	62
Four or more	52
Total	1,464

Source: 1984 General Social Survey.

Compute the cumulative frequency distribution and cumulative percentage distribution, and give a verbal interpretation.

Problems Requiring the 1987 General Social Survey Data

11. The GSS asks its respondents whether they belong to any of 16 different types of organizations (MEMNUM). Find how many persons belong to none, one, two, three, or more organizations, and display the results both as a percentage table and as a histogram.

12. Show how to decide whether support for freedom of speech by a racist (SPKRAC), by a militarist (SPKMIL), or by a homosexual (SPKHOMO) receives greater public support by displaying the percentage distributions of these three items.

13. Historically, women have been more religious than men. See if this remains true today, by using SEX to select sub-samples of women and men, and comparing the relative proportions who PRAY with differing frequency.

14. Compare respondents' regions of residence when they were growing up (REG16) and current region of residence (REGION). Is there any noticeable population shift?

15. Were blacks or whites (RACE) more likely to vote for Ronald Reagan in 1984 (PRES84)?

Problems Requiring the 50-States Data Set

16. Recode state population (POPULAT) into three categories that differ by a factor of 10, beginning with 100,000 (that is, 100,000 to 999,999; 1,000,000 to 9,999,999; and 10,000,000 to 99,999,999). How many states fall into each of these three categories?

17. What is the distribution of murders across the states? Recode MURDER into groups of 50 per million residents (i.e., 0 to 50; 51 to 100; 101 to 150; etc.), and display as a percentage distribution.

18. Show the state election returns for Reagan in 1980 (VOTE) as a cumulative percentage distribution from the lowest to highest values in categories of 10% (e.g., 30.0 to 39.9; 40.0 to 49.9; 50.0 to 59.9; etc).

3

Describing Frequency Distributions

By nature, we try to simplify the world so we can understand and describe it better. The social scientist, for example, uses average income, median age of the U.S. population, and other useful shorthand descriptions to evaluate entire distributions of data. This chapter presents a number of **statistics** for summarizing distributions of discrete and continuous variables. As we noted in Chapter 1, discrete variables classify persons, objects, or events by the *quality* of their attributes, and continuous variables classify them according to *quantity*.

Statistics that summarize or describe frequency distributions have two broad purposes. We want to find a single number or label to describe the average or **central tendency** of a distribution (e.g., "The average age of persons who smoke crack at least once a week is . . . "; "The most common category of religious preference in Germany is . . . "). We also want to know how typical that number or label is of the other members of the sample. Therefore, we need a second type of statistic to judge the amount of **variation** in the distribution. For example, we may want to know whether most persons' scores are close to the average score or whether the cases are spread widely away from it. If the scores are close to the mean, that measure describes the typical element in the distribution much better than if the scores are dispersed.

3.1   Measures of Central Tendency

Commonly used measures of central tendency include the mode, the median, and the mean. The choice of a central tendency measure to describe a set of scores depends on the types of variables. The description and use of these three statistics are presented in this section.

3.1.1   Mode

The most basic measure of central tendency is the mode. The **mode** has the largest number (or percentage) of observations among the various categories (K) in the distribution. For example, if the number of persons saying that their favorite color is red is 8, yellow is 5, and blue is 10, then the modal category is "blue." Do not confuse the modal frequency (number of cases) with the modal category. Note that a modal category is not required to contain a majority of the cases, only *more* than any other single category. Some distributions are said to be *bimodal* (i.e., to have *two* modes). Strictly speaking, in a bimodal distribution the largest two categories must each have exactly the same number of observations. In practice, this equality very rarely occurs, and scientists use the term "bimodal" to describe any distribution where two categories are roughly equal and contain the greatest number of cases.

- **mode**
the value of the category in a frequency distribution that has the largest number, or percentage, of cases

An example of a distribution that is not strictly bimodal, but would be said to be, is shown in Figure 3.1 for an orderable discrete variable. The 1984 GSS respondents were asked about their agreement with the statement, "If social welfare benefits such as disability, unemployment compensation, and early retirement pensions are as high as they are now, it only makes people not want to work anymore." As Figure 3.1 shows, respondents tended to say either "somewhat agree" or "somewhat disagree," while far fewer persons chose the "strongly agree" or "strongly disagree" categories.[1]

Any statistic that can be used to describe discrete measures can also be used to describe continuous measures. For example, the modal state of residence (a discrete variable) is Califor-

---

[1]SPSS will only report as the mode that category with the largest number of cases, in this example "Strongly Disagree." Thus, it is important for you to inspect the results to determine if a distribution contains other "peaks" that make it close to a bimodal or multimodal distribution.

Distributions of Responses to Social Welfare Benefits

FIGURE 3.1

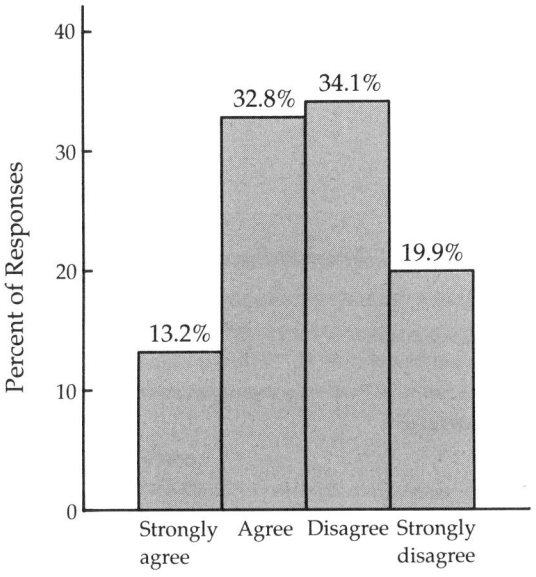

Attitude toward Social Welfare Benefits

Source: Data derived from 1984 General Social Survey.

nia, since more people live there than any other state. And, the modal number of automobiles (an ordered discrete variable) owned by American families is two, since more families have two cars than have either fewer or more. Thus the mode is a central tendency statistic for both types of variables.

3.1.2   Median

The median, another measure of central tendency, is useful for describing central tendency in distributions where the categories of the variable can be ordered from lowest to highest. The **median** is ordinarily defined as the value that divides an ordered distribution exactly into two parts; that is, the cases will be split into two equal parts, those above the median and those

● **median**
the value or score that exactly divides an ordered frequency distribution into equal halves; the value of the category at which the cumulative percentage equals 50%

below the median. Determination of the median value depends on whether the number of observations is odd or even. Consider the following three examples:

Distribution A: 1, 4, 6, 7, 9, 10, 22, 24, 24
Distribution B: 1, 4, 6, 7, 9, 10, 22, 24, 24, 25
Distribution C: 1, 4, 6, 7, 7, 7, 7, 24, 24

Distribution A has an odd number of cases (9); the median is the score of the fifth observation, or 9. Distribution B has an even number of cases (10), so the median falls halfway between the scores of the fifth and sixth cases. Its value is the average of the values of these two cases, $(9 + 10)/2 = 9.5$. For distribution C, the value of the median case (7) also happens to be shared by several other observations. In this instance, we can still apply the rule that the median is either the score of the middle case (for an odd number of observations), or the average of the scores for two cases (for an even number of cases). In these three examples, the small number of observations makes the median easy to calculate.

Matters can become more difficult when data are sorted in a grouped frequency distribution. Many statistics textbooks recommend using the complex formula in Box 2.4 for calculating the 50th percentile as the median value of a grouped frequency distribution. We offer a simpler and more accurate approach to finding the median of a grouped distribution: For any grouped frequency distribution, the median is the value of that category at which the cumulative percentage equals 50.0% (see Box 3.1 on grouped data). (This approach also agrees with the SPSS computer program calculation of the median; see Box 2.1.) In general, the value of the median calculated using ungrouped data will not equal the median that results when these data are grouped. This occurs because information on all the individual case values is lost by the grouping process. However, in many instances a researcher has only the grouped data available (for example, in printed census tables or from newspaper tables), and these tabled data cannot be broken down into the original ungrouped data. Thus, the median for the grouped data can be computed as the score of the category in which the cumulative percentage equals 50.0%.

In most data distributions, rarely will one category precisely cumulate to 50.0%. In those situations, the median is the value of the first category in the cumulative distribution that exceeds

Box 3.1   Medians with Grouped Data

Many times data involving large numbers of cases are available only in grouped distributions, for example, as computer tabulations or displays in newspapers and government documents such as census reports. In these circumstances, social scientists can still calculate median values.

Because the median is the score above and below which half the cases fall, it is the 50th percentile, or P_{50}. (See Box 2.4 in Chapter 2 for a review of percentiles.)

50.0%. Table 3.1 shows the amount of satisfaction that GSS respondents said they received from their families. The modal response category, with 606 cases, was "a very great deal" (coded 7). With 1,452 total respondents, the median value must fall between case 726 and case 727. As the cumulative frequency and cumulate percentage distributions reveal, both of these cases are in the response category "a great deal" (coded 6). Hence, we say the median value for this distribution is 6.

Distribution of Degree of Satisfaction Derived from the Family, GSS Respondents

TABLE 3.1

Code	Response category	f	%	cf	$c\%$
1	None	21	1.4	21	1.4
2	A little	33	2.3	54	3.7
3	Some	45	3.1	99	6.8
4	A fair amount	107	7.4	206	14.2
5	Quite a bit	169	11.6	375	25.8
6	A great deal	471	32.4	846	58.3
7	A very great deal	606	41.7	1,452	100.0

Source: 1987 General Social Survey (coding was reversed from original).
Note: 14 persons who reported "don't know" or gave no answer have been eliminated from this analysis.

skewed distribution
a frequency distribution that is asymmetric with regard to its dispersion

positive skew
an asymmetrical frequency distribution characteristic whereby, in a graphic display, larger frequencies are found toward the negative end and smaller frequencies toward the positive end

negative skew
a property of a frequency distribution whereby larger frequencies are found toward the positive end and smaller frequencies toward the negative end

mean
a measure of central tendency for continuous variables calculated as the sum of all scores in a distribution, divided by the number of scores; the arithmetic average

When the distribution of an ordered variable is plotted, the plot may be asymmetric about its median value; that is, there may be more categories with small numbers of observations at one side of the median than at the other side. Whenever this condition occurs, and one end of the distribution has a long "tail" (i.e., there are many categories with few cases), the result is a **skewed distribution.** Thus, the distribution of satisfaction with family shown in Figure 3.2, using data from Table 3.1, is skewed. When distributions are skewed, the mode and the median differ, as they do in this example. When the long tail is to the right of the median, the distribution is said to have **positive skew;** when the tail is to the left, the distribution has **negative skew.** (In other words, a positive skew has more categories above the median than below, while a negative skew has more categories below the median than above.) Convince yourself that satisfaction with family has a negative skew by studying Table 3.1 and Figure 3.2.

3.1.3   Mean

By far the most commonly used measure of central tendency is the arithmetic mean, which can be calculated only for continuous measures. The **mean** is commonly called the average. The formula for the mean adds all the scores in the Y distribution and divides by the number of cases, N. If the mean of a sample of observations is represented by $\overline{Y}$, then the formula for the mean statistic is the following:

$$\overline{Y} = \sum_{i=1}^{N} \frac{Y_i}{N}$$

The Greek capital letter sigma (Σ) is widely used as a symbol to signify the operation of summation. Appendix A, "The Use of Summations," provides rules on its use.

To illustrate the mean, we can use the 1980 murder rates of the 16 southern states in the 50-States Data Set (see Box 3.2). The murder rates for each southern state appear in Table 3.2.

Distribution of Satisfaction Derived from the Family

FIGURE 3.2

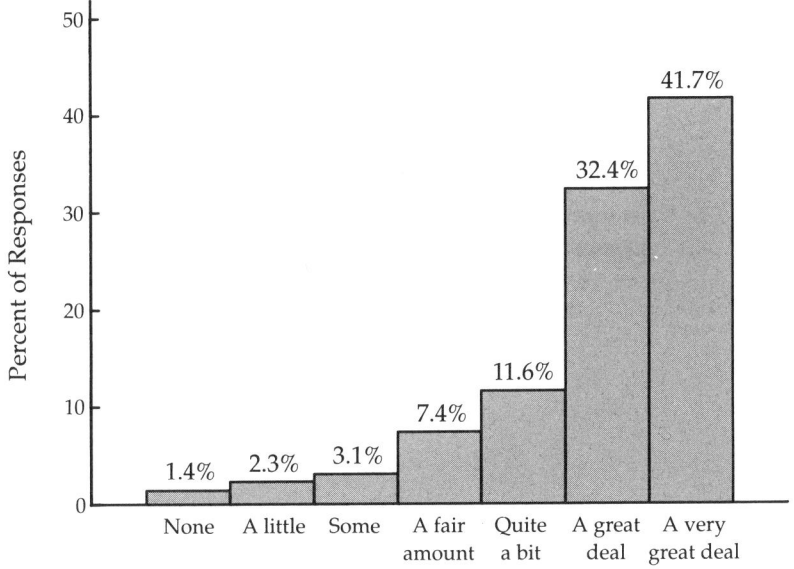

Source: Data derived from Table 3.1.

Although two states (Florida and Mississippi) have identical rates, this modal value does not convey much about the distribution. Because murder rates are continuous variables, we can also calculate the mean, as follows:

$$\overline{Y} = (51 + 69 + 71 + 86 + 88 + 92 + 95 + 106 + 108$$
$$+ 114 + 132 + 138 + 145 + 145 + 157 + 169)/16$$
$$= (1776)/16$$
$$= 110.38, \text{ or, rounding, } 110.4$$

When the data are presented as a grouped frequency distribution, as is often the case, we must take into account the

TABLE 3.2   Murder Rate per 1,000,000 Population in 16 Southern States

State name	Murder rate
Oklahoma	51
Delaware	69
West Virginia	71
Virginia	86
Kentucky	88
Arkansas	92
Maryland	95
North Carolina	106
Tennessee	108
South Carolina	114
Alabama	132
Georgia	138
Florida	145
Mississippi	145
Louisiana	157
Texas	169

Source: 50-States Data Set.

frequency of each value when calculating the mean. When confronted with group data, we must use the following formula:

$$\overline{Y} = \frac{\sum_{i=1}^{K} (f_i Y_i)}{N}$$

Where:

f_i = the frequency of cases of Type Y_i.

K = the number of outcomes in the distribution.

The next example shows how to use this version of the mean formula. In both the 1978 and 1986 General Social Surveys, respondents were asked how many hours of television they

Box 3.2   The 50-States Data Set

Sometimes we want to show relationships between variables with a much smaller data set than the typical 1,500-respondent surveys of the General Social Survey. For these purposes, the 50-States data are ideal. We chose 33 variables from Census Bureau and other federal agency documents and created an SPSS/PC+ computer file. The program cards and data appear in Appendix G and are also available on diskette from the publisher. Several chapter assignments are built around these data. We urge instructors and students to use these variables for classroom problems. New variables can be added to this data set for both instructional and research purposes.

watch on an average day. The two distributions appear in Table 3.3. Applying the mean formula, we find that the mean number of hours watched in 1978 is computed as follows:

$$\overline{Y}_{1978} = [0(91) + 1(316) + 2(418) + 3(287)$$
$$+ 4(194) + 5(99) + 6(55) + 7(8) + 8(30)$$
$$+ 9(3) + 10(12) + 11(0) + 12(10) + 13(1)$$
$$+ 14(0) + 15(1) + 16(0) + 18(1) + 20(1)$$
$$+ 24(1)]/1,528$$
$$= 2.79 \text{ hours per day}$$

Similarly, the mean number of television hours in 1986 is as follows:

$$\overline{Y}_{1986} = [0(65) + 1(261) + 2(389) + 3(298)$$
$$+ 4(193) + 5(100) + 6(61) + 7(18) + 8(33) + 9(2)$$
$$+ 10(22) + 11(3) + 12(11) + 13(1) + 14(2) + 15(1)$$
$$+ 16(3) + 18(2) + 20(1) + 24(0)]/1,466$$
$$= 3.09 \text{ hours per day}$$

TABLE 3.3

Distribution of Hours Spent Watching Television

Number of hours	1978		1986	
	f	%	f	%
0	91	6.0	65	4.4
1	316	20.7	261	17.8
2	418	27.4	389	26.5
3	287	18.8	298	20.3
4	194	12.7	193	13.2
5	99	6.5	100	6.8
6	55	3.6	61	4.2
7	8	0.5	18	1.2
8	30	2.0	33	2.3
9	3	0.2	2	0.1
10	12	0.8	22	1.5
11	0	0.0	3	0.2
12	10	0.7	11	0.8
13	1	0.1	1	0.1
14	0	0.0	2	0.1
15	1	0.1	1	0.1
16	0	0.0	3	0.2
18	1	0.1	2	0.1
20	1	0.1	1	0.0
24	1	0.1	0	0.0
Total	1,528	100.0	1,466	100.0

Source: 1978 and 1986 General Social Surveys.

These statistics suggest that over a nine-year span Americans watched about $3.09 - 2.79 = 0.30$ hours, or (0.30) $(60$ minutes$) = 18$ minutes more television per day. An important question, however, is whether or not this small increase is due to sampling chance (an issue discussed in Chapter 4).

A special case of the mean for a grouped frequency distribution occurs when the variable is measured as a dichotomy. If one category is assigned the score 1 and the second category the score 0, then the mean of the distribution is simply the proportion of cases having the score 1. The formula for the mean of a grouped frequency distribution reduces to the following:

$$\overline{Y} = \frac{\Sigma f_i Y_i}{N}$$

$$= \frac{(0)(f_0) + (1)(f_1)}{N}$$

$$= p_1$$

$$P = \frac{\Sigma_i}{N}$$

$$\% = \frac{\Sigma_i}{N}(100)$$

Where:

f_0 = the number of cases coded 0.

f_1 = the number of cases coded 1.

p_1 = the proportion of cases coded 1.

To see this, look at the gender distribution of the 1987 GSS respondents (see Table 2.5). There were 825 women and 641 men in the sample. If the women are coded 1 and the men coded 0, the mean score is [(1) (825) + (0) (641)]/1,466 = .563, which is identical to the proportion of women in the sample.

3.1.4   Relationships among Central Tendency Measures

Now that we have considered the three basic measures of central tendency, the question arises: Is there any systematic relationship among their values in a distribution of continuous scores? The answer depends on whether the distribution is symmetrical or skewed.

When a distribution of scores is relatively symmetric, the mean, median, and mode will be very close to one another in value. However, when the distribution is skewed, the three can differ rather sharply.

In the 1986 GSS, respondents were asked to rate their liking of a series of countries on a scale from −5 (dislike very much) to +5 (like very much). To illustrate our point more easily, we eliminate the negative scores by recoding the ten ordered categories from 0 for dislike to 9 for like. (Note that the original GSS scoring of these variables did not contain a zero point, which created an interval of width two between −1 and +1, while our recoding makes all intervals equal to width one.) The distributions of responses for two countries, China and Russia, are shown in Table 3.4, and these distributions are graphed in Figure 3.3.

The distribution of responses for China is roughly symmetric, and the mean, median, and mode are 4.96, 5, and 5, respectively. By contrast, the mean, median, and mode for Russia are 3.06, 3, and 0, reflecting the obvious positive skew to U.S. citizens' evaluations of Russia (see Section 3.1.2). A substantial minority of Americans rated Russia in the most negative category, perhaps because of stronger anticommunist feelings directed at the Soviet Union than at China. Perhaps China's

TABLE 3.4   Distribution of Liking Scores for China and Russia, GSS Respondents

		China				Russia			
Score	Code	f	%	cf	c%	f	%	cf	c%
−5	0	83	5.9	83	5.9	387	27.5	387	27.5
−4	1	52	3.7	135	9.6	83	5.9	470	33.5
−3	2	86	6.1	221	15.7	165	11.7	635	45.2
−2	3	90	6.4	311	22.2	103	7.3	738	52.5
−1	4	157	11.2	468	33.3	193	13.7	931	66.3
+1	5	352	25.1	820	58.4	229	16.3	1,160	82.6
+2	6	223	15.9	1,043	74.3	107	7.6	1,267	90.2
+3	7	217	15.5	1,260	89.7	102	7.3	1,369	97.4
+4	8	77	5.5	1,337	95.2	17	1.2	1,386	98.6
+5	9	67	4.8	1,404	100.0	19	1.4	1,405	100.0

Source: 1986 General Social Survey.
Modes: China = 5; Russia = 0.
Medians: China = 5; Russia = 3.
Means: China = 4.96; Russia = 3.06.

Distributions of Scores Measuring Degree of
Liking by U.S. Citizens for China and Russia

FIGURE 3.3

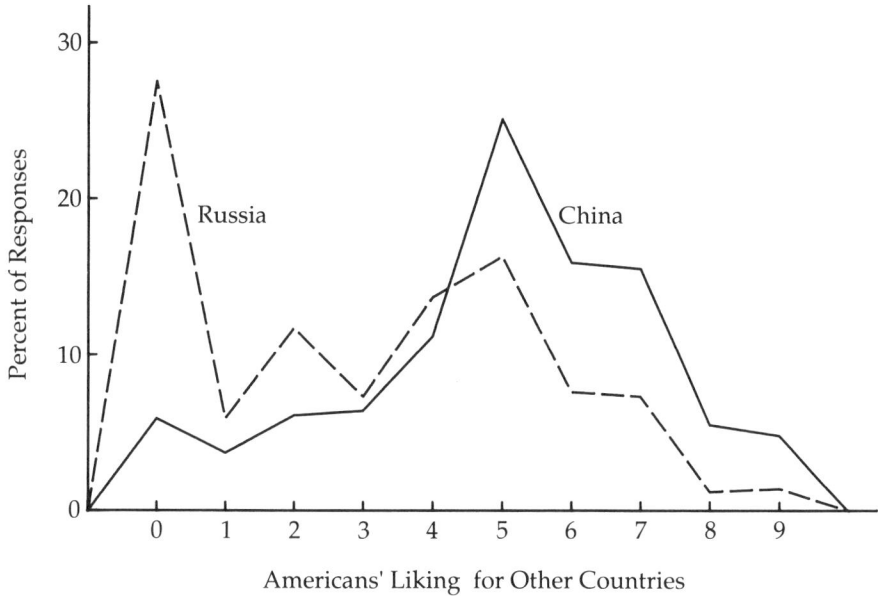

Source: Data derived from Table 3.4.

friendly relations with the U.S. at that time and its more market-oriented economic experiments inclined Americans toward more neutral ratings. (These ratings may be in the process of change, with respect to significant political events particularly the international popularity of Mikhail Gorbachev's experiments with democracy in the Soviet Union, and the Chinese government's massacre of Beijing student demonstrators in 1989.)

In general, for distributions with a positive skew, the mean is the highest, the median the second highest, and the mode the lowest statistic. The opposite ordering holds for distributions with a negative skew. The mean and median differ because the mean is a weighted average—extreme values affect it—whereas the median is not. Every score in a distribution enters into the calculation of the mean, with the result that very large or very small scores will tend to move the mean toward a higher or lower value, respectively. In the last example, if we had recoded a 9 to a 20, the medians would be unchanged, but the means would change rather dramatically. To reassure yourself of this, change the code 9 in Table 3.4 to 20, and recompute the medians and the means. Or change the 0 to −10 and notice changes to those measures of central tendency. Figure 3.4 illustrates the effect that a single extreme case (an outlier) can have on central tendency measures for a distribution. In both diagrams, the median value of the five cases is the score of the third case (3). In the top diagram, the mean of the five cases is also 3.0. But, in the bottom diagram a change in only one case's value, from 5 to 10, increases the mean to 4.0 while leaving the median score unchanged.

Because the mean is a weighted average, some scientists favor using the median as a measure of central tendency in distributions that are highly skewed, such as distributions of personal income. For example, the U.S. Census Bureau's analyses of earnings by Americans of different races, genders, ages, or regions typically report median values for people in these categories, to avoid distortions that the use of means would create.

FIGURE 3.4   The Effect of an Outlier Case on the Mean
                    and Median of a Distribution

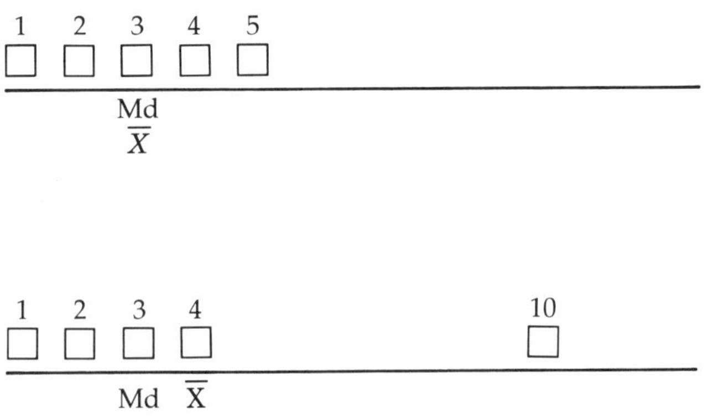

3.2   Measures of Variation

Central tendency measures are important in identifying a typical value for a frequency distribution. But, a more complete description must take account of variation—the extent to which a distribution's scores are close in value to the central measure or far from it. This section will discuss several statistics that describe the degree of dispersion among a distribution's scores.

3.2.1   Range

Variation in continuous variables can be measured in several ways; the simplest is the **range,** which uses only the two extreme scores between which all other responses are found in a given sample. The range of the outcomes of a distribution is defined as the difference between the largest and the smallest outcomes. The range of the years of education shown in Table 3.5 is from 0 to 20 years, or $20 - 0 = 20$.

● **range**
a measure of dispersion based on the difference between the largest and smallest outcomes in a distribution

Although the range is a quick and easy measure, it communicates relatively little information about the sample, since it is based on only the two extreme scores. It does not tell us how much the other persons or events are spread out or bunched up on the scale values between the highest and lowest scores. Although a village of 30 paupers and 30 millionaires may have an income range equal to that of a village with one pauper, one millionaire, and 58 middle income residents, these are quite different places. In Table 3.5, we see that very few cases have fewer than 8 or more than 17 years of education, indicating that most of the sample is bunched in the middle of the range. We turn next to some statistics useful for summarizing the amount of spread among scores in a distribution.

3.2.2   Average Deviation

The mean as a measure of central tendency representing the value of every observation in a distribution is highly useful in developing a measure of variation for continuous data—the spread or dispersion of scores away from the mean. The range, as we have noted, uses only the two extreme scores to tell us about variability. But, a good measure of variation should also take into account all the scores' relations to the mean, that is, how close or far each is from the mean.

First, note that the deviation, or distance, of a score, Y_i, from the mean, $\overline{Y}$, is commonly calculated as follows:

$$d_i = Y_i - \overline{Y}$$

This formula results in positive and negative deviations, depending on whether a given observation is above or below the mean. If we try to calculate the average deviation of all N scores from the mean, we would always find 0. This occurs because another feature of the mean is that it equalizes the deviations in both positive and negative directions. (Test this with an exercise using Table 3.5.) Therefore, the average deviation is unsuitable as a statistical measure of variation for continuous variables, since all distributions will give the same value (zero). We need some other way to capture the typical deviation of every observation from the mean without allowing the mean's balancing property to cancel all that information. By taking the absolute values of the deviations before averaging them, we can remove the problem of positive and negative deviations. This calculation is called the **average deviation** (AD) about the mean. Following is the formula for AD, where the vertical bars indicate the absolute values of d_i:

● average
deviation
the mean of the
absolute values of
the difference
between a set of
continuous measures
and their mean

$$AD = \frac{\Sigma \mid d_i \mid}{N}$$

Suppose that the mean for a set of scores is 4. Then, an observation with a value of 1 has a deviation from the mean of − 3. Its absolute deviation is the absolute value of −3, or 3. If we sum all the absolute deviations for the distribution and divide by the number of observations, then we obtain an AD for the distribution. It must have a value larger than zero, unless all N observations have exactly the same score.

As useful as this alternative is, it does not fulfill an important criterion for a measure of variation. Because we use the mean as the basic measure of central tendency in many statistical analyses, we prefer a measure of variation that also uses the mean as its reference point. However, the variation formula we

Distribution of Years of Education, GSS Respondents

TABLE 3.5

Years	f	%	c%
0	3	.2	.2
1	2	.1	.3
2	2	.1	.5
3	7	.5	1.0
4	7	.5	1.4
5	10	.7	2.1
6	23	1.6	3.7
7	26	1.8	5.5
8	85	5.8	11.3
9	65	4.5	15.8
10	67	4.6	20.3
11	71	4.9	25.2
12	481	32.9	58.2
13	111	7.6	65.8
14	150	10.3	76.0
15	57	3.9	79.9
16	153	10.5	90.4
17	54	3.7	94.1
18	45	3.1	97.2
19	16	1.1	98.3
20	25	1.7	100.0
Total	1,460	100.0	100.0

Source: 1987 General Social Survey.
Missing data: 6.

choose must have a property that the dispersion of scores around the mean should be *smaller than* the dispersion calculated with that formula around any other central tendency statistic. Unfortunately for the average deviation formula, the value of AD when the median is used to calculate the deviations (d_i) is smaller than the value when the mean is used to calculate the d_i. To illustrate this problem, consider the education data in Table 3.5 that have a mean of 12.53 and a median of 12 (the cumulation to 50.0% falls into this category). As a rule the average deviation about the mean is larger than the average deviation about the median and this is true here (the AD about the mean is 2.53 and the AD about the median is 2.39). Thus, the AD fails to meet the criterion for an acceptable variation measure.

Although the average deviation is a meaningful statistic, it has certain points that are less desirable as a variability measure than the variance and standard deviation measures introduced in the following section. The average deviation, therefore, rarely is used in most analyses of social data.

3.2.3   Variance and Standard Deviation

As well as an average, as defined in Section 3.1.3, the mean is the number that makes the average squared distance from all the numbers in a distribution a minimum. No other number than the mean (including the median) produces a smaller value when we calculate the deviations from it, square them (to eliminate negative signs), and average them over all observations. This feature of the mean is useful for building a highly desirable measure of variability for a distribution—the **variance** of the scores about the mean. This statistic is the average of the squared deviations of a set of continuous scores; that is, the variance of a variable Y (denoted s_Y^2) is the mean squared deviation. Although the formula for the variance can be written several ways, we present two:

● **variance**
a measure of dispersion for continuous variables indicating an average of squared deviations of scores about the mean

$$s_Y^2 = \frac{\sum\limits_{i=1}^{N} d_i^2}{N-1}$$

$$s_Y^2 = \frac{\sum\limits_{i=1}^{N} (Y_i - \overline{Y})^2}{N-1}$$

Replacing the mean, $\overline{Y}$, in the formulas with any other measure of central tendency will always result in a larger value for s_Y^2. [Note that, unlike the calculation of the mean, we used $(N-1)$ in the denominator of the variance formulas because the result is an *unbiased* value, which we discuss in Chapter 6.] Table 3.6 shows the step-by-step calculation of the variance for murder rates in the 16 southern states (shown in Table 3.2), using the

Calculation of Variance for Murder Rates
Listed in Table 3.2

TABLE 3.6

$(Y_i - \bar{Y})$		d_i	d_i^2
51 − 110.375	=	− 59.375	3,525.39
69 − 110.375	=	− 41.375	1,711.89
71 − 110.375	=	− 39.375	1,550.39
86 − 110.375	=	− 24.375	594.14
88 − 110.375	=	− 22.375	500.64
92 − 110.375	=	− 18.375	337.64
95 − 110.375	=	− 15.375	236.39
106 − 110.375	=	− 4.375	19.14
108 − 110.375	=	− 2.375	5.64
114 − 110.375	=	3.625	13.14
132 − 110.375	=	21.625	467.64
138 − 110.375	=	27.625	763.14
145 − 110.375	=	34.625	1,198.89
145 − 110.375	=	34.625	1,198.89
157 − 110.375	=	46.625	2,173.89
169 − 110.375	=	58.625	3,436.89

$$\Sigma d_i^2 = 17{,}733.74$$

$$s_Y^2 = \frac{\Sigma d_i^2}{N-1}$$

$$= \frac{17{,}733.74}{15}$$

$$= 1{,}182.249$$

precise mean value of 110.375 to preserve accuracy in the arithmetic. *The variance is always a nonnegative number, due to the squaring.* Note that the variance, as an average of squared distances from the mean, is a large number relative to the original scores ($s_Y^2 = 1{,}182.25$ with a scale whose highest reported score is only 169). Thus, an intuitively meaningful interpretation of the variance is difficult to make.

To return the measure of variance to the original units of measurement, we take its positive square root, which is called the **standard deviation.** This is given by the following:

$$s_Y = \sqrt{s_Y^2}$$

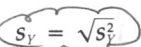

For the 16-state murder rate data, the standard deviation is 34.38 murders per million population, since $\sqrt{1,182.25} = 34.38$. (Some useful properties of the standard deviation will be shown in Chapter 6, which discusses inferential statistics).

The formulas for the variance and standard deviation are tedious to use when a large number of cases are involved. But, the steps can be simplified by a few algebraic manipulations to result in the following computing formula for s^2:

$$s_Y^2 = \left(\frac{\Sigma \, Y_i^2}{N-1} \right) - \left(\frac{N}{N-1} \right)(\overline{Y})^2$$

We now move to our example of murder rates in 16 southern states to show how the computing formula for the variance can be used with actual data. Table 3.7 displays the sum of the squared scores, their average, and the subtraction of the squared mean. Note that the computing formula avoids the subtraction of the mean from each score before squaring and then summing.

When data are grouped in a frequency distribution, as they are in Tables 3.3 and 3.4, a different formula for the variance is needed.

$$s_Y^2 = \frac{\sum\limits_{i=1}^{K} d_i^2 \, f_i}{N-1} = \frac{\sum\limits_{i=1}^{k} (Y_i - \overline{Y})^2 f_i}{N-1}$$

Grouped data

Computing Formula Calculation of Variance   TABLE 3.7
or Murder Rates

Y_i	Y_i^2
51	2,601
69	4,761
71	5,041
86	7,396
88	7,744
92	8,464
95	9,025
106	11,236
108	11,664
114	12,996
132	17,424
138	19,044
145	21,025
145	21,025
157	24,649
169	28,561

$$\Sigma Y_i^2 = 212,656$$

$$= \frac{\Sigma Y_i^2}{N-1} = \frac{212,656}{15} = 14,177.067$$

$$\overline{Y} = 110.375$$

$$\left(\frac{N}{N-1}\right)(\overline{Y})^2 = \left(\frac{16}{15}\right)(12,182.64) = 12,994.816$$

$$s_Y^2 = 14,177.067 - 12,994.816 = 1,182.251$$

To use this formula, we first form each deviation. Then we square it, multiply it by the frequency of cases of type i, sum the weighted squared deviations for the K outcomes of Y, and divide the sum by $(N-1)$. This is done in Table 3.8 for the data

TABLE 3.8   Calculation of Variance for Data in Table 3.4 on Liking for China

$(Y_i - \overline{Y})$	d_i	d_i^2	f_i	$d_i^2 f_i$
(0 - 4.9558)	-4.9558	24.5599	83	2,038.4717
(1 - 4.9558)	-3.9558	15.6484	52	813.7168
(2 - 4.9558)	-2.9558	8.7368	86	751.3648
(3 - 4.9558)	-1.9558	3.8252	90	344.2680
(4 - 4.9558)	-0.9558	.9136	157	143.4352
(5 - 4.9558)	.0442	.0020	352	0.7040
(6 - 4.9558)	1.0442	1.0904	223	243.1592
(7 - 4.9558)	2.0442	4.1788	217	906.7996
(8 - 4.9558)	3.0442	9.2672	77	713.5744
(9 - 4.9558)	4.0442	16.3556	67	1,095.8252

$$\Sigma d_i^2 f_i = 7{,}051.3189$$

$$s_Y^2 = \frac{\Sigma d_i^2 f_i}{N-1} = \frac{7{,}051.3189}{1{,}403}$$

$$= 5.0259$$

$$s_Y = \sqrt{s_Y^2} = 2.24$$

on China from Table 3.4. As the computations indicate, the variance is 5.025, and the standard deviation is 2.24.

As with the variance for ungrouped data, a more convenient computing formula also exists for a grouped frequency distribution.

$$s_Y^2 = \left(\frac{N}{N-1} \right) \left(\frac{\Sigma Y_i^2 f_i}{N} - \left(\frac{\Sigma Y_i f_i}{N} \right)^2 \right)$$

Note the adjustment ratio, $(N/(N-1))$, which is required to re-move the bias in the sample variance. Table 3.9 illustrates the application of this calculation formula to the liking for China example.

Convince yourself that the variance and standard deviation for the data on Russia in Table 3.4 are 6.25 and 2.50. These figures, when compared to those for China, make it clear that there is less variability in liking for China than there is in liking

Computing Formula Calculation of Variance for Liking for China

TABLE 3.9

Y_i	f_i	$Y_i f_i$	Y_i^2	$Y_i^2 f_i$
0	83	0	0	0
1	52	52	1	52
2	86	172	4	344
3	90	270	9	810
4	157	628	16	2,512
5	352	1,760	25	8,800
6	223	1,338	36	8,028
7	217	1,519	49	10,633
8	77	616	64	4,928
9	67	603	81	5,427
Total	1,404	6,958		41,534

$$s_Y^2 = \left(\frac{N}{N-1}\right)\left(\left(\frac{\Sigma Y_i^2 f_i}{N}\right) - \left(\frac{\Sigma Y_i f_i}{N}\right)^2\right)$$

$$= \left(\frac{1,404}{1,403}\right)\left(\left(\frac{41,534}{1,404}\right) - \left(\frac{6,958}{1,404}\right)^2\right)$$

$$= 5.0258$$

$$s_Y = 2.24$$

for Russia. A substantial proportion of all Americans in 198●
were relatively neutral about China, but opinions on Russia wer●
much more variable. Many strongly disliked the Soviet nation●
but many others were more favorable.

We can make direct comparisons of the variances and stan
dard deviations for liking of China and Russia because both vari
ables were measured using the same 10-point scale, and thu●
they have the same original units of measurement. But, if w●
have two variables with different units of measurement, for ex
ample years of education and dollars of annual income, we can
not make meaningful comparisons of the difference in thei●
variances and standard deviations. Thus, while a 3.0 standard
deviation of education is certainly smaller than a $5,000 stan-
dard deviation of income, these values just do not refer to the
same thing.

A special case of the variance for a grouped frequency distribution occurs when the variable is measured as a dichotomy.
If one category is assigned the score 1 and the second category
the score 0, then the formula for variance of the distribution is
as follows:

$$s_Y^2 = (p_0)(p_1)$$

Where:

p_0 = the proportion of cases coded 0.

p_1 = the proportion of cases coded 1.

The standard deviation is simply the positive square root of the
variance. To continue the gender example with 825 women
coded 1 and 641 men coded 0 in the 1987 GSS, the value of the
variance is $(825/1466)(641/1466) = (.563)(.437) = .246$ and the
standard deviation is .496. To convince yourself that the formula
for the variance of a proportion is identical to that for the variance of a grouped frequency distribution given earlier, you
should calculate the variance of this gender example using the
latter formula.

3.3   Z Scores

Researchers often want to compare scores across distributions that have different means and standard deviations. When
two distributions have different means and standard deviations,
however, the same score can mean something quite different
in each case. For example, in Table 3.4 a recoded score of 4
means something quite different in the data on liking for China
than it does in the data on liking for Russia. A 4 in the data on
China means the respondent likes China somewhat less than
the average American ($\overline{Y} = 4.96$). But a 4 in the data on Russia
means that the person likes Russia somewhat *better* than the
average American, since for these data $\overline{Y} = 3.06$.

To make comparisons across distributions, while allowing
for varying means and standard deviations, we compute *standard scores*, more commonly called **Z scores**. These transformations put the scores from different distributions on the same
scale, using each distribution's standard deviation as the common yardstick. The Z score formula is as follows:

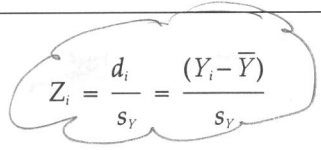

$$Z_i = \frac{d_i}{s_Y} = \frac{(Y_i - \overline{Y})}{s_Y}$$

● **Z scores
(standard scores)**
a transformation of
the scores of a
continuous
frequency
distribution by
subtracting the mean
from each outcome
and dividing by the
standard deviation

The Z score for a given Y_i score represents the number of
standard deviations above or below the mean of the distribution. The larger the Z score, the further away that case is from
the mean. A Z score of 0, however, occurs when a score falls
exactly on the mean of the distribution.

Table 3.10 shows the Z scores for the data on liking of China
and Russia presented in Table 3.4. The Z score for a recoded
score of 2 in the Russia data (-0.42) is comparable to the Z score
for a recoded score of 4 in the China data (-0.43), relative to
what the average American feels for these two countries.

Because data are standardized when using Z scores, you
should not be surprised that a distribution of Z scores has the
same mean and standard deviation. In particular, when Z scores

TABLE 3.10 Standard Scores (Z Scores) for Data in Table 3.4 on Liking for China and Russia

	Liking for China			Liking for Russia	
Recoded scores	$(Y_i - \bar{Y})/s_Y$	Z_i	Recoded scores	$(Y_i - \bar{Y})/s_Y$	Z_i
0	(0 − 4.96)/2.24	−2.21	0	(0 − 3.06)/2.50	−1.2
1	(1 − 4.96)/2.24	−1.77	1	(1 − 3.06)/2.50	−0.8
2	(2 − 4.96)/2.24	−1.32	2	(2 − 3.06)/2.50	−0.4
3	(3 − 4.96)/2.24	−0.88	3	(3 − 3.06)/2.50	−0.0
4	(4 − 4.96)/2.24	−0.43	4	(4 − 3.06)/2.50	0.3
5	(5 − 4.96)/2.24	0.02	5	(5 − 3.06)/2.50	0.7
6	(6 − 4.96)/2.24	0.46	6	(6 − 3.06)/2.50	1.1
7	(7 − 4.96)/2.24	0.91	7	(7 − 3.06)/2.50	1.5
8	(8 − 4.96)/2.24	1.36	8	(8 − 3.06)/2.50	1.9
9	(9 − 4.96)/2.24	1.80	9	(9 − 3.06)/2.50	2.3

are computed on *any* distribution, the mean of the Z-score distribution will always be zero, and the standard deviation will always be 1. This is difficult to see from the data in Table 3.8 because the observations are grouped. But, if we use the data in Table 3.2 on murder rates in the southern states, we can change these 16 observations to Z scores using the rounded values for the mean of 110.4 and for the standard deviation of 34.4. These Z scores appear in Table 3.11. The mean of these 16 Z scores is −0.00125 and the standard deviation is 0.9996, both differing from the expected values of 0 and 1 only because of rounding error.

Standardized scores are constructed from two descriptive statistics for continuous variables—the mean and the standard deviation—which summarize all the scores in a frequency distribution. These three descriptive statistics play crucial roles in allowing social scientists to make inferences from sample data to populations from which sample observations are selected, as you will learn in later chapters. Because Z scores are used very often in this text, you should be certain you understand this section clearly.

Z Scores for Murder Rates in 16 Southern States

TABLE 3.11

State name	Murder rate
Oklahoma	−1.73
Delaware	−1.20
West Virginia	−1.15
Virginia	−0.71
Kentucky	−0.65
Arkansas	−0.53
Maryland	−0.45
North Carolina	−0.13
Tennessee	−0.07
South Carolina	+0.10
Alabama	+0.63
Georgia	+0.80
Florida	+1.01
Mississippi	+1.01
Louisiana	+1.35
Texas	+1.70

Source: Table 3.2.

Key Concepts and Symbols

These key concepts and symbols are listed in the order of appearance in the chapter. Combined with the definitions in the margins, these will help you review the material and can serve as a self-test for mastery of the concepts.

statistics

central tendency

variation

mode

median

skewed distribution

positive skew

negative skew

mean

range

average deviation

variance

standard deviation

Z scores (standard scores)

$\overline{Y}$

d_i

AD

s_Y^2

s_Y

Z_i

Problems

General Problems

1. Following are data from the 14 largest American states in 1980:

State	Per capita income ($00's)	Unionized workers (%)	Prisoners per 100,000 (N)
California	109	27.0	98
Florida	90	11.7	208
Georgia	81	15.0	219
Illinois	105	30.6	94
Indiana	89	30.4	114
Massachusetts	101	24.9	56
Michigan	100	37.4	163
New Jersey	109	25.6	76
New York	103	38.7	123
North Carolina	78	9.6	244
Ohio	95	31.5	125
Pennsylvania	94	34.6	68
Texas	95	11.4	210
Virginia	94	14.7	161

Find the mode, median, mean, and range for (a) per capita income, (b) percent unionized workers, and (c) prisoners per 100,000 population.

2. Consider the leading four methods of suicide in 1977 for men and women, according to the National Center for Health Statistics listed in the following table:

Method of death	Men	Women
Firearms	12,124	2,598
Strangulation	2,827	859
Poisoning by gas	1,637	815
Solid or liquid poison	1,423	2,253
Total	18,011	6,525

What were the modal methods of self-destruction for men compared to women?

3. In 1987, the General Social Survey found the following data on household size, by number of persons in the household: one = 327; two = 444; three = 288; four = 236; five = 112; six = 40; seven = 11; eight = 4; nine = 1; ten = 3. What is the mode, median, mean, skew, and range of this distribution?

4. Find the average deviation, variance, and standard deviation of the following scores on a midterm statistics exam: 62, 67, 73, 77, 78, 78, 83, 84, 89, 92, 93, 97

5. Find the standard deviations using the data in Problem 1 for each of the three variables.

6. Following is a grouped frequency distribution of number of children ever born to 1987 GSS respondents:

N	f_i
0	422
1	227
2	335
3	246
4	114
5	45
6	26
7	15
8	31

What are the (a) mode, (b) median, (c) mean, (d) range, (e) variance, (f) standard deviation, and (g) Z score for a family with three children?

7. Find the Z scores for the following:

	$\overline{Y}$	s_Y^2	Y_i
a.	40	9	55
b.	40	9	35
c.	100	36	84
d.	12	1.69	10
e.	50	6.25	55

8. For a sample with $Y = 24$ and $s^2 = 6$, give the observed scores (Y_i) corresponding to the following Z scores:

a. Z = + 2.00   c. Z = +4.50
b. Z = −1.33   d. Z = −0.75

9. The GSS asks whether respondents favor or oppose capital punishment for murder. Following are the responses for 1972, 1980, and 1987:

	1972	1980	1987
Yes = 1	852	982	1,012
No = 0	632	390	354

a. Compute the means and standard deviations for all three time periods. Does there appear to be a trend across time?

b. Compute the proportion "yes" for all three years and compare your results to the mean computed above. What have you discovered?

10. Tuition at six public universities in a state were (in thousands of dollars) $5, $7, $6, $7, $4, and $8. At six private colleges, tuition was $8, $11, $9, $13, $10, and $14. What differences do you see in these schools, based on central tendency and variation statistics for the two distributions?

Problems Requiring the 1987 General Social Survey

11. Describe the distribution of respondents' occupational prestige scores (PRESTIGE), using all the central tendency and variation statistics discussed in this chapter.

12. For the respondents' years of schooling (EDUC) find the (a) mode, (b) median, (c) range, (d) mean, (e) variance, (f) standard deviation, and (g) Z score for 14 years of education.

13. Compare respondents' satisfaction with their family life (SATFAM) to their satisfaction with friends (SATFRND), using whatever statistics you think appropriate.

14. Compare the liberal-conservative self-images (POLVIEWS) of Republicans, Democrats, and Independents (PARTYID).

15. What differences occur between married men and women (SEX) when they judge their happiness with marriage (HAPMAR)? In their happiness in general (HAPPY)?

Problems Requiring the 50-States Data Set

16. America is one of the more heavily urbanized nations, but considerable variation remains across states. Use the SPSS/PC+ FREQ program to calculate mode, median, mean, range, standard deviation, and variance for the percentage of state populations living in urban areas (URBAN).

17. A traffic researcher hypothesizes that in smaller eastern states fewer auto fatalities occur than in larger western states, primarily because of differences in speeding and safety belt use. As a first step in examining this hypothesis, calculate the mean and standard deviation for FATALITY. Then compare Z scores for Wyoming (4.89 fatalities per 100 million miles), Texas (4.01), Connecticut (2.87), and Rhode Island (2.38). What do you observe?

18. Population growth and migration patterns have been redistributing people among the states. Compare the means and standard deviations of population growth from 1970–80 (POPCHNG) in the four main regions (REGION4).

4

Crosstabulation

Frequency distributions are useful displays of the quantitative attributes of continuous variables or the qualitative attributes of discrete variables. But, social scientists are usually more interested in identifying and questioning *relationships* between distributions: Are teenagers who have sexual intercourse more likely to drop out of school than those who don't have sexual intercourse? Are younger couples happier with their marriages than older couples? Do most blacks vote for Jesse Jackson and most whites for other candidates? On the basis of theory, past research, or just plain intuition, we typically form hypotheses about the covariation of two variables. When we posit that variable X and variable Y are related, we are suggesting that a pattern exists in which the scores observed on one variable are systematically connected to the scores observed on the second variable.

4.1 Bivariate Crosstabulation

One of the most widespread and useful tools that social researchers have in their kit bags is the **crosstabulation** or **joint contingency** table. Such a table offers a way to determine whether a bivariate relationship exists; that is, whether the two variables are in fact related as hypothesized.

● **crosstabulation (joint contingency table)** a tabular display of the joint frequency distribution of two discrete variables which has r rows and c columns

As a simple example of crosstabulation consider the relationship between two variables: state rates of poverty and the number of women in the paid labor force. We take the 50 American states and classify each one according to whether the proportion of women in the paid labor force is above or below average. At the same time, we also classify every state according to its rate of poverty, high (above average) or low (below average) and assign each of the 50 states to one of four paired combinations: high working women/high poverty, low working women/low poverty, high working women/low poverty, and low working women/high poverty. These data, appearing in Table 4.1, can be used to test this hypothesis.

TABLE 4.1   Raw Data on Poverty and Working Women for 50 American States

State	Poverty	Working women	State	Poverty	Working women
Alabama	Hi	Lo	Montana	Hi	Lo
Alaska	Hi	Hi	Nebraska	Lo	Hi
Arizona	Hi	Lo	Nevada	Lo	Hi
Arkansas	Hi	Lo	New Hampshire	Lo	Hi
California	Lo	Hi	New Jersey	Lo	Lo
Colorado	Lo	Hi	New Mexico	Hi	Lo
Connecticut	Lo	Hi	New York	Hi	Lo
Delaware	Hi	Lo	North Carolina	Hi	Hi
Florida	Hi	Lo	North Dakota	Hi	Lo
Georgia	Hi	Hi	Ohio	Lo	Lo
Hawaii	Lo	Hi	Oklahoma	Hi	Lo
Idaho	Hi	Lo	Oregon	Lo	Hi
Illinois	Lo	Hi	Pennsylvania	Lo	Lo
Indiana	Lo	Hi	Rhode Island	Lo	Hi
Iowa	Lo	Hi	South Carolina	Hi	Lo
Kansas	Lo	Hi	South Dakota	Hi	Hi
Kentucky	Hi	Lo	Tennessee	Hi	Lo
Louisiana	Hi	Lo	Texas	Hi	Lo
Maine	Hi	Lo	Utah	Lo	Lo
Maryland	Lo	Hi	Vermont	Hi	Hi
Massachusetts	Lo	Hi	Virginia	Hi	Hi
Michigan	Lo	Lo	Washington	Lo	Lo
Minnesota	Lo	Hi	West Virginia	Hi	Lo
Mississippi	Hi	Lo	Wisconsin	Lo	Hi
Missouri	Hi	Lo	Wyoming	Lo	Hi

H1: States with larger proportions of working women have lower levels of poverty than states with small proportions of working women because more women are making larger contributions to household incomes.

The data displayed in Table 4.1 do not allow us to tell whether or not the hypothesis is supported. To indicate the relationship among the two variables, we must build a crosstabulation in the following way: We count the number of observations occurring for each of the four joint outcomes. For example, from Table 4.1 we see that Alabama has a low proportion of working women and high rate of poverty, as does Arizona, Arkansas, Florida, and 16 other states, that is, 20 states constitute the low working women/high poverty category. The following joint frequency results consolidate the data:

Joint outcomes	f
High working women/High poverty	6
High working women/Low poverty	18
Low working women/High poverty	20
Low working women/Low poverty	6

The raw data are arranged in crosstabulated form in Table 4.2, panel A. For ordered discrete variables, column values increase from left to right, and row values increase from bottom to top. These sequences of numerical values are consistent with the way we will graph continuous variables in Chapter 9. (You should order your variables in tables and graphs in the same directions.[1]) A crosstabulation of two variables, each of which has only two categories (a dichotomy) is called a 2 × 2 *table* (read as a "two by two table"). The **cells** of any crosstabulation show the joint outcomes (intersection) of the two variables. The **marginal distributions** (or as they are more simply called, *the marginals*) are the **row marginals** (row totals) shown on the right and the column totals (**column marginals**) shown at the bottom of the table. The grand total of all cases, 50 states, appears in the lower right cell. If one or both of the variables have missing

● **cells**
intersections of rows and columns in crosstabulations of two or more variables. Numerical values contained within cells may be cell frequencies, cell proportions, or cell percentages

● **marginal distributions**
the frequency distributions of each of two crosstabulated variables

● **row marginals**
the frequency distribution of the variable shown across the rows of a crosstabulation

● **column marginals**
the frequency distribution of the variable shown across the columns of a crosstabulation

[1] Unfortunately, SPSS and other computer crosstabulation programs tend to print their tables with the row values increasing from top to bottom. You should get in the habit of rewriting tables by hand to rearrange their rows and columns in the proper sequences.

TABLE 4.2   Crosstabulation of Poverty and Working
             Women for 50 American States

A. Raw data

		Working women		
		Low	High	Total
Poverty	High	20	6	26
	Low	6	18	24
	Total	26	24	50

B. Percentaged data

		Working women		
		Low	High	Total
Poverty	High	76.9%	25.0%	52.0%
	Low	23.1	75.0	48.0
	Total	100.0%	100.0%	100.0%
	(N)	(26)	(24)	(50)

information for any reason, then we cannot classify that case
and the total number of cases appearing in the crosstabulation
will be smaller than the sample size. Missing data frequencies
can be reported in a footnote to the table (such as in Table 4.3).

The marginal distributions are the frequency distributions
of each of the two crosstabulated variables. Although the particular example in Table 4.2 displays equal dichotomies, row
marginals and column marginals do not always have the same
distributions. In fact, whether a frequency crosstabulation has
equal or unequal marginals gives little or no indication of how
strongly the variables may be related. For example, if all of the
26 high poverty states had low levels of working women, then
the marginal distribution for the columns would have 32 low
working women and 18 high working women states. The distribution of the column marginals would be more skewed than
the nearly equal distribution of the row marginals, making a

judgment about the degree of covariation difficult to reach. We need some way to *standardize* the frequency table to a common denominator so that the pattern of covariation is clearer.

A *percentage crosstabulation* permits such a pattern to surface. As you recall from Chapter 2, calculating percentages for a frequency distribution results in a standardized distribution totalling to 100%. For two-variable crosstabulations, we have a choice of standardizing within rows, within columns, or by the total number of cases in the table. However, for examining research hypotheses, the clear preference is to calculate percentages within categories of the independent variable. Here we chose working women as the independent variable, on the assumption that states which have a larger proportion of their female population in the labor force are likely to have lower poverty rates than are states where fewer women are earning incomes. Because we want percentages for each of the two categories of working women, we first locate the column total for "low" working women (26), in the last row of the frequency distribution in panel A. Then, we divide this total into each of the cell frequencies in that column and multiply by 100 to change the proportion to a percentage. For the high poverty states, the percentage is $(20/26)(100) = 76.9\%$ and for the low poverty states, the percentage is $(6/26)(100) = 23.1\%$. Next, we find the percentages within the column of "high" working women: $(6/24)(100) = 25.0\%$ and $(18/24)(100) = 75.0\%$. Finally, we also calculate the percentage distribution in the total column, dividing each of the row totals by the grand total and multiplying by 100.

If the poverty level were unrelated to working women among the 50 states, then we would expect to find the percentages within each category of the independent variable to be equal to one another and to equal the percentages in the row marginal. Because 52% of all states have a high poverty level, we would expect that 52% of states with low rates of working women and 52% of states with high rates of working women would also have high poverty levels. The fact that the observed distributions within columns of Table 4.2 differ so widely—the high poverty percentages are three times greater among states with fewer working women compared to states with many working women—indicates that the two variables are indeed related. (Later in this chapter and elsewhere in this book you will learn statistics useful for summarizing other aspects of relationships in crosstabulations.)

4.1.1   An Example: Church Attendance and Marital Status

Another example of crosstabulation is taken from the sociology of religion. Although the United States is one of the most religious nations in the world as shown by high levels of church attendance, not all persons are equally observant. Researchers have known that various social characteristics are related to frequency of participation in religious services. For example, women attend more often than men, blacks more often than whites, older people more often than younger. In this example, we look at the following proposition involving marital status:

P: Marital status is related to church attendance.

This proposition does not specify the precise form of the expected relationship; it merely states that church attendance will not be the same for all categories of current marital situation. Based on other research findings, we can expect that currently married persons and widows are likely to attend church more often than are the formerly married (divorced and separated), while never married persons go to church or synagogue least often. This pattern may occur, in part, because of the greater age of widowed and married persons than of single persons, because religious involvement tends to increase with age. Although age provides an interesting hypothesis for further research, we will not test that explanation in this example.

Using the percentage distributions of 1987 GSS respondents for four categories of marital status and the recoded church attendance variables shown in Tables 2.5 and 2.6 in Chapter 2, we compile a raw data crosstabulation for the proposition, as shown in Table 4.3. Categories of church attendance are arranged in the rows and categories of marital status in the columns. We chose marital status as the independent variable because we believe it is more likely that a person's marital situation affects his or her level of religious activity than religious participation affecting a change in a person's marital status. When these frequency data are expressed as percentages within columns of the independent variable, the crosstabulation shown in Table 4.4 results. The percentages in the "total" column for

Crosstabulation of Observed Frequencies for
Marital Status and Church Attendance,
GSS Respondents

TABLE 4.3

Church attendance	Marital status					
	Never	Separated	Divorced	Widowed	Married	Total
Never	34	6	32	16	85	173
Annually	129	18	74	43	269	533
Monthly	50	10	30	26	149	265
Weekly	63	17	34	80	289	483
Total	276	51	170	165	792	1,454

Source: 1987 General Social Survey.
Missing data: 12 cases.

these variables do not agree with those shown in Table 2.5 because 12 respondents with no information on church attendance were eliminated from Tables 4.3 and 4.4, as stated in the table footnote.

With the data in this form, we can now examine the hypothesis that marital status is related to church attendance. In interpreting the results, we compare each value with the others in the same row. For example, looking at the five percentages within the row of those who never attend church, we see that the smallest percentage is widowed (9.7%) and the largest percentage is divorced (18.8%). Similarly looking across the weekly attendance row, the highest rates are for the widowed and currently married (48.5% and 36.5%, respectively), while divorced and single people have the lowest level of weekly attendance (20.0% and 22.8%, respectively). The rate of weekly church attendance for the separated falls in between (33.3%). Thus, the hypothesis appears to be supported by the evidence from the 1987 GSS.

Figure 4.1 displays one way to present data from bivariate crosstabulations as a bar chart (see Section 2.2.1). Bars representing the same category on the independent variable (marital status) are grouped together and given different shadings to stand for the various categories of the dependent variable (church attendance).

FIGURE 4.1   Bar Chart Showing Church Attendance and
                  Marital Status

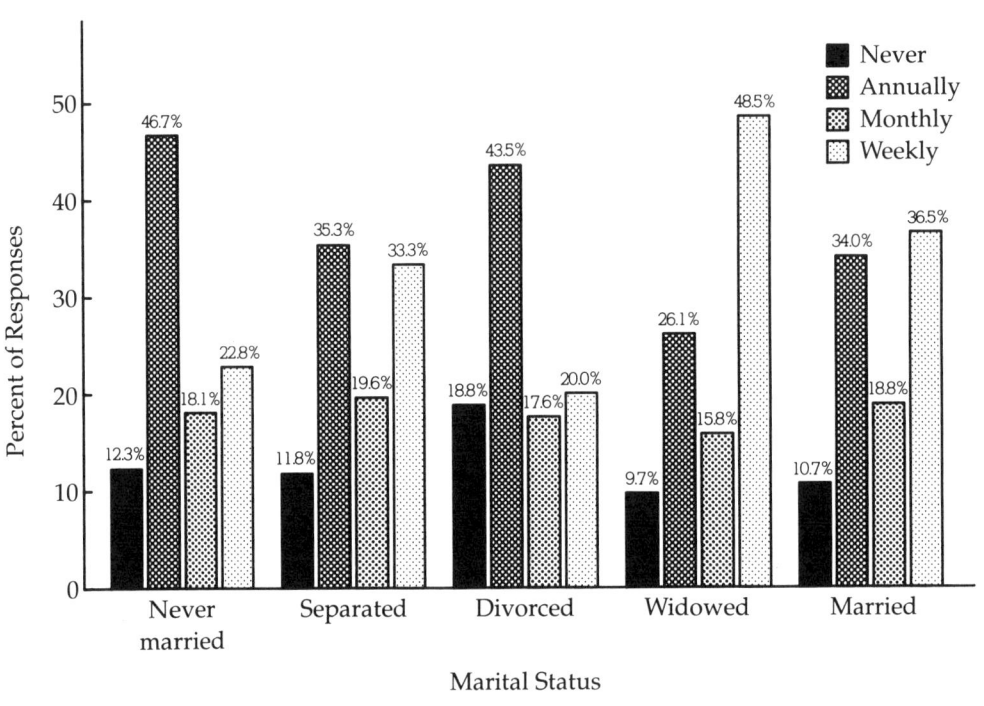

Source: Data from Table 4.4.

4.2   Population Inference from Samples

The data displayed in Table 4.4 came from the 1987 GSS
of a cross-sectional sample of the American adult population.
Despite the large sample size (1,466 respondents), these cases
are only a fraction of the 160 million American adults in the
population from which persons to be interviewed were selected.
Literally trillions of different samples of the same size might have
been drawn by the National Opinion Research Center. Because
only one of these possible samples was actually drawn, we are
faced with the question of whether the conclusions based on

Percentage Crosstabulation of Marital Status and Church Attendance

TABLE 4.4

Church attendance	Marital status					
	Never	Separated	Divorced	Widowed	Married	Total
Never	12.3%	11.8%	18.8%	9.7%	10.7%	11.9%
Annually	46.7	35.3	43.5	26.1	34.0	36.7
Monthly	18.1	19.6	17.6	15.8	18.8	18.2
Weekly	22.8	33.3	20.0	48.5	36.5	33.2
Total	99.9%*	100.0%	99.9%*	100.1%*	100.0%	100.0%
(N)	(276)	(51)	(170)	(165)	(792)	(1,454)

Source: 1987 General Social Survey.
* Does not total to 100.0% due to rounding.
Missing data: 12 cases.

this data can be meaningfully *generalized* to the entire U.S. adult population. In other words, what sort of *inference* can we make about marital status and church attendance from this sample to the U.S. population as a whole? This chapter introduces some basic concepts necessary for understanding the topic of statistical inference.

Statistical significance tests allow us to be reasonably certain that conclusions based on a sample of observations would also apply to the population from which that sample was drawn. We can never be entirely certain that the sample findings accurately reflect the population situation, for we might by chance have selected an unusually deviant set of observations. But, if the sampling of observations from the population is done randomly, we can make an inference to the entire population, with a calculable chance that this inference is incorrect.

The typical requirement is that a sample from a population be created by **random sampling**. (The concept of a random sample was introduced in Chapter 1.) In simple random sampling, each observation (i.e., a person, an object, or an event) in the population has an equal chance of being selected for the sample. If the population consists of *N* units, each unit has the probability of exactly *1/N* of being chosen for the sample. If, as is typically the situation in national surveys, the American adult population has an *N* of 160 million and the sample of persons

● **statistical significance tests**
tests of inference that conclusions based on samples of observations also hold true for the populations from which the samples were selected

● **random sampling**
a procedure for selecting a set of representative observations from a population, in which each observation has an equal chance of being selected for the sample

to be interviewed is only 1,500 observations, then each person has less than one chance in 100,000 – or a probability lower than .00001 – of being drawn for a given national survey. No wonder that so few people say they have ever been interviewed for a Gallup Poll!

It would be ideal to use a national sample drawn by simple random sampling, but this method requires a complete list of all sample candidates, which is too costly to create for a national or even a city population. Instead, survey research organizations such as Harris, Gallup, and NORC use more cost-efficient sampling methods which are beyond the scope of our discussion. In this text, we will treat the GSS data as though they had been drawn using simple random procedures. The amount of error this creates for inference is small and calculable.

4.3   Probability and Null Hypotheses

Suppose that we draw a sample of observations, form a bivariate crosstabulation, compute percentages for the table, and find that the variables are related. Now, we want to know whether we are justified in concluding that this relationship also occurs in the population from which the sample data came. The basic question of statistical inference is this: What is the probability that the relationship observed in the sample data could come from a population in which there is *no* relationship between the two variables? If we can show that this probability is very high, then, even though a relationship exists in the sample, we would be extremely hesitant to conclude that the two variables are related. If the chance were small (perhaps less than 1 in 20 or less than 1 in 100) that the sample relationship could have been created by sampling from a population in which no relationship exists, we would decide that the hypothesis should be accepted.

When samples are small, the probability of observing a relationship in the sample where none exists in the population is greater than when samples are large. Suppose, for example, that in a population of 1,000 no relationship exists between a pair of variables. If we choose a sample of 900 observations, the probability that we would find sample results indicating a relationship among two variables is much smaller than if we draw a sample of only 50 observations. Conversely, if a relationship *does* exist in a population, the probability is much greater in a larger sample than in a smaller sample that we would observe a sample outcome which indicates a relationship.

Suppose we have an hypothesis that two variables (for example, marital status and church attendance) are related in a population of interest (e.g., adult Americans). One way to determine if two variables are related in the population is to test the hypothesis that they are *unrelated* using the sample observations (as we noted in Chapter 1). The way to make this test is to state a **null hypothesis** that *no* relationship between the variables exists in the population. This statement is contrary to the research hypothesis that states there is an expected relationship between variables, either based on theory or past research. Even though, as social scientists, we firmly believe that the research hypothesis is correct, we actually perform the statistical inference test on the null hypothesis, because we hope to show that it is a false statement about the situation. In other words, we expect to "nullify" that hypothesis. For discrete data in cross-tabulation form (such as Table 4.3), the basic question of inference arises: What is the probability that the relationship found in the sample data could have come from a population in which there was no relationship between the two variables? In the example on marital status and church attendance in Section 4.1.1, the research hypothesis can be restated as a null hypothesis, using the symbol H_0 (where the subscript is a zero, standing for "null"):

● **null hypothesis** a statistical hypothesis that one usually expects to reject. Symbolized H_0

> H_0: Marital status is not related to church attendance.

We really expect to show that this null hypothesis is an untrue statement about the population of adult Americans in 1987. If the probability is small — less than .05 (that is, less than 1 chance in 20) — that the sample evidence could have happened as the outcome of a random sampling from such a population, then we reject this null hypothesis. In concluding that H_0 is false, we accept its alternative H_1 — the research hypothesis stating that the two variables do in fact covary in the population. From a scientific point of view, the acceptance of an **alternative hypothesis** is conditional, because the truth about social relationships can only be assessed indirectly, through the rejection of false hypotheses (as expressed in Chapter 1).

● **alternative hypothesis** a secondary hypothesis about the value of a population parameter that often mirrors the research or operational hypothesis. Symbolized H_1

As another example of a null hypothesis, consider research on the relationship between social class and use of illegal drugs. If you suspect that a relationship exists between these two variables—for example, that lower-class people consume more illegal drugs than do upper-class people—then you might formulate a research hypothesis in these terms:

> H3: The higher the social class, the lower the illegal drug use.

However, in testing that relationship with a random sample of observations drawn from some population, you would restate the research hypothesis as a null relationship in which the two variables do not covary:

> H_0: Social class is unrelated to use of illegal drugs.

Notice that we have set up the research and null hypotheses so that we are expecting to find evidence that social classes differ in their levels of illegal drug use. We hope to reject the null hypothesis and support the research hypothesis, thus lending weight to the original social relationship we felt to exist between class and drug use.

If the research hypothesis is correct, then you would find evidence in the sample to reject the null hypothesis. On the other hand, if social class and drug use really *are* unrelated—as some studies indicate—then your sample data should turn up insufficient evidence to reject this H_0. You would then conclude that the original research hypothesis is probably not true. That conclusion, however, always carries a probability of being incorrect. We turn next to procedures for deciding the level of probability for a false conclusion.

● **probability level**
the probability selected for rejection of a null hypothesis, which is the likelihood of making a Type I error

● **alpha**
the probability level for rejecting a null hypothesis when it is true, conventionally set at .05 or lower

4.3.1   Type I and Type II Errors

Whenever we deal with probabilities, we run the risk of making an incorrect decision. Otherwise we would be dealing with certainties, which is never the case. A **probability level** (α, or **alpha**) for rejection of a null hypothesis is usually set at .05 (that is, one chance in 20) or lower. By setting this α level before beginning to examine the data, we make a deliberate choice to run a given risk of an incorrect inference from a sample relationship to a population relationship.

In making inferences, we might make two different types of judgment errors. First, based on the significance test results, we might reject a null hypothesis which in fact is true; that is, we might reject the hypothesis that two variables are unrelated, based on the sample results, when in the population they are in fact unrelated. In other words, if we had known the truth about the population, we would not have rejected the H_0, but unfortunately we did reject the H_0 and thus made an error. Such an error occurs when, simply by chance, the sample we draw contains many of the most deviant observations in the population from which it was selected. Even when sampling is done randomly, there is always some chance that one will select a sample whose variables show a relationship that is quite different from the population relationship. Concluding that H_0 is false when in the population it is really true leads to a **Type I error**, or **false rejection error**. The chance of making this mistake is the same as the probability level that we set for rejection of the null hypothesis (α). Thus, Type I error is often called α *error*, or *alpha error*.

● **Type I error (false rejection error)** a statistical decision error that occurs when a true null hypothesis is rejected; its probability is alpha

The second type of error is a **Type II error**, which may also be called a **false acceptance error**. This occurs in the opposite fashion: Although the null hypothesis is actually false, we fail to reject it on the basis of the sample data. This type of decision-making error is also called β *error*, or *beta error*. Box 4.1 offers some help in keeping the two types of error distinct.

● **Type II error (false acceptance error)** a statistical decision error that occurs when a false null hypothesis is not rejected; its probability is beta

The probability of making a Type II error is not simply 1.0 minus the probability of a Type I error; that is, if α is .05, β is *not* just $1.00 - .05 = .95$. It is more complicated than that. A complete account of how to find the probability of a Type II error would take us into a long discussion of the "power" of statistical tests and lead us away from our immediate goal, which is to show the basis of significance tests for crosstabulations.

Although there is not a simple mathematical relationship between Type I and Type II errors, it is important to note that they are related to one another. Reducing the potential probability of making a false rejection error—setting α at a very low level, such as .001—tends to increase the risk of making a false acceptance error. Standard methods for offsetting false accepting error are (1) to increase the sample size, thus reducing sampling error in making inferences about population relationships

Box 4.1   Type I and Type II Errors

Type I and Type II errors are often confused. One way to keep them straight is to memorize this table.

		Based on sample results, the decision made is	
		Reject null hypothesis	Do not reject null hypothesis
In the population from which the sample is drawn, the null hypothesis is	True	Type I or false rejection error (α)	Correct decision
	False	Correct decision	Type II or false acceptance error (β)

from sample data; or (2) to repeat the study using another, independently drawn sample, so that consistent results strengthen our belief in the findings.

4.4   Chi-Square: A Significance Test

● **chi-square test** a test of statistical significance based on a comparison of the observed cell frequencies of a joint contingency table with frequencies that would be expected under the null hypothesis of no relationship

For bivariate crosstabulations, we can calculate a simple statistic that allows us to determine the probability that two variables in the sample are also related in the population. This statistic is the **chi-square test** (χ^2) of statistical significance. If the null hypothesis to be tested is that no relationship exists between two crosstabulated variables, the probability associated with χ^2 reveals the Type I error.

This test is made by comparing the observed cell frequencies of a crosstabulation or joint contingency table with the frequencies that one expects if the null hypothesis of no

Percentage Crosstabulation of Two
Unrelated Variables, Time of Birth and
Voting for President

TABLE 4.5

Presidential vote	Time of birth		Total
	Jan.–June	July–Dec.	
Reagan	59.7%	58.6%	59.2%
Mondale	40.3	41.4	40.8
Total	100.0%	100.0%	100.0%
(N)	(459)	(459)	(918)

Source: 1987 General Social Survey.
Missing data: 548 cases.

relationship were in fact true. The key to the calculation of the χ^2 statistic is to find these expected frequencies.

What would a contingency table look like if no relationship whatsoever existed between the two variables? That is, what would we expect to find in a situation of **statistical independence**?

> If two variables are statistically independent, within categories of the independent variable in a contingency table there are identical percentages of the dependent variable. Similarly, within each category of the dependent variable the same percentages of the independent responses occur.

● **statistical independence** a condition of no relationship between variables in a population

To take an obvious example where we would expect two variables to be independent, consider the crosstabulation in Table 4.5 between the time of year in which people were born and their choice for president in 1984. For the sample of voters as a whole, 59.2% voted for Reagan and 40.8% voted for Mondale (row marginals). Among those persons born in the first half of the year, 59.7% were Reagan voters; among those born in the last half of the year, 58.6% were Reagan voters.

The observed 1.1% difference in these sample vote distributions is very small, as shown by the χ^2 of .072. This value is probably too small to reflect real differences in the population

TABLE 4.6   Expected Frequencies for Marital Status by
                         Church Attendance, under Null Hypothesis
                         of Independence

| | | | Marital status | | | | |
Church attendance	Never	Separated	Divorced	Widowed	Married	Total	(N)
A. Expected frequencies							
Never	32.8	6.1	20.2	19.6	94.2	172.9*	
Annually	101.2	18.7	62.3	60.5	290.3	533.0	
Monthly	50.3	9.3	31.0	30.1	144.3	265.0	
Weekly	91.7	16.9	56.5	54.8	263.1	483.0	
Total	276.0	51.0	170.0	165.0	791.9*	1,454.0	
B. Column percentages							
Never	11.9%	11.9%	11.9%	11.9%	11.9%	11.9%	
Annually	36.7	36.7	36.7	36.7	36.7	36.7	
Monthly	18.2	18.2	18.2	18.2	18.2	18.2	
Weekly	33.2	33.2	33.2	33.2	33.2	33.2	
Total	100.0%	100.0%	100.0%	100.0%	100.0%	100.0%	
(N)	(276)	(51)	(170)	(165)	(792)	(1,454)	
C. Row percentages							
Never	19.0%	3.5%	11.7%	11.3%	54.5%	100.0%	(173)
Annually	19.0	3.5	11.7	11.3	54.5	100.0	(533)
Monthly	19.0	3.5	11.7	11.3	54.5	100.0	(265)
Weekly	19.0	3.5	11.7	11.3	54.5	100.0	(483)
Total	19.0%	3.5%	11.7%	11.3%	54.5%	100.0%	(1,454)

* Totals do not agree with those in Table 4.3 due to rounding.

● **expected frequencies** in chi-square tests, the values that cell frequencies are expected to take, given the hypothesis under study (ordinarily, the null hypothesis)

of all voters from which this sample came. Later in this chapter you will learn how to use chi-square as a statistical test for determining the probability of such a sample relationship if none exists in the population.

We can also calculate what the frequencies of a crosstabulation would look like *if* the two variables were independent, that is, if the H_0 of no relationship were true. Panel A of Table 4.6 shows what such an independence relationship would look like for the marital status and church attendance crosstabulation in Table 4.3. The cell entries are the **expected frequencies** under the null hypothesis of independence. If we calculate the percentages within each column using these expected frequencies, as shown in panel B, we find that 11.9% never attend church, 36.7% attend annually, 18.2% attend monthly, and 33.2% are weekly churchgoers. These percentages exactly equal the values found when calculating the rates of attendance for the row marginals (in the last column of Table 4.6). In other words, if the two variables are independent, there is no difference in the distributions of the dependent variable within every category of the independent variable. And, as panel C shows, no differences occur when the percentages are calculated in the other direction. Within any category of church attendance, there are 19.0% never married, 3.5% separated, 11.7% divorced, 11.3% widowed, and 54.5% married. Again, the identical percentage distribution occurs for the column marginals (last row). The marginal totals for both variables in Table 4.3 were the basis for calculating the 20 expected frequencies in the cells of panel A in Table 4.6. If the two variables in any crosstabulation, X and Y, are independent, the formula for the expected frequency in row i and column j is as follows:

$$\hat{f}_{ij} = \frac{(f_{i.})(f_{.j})}{N}$$

Where:

$\hat{f}_{ij}$ = the expected frequency of the cell in the ith row and the jth column.

$f_{i.}$ = the total in the ith row marginal.

$f_{.j}$ = the total in the jth column marginal.

N = the grand total, or sample size for the entire table.

To illustrate, the expected frequency of never married persons who never attend church under the null hypothesis that the two variables are unrelated is

$$\frac{(173)(276)}{1{,}454} = 32.84$$

You should calculate a few of the other expected frequencies to check on your understanding of this concept.

Tables 4.3 and 4.6, respectively, give the observed frequencies and the expected frequencies under the null hypothesis of independence. The χ^2 statistic summarizes the differences between these two tables across all 20 cells in the body of each table. (The row and column marginals in the two tables are identical, so no comparisons there are helpful.) These discrepancies are noted by comparing the observed and expected frequencies in the corresponding cells of the two tables. If $\hat{f}_{ij}$ is the expected frequency under the null hypothesis and the observed frequency is f_{ij} for the same cell, then the χ^2 statistic for the table is found by the formula:

$$\chi^2 = \sum_{i=1}^{R} \sum_{j=1}^{C} \frac{(\hat{f}_{ij} - f_{ij})^2}{\hat{f}_{ij}}$$

Where:

$\hat{f}_{ij}$ = the expected frequency of the cell in the ith row and jth column.

f_{ij} = the observed frequency of the cell in the ith row and jth column.

C = the number of columns in the crosstabulation.

R = the number of rows in the crosstabulation.

The difference between the observed and expected frequencies in a cell is first squared (to remove plus and minus signs) and then is divided by the expected frequency for that cell. After this operation has been performed for all cells, the results are summed for all cells of the table.

The formula for finding the χ^2 statistic uses double summation signs, which have not been used before in this book. (Appendix A describes how to use summation.) Following are some rules for using double summation in the formula:

1. Set $i = 1$ and $j = 1$, and calculate the first term. In this case, the term is

$$\frac{(\hat{f}_{11} - f_{11})^2}{\hat{f}_{11}} = \frac{(32.84 - 34)^2}{32.84}$$

$$= 0.041$$

2. The index of the second, or inside, summation operator changes from 1 to C one step at a time before the index of the first, or outside, summation operator changes to its next value. Thus, the second element has $i = 1$ and $j = 2$; the third element has $i = 1$ and $j = 3$; etc.
3. At each step, as the index i changes to the next higher value, index j must pass through its *entire* cycle from 1 to C.
4. The process ends with $i = R$ and $j = C$.

If we follow these procedures using the observed frequencies (f_{ij}) in Table 4.3 and the corresponding expected frequencies ($\hat{f}_{ij}$) in Table 4.6, we find

$i = 1, j = 1$ $(32.8 - 34)^2/32.8$ $= 0.04$
$i = 1, j = 2$ $(6.1 - 6)^2/6.1$ $= 0.00$
$i = 1, j = 3$ $(20.2 - 32)^2/20.2$ $= 6.89$
$i = 1, j = 4$ $(19.6 - 16)^2/19.6$ $= 0.66$
$i = 1, j = 5$ $(94.2 - 85)^2/94.2$ $= 0.90$
$i = 2, j = 1$ $(101.2 - 129)^2/101.2 = 7.64$
$i = 2, j = 2$ $(18.7 - 18)^2/18.7$ $= 0.03$
$i = 2, j = 3$ $(62.3 - 74)^2/62.3$ $= 2.20$
$i = 2, j = 4$ $(60.5 - 43)^2/605$ $= 5.06$
$i = 2, j = 5$ $(290.3 - 269)^2/290.3 = 1.56$
$i = 3, j = 1$ $(50.3 - 50)^2/50.3$ $= 0.00$
$i = 3, j = 2$ $(9.3 - 10)^2/9.3$ $= 0.05$
$i = 3, j = 3$ $(31.0 - 30)^2/31.0$ $= 0.03$
$i = 3, j = 4$ $(30.1 - 26)^2/30.1$ $= 0.56$
$i = 3, j = 5$ $(144.3 - 149)^2/144.3 = 0.15$
$i = 4, j = 1$ $(91.7 - 63)^2/91.7$ $= 8.98$
$i = 4, j = 2$ $(16.9 - 17)^2/16.9$ $= 0.00$
$i = 4, j = 3$ $(56.5 - 34)^2/56.5$ $= 8.96$
$i = 4, j = 4$ $(54.8 - 80)^2/54.8$ $= 11.59$
$i = 4, j = 5$ $(263.1 - 289)^2/263.1 = 2.55$

TABLE 4.7   Chi-Square Components for Marital Status
                   by Church Attendance

Church attendance	Marital status				
	Never	Separated	Divorced	Widowed	Married
Never	.04	.00	6.89	.66	.90
Annually	7.64	.03	2.20	5.06	1.56
Monthly	.00	.05	.03	.56	.15
Weekly	8.98	.00	8.96	11.59	2.55

We have arranged these 20 chi-square components in the cells of Table 4.7. The larger the value, the greater the relative difference between observed and expected frequencies for that cell.

The largest differences in Table 4.7 are underscored to highlight where the major deviations from independence occur. You must look at both Tables 4. 3 and 4.6 to determine where the excesses and deficits occur, because the squaring step hides the directions of these differences. The never married and the divorced respondents are less likely than expected under the null hypothesis to attend church every week. The never married are more likely to go only annually and the divorced not to go to church at all. Widowed persons go more often than expected on a weekly basis and less often annually. Both the separated and the married have church attendance patterns close to what would occur if the two variables were statistically independent.

The sum of all the entries in Table 4.7 is 57.55. Thus, we say that $\chi^2 = 57.85$ for the null hypothesis of independence in this crosstabulation. To understand the meaning of this number in making a decision about whether or not to reject the null hypothesis, we must first ask how χ^2 values are distributed under the null hypothesis. The chi-square statistic for a large N (30 or greater) follows a **chi-square distribution**, which is the topic of the next section.

● **chi-square distribution**
a family of distributions, each of which has different degrees of freedom, on which the chi-square test statistic is based

4.5   Sampling Distributions for Chi-Square

A central idea in statistical inference is the sampling distribution of a test statistic. A **test statistic** is used to evaluate a hypothesis about a population, given evidence drawn from a particular sample (see Section 4.2). In the example in Section 4.4, the sample value of the χ^2 test statistic is 57.85. Each test statistic has a characteristic sampling distribution that depends on the sample size and the degrees of freedom which will be discussed shortly. You will see different sampling distributions in this book as we look at different test statistics. For now, our attention is focused on the sampling distribution of χ^2.

● **test statistic**
a number used to evaluate a statistical hypothesis about a population, calculated from data on a sample selected from a population

In general, a **sampling distribution** is a theoretical frequency distribution of a test statistic, under the assumption that all possible random samples of a given size have been drawn from some population. For example, assume that we have a population of 50 from which we draw a single sample of 45 cases. It can be shown that there are 2,118,760 *different* samples of size 45 from a population of 50 cases. Suppose we collect data on two variables, X and Y, for each of these different samples. Then we compute a χ^2 test statistic for each of the X by Y crosstabulations. In principle, we could build a frequency distribution of the 2,118,760 χ^2 values, although in practice that would be a long task.

● **sampling distribution**
a theoretical frequency distribution of a test statistic, under the assumption that all possible random samples of a given size have been drawn from some population

This imaginary distribution would look much like a sampling distribution for χ^2. We say it would look much like a sampling distribution because an actual sampling distribution of χ^2 also assumes that the population from which the samples were drawn was normally distributed. At this point you may not know what a normal distribution is. We will discuss this concept in Chapter 6; for now, you need only know that a normal distribution is a smooth, bell-shaped curve. (Figure 6.2 shows two normal distributions.) Obviously, in a population composed of only 50 elements, there are too few observations for a distribution of them to form a smooth, bell-shaped curve. For that reason, our distribution of 2,118,760 χ^2 values technically would *not* be a sampling distribution.

However, our distribution would look much like a member of a family of theoretical distributions called *chi-square distributions* (discussed in more detail in the next section; three are displayed in Figure 4.2). We say that our distribution would look

FIGURE 4.2   Three Chi-Square Distributions

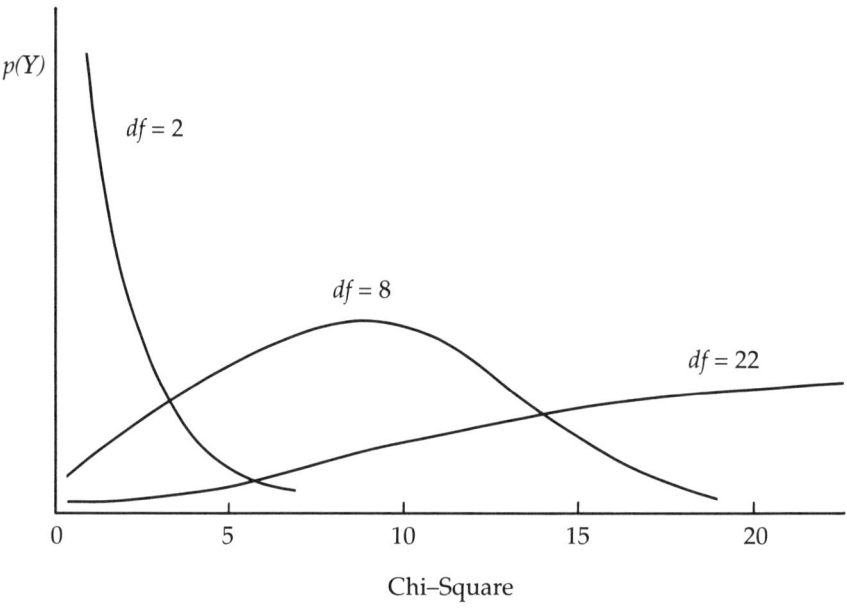

much like a chi-square distribution because the formula that generates it is only an approximation of the actual sampling distribution of χ^2, and the approximation improves only as the population size and the sample size both get larger.

Notice in the preceding paragraph the use of the plural chi-square distributions. Instead of a single distribution, there is an entire family of χ^2 distributions similar to, but slightly different from, one another, according to the degrees of freedom involved. The best way to introduce the concept of degrees of freedom is with reference to the crosstabulation of marital status and church attendance. In a crosstabulation table, **degrees of freedom** (*df*) refers to the potential for cell entries to vary freely, given a fixed set of marginal totals.

Table 4.3, for example, includes data on a total of 173 respondents who say that they never attend church. We could choose any 4 numbers that add up to 173 or less for any 4 marital status categories. But once we knew any 4 numbers, the fifth value

● **degrees of freedom**
the number of values free to vary when computing a statistic

would be strictly determined by the difference of their sum from the row total. Thus we can speak of 4 degrees of freedom in the 5 cells of each row in Table 4.3. For example, in row 1 we know that the column total is 173. If we know there are 34 never married, 6 separated, 32 divorced, and 16 widowed we know there *must* be 173 − (34 + 6 + 32 + 16) = 85 married persons who never attend church.

Similarly, in each column of 4 entries there are 3 degrees of freedom. For the 5-column and 4-row table as a whole there are 12 degrees of freedom (df = 12). Once 12 independent cell entries are known, the remaining 8 entries are not free to vary within the constraints set by the row and column marginal sums. For *any* two-variable crosstabulation, the degrees of freedom for the chi-square statistic equal the product of the number of rows less 1, times the number of columns less 1. The formula is as follows:

$$df = (R - 1)(C - 1)$$

In Table 4.3 there are (5 − 1)(4 − 1) = 12 df, as noted earlier. Thus, the sampling distribution appropriate to evaluating the χ^2 obtained for Table 4.3 is a sampling distribution of chi-square with 12 degrees of freedom.

What do theoretical χ^2 sampling distributions look like, and how are they used to evaluate hypotheses? Figure 4.2 shows 3 different sampling distributions for χ^2 statistics with 2, 8, and 22 degrees of freedom, under the assumption that the null hypothesis is true. Three features of χ^2 distributions can be seen in this figure. First, notice that *chi-square values are always nonnegative*, i.e., they vary in value from zero to plus infinity (+ ∞). (This is not true of all the sampling distributions we will discuss in this text, however.)

Second, the χ^2 value that is the most common (and therefore has the highest probability of being observed) lies near its *degrees of freedom value*. Thus, a given χ^2 value has meaning only relative to the degrees of freedom involved. In a 2 × 2 crosstabulation or joint contingency table, that has 1 degree of freedom (why?), an observed χ^2 of 8 or more would be an extremely rare event. It would occur fewer than five times in a thousand chi-square distributions with 1 degree of freedom. But, a χ^2 of 8 in a 3 × 5 table (how many *df*?) would be a relatively common outcome. Indeed, we would expect to observe a χ^2 of 8 or greater in nearly half of all chi-square distributions with 8 *df*.

Third, as the number of degrees of freedom increases, the shape of chi-square distributions becomes more bell-like. This means that the larger the degrees of freedom, the lower the probability of observing a chi-square value in either the extreme left or right tail of the distribution. In a sampling distribution with only a few degrees of freedom, in contrast, rare events occur only in the extreme right tail of the distribution. For example, with 21 *df* an observed χ^2 value of either less than 1 or greater than 40 would be almost as rare. But with 2 *df* an observed value of 3 or greater is much less probable than an observed value of 1 or less.

Finding the probabilities for specific χ^2 values in a sampling distribution with a given *df* requires the use of the chi-square table in Appendix B. To use this table, follow these steps:

> 1. Choose an α level for rejection of the null hypothesis.
> 2. Calculate the degrees of freedom (*df*) in the crosstabulation of observations.
> 3. Enter the chi-square table in Appendix B at the corresponding *df* in the row and corresponding α in the column and find the numerical entry. This value tells you how large the chi-square calculated from the data table must be in order to reject the null hypothesis, while running a chance of α of making a Type I or false rejection error (i.e., rejecting a null hypothesis that really is true—no relationship exists in the population).

● **critical value**
the minimum value of a test statistic that is necessary to reject the null hypothesis at a given probability level

The value for χ^2 determined in step 3 is called the **critical value** (c.v.). In the example in Table 4.7 of the relation between church attendance and marital status, we calculated a χ^2 value of 57.85. For *df* = 12 and α = .05, we needed to have a chi-square only equal to or larger than the c.v. of 21.03 in order to reject the null hypothesis. Even setting α = .001, we are well above the c. v. of 32.91 necessary to reject the hypothesis that no relationship between marital status and church attendance exists in the population. We can conclude that not only are marital and religious behavior both related in the GSS sample (as we established in Section 4.1.1), but this relationship is statistically significant; that is, these two variables most probably are related in the population from which the sample was drawn.

One reason the relationship in the crosstabulation is highly significant (and the chance of a Type I error is so remote) is its large sample size. The χ^2 statistic is directly proportional to sample size. For example, doubling the cell frequencies in a table will double the calculated value of chi-square while the *df* remain unchanged.

The sensitivity of χ^2 to the size of the sample in a cross-tabulation points to an important difference between statistical significance and substantive importance. One hopes that if the sample size is large enough, then it provides a good basis for making an inference to the population from which the sample was drawn. But, in the population the magnitude of the relationship could be too small to be of much sociological importance. Although a large sample size allows us to reject the H_0 of no relationship in the population, that decision does not give us much information about the strength, or magnitude, of the population relationship. Statistical significance is only the first part of an answer to the question, "How are two social variables related?" When a statistical significance test tells us that the variables are probably related in the population, then we can turn our attention to the second part of the answer, which requires us to find out how strongly the variables are related.

4.5.1   Another Example Using Chi-Square

The χ^2 distribution can also be used to investigate the changes in political partisanship following a presidential election year. We formulate this hypothesis.

> H_0: People do not change their political party identifications after a presidential election.

Two kinds of change might be expected. First, fewer individuals might declare themselves Independent and align themselves with one of the major political parties. And, second, those who changed their Independent identification might be more likely to align themselves with the party of the presidential victor, a bandwagon effect.

TABLE 4.8   Distributions of Party Identification,
GSS Respondents

A. Observed distributions

	1984	%	1985	%
Democrat	545	37.8	595	39.3
Independent	528	36.6	462	30.6
Republican	370	25.6	455	30.1
	1,443	100.0	1,512	100.0

B. Expected distributions under independence

	1984	1985
Democrat	556.69	583.31
Independent	483.44	506.56
Republican	402.87	422.13

$$\chi^2 = 13.75$$

Source: 1984 and 1985 General Social Surveys.

The 1984 and 1985 General Social Surveys can help to test these hunches. In 1984 Ronald Reagan, the Republican incumbent, was reelected president. What happened to party identifications in the following year? Panel A of Table 4.8 suggests support for the first of our hypotheses; the data indicate 6.0% fewer Independents in 1985, following the 1984 election. There also are 1.5% more declared Democrats in the 1985 data, much smaller than the 4.5% increase for the number of declared Republicans. The difference between these increases is in the predicted direction.

An important question is whether the difference between these two distributions is due to chance, that is, to mere sampling variability, or whether the distribution of political identification actually changed between 1984 and 1985. To examine this question we determine what the number of expected Democrats, Independents, and Republicans would have been under the assumption of statistical independence. If the 1984 and 1985 distributions are statistically independent, then we should have expected the joint distribution shown in panel B of Table 4.8. Are the observed frequencies significantly different from those expected on the assumption of independence? We can use χ^2 to find out.

First, convince yourself that in this case $df = 2$. Second, note that we subscript chi-square with its df — a common practice. We use the formula to compute the following:

$$\chi_2^2 = (556.69 - 545)^2/556.69 + (483.44 - 528)^2/483.44 + (402.87 - 370)^2/402.87 + (583.31 - 595)^2/583.31 + (506.56 - 462)^2/506.56 + (422.13 - 455)^2/422.13$$
$$= 13.748$$

A check of the chi-square table in Appendix B indicates that for $\alpha = .05$, and $df = 2$ an observed χ^2 value must be at least 5.99 to reject the null hypothesis. Hence, we can easily reject the hypothesis that the distributions are the same. We conclude that more persons affiliated with the major parties, and fewer declared themselves Independents, in the year after the 1984 presidential election. To be more certain that these differences represent real changes in voter affiliations and are not the result of younger voters entering and older voters leaving the population between 1984 and 1985, we might wish to compare the relationship within age groups.

4.5.2   Chi-Square as a Goodness-of-Fit Test

The chi-square statistic can also be used to test whether an observed frequency distribution could have been randomly sampled from a *known* population distribution. For example, minority groups may question whether admissions to programs in higher education or vocational training are unfair, in the sense that the proportions of admitted candidates by race and ethnicity are not the same as the proportions of these groups among the program applicants. One way to test whether or not these perceptions are accurate would be to classify the admitted candidates according to their race and ethnic groups (such as white, black, Hispanic, Asian, and native American). Then this observed distribution would be compared to the distribution of cases expected if its proportions were the same as the proportions among the applicants. If the χ^2 test were significant at a given α level, then you would reject the null hypothesis that admissions by race or ethnic status followed the same proportions as those occurring in the applicant pool. Whether the admission process was biased against certain race or ethnic groups could be determined by examining which categories had fewer admissions than expected.

In this example the known distribution is an empirical distribution, created by whatever social processes generated the applications. In a very rare instance, a social distribution might exhibit an **equiprobable distribution**, in which each outcome category has an equal probability of occurring. For example, a population might be exactly 50% male and 50% female, in which case a randomly drawn sample would have an expected equiprobable distribution of 50% men and 50% women. When χ^2 is used as a **goodness-of-fit test**, the degrees of freedom are $K - 1$, where K is the number of outcomes (categories) associated with the distribution being examined. If there were 5 race-ethnic groups in the example cited earlier, $df = 4$.

● **equiprobable distribution**
a probability distribution in which each outcome has an equal chance of occurrence

● **goodness-of-fit test**
the chi-square statistic applied to a single discrete variable, with K-1 degrees of freedom, where expected frequencies are generated on some theoretical basis

A second example using χ^2 as a goodness-of-fit statistic might concern a demographer interested in whether or not equal numbers of people are born each month or more births occur in some months than in others. In this example the known theoretical distribution (the expected outcome) is again the equiprobable one; that is, the probability of being born in any given month is 1/12 if births occur randomly throughout the year.

We can use data from the 1987 GSS, which codes the months of respondents' births, to test the hypothesis that the distribution of births could have been generated by an equiprobable population distribution. The distribution of births for the sample of $N = 1,455$ respondents is shown in Table 4.9. Since $N = 1,455$, the expected frequency for each outcome is (1/12) (1,455) = 121.25 under the assumption of an underlying equiprobable population distribution.

In this example there are $12 - 1 = 11$ df, and $\chi^2 = (121.25 - 118)^2/121.25 + (121.25 - 109)^2/121.25 + \ldots + (121.25 - 117)^2/121.25 = 7.26$. If we set $\alpha = .05$, we can use Appendix B to determine that the critical value for 11 degrees of freedom is 19.7. Therefore we cannot reject the hypothesis that births in the population of adult Americans are distributed randomly across the months of the year, based on these sample results. Remember, however, that in reaching this conclusion we run some risk of Type II error—the false acceptance of the null hypothesis of equiprobable birth months.

4.6   Two Meanings of Statistical Inference

The examples presented in this chapter demonstrate the different meanings that can be attached to the term statistical inference (see Chapter 6). Early in this chapter, when we discussed inference, we referred to generalizing from a given sample to a large population from which the sample was drawn. This is the most common use of the term. However, the examples in Sections 4.5.1 and 4.5.2 illustrate a second, less common,

Distribution of Births by Months, GSS Respondents

TABLE 4.9

Month of Birth	f	%
January	118	8.1
February	109	7.5
March	125	8.6
April	130	8.9
May	106	7.3
June	122	8.4
July	115	7.9
August	131	9.0
September	132	9.1
October	121	8.3
November	129	8.9
December	117	8.0
Total	1,455	100.0 %
	$\hat{f} =$	121.25
	$\chi^2 =$	7.26

Source: 1987 General Social Survey.
Missing data: 11.

application of the inference concept—a test of an hypothesis that the process which generated the data is a random rather than a systematic one. If the process is random, we could expect the two variables being studied to be statistically independent and a χ^2 test to be nonsignificant.

Keep these two notions of statistical inference in mind for the other tests of significance considered in the remaining chapters of this text. Both will be used.

You may have noticed that all the tests for statistical significance we have computed follow a set pattern. This routine is summarized in Box 4.2. Since the procedure for testing statistical significance is the same for all the statistics employed in this text, you would do well to commit the steps in this box to memory.

Box 4.2   Testing for Statistical Significance

Step 1. State the research hypothesis believed to be true.

Step 2. State the null hypothesis (H_0) that is expected to be rejected.

Step 3. Choose an α level (probability for a Type I or false rejection error) for the null hypothesis.

Step 4. Examine the tabled values of the statistic to see how large the test statistic would have to be in order to reject the null hypothesis. This is called the critical value, or c.v., for that test statistic.

Step 5. Calculate the test statistic, applying its formula to the observed data.

Step 6. Compare the test statistic with the critical value. If the test statistic is as large or larger than the c.v., then reject the null hypothesis, with an α-probability of a Type I (false rejection) error. If it is smaller, then do not reject the null hypothesis, with a β-probability of a Type II (false acceptance) error.

Key Concepts and Symbols

These key concepts and symbols are listed in the order of appearance in the chapter. Combined with the definitions in the margins, these will help you review the material and can serve as a test for mastery of the concepts.

crosstabulation (joint contingency table)
cells
marginal distributions
row marginals
column marginals
statistical significance tests
random sampling
null hypothesis
alternative hypothesis
probability level
alpha
Type I error (false rejection error)
Type II error (false acceptance error)

chi-square test
statistical independence
expected frequencies
chi-square distribution
test statistic
sampling distribution
degrees of freedom
critical value
equiprobable distribution
goodness-of-fit test
α
β
χ^2
df
c.v.

Problems

General Problems

1. A political scientist hypothesizes that region was an important factor in the 1988 election. She finds the following results in a national sample: among "Sunbelt" respondents, 80 Bush voters, 50 Dukakis voters, and 40 nonvoters; among "Frostbelt" respondents, 120 Dukakis voters, 90 Bush voters, and 90 nonvoters. Set up both the raw data and percentage crosstabulations to display the region-by-vote relationship, treating region as the independent variable. Give a verbal interpretation.

2. For the data in Problem 1, what are the expected frequencies under the hypothesis of statistical independence between region and vote?

3. State the following research hypotheses as null hypotheses:

    a. Women work more hours at home and on the job than do men.
    b. Lower-class people drink alcoholic beverages more often than upper-class people.
    c. Homeowners in wet climates consume more water than those in dry climates.
    d. The more intense a community's law enforcement effort against illegal drugs, the more plentiful the supply.

4. Find the degrees of freedom and the critical values of chi-square for the following:

	Rows	Columns	α
a.	3	4	.05
b.	4	5	.05
c.	8	4	.01
d.	5	4	.001
e.	12	2	.01
f.	13	11	.001
g.	3	7	.001

5. How large must χ^2 be in a 4 × 6 crosstabulation to reject the independence hypothesis (a) at α = .05, (b) at α = .01, and (c) at α = .001?

6. Calculate the observed χ^2 value for the data in Problem 1, state the *df*, and report the lowest α level at which the null hypothesis of no relationship between region and vote can be rejected.

7. In 1988, U.S. public health officials reported that the acne treatment drug Accutane had been found to produce significantly more birth defects among children whose mothers had used it while pregnant than mothers who did not use it. Suppose the observed sample difference in birth defects had an α level of only .20 of occurring in the population. What decision should be made about allowing continued use of the drug? What criteria should enter into public policy decisions involving harmful substances?

8. Surveys conducted in the United States and Hungary found the following frequencies in response to a question about whether getting ahead in life depended on "knowing the right people":

	United States	Hungary
Essential	99	369
Very important	413	656
Fairly important	579	849
Not very important	161	483
Not important at all	23	125

Are the differences statistically significant? If so, at what α level?

9. State the level of significance at which you can reject the null hypothesis that drinking and smoking too much are unrelated, in a sample of 30 college students who gave these responses:

		Smoke too much?	
		Yes	No
Drink	Yes	6	6
too much	No	6	12

10. Suppose that you toss a six-sided die and find the following results after 50 tosses where the "face" column represents the number of dots obtained:

Face	f
1	6
2	7
3	10
4	8
5	9
6	10

Is this a "fair" die? Why or why not?

Problems Requiring the 1987 General Social Survey

11. Given the Surgeon General's warnings about tobacco smoking, are people's healths likely to be worse if they smoke? Crosstabulate HEALTH by SMOKE and calculate χ^2 to test the null hypothesis of no health differences between smokers and nonsmokers. Use $\alpha = .05$.

12. Now test whether people who say they drink too much (DRUNK) have worse health than those who don't. Set $\alpha = .05$.

13. How does education affect racial attitudes? Recode EDUC into three categories (less than 12 years of school; 12 years; more than 12 years) and crosstabulate with responses to the statement that "white people have a right to keep blacks out of their neighborhoods if they want to, and blacks should respect that right" (RACSEG). Set $\alpha = .001$.

14. Do women or men (SEX) more strongly favor capital punishment for murder (CAPPUN)? Crosstabulate, using $\alpha = .05$.

15. Are there any significant differences among the main religious groups (RELIG) in their belief in a life after death (POSTLIFE)? Set $\alpha = .001$.

Problems Requiring the 50-States Data Set

16. Education and poverty are known to be inversely related. Show this for the 50 states by dichotomizing HSGRAD (at 67.5%) and POVERTY (at 11.5%) and crosstabulate them. Set $\alpha = .001$.

17. Do states with so-called right-to-work laws (which ban compulsory union membership, or "closed shops") have lower rates of unionized working forces? Dichotomize UNION (at 21.8%) and crosstabulate with RT2WORK, with $\alpha = .05$ to reject the null hypothesis.

18. Can automobile abuse be fatal to your health? Dichotomize SPEED (at 48.8%) and FATALITY (at 3.34), crosstabulate, and use $\alpha = .01$ to test the null hypothesis of no effect of excessive speeding on states' automobile deaths.

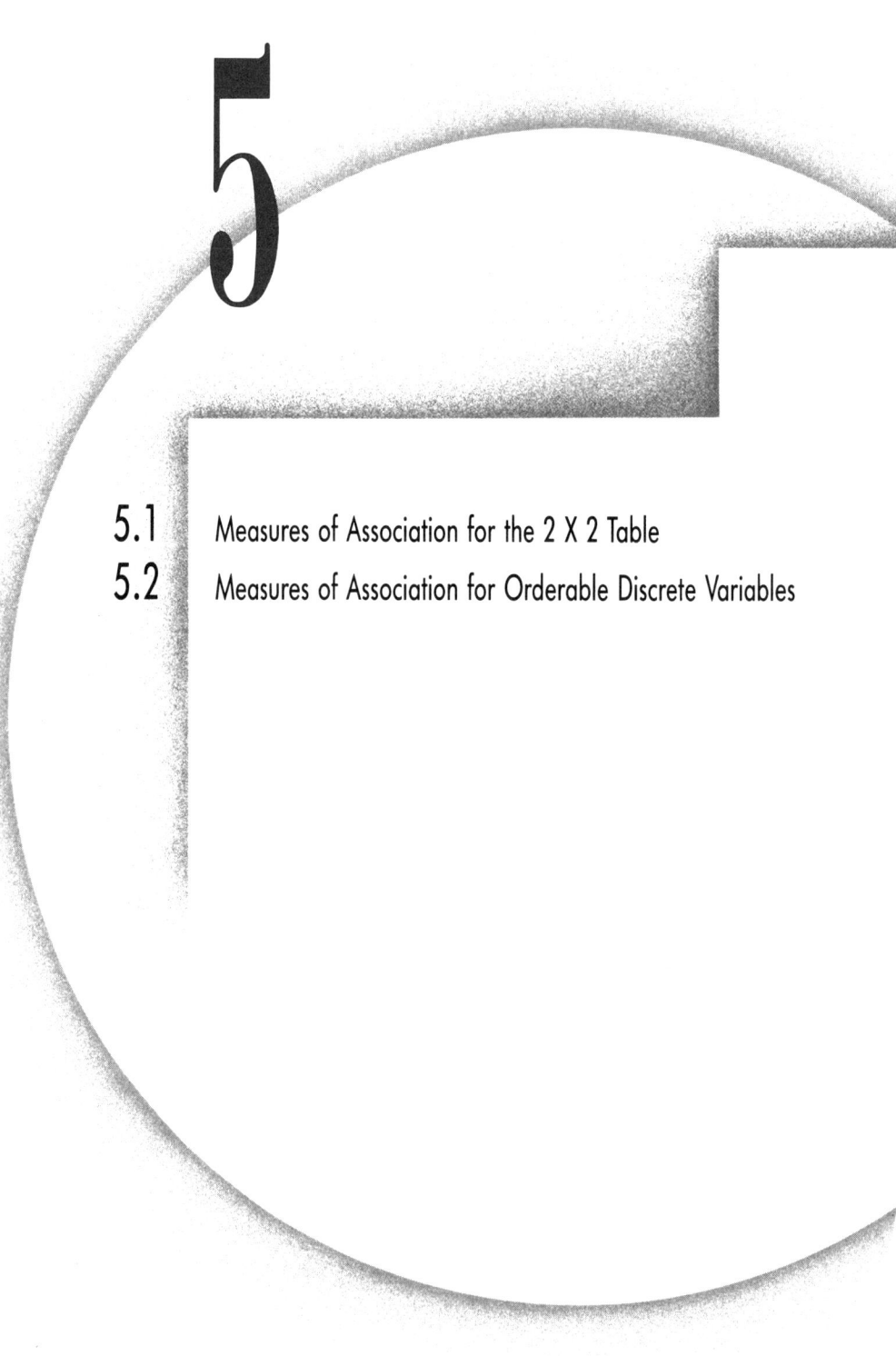

5

Measures of Association

The existence of a relationship between two discrete variables can be tested with the χ^2 statistic introduced in Chapter 4. Use of chi-square is limited because it shows only whether or not the two variables are likely to be dependent in the population from which the sample was drawn; it does not show whether the two variables are very strongly, moderately, or only weakly related. This chapter considers **measures of association,** statistics that reveal the strength of the relationship between pairs of discrete variables. To introduce this set of measures, we begin with the most basic type of crosstabulation, the 2 X 2 table which crosstabulates a pair of dichotomous variables.

● **measures of association** statistics that show the direction and/or magnitude of a relationship between variables

5.1 Measures of Association for the 2 X 2 Table

In standard labeling for 2 X 2 tables, the first four italic letters are used to designate cell frequencies, as follows:

		Variable X		
		1	2	Totals
Variable Y	2	a	b	$a + b$
	1	c	d	$c + d$
	Totals	$a + c$	$b + d$	$a + b + c + d$

Notice that this table is set up in a standard format so that (1) the "higher"-valued row categories are located above the "lower"-valued row categories; and (2) the "higher"-valued column categories appear to the right of the "lower"-valued column categories.[1] Therefore, we can write an approximate formula for χ^2 for a 2 X 2 table in the notation.[2]

$$\chi_1^2 = \frac{N(bc - ad)^2}{(a+b)\,(a+c)\,(b+d)\,(c+d)}$$

Cells b and c are given a special label as the *main diagonal* cells, while a and d are referred to as the *off-diagonal* cells. Thus, the numerator of the χ^2 formula involves the *cross-product differences* between the main and off-diagonal cells. These values appear in several statistical formulas that follow in this chapter.

In general, the degree of freedom for a χ^2 test of an R X C table is $(R - 1)\,(C - 1)$. Thus, for a 2 X 2 table, $df = (2 - 1)(2 - 1) = 1$.

5.1.1   An Example: Political Intensity and Voting

For investigating measures of association for 2 X 2 tables, we will use an example from political science. Americans differ in their identification as supporters of one of the two major po-

---

[1]The SPSS/PC+ computer program CROSSTABS prints its tables with "higher" valued rows *below* the "lower" rows, but it compensates for this change by treating cells a and d as the main diagonal and cells b and c as the off-diagonal when calculating measures of association. Thus, positive and negative signs are correctly attached to the statistics printed by SPSS/PC+ CROSSTABS.

[2]Many earlier statistics texts advised that something called "Yates's correction for continuity" should be applied when the expected frequency in a cell is equal to or less than 5.0. Recent studies indicate that both the uncorrected χ^2 formula and Yates's correction give biased estimates of true α levels. Formulas that give better estimates of the true α levels for 2 X 2 tables are too cumbersome to present here.

Unfortunately, SPSS/PC+ CROSSTABS automatically applies Yates's correction for continuity to all 2 X 2 tables with $N \geq 20$. All we can do is caution you that this problem exists.

litical parties. Some people claim to be strong supporters of the Democratic or Republican party, while others say they are not strong supporters or are Independents. Political scientists have found that strength of party identification is related to turnout on election day. As a hypothesis this can be stated the following way:

> H1: Persons who strongly identify with the Republican or Democratic parties are more likely to vote in presidential elections than are people who do not strongly identify with either party.

Using 1987 GSS data, we test this hypothesis by measuring a respondent's party identification with two questions: "Generally speaking, do you usually think of yourself as a Republican, Democrat, or Independent?" and (if Republican or Democrat) "Would you call yourself a strong Republican/Democrat or not a very strong Republican/Democrat?" Respondents saying they were strong supporters of either party were classified as "strong" identifiers and all other respondents were classified as "not strong" identifiers. Voting turnout was dichotomized into those who said that they had voted in the 1984 presidential election and those who said they were eligible to vote but did not do so. Table 5.1 displays the crosstabulation of these two dichotomous measures. There is nearly a 20% difference in voting turnout rates between the strong and not strong party identifiers. Note also that the overall relative frequency of voting claimed by the GSS respondents (71.7%) is much higher than the actual 1984 voting turnout measured at the polling places (approximately 53%). Perhaps many nonvoters were not selected for the GSS sample, or many nonvoters in the sample may have given the more socially desirable response. Not surprisingly, the χ^2 for this table is very large.

$$\chi^2 = \frac{(1,331)\,[(318)\,(339) - (615)\,(59)]^2}{(398)\,(933)\,(377)\,(954)} = 50.97$$

Since the degrees of freedom for a 2 X 2 table is $(2 - 1)\,(2 - 1) = 1$, and the critical value is only 3.84 at $\alpha = .05$, this value is highly significant. This formula for χ^2 is only an approximation, and it may fit poorly when sample size is small. The following sections discuss statistics suitable for measuring the degree of association between two nonorderable discrete variables in a 2 X 2 table.

TABLE 5.1   Crosstabulation of Party Identification
                            and Voting

| Voting turnout | Party identification | | Total |
	Not strong	Strong	
Voted	65.9%	85.2%	71.7%
(N)	(615)	(339)	(954)
Not voted	34.1	14.8	28.3
(N)	(318)	(59)	(377)
Total	100.0%	100.0%	100.0%
(N)	(933)	(398)	(1,331)

Source: 1987 General Social Survey.

5.1.2   Yule's Q

● **Yule's Q**
a symmetric
measure of
association for 2 X 2
crosstabulations,
equivalent to gamma

One measure of 2 X 2 association is **Yule's Q**, which makes use of the cross-product difference that we encountered with the chi-square formula. As noted earlier, by convention the four cells of a 2 X 2 table are identified by italic letters: starting at the upper left and ending at the lower right, these labels are *a*, *b*, *c*, and *d*. The two cross products, (*ad*) and (*bc*), are then combined in two different ways.

$$Q = \frac{(bc) - (ad)}{(bc) + (ad)}$$

When the two products in the numerator equal one another, the value of *Q* is zero, meaning that no relationship exists between the two variables. In this case, the value of chi-square will be zero, since the cross-product term also appears in its numerator. And the expected cell frequencies will have the same percentage distributions as the row marginal and the column marginal distributions.

Note that if one of the four cell frequencies is zero, the value of *Q* must either be −1.00 or +1.00. Yet less than a "perfect" relationship may exist between the two dichotomous variables. In this case *perfect* means that all cases fall either only into the two main diagonal cells or only into the two off-diagonal cells.

Clearly, Q can give misleading information when cells with a frequency of zero are present. This is shown in hypothetical illustrations in Table 5.2. In example A, a maximum negative relationship is shown, with all 40 observations located in the two off-diagonal cells. Q attains its maximum value, -1.0. In example B, Q also has a value of -1.0, but the cell entries show that the majority of the cases in the high level of variable Y are concentrated in the main diagonal cell. Example C shows that if just a single observation from example B were to be shifted from d to c, the value of Yule's Q would drop substantially to -0.65.

These illustrations underscore one of the defects of Yule's Q—its sensitivity to distortion due to cell frequencies of zero. This is particularly problematic when the sample size is small (as in these hypothetical illustrations) or when the frequencies in some variable categories are rare. For these reasons, you should always carefully inspect the cell frequencies in a 2 X 2 table and examine it for the presence of zero cell frequencies. If a zero cell is present, then some alternative measure of association should be chosen.

Three Hypothetical Examples of Q TABLE 5.2

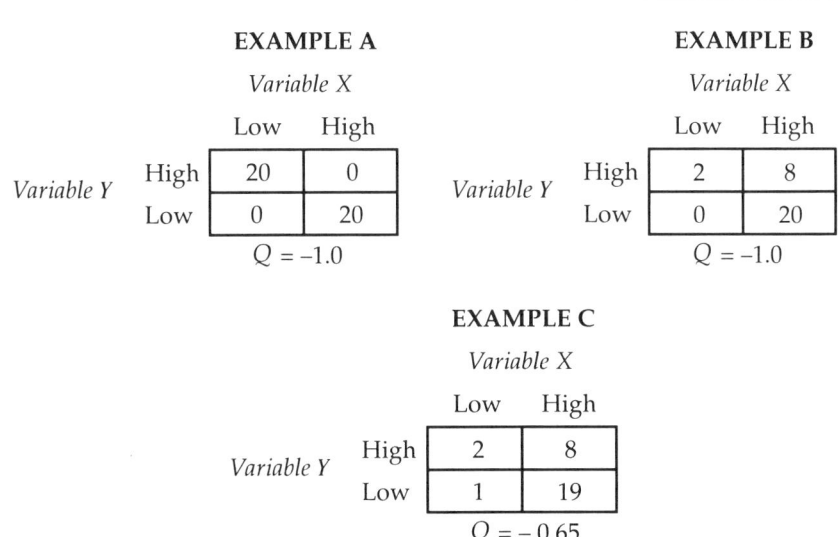

Source: George Bohrnstedt and David Knoke, *Statistics for Social Data Analysis* (Itasca, Ill.: F. E. Peacock Publishers, Inc., 1988), 331.

Using the real data in Table 5.1, we can readily calculate the following:

$$Q = \frac{(339)\,(318) - (615)\,(59)}{(339)\,(318) + (615)\,(59)}$$

$$= +.496$$

Interpreting the magnitude of a Yule's Q is somewhat arbitrary. We suggest the following verbal labels be applied to absolute values of Q that fall into these ranges.

.00 to .24   "no relationship"
.25 to .49   "weak relationship"
.50 to .74   "moderate relationship"
.75 to 1.00   "strong relationship"

Thus, the Q of $+.496$ represents a moderate positive covariation between party identification strength and voting turnout: Strong partisans were more likely to vote than were not strong partisans.

The signs of Yule's Q and other measures of association in a crosstabulation depend on how the values of the two variables are coded. When both variables are orderable discrete measures, a positive sign indicates that the two high categories are associated, as are the two low categories. A negative sign indicates an inverse relationship, meaning that the high category on one variable is associated with the low category on the other variable. However, if one or both variables in a 2 X 2 table are nonorderable discrete measures, the interpretation of the sign is more complicated. It depends on which categories are arbitrarily assigned to the columns and rows representing the four cell frequencies used to calculate the measure of association. Table 5.3 gives two examples using the 1987 GSS data. Respondents were crosstabulated by gender and whether they favored requiring a person to obtain a police permit before buying a gun. In panel A, where "women" is treated as the high category, the positive Yule's Q of $+.34$ means that women are more likely than men to favor gun control. In panel B, where the columns are rearranged so that "men" is now the high category, the negative Yule's Q of $-.34$ *also* means that women favor gun control more than men. This reversal of signs without any change in

Two Crosstabulations of Gender TABLE 5.3
and Gun Permit

A. With women "high"

Gun permit opinion	Gender		
	Men	Women	Total
Favor	63.3%	77.8%	71.5%
(N)	(397)	(628)	(1,025)
Oppose	36.7	22.2	28.5
(N)	(230)	(179)	(409)
Total	100.0%	100.0%	100.0%
(N)	(627)	(807)	(1,434)

Yule's Q = .34

B. With men "high"

Gun permit opinion	Gender		
	Women	Men	Total
Favor	77.8%	63.3%	71.5%
(N)	(628)	(397)	(1,025)
Oppose	22.2	36.7	28.5
(N)	(179)	(230)	(409)
Total	100.0%	100.0%	100.0%
(N)	(807)	(627)	(1,434)

Yule's Q = −.34

Source: 1987 General Social Survey.
Missing cases = 32.

the interpretation of the relationship should caution you always to inspect carefully how tabular data are arranged before you proceed to calculate and interpret a measure of association.

5.1.3   Phi

Phi (ϕ) is another statistic used to estimate association in a 2 X 2 table (in fact, it is identical to r, the correlation coefficient in a sample; see Section 9.4.2). As with Yule's Q, the range of ϕ lies between −1.00 and +1.00, with 0.00 indicating no relationship.

● **phi**
a symmetric measure of association for 2 X 2 crosstabulations, equivalent to the correlation coefficient

Unlike Yule's Q, ϕ is sensitive to the distribution of cases in the row and column marginals of the table, as can be seen by its formula, which also makes use of the cross products.

$$\phi = \frac{bc - ad}{\sqrt{(a + b)(c + d)(a + c)(b + d)}}$$

Phi shares with Q the cross-product difference in its numerator, but its denominator is the square root of the product of the four marginal totals. For any 2 X 2 table with a specific set of row and column totals, ϕ can attain a maximum or minimum value that may be considerably short of the hypothetical range between -1.00 and $+1.00$. Some researchers prefer to adjust ϕ to remove this limitation so that the relative magnitude of an association can be revealed. **Phi adjusted (ϕ_{adj})** is determined by dividing the observed value of ϕ by the maximum absolute value, **phi maximum,** with the given set of marginals (ϕ_{max}).

- **phi adjusted**
a symmetric measure of association for a 2 X 2 crosstabulation in which phi is divided by phi maximum to take into account the largest covariation possible, given the marginals

$$\phi_{adj} = \frac{\phi}{|\phi_{max}|}$$

- **phi maximum**
the largest value that phi can attain for a given 2 X 2 crosstabulation; used in adjusting phi for its marginals

To find ϕ_{max}, we simply reduce the entries in any one of the four cells to zero and correspondingly adjust the frequencies in the other three cells, keeping the row and column marginal totals unchanged. Table 5.4 gives an illustration of this procedure with hypothetical data. The observed ϕ value is -0.41. The maximum value, obtained by removing all cases from cell c (any of the four cells could be used as the focal cell), is -0.82. Then $\phi_{adj} = -0.41/|-0.82| = -0.50$. This indicates a somewhat stronger inverse relationship than suggested in the observed data. In the party and vote data in Table 5.1, ϕ is $+0.196$, ϕ_{max} is $+0.411$, and therefore $\phi_{adj} = +0.477$. Note that the unadjusted value of ϕ is much lower than the value of Yule's Q for this table, but the adjustment to ϕ brings them closer in

Observed Value and Maximum Absolute   **TABLE 5.4**
Value of Phi, Hypothetical Data

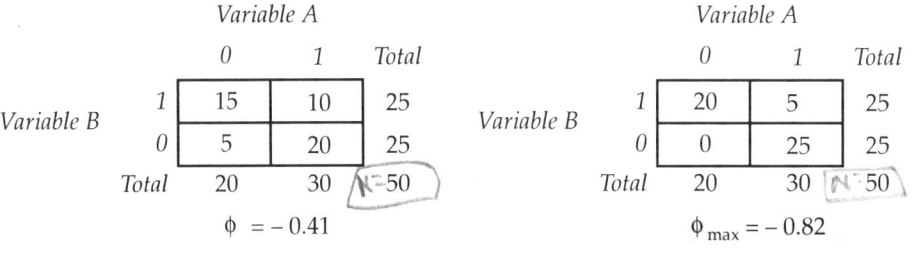

A. OBSERVED VALUE   **B. MAXIMUM VALUE**

		Variable A		
		0	1	Total
Variable B	1	15	10	25
	0	5	20	25
	Total	20	30	N = 50

$\phi = -0.41$

		Variable A		
		0	1	Total
Variable B	1	20	5	25
	0	0	25	25
	Total	20	30	N = 50

$\phi_{max} = -0.82$

Source: George Bohrnstedt and David Knoke, *Statistics for Social Data Analysis* (Itasca, Ill.: F. E. Peacock Publishers, Inc., 1988), 333.

magnitude. Although ϕ_{adj} is sometimes reported in the analyses of data from a 2 X 2 table, our recommendation is to report the original and adjusted values.

5.1.4   Odds and the Odds Ratio

Most of us are familiar with odds in everyday life, from games of chance or gambling on horse races. An **odds** is the ratio of the frequency of being in one category to the frequency of not being in that category.[3] For example, the odds that a fair die will come up "3" when rolled are 1/5. (Note that a probability differs from an odds; the former is a ratio of a category's frequency to the total of *all* frequencies, while an odds is a ratio between a category's frequency and the total of the *other* categories' frequencies.) The odds that a pair of tossed coins will both land heads up is 1/3 since there are four possible

● **odds**
the frequency of an outcome occurring divided by the frequency of that outcome not occurring

[3]For basic expositions, see Y.M.M. Bishop, S.E. Feinberg, and P.W. Holland, *Discrete Multivariate Analysis: Theory and Practice* (Cambridge: MIT Press, 1975); S.E. Feinberg, *The Analysis of Cross-Clarified Data* (Cambridge: MIT Press, 1977); S.J. Haberman, *Analysis of Qualitative Data*, Vols. 1 and 2 (New York: Academic Press, 1978); L.A. Goodman and W.H. Kruskal, *Measures of Association for Cross-Classifications* (New York: Springer-Verlag, 1979); D. Knoke and P.J. Burke, *Log-Linear Models* (Beverly Hills: Sage, 1980); and L.A. Goodman, *The Analysis of Cross-Classified Data Having Ordered Categories* (Cambridge, MA: Harvard University Press, 1984).

outcomes—HH, HT, TH, and TT. Odds are always stated in terms of one specific category of a variable relative to the sum of all the remaining categories. Thus, returning to our example of marginals for voting in Table 5.1, we find the odds that a randomly selected respondent voted are 954/377 = 2.53, while the odds of being a strong party identifier are 398/933 = 0.43. Odds can also be calculated for the alternative categories: nonvoter (377/954 = 0.40) and not strong party identifier (933/398 = 2.34).

A percentage can always be transformed to odds by calculating the ratio of the corresponding proportion to the proportion remaining when subtracted from 1.00. If we know that 55% of the American electorate voted for George Bush in 1988, then the odds that a randomly selected voter was a Bush supporter is simply .55/(1.00 − .55) = .55/.45 = 1.22. In other words, a person selected at random is 1.22 times more likely to have voted for Bush than to have voted for someone else. Note also that in a dichotomous percentage distribution with exactly 50% in both categories, the odds ratio is (.50/.50) = 1.00. An odds with a value of exactly 1.00 means that the chances are equal that a randomly selected case would be found in either category. This ability to calculate odds from either numerical frequencies or percentages permits many published data displays to be reanalyzed in terms of odds.

Thus far we have discussed only simple odds, such as those for a frequency distribution of a single variable or the margins of a crosstabulation. We can also calculate **conditional odds** within the cells of a table, comparable to the crosstabulation percentages with which you are by now familiar. Conditional odds are the chances of being in one category of a variable relative to the remaining categories of that variable, given a specific category of a second variable. Distinct conditional odds may be calculated for each category of the second variable. In Table 5.1, assume that party identification is the first variable and voting is the second variable. The conditional odds for voting among the strong identifiers are 339/59 = 5.75, nearly six times greater than nonvoting. The odds for voting among the not strong identifiers are 615/318 = 1.93, less than twice the chance of voting than nonvoting. The odds are certainly much higher among the strong partisans than the not strong partisans, a conclusion also supported by the percentages. Thus, by knowing a person's party strength, we can better predict the chances that she or he voted. If the two variables had not been related, the conditional odds for voting would have been identical across both groups

● **conditional odds** the frequency of an outcome occurring divided by the frequency of that outcome not occurring within a given category of a second variable

(and thus equal to the marginal odds of 2.53). In such an instance, knowing the state of the first variable does not improve our ability to predict the state of the second variable.

When variables in a 2 X 2 table are associated, their conditional odds are unequal, as we have just seen. To compare directly two conditional odds, a single summary statistic called the **odds ratio** can be formed by dividing one conditional odds by another. In terms of the standard symbols for the cell frequencies of a 2 X 2 table, once again we see that cross products are used.

● **odds ratio (cross-product ratio)** the ratio formed by dividing one conditional odds by another conditional odds

$$\text{odds ratio} = \frac{b/d}{a/c} = \frac{bc}{ad}$$

Notice that the simplified formula on the right divides the product of the main diagonal cell frequencies by the product of the off-diagonal cell frequencies. Thus, the odds ratio is sometimes called the **cross-product ratio.** (Note its contrast with the chi-square formula, which uses the difference of the cross-products in its numerator.) The odds ratio for Table 5.1 is $(339)(318)/(615)(59) = 2.971$, which means that the strong party identifiers were just under three times more likely to have voted than were the not strong party identifiers.

You might wonder what would be the results if our analysis of Table 5.1 had been set up with the row labeled "not voted" interchanged with the row labeled "voted." In this case cell b would have counted those respondents who have strong party preferences but did not vote in 1984 ($N = 59$) and the odds ratio would have been $(59)(615)/(339)(318) = 0.336$; that is, those persons who are not strong identifiers are .336 times or about one-third as likely to vote as those who are strong identifiers. Is this finding any different from the finding that strong partisans are 2.971 times more likely to vote than those who are not strong partisans? Since all we have done is to switch the response categories for the voting variable, we hope not! And, indeed, these findings turn out to be the same. Note that $1/2.971 = 0.335$ and $1/0.336 = 2.976$, where the differences are due only to rounding error. Because the inverse of one odds ratio equals the other, we can use this fact to rephrase a finding in terms of a different category of the "dependent variable" (voting turnout, in this case) by simply taking the inverse of the computed odds ratio. This exercise should convince you that an odds ratio formed between two dichotomous variables is basically unchanged regardless of which categories are considered "high" or "low."

Suppose you choose to think of party identification as the dependent variable. What are the odds of being a strong partisan for someone who voted, compared to the odds of those who did not vote?

Notice that if either cell of the main diagonal has zero frequency, the odds ratio will be undefined, since division by zero is impossible. The odds ratio shares with Yule's Q a difficulty in dealing with empty cells. Unlike Yule's Q and ϕ, which are constrained between -1.00 and $+1.00$ with 0.0 indicating no association, the range of the odds ratio is asymmetric. It is always positive, has an unlimited upper range, and 1.00 means no association (i.e., equal conditional odds). Thus, the values for negative covariation along the off diagonal have a much more restricted range (between zero and 1.00) than do the values for positive covariation (which can range between 1.00 and positive infinity). Comparing the strengths of association for two relationships of opposite direction is thus very difficult unless you first form the reciprocal of one of the odds, then compare their values. For example, if variables W and X have an odds ratio of .50 and variables Y and Z have an odds ratio of 1.50, which pair has the stronger degree of association? Although both pairs seem to be equally distant from 1.00 (no association), if we invert the $W-X$ odds ratio $(1/.50) = 2.00$, we see that its magnitude is considerably higher than that of the $Y-Z$ association.

The statistical significance of an odds ratio is determined by the standard χ^2 test for 2 X 2 tables. If you take an advanced social statistics course that covers log-linear models, you will learn how the odds ratio can be used in computing expected cell frequencies for crosstabulations whose fit to observed data is then tested by chi-square.

5.2   Measures of Association for Orderable Discrete Variables

In variables measured with several categories at the orderable discrete level, as we noted in Section 2.3, response categories are arranged in an ascending or descending sequence but lack continuous measurement properties. Several appropriate measures of association are available. As with Yule's Q and ϕ, these measures have the useful property of indicating the *direction* of association between the two orderable discrete variables.

By direction we mean that cases in the crosstabulation tend to fall into the main diagonal cells, c and b, indicating a positive relationship (maximum value = +1.00); into the off-diagonal cells, a and d, indicating a negative relationship (maximum value = -1.00); or to have no relationship (value = 0.0). This section presents three measures of association suitable for orderable discrete variables: gamma, tau c, and Somers's d.

5.2.1   An Example: Social Class and Financial Satisfaction

One of the important issues in social stratification and work is the relationship between social position and perceptions or feelings. Researchers have generally found that people occupying more advantaged positions express greater enjoyment and satisfaction with various features of their lives. Our general proposition is as follows:

> P1: The higher a person's position in a social system, the greater his or her satisfaction.

Using the 1987 GSS, social position is operationalized (see Section 1.3) by an item about the respondent's subjectively perceived social class: "If you were asked to use one of four names for your social class, which would you say you belong in: the lower class, the working class, the middle class, or the upper class?" Similarly, satisfaction is operationalized by an item asking the following:

> We are interested in how people are getting along financially these days. So far as you and your family are concerned, would you say that you are pretty well satisfied with your present financial situation, more or less satisfied, or not satisfied at all?

Using these two indicators, a testable hypothesis can be specified in operational terms.

> H2: The higher a person's subjective social class position, the greater his or her family financial satisfaction.

TABLE 5.5   Crosstabulation of Social Class
                     and Financial Satisfaction

Financial satisfaction	Social class				
	Lower	Working	Middle	Upper	Total
Very well	13.9%	20.8%	37.0%	58.1%	29.7%
(N)	(10)	(131)	(251)	(36)	(428)
More or less	26.4	49.0	50.6	30.6	47.9
(N)	(19)	(309)	(343)	(19)	(690)
Not at all	59.7	30.2	12.4	11.3	22.5
(N)	(43)	(190)	(84)	(7)	(324)
Total	100.0%	100.0%	100.0%	100.0%	100.0%
(N)	(72)	(630)	(678)	(62)	(1,442)

Source: 1987 General Social Survey.

Table 5.5 displays the crosstabulation of these two measures, with social class treated as the independent variable. The two variables are plainly related, as, taken together, 58% of those in the upper class but only 14% of those in the lower class are very well satisfied with their financial situations, while the working and middle class respondents' satisfaction levels are in between. For this 3 X 4 table, $\chi^2 = 159.1$ ($df = 6$), leading us to reject the null hypothesis of no relationship between the two variables.

When orderable discrete variables are displayed in tabular form, we would expect to find the largest number of cell frequencies along the *main diagonal* if the relationship is one of positive covariation. (In a nonsquare crosstabulation that has been set up in standard format, the main diagonal is the set of cells from lower left to upper right; in Table 5.5, the frequencies are 43, 309, 343, and 36.) In contrast, if the class-satisfaction relation were inverse or negative, we would expect to observe a concentration of frequencies in the off-diagonal cells running from upper left to lower right. A look at the table reveals the tendency toward a positive relationship, although that relationship seems to be weak.

As discussed earlier, one desirable feature of orderable discrete measures of association is that the direction of the relationship should be indicated by the *sign* of the coefficient. A plus sign shows a positive covariation and a minus sign indicates an inverse or negative relationship. Like nonorderable discrete measures of association, orderable measures of association should also be normed to vary between zero (for no relationship) and 1, to provide maximum predictability of the dependent variable values from the independent variable. Norming an association measure restricts its values to a limited range, for convenience of interpretation. Thus, these measures of association should take on values ranging between -1.00 and $+1.00$.

5.2.2   Gamma

All good measures of association make use of a *proportionate reduction in error* (PRE) approach. The PRE family of statistics is based on comparing the errors made in predicting the dependent variable with knowledge of the independent variable, to the errors made without information about the independent variable. Thus, every PRE statistic reflects how well knowledge of one variable improves prediction of the second variable. The general formula for any PRE statistic is given in terms of decision rules about expected values of one variable, Y, conditioned on the values of a second variable, X. In terms of first and second variables, the formula is a ratio between two decision rules.

$$\text{PRE statistic} = \frac{\substack{\text{Error without} \\ \text{decision rule}} - \substack{\text{Error with} \\ \text{decision rule}}}{\text{Error without decision rule}}$$

When variables Y and X are unrelated, we are completely unable to use our knowledge of the first variable to reduce errors when we try to estimate values of the second variable. Thus, the PRE statistic's value is zero. In the opposite case, when a perfect prediction from one variable to the other is possible, we make no errors, and the PRE statistic takes its maximum value of 1.00. Intermediate values of the PRE measure show that we have greater or lesser degrees of predictability.

Gamma is the most frequently used measure of ordered crosstabular association. It is a *symmetric* PRE measure of association, so that predicting the second variable from the first yields

● **gamma**
a symmetric measure of association for orderable discrete variables that takes into account only the number of untied pairs

the same gamma value as the opposite order of prediction, even for non-square crosstabulations. Gamma has the desired characteristic of ranging between +1.00 and −1.00, with zero indicating no relationship. Gamma is also a "margin-free" measure of association; its value does not depend on the row or column marginal totals.

The calculation of gamma uses the observed cell frequencies in a crosstabulation. This statistic systematically compares *every* pair of observations, eliminating those pairs that are identical on at least the categories of one variable (i.e., *tied* cases). Only the untied pairs of cases are used to calculate gamma. The total number of untied pairs consist of two types, concordant and discordant. To understand what these terms mean, look at Table 5.5 where two ordered variables are crosstabulated. Consider first a pair in which one person is upper-class and very well satisfied financially and the second person is lower-class and not at all satisfied. This is a **concordant pair** because the first member is higher on both variables than the second member. Then consider another pair consisting of a middle-class person not at all satisfied and a working-class person who is more-or-less satisfied. This is a **discordant pair** because one member is higher than the other on the first variable (social class) but lower than the other on the second variable (financial satisfaction). In calculating gamma, we must identify the total number of pairs having the same rank on both variables (n_s), or concordant pairs, and the total number of pairs having different ranks on the two variables (n_d), or discordant pairs.

● **concordant pairs** in a crosstabulation of two orderable discrete variables, the number of pairs having the same rank order of inequality on both variables

● **discordant pairs** in a crosstabulation of two orderable discrete variables, the number of pairs having reverse rank order of inequality on both variables

Using these two sets of untied pairs, the formula for the sample statistic for gamma (G) is as follows:

$$G = \frac{n_s - n_d}{n_s + n_d}$$

The PRE nature of gamma can be clearly seen in this formula. If any pair of cases is drawn at random from the crosstabulation table and we try to predict whether the same or reverse order occurs, our chances of being correct depend on the numbers of concordant and discordant pairs in the table. If $n_s = n_d,$

we will be unable to predict at better than chance, and gamma will equal zero. But if n_s is much larger than n_d, gamma will be positive, and we will be more successful in predicting that the respondent with the higher value on one variable will also have the higher value on the second variable, compared to the other respondent in the pair. Note especially that when $n_d = 0$ (i.e., there are no discordant pairs), gamma equals unity (1.00). The rate of prediction error is reduced, however, when n_d is substantially larger than n_s. In this case, gamma will be negative. For a negative gamma we predict that if person A is higher than person B on variable X, the reverse order holds for the pair on variable Y. The maximum negative value of gamma (-1.00) occurs when n_s is zero, and there are no concordant pairs.

Although the calculation of gamma is simple once we have the numbers of concordant and discordant pairs, obtaining these values from a crosstabulation requires a lot of arithmetic. To illustrate the general procedure, think of three respondents—A, B, and C. Suppose that person A is upper class and very well satisfied financially; person B is middle class and more or less satisfied; and person C is upper class but not at all satisfied. If we examine all three pairs of respondents, we find first that A is higher than B, both in social class and in financial satisfaction. Hence, this pair should be counted in the concordant, or n_s, group. Since there are 36 people like A and 343 like B in Table 5.5, there is a total of (36)(343) = 12,348 concordant pairs exactly like this one. Next, although A and C have different levels of satisfaction, they belong to the same social class; hence, this pair is tied on one of the variables and must be dropped from further consideration. Altogether, 252 pairs of this kind will be eliminated (i.e., the 36 respondents in the upper-right cell and the 7 in the lower-right cell form [36][7] = 252 pairs). The B–C pair is "untied," but the direction is not consistent for both variables; B has a lower class position than C, but B shows more satisfaction compared to C. Hence, this pair should be counted in the n_d (discordant) sum. There are (343)(7) = 2,401 pairs identical to this one.

For an ordered crosstabulation with N cases, the total number of possible pairs of cases equals the square of N. However, this set includes each case paired with itself, so we must subtract N from N^2. And, because the pair consisting of A and B is the same as the pair consisting of B and A, we must divide by two to find the number of unique pairs. Hence, the formula for unique pairs in N cases is $(N^2 - N)/2$. In Table 5.5, there are $[((1,442)^2 - (1,442))/2] = 1,308,961$ unique pairs of respondents to be sorted into the n_s, n_d, or eliminated groups. Such a task would be impossible if every pair had to be individually inspected one at a time, as described in the previous paragraph. Fortunately, a very easy method exists for making these comparisons rapidly, even when a computer is not handy. This *algorithm*, or procedure, for determining n_s and n_d is as follows, using Table 5.5:

1. With the ordered table laid out in standard format, begin at the *upper-right* cell. Ignoring all entries in the same row and column, add the remaining cell frequencies, that is, those frequencies in the cells below and to the left. For example, in Table 5.5 the sum of all entries below and to the left of the 36 respondents who are upper class and also very well satisfied is 19 + 309 + 343 + 43 + 190 + 84 = 988. Multiply this sum by the cell frequency in the upper-right cell (e.g., 36), and add the product to the n_s total. All these pairs have the same order of inequality on both variables (concordant), and thus (988)(36) = 35,568 pairs forms the first count to be added to the n_s total.

2. Still within the top row of the table, move over one column to the *left* and again add up all cell frequencies below and to the left. The sum of all entries below and to the left of the 251 respondents who are middle class and very well satisfied is 309 + 19 + 43 + 190 = 561. Once again obtain the product of this sum and the frequency in the initial cell, and add it to the n_s total: (251)(561) = 140,811; thus far we have 35,568 + 140,811 = 176,379 in n_s.

3. Proceed in this fashion, moving to the left across the first row, multiplying the cell frequency by the sum of all frequencies below and to the left, and cumulating the total count of same order pairs. When any row has been completed, move to the row below, always starting with the right most column. There are six elements in this example.

$$(36)(988) = 35,568$$
$$(251)(561) = 140,811$$
$$(131)(62) = 8,122$$
$$(19)(317) = 6,023$$
$$(343)(233) = 79,919$$
$$(309)(43) = 13,287$$
$$\text{Total} = 283,730$$

4. To calculate the number of *discordant untied pairs*, n_d, follow the same process but begin with the *upper-left* cell and multiply it by the sum of all cell frequencies below and to the *right*. Target the upper-left cell—10 cases. Find the sum of cell frequencies in cells below and to the right of the first row and first column: $309 + 343 + 19 + 190 + 84 + 7 = 952$ cases. Multiply this sum by the number of cases in the targeted cell to obtain the number of discordant pairs associated with that cell: $(952)(10) = 9,520$.

5. Still within the top row, move one column to the *right* and again add up all cell frequencies below and to the right. The target cell has 131 cases, and the sum of cases below and to the right is 453. Their product is $(131)(453) = 59,343$ discordant pairs. Add this to the number obtained in the preceding step: $9,520 + 59,343 = 68,863$.

6. Continue in this fashion until all discordant pairs have been calculated. Following are the six elements in this example:

$$(10)(952) = 9,520$$
$$(131)(453) = 59,343$$
$$(251)(26) = 6,526$$
$$(19)(281) = 5,339$$
$$(309)(91) = 28,119$$
$$(343)(7) = 2,401$$
$$\text{Total} = 111,248$$

Using the formula for gamma, we can now find the association between social class and financial satisfaction.

$$G = \frac{(283,730) - (111,248)}{(283,730) + (111,248)} = +0.437$$

Because the maximum positive value that gamma can reach is 1.00 we interpret this result as indicating a moderate positive association between the two variables. And this supports the hypothesis that the higher a person's subjective social class, the greater the family financial satisfaction. Note that when the formula for G is applied to a 2 X 2 table, its value is identical to Yule's Q, indicating that Yule's Q is a special case of the more general gamma measure of association.

5.2.3   Tau c

● **tau c**
a symmetric measure of association for two orderable discrete variables with unequal numbers of categories that takes into account only the number of untied pairs

Like gamma, **tau c** (τ_c) uses information about two orderable discrete variables by considering every possible untied pair of observations in the crosstabulation table. Although it is not a PRE-type measure of association, tau c also ranges in value from -1.00 to $+1.00$ and it equals zero if the two variables being analyzed are unrelated. The formula for computing this statistic in the sample is as follows:

$$t_c = \frac{2m(n_s - n_d)}{N^2(m - 1)}$$

Where:

$$m = \text{the smaller of } R \text{ or } C.$$

To compute t_c, the sample estimate, for Table 5.5 we need only n_s and n_d.

$$t_c = \frac{(2)\,(3)\,(283,730 - 111,248)}{(1,442)^2\,(3 - 1)} = +0.249$$

We see that the value of tau c is smaller than that for gamma using the same data. The reason is that G's denominator counts only the number of concordant and discordant pairs, whereas t_c's denominator basically counts *all* pairs, including those that are tied ($N^2/2$). To the extent that substantial numbers of tied pairs occur in a table, the value of gamma will be much larger than tau c. Neither value can be considered more "accurate" or "correct" than the other. Each simply conceptualizes the meaning of a tabular relationship in different terms.

5.2.4   Somers's d_{yx}

Unlike gamma, which yields the same value regardless of which variable is considered independent and which is considered dependent, **Somers's d_{yx}** is an *asymmetric* measure of ordinal association whose value depends on which variable plays which role. Suppose we are trying to predict the value of variable Y from our knowledge of variable X. We can take into account those pairs of observations that are tied on variable Y, the dependent variable, but we ignore any pairs on which both observations are tied in the independent variable, X. Somers's d for predicting Y from X, assuming Y is the row variable and X is the column variable in a crosstabulation, is given by the following:

● Somers's d_{yx} an asymmetric measure of association for two orderable discrete variables that takes into account the numbers of untied pairs and of pairs tied only on the dependent variable

$$d_{yx} = \frac{n_s - n_d}{n_s + n_d + T_r}$$

Where:

T_r = the number of ties associated with the row variable.

Somers's d_{yx} is a PRE-type measure of association that predicts the ranking on the dependent variable from a prediction rule that includes one type of tie among the variables. Following are the steps to be followed in computing T_r using Table 5.5:

1. Target the upper-left cell. Multiply this cell frequency times the sum of all the other cell frequencies in the *same row* and to the right of the cell: $(10)(131 + 251 + 36) = 4,180$. Call this term R_{11}.

2. Target the next cell to the right and in the same row. Multiply this cell frequency times the sum of the other cell frequencies to the right and in the same row: $131 (251 + 36) = 37,597$. Call this term R_{12}.

3. Continue this process of targeting a given cell and multiplying its frequency times the sum of all cell frequencies to the right of it and in the same row until all cells have been targeted, except for those in the last column. There will be $(R) (C) - R = R(C - 1)$ terms in all.

4. Add all of the $C (R - 1)$ terms together to form T_r. If the term associated with a given cell is labeled R_{ij}, then $T_r = \Sigma\Sigma R_{ij}$

In the example, verify the following:

$R_{11} = 4,180$	$R_{12} = 37,597$	$R_{13} = 9,036$
$R_{21} = 12,749$	$R_{22} = 111,858$	$R_{23} = 6,517$
$R_{31} = 12,083$	$R_{32} = 17,290$	$R_{33} = 588$

Then

$$T_r = 211,898$$

Now we have all the information we need to compute d_{yx}.

$$d_{yx} = \frac{283,730 - 111,248}{283,730 + 111,248 + 211,898}$$

$$= +0.284$$

Again, we see that the presence of numerous tied pairs means the value of Somers's d will be smaller than the value of G for the same tabular data.

The asymmetric nature of Somers's d means that two different values are likely to be computed from any table larger than 2 X 2. (For d_{xy} instead of d_{yx}, T_r is replaced in the denominator with T_c, the number of ties associated with the column variable. A procedure identical to that described above is used to calculate T_c.) Therefore, when reporting this statistic you must state which variable is assumed to be the dependent measure.

The measures of association and their statistical tests in this chapter are suitable only to crosstabulated frequency distributions. If data are measured as continuous variables, the more powerful statistical techniques described in the following chapters can be used.

Key Concepts and Symbols

These key concepts and symbols are listed in the order of appearance in the chapter. Combined with the definitions in the margins, these will help you review the material and can serve as a self-test for mastery of the concepts.

measures of association	Somers's d_{yx}
Yule's Q	Q
phi	ϕ
phi adjusted	ϕ_{adj}
phi maximum	ϕ_{max}
odds	n_s
conditional odds	n_d
odds ratio	G
(cross-product ratio)	τ_c
gamma	t_c
concordant pairs	d_{yx}
discordant pairs	d_{xy}
tau c	T_r

Problems

General Problems

1. In the 1984 presidential election, there was talk of a "gender gap," in which allegedly men supported Ronald Reagan more than did women. Test this hypothesis by calculating Yule's Q for these frequencies from the 1987 General Social Survey.

Vote by Gender

	Gender	
Vote	Men	Women
Reagan	223	320
Mondale	166	210

Source: 1987 General Social Survey.
Missing data = 547.

2. Is contact with people of other races related to attitudes toward integration? Here are data on 1987 GSS respondents who had brought a person of a different race home to dinner in recent years and their positions on a hypothetical open housing law that would allow owners to discriminate on the basis of race.

Open Housing by Dinner Guest

Position on open housing law	Ever brought a white/black home to dinner?	
	Yes	No
Owner has right to decide	130	503
Can't discriminate on race	301	463

Source: 1987 General Social Survey.
Missing data = 69.

How strongly are these two variables related, using Yule's Q?

3. Support and opposition to women's rights to abortions are known to vary by education levels. Using this crosstabulation from the 1987 GSS, calculate both ϕ and ϕ_{adj}.

Abortion Attitude by Education

Should abortion be legal for a poor woman who doesn't want more children?	Education	
	Less than college	Some college
Yes	304	330
No	512	255

Source: 1987 General Social Survey.
Missing data = 65.

4. Does personal experience with violence lead to support for tougher controls on firearms? Apply ϕ and ϕ_{adj} to this table from the 1987 GSS.

Gun Permit by Beating

Should people be required to obtain a police permit before buying a gun?	Have you ever been punched or beaten by another person?	
	No	Yes
Yes	678	345
No	234	175

Source: 1987 General Social Survey.
Missing data = 34.

5. In the 1985 GSS, respondents were asked whether the government should support declining industries to protect jobs. Of the 668 respondents, 343 supported such action, 178 were opposed, and 147 were neither for nor against the proposal. What were the odds of a respondent taking each of these positions?

6. Tolerance for civil liberties is a function of education. For this table from the 1987 GSS, calculate the conditional odds in favor of allowing a homosexual to speak in public for both levels of education, and the odds ratio for the table.

Homosexual Speech by Education

Should an admitted homosexual be allowed to make a speech in your community?	Education	
	Less than college	Some college
Yes	482	507
No	334	98

Source: 1987 General Social Survey.
Missing data = 45.

7. Does an exciting life make for greater happiness? Calculate gamma and t_c for this crosstabulation from the 1987 GSS.

Happiness by Life Excitement

Happiness	Life is		
	Dull	Routine	Exciting
Very happy	2	130	307
Pretty happy	15	475	301
Not too happy	38	104	31

Source: 1987 General Social Survey.
Missing data = 63.

8. Now consider whether happiness is related to feelings of closeness to God, again applying gamma and t_c to this table from the 1987 GSS.

Nearer to God by Happiness

Near to God	Happiness		
	Not too	Pretty	Very
Extremely close	53	217	175
Somewhat close	85	444	231
Not very close	24	74	25
Not close at all	8	42	11

Source: 1987 General Social Survey.
Missing data = 77.

9. Are people in better health more likely to lead exciting lives (and vice versa)? Apply Somers's d to the following table from the 1987 GSS, using first life and then health as the dependent variable.

Health by Life Excitement

Health	Life is		
	Dull	Routine	Exciting
Excellent	4	192	290
Good	14	334	259
Fair	20	160	80
Poor	18	34	22

Source: 1987 General Social Survey.
Missing data = 39.

10. How strongly are job satisfaction and social class related, according to Somers's d applied to this table from the 1987 GSS?

Job Satisfaction by Social Class

	Social class			
Job satisfaction	Lower	Working	Middle	Upper
Very satisfied	13	213	250	29
Moderately satisfied	15	215	206	8
Little dissatisfied	19	75	51	3
Very dissatisfied	8	25	19	2

Source: 1987 General Social Survey.
Missing data = 315.

Problems Requiring the 1987 General Social Survey

11. Who smokes more—women or men? Crosstabulate SEX and SMOKE and compute χ^2 and ϕ. Set α = .05. What do you conclude?

12. Are there any significant racial differences (RACE) in toleration of a racist teaching at a local college (COLRAC)? Calculate χ^2 and gamma. Use α = .01.

13. Religious fundamentalists (FUND) are likely to attend church (ATTEND) more frequently than moderates or liberals. How strong is this relationship, using gamma and t_c? Use α = .001.

14. Are workers who supervise others on the job (WKSUP) more likely than workers without subordinates to believe that hard work or luck is the key to getting ahead? Crosstabulate these variables and calculate Somers's d with GETAHEAD as dependent. Use α = .01.

15. How strongly is education related to beliefs that homosexuality is wrong? Recode EDUC into three categories (less than 12 years; 12 years; more than 12 years), crosstabulate with HOMOSEX, and calculate Somers's d with HOMOSEX dependent. Use α = .001.

Problems Requiring the 50-States Data Set

16. Crime seems to be more an urban than a rural problem. Dichotomize state ROBBERY rates (at 1279), URBAN percentage (at 66.8%), crosstabulate and calculate χ^2, ϕ, gamma, t_c, and Somers's d. Use $\alpha = .05$.

17. In the present era of industrial restructuring, states with a manufacturing base (MFGING) may be growing less rapidly (POPCHNG) than those states without such economic foundations. Dichotomize these variables (20.3% MFGING and 13.3% POPCHNG), crosstabulate and calculate χ^2, ϕ, gamma, t_c, and Somers's d. Use $\alpha = .05$.

18. How are crime and poverty linked? Dichotomize MURDER (at 69) and POVERTY (at 11.1%), crosstabulate and calculate χ^2, ϕ, gamma, t_c, and Somers's d. Use $\alpha = .05$.

6

Statistical Inference and Hypothesis Testing

Some basic concepts necessary for understanding statistical inference, which makes it possible to generalize from a sample to a population in order to test a hypothesis, were introduced in Chapter 4. In this chapter we will more precisely address the problem of making inferences about a population from sample data. First we begin with a general, elementary discussion of probability distributions. Then we give a short description of discrete probability distributions but present in detail two continuous probability distributions which are useful for drawing inferences about sample means: the normal distribution and the t distribution.

6.1   Probability Distributions

When a researcher draws a random sample from some population of interest, the goal is to be able to make accurate inferences about characteristics of the population from which the sample was drawn. The researcher hopes that the distribution of outcomes is a good approximation of the population distribution from which the sample was drawn. If it is a good approximation, the sample mean and standard deviation, for example, would also be expected to be good approximations of the population mean and standard deviation. (These concepts were described in Chapter 3.)

● **discrete probability distributions**
probability distributions for discrete variables

● **probability distribution**
a set of outcomes, each of which has an associated probability of occurrence

● **continuous probability distributions**
probability distributions for continuous variables with no interruptions or spaces between the outcomes of the variables

As was described in Chapter 1, a *discrete variable* classifies persons, objects, or events according to the kind or quality of their attributes. In considering **discrete probability distributions,** however, we are concerned with another characteristic of a discrete measure, that is, its outcomes are countable. Examples of discrete outcomes include the number of Democrats in Chicago, the number of women enrolled in Ph.D. programs in the U.S., and the number of heads observed if three coins are tossed simultaneously.

Every population has a **probability distribution** associated with it. And every outcome in that distribution has a probability of occurrence associated with it. For example, if a die is fair the probability associated with any of the six possible outcomes is $1/6 = .167$. Note that the sum of the probabilities across all outcomes is unity (i.e., $1/6 + 1/6 + 1/6 + 1/6 + 1/6 + 1/6 = 1.0$). This is an important fact for all probability distributions.

Let's examine a couple of other examples. The probability of flipping a coin and observing heads is $1/2 = 0.5$. If we toss two coins simultaneously, there are four possible outcomes – HH, HT, TH, and TT where H = Heads and T = Tails. The probability of observing any of these four outcomes is $1/4 = 0.25$. In a deck of cards there are 13 cards of each suit, 4 suits, and therefore 52 cards in total. The probability of picking a card at random and observing a club is $13/52 = 1/4 = 0.25$. This last example suggests that it also makes sense to think of the probability of discrete outcomes as a *relative frequency*. Thus the relative frequency of observing a club when drawing a card at random from a deck of cards is 13 of 52 cards, or as seen above, $13/52 = 0.25$. And the probability (or relative frequency) of observing a queen when picking a card at random is just 4/52 or $1/13 = .077$.

Many of the variables in the social sciences can be thought of as continuous – grade point average, social status, and religiosity, for example. In Chapter 1 we noted that continuous variables are used to classify persons, objects, or events according to the *magnitude or quantity* of their attributes. When we are considering **continuous probability distributions,** however, *continuous* also means that there are no interruptions or spaces between the outcomes of a variable. In fact, we must make some decision about how precisely to measure an underlying continuous variable. For example, grade point average is rarely computed beyond the nearest hundredth (e.g., 3.27), age is rarely measured beyond the nearest month, and so on.

Since the distribution of outcomes is continuous, the probability associated with the various outcomes can be connected by a single continuous line, as has been done in the hypothetical example in Figure 6.1. As a continuous variable is measured more and more precisely (such as a grade point average of 3.4276), the number of cases associated with an outcome becomes smaller and smaller and the probability of observing that outcome approaches zero. For this reason, when considering probabilities for continuous variables, we look at the area between two outcomes, a and b. Notice that the probability of observing an outcome of Y that lies between points a and b is labeled alpha (α); that is, $p(a \leq Y \leq b) = \alpha$. (Read this as, "The probability of observing an outcome of Y that is greater than or equal to a and less than or equal to b is alpha.")

Several *continuous probability distributions* are of great use when a scientist attempts to draw inferences about a population from characteristics observed in a sample. Later in this chapter we will introduce two of those distributions—the normal and the t. Another one is the χ^2 distribution discussed in Chapter 4. Still another—the F distribution—will be introduced in Chapter 8. These four theoretical probability distributions are extremely important for the field of **inferential statistics.** This is the part of statistics that is concerned with generalizing from sample estimates to descriptive characteristics of a population.

● **inferential statistics** numbers that represent generalizations, or inferences, drawn about some characteristic of a population, based on evidence from a sample of observations from the population

A Continuous Probability Distribution

FIGURE 6.1

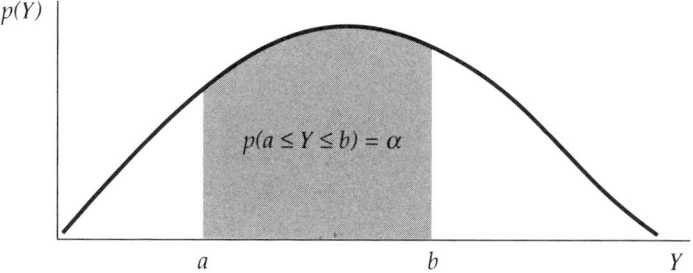

$p(Y)$

$p(a \leq Y \leq b) = \alpha$

a b Y

Source: George Bohrnstedt and David Knoke, *Statistics for Social Data Analysis* (Itasca, Ill.: F. E. Peacock Publishers, Inc., 1988), 138.

6.2   Describing Discrete Probability Distributions

● **population parameters**
descriptive characteristics of populations, such as means, variances, or correlations; usually designated by Greek letters

In the same way researchers can describe and summarize a sample with statistics such as the mean, as we noted in Chapter 3, they can also summarize and describe population distributions. The three major population descriptors are the mean, standard deviation, and variance. These descriptors are called **population parameters.** A parameter is a constant and in a population, the mean, standard deviation, and variance are *constants*. Each sample drawn from the same population, however, will have its own mean and variance, which can differ from corresponding population parameters. For this reason, statistics (e.g., the sample mean and standard deviation) are used as *estimators* of population parameters, and the sample mean and variance are estimators of the population mean and variance, respectively.

6.2.1   The Mean of a Probability Distribution

● **mean of a probability distribution**
the sum of all N observations in a population divided by N

The single outcome that best describes a probability distribution is the **mean of a probability distribution,** labeled μ_Y (Greek letter *mu*). It is computed the same way as the mean of a sample, except that all N of the observations in the *population* are added together and divided by the total number of observations in the population. Specifically the formula for computing the mean of a probability distribution where each outcome has the same probability of being observed is expressed as follows:

$$\mu_Y = \frac{\sum\limits_{i=1}^{N} Y_i}{N}$$

The mean of the distribution of outcomes of a die toss, for example, is $\mu_Y = (1 + 2 + 3 + 4 + 5 + 6)/6 = 21/6 = 3.5$. This example should make it clear that the mean of a probability distribution often will *not* equal one of the possible outcomes. Clearly we cannot observe an outcome of 3.5 when tossing a die! Nevertheless, 3.5 *is* the mean of all possible die tosses.

6.2.2   The Variance of a Probability Distribution

The **variance of a probability distribution,** which is labeled σ_Y^2 (Greek letter *sigma*), is similar but not identical to the sample variance. In particular, the population variance is given by this equation:

● **variance of a probability distribution** the spread or dispersion in a population of scores

$$\sigma_Y^2 = \sum_{i=1}^{N} \frac{(Y_i - \mu)^2}{N}$$

As in a sample, the variance of a probability distribution is a measure of spread or dispersion, but this case uses the population.

Recall from Chapter 3 that the square root of the variance is called the *standard deviation*. For a population, the standard deviation is symbolized σ_Y and is expressed as follows:

$$\sigma_Y = \sqrt{\sigma_Y^2}$$

Since researchers do not ordinarily observe populations, the parameters μ_Y and σ_Y^2 are of largely theoretical interest. You need to understand the concept of a population mean and variance, however, in order to understand the discussion of inference in the sections and chapters that follow. Box 6.1 provides a summary of symbols for the sample statistics introduced in Chapter 3 and the population parameters used thus far in this chapter.

Box 6.1   Population and Sample Symbols

Formulas can apply to data for an entire population and for a sample of observations drawn from a population. While the formulas are often the same or similar, the symbolic notation differs. Italic letters are used to stand for statistics calculated on sample data, while lower-case Greek letters stand for the population values, called *parameters*. For some of the statistics and parameters we have introduced, the symbols are the following:

Name	Sample statistics	Population parameter
Mean	$\overline{Y}$	μ_Y *(mu)*
Variance	s_Y^2	σ_Y^2 *(sigma)*
Standard deviation	s_Y	σ_Y *(sigma)*

6.3   Normal Distributions

One family of unimodal, symmetric distributions that is especially important in inferential statistics is comprised of **normal distributions,** noted in Chapter 4. The term *normal* is really a misnomer, however, since normal distributions are rarely, if ever, found in real data. Normal distributions are all described by a rather formidable equation.

● **normal distributions**
smooth, bell-shaped theoretical probability distributions for continuous variables that can be generated from formulas

---

$$p(Y) = \frac{1}{\sqrt{2\pi\sigma_Y^2}}\, e^{-(Y-\mu_Y)^2/2\sigma_Y^2}$$

The shape of any given normal curve is determined by two values, the population's mean, μ_Y, and variance, σ_Y^2.

Two normal curves are shown in Figure 6.2, one with $\sigma_Y^2 =$ 10 and the other with $\sigma_Y^2 = 15$, and both with $\mu_Y = 0$. Notice that the smaller the variance, the closer the population scores are to the mean, and the "thinner" the tails of the normal distribution are. Although the tails of the normal curve appear to touch the horizontal axis, in fact, the theoretical distribution of values ranges from $-\infty$ to $+\infty$; that is, the tails approach but never actually touch the horizontal axis.

We will refer to probabilities associated with outcomes of normal distributions very often in this text. Figuring out the probability of outcomes for different values of μ_Y *and* σ_Y^2 can be very tedious and time-consuming, but any distribution of outcomes can easily be converted to Z scores. For population values, $Z = (Y - \mu_Y)/\sigma_Y$. Therefore, one table of probabilities associated with normal distributions will suffice—the one associated with Z scores. When a normal curve has been converted to Z scores with a mean of zero and a standard deviation of one, it is called the **standard normal distribution.** However, converting a distribution to Z scores does not turn that distribution into a normal distribution in general. In the case under discussion, we are converting one normal distribution into another and only the values of the mean and standard deviation change, not the

● **standard normal distribution**
the normal distribution of a Z variable (score)

Two Examples of Normal Distributions   FIGURE 6.2

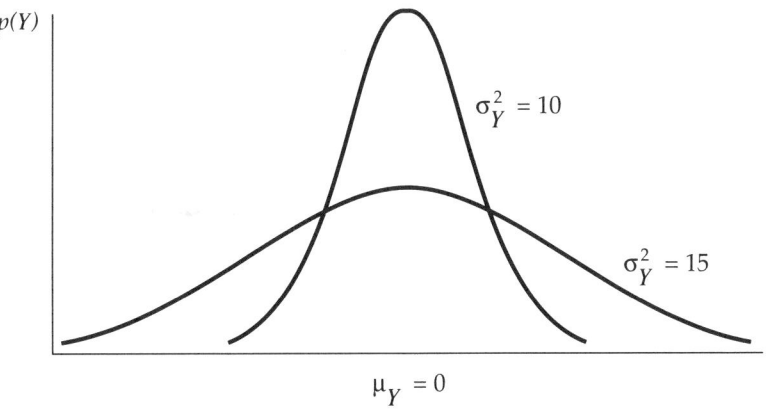

Source: George Bohrnstedt and David Knoke, *Statistics for Social Data Analysis* (Itasca, Ill.: F. E. Peacock Publishers, Inc., 1988), 145.

shape of the distribution. The table of probabilities for the standard normal distribution is in Appendix C, "Area under the Normal Curve," and a schematic of it is shown in Figure 6.3.

The probability associated with the set of outcomes for a normal curve is given by the area under the curve. Since the probabilities of all possible outcomes must sum to unity, the total area under the curve shown in Figure 6.3 is unity (1.0). Half the area lies left of its mean (which is zero, since the mean of a Z-score distribution is zero) and half to the right of the mean. As a result, in any normal distribution the probability of observing an outcome less than or equal to zero (the midpoint of the distribution) is 0.5, and the probability for observing an outcome equal to zero or greater is 0.5, as well.

The shaded area in Figure 6.3 refers to the probability of a value between zero and Z_a. For example, suppose we want to know the probability of an outcome being at least 1.55 standard deviations above the mean, assuming a normal distribution. In this case, $Z_\alpha = 1.55\sigma = 1.55$, since the standard deviation of Z scores is always 1.0, as we saw in Chapter 3. To determine the probability of this occurrence, turn to Appendix C. Look *down* the stub, or first column, of the table until you find 1.5. At that point look *across* the table, to the column labeled .05. The number you should see under this column is .4394. This is the probability of an outcome being between zero and Z_a (1.55 in this example). The probability of Z_a being 1.55 or greater is the unshaded area in the right tail of the distribution. This probability is .5000 − .4394 = .0606, since as we discussed above, the probability for the entire upper half of the distribution equals .5000. Since a normal distribution is symmetric, it should be clear that the probability of an observation being at least 1.55 standard deviations *below* the mean is also .0606. Thus, .8788 of the standard normal curve area lies between −1.55 and +1.55, while only .1212 of the area lies in both tails beyond Z scores of −1.55 and +1.55.

6.3.1   The Alpha Area

The alpha we introduced in Chapter 4—the probability of a Type I or false rejection error (or the probability of rejecting the null hypothesis when it is in fact true)—will assume a more formal definition here. The area from a given Z_a to the tail of a distribution, alpha, or α, is defined mathematically as follows:

$$p(|Z|) \geq p(|Z_a|) = \alpha$$

Example of the Probability of Observing an
Outcome in a Normal Distribution

FIGURE 6.3

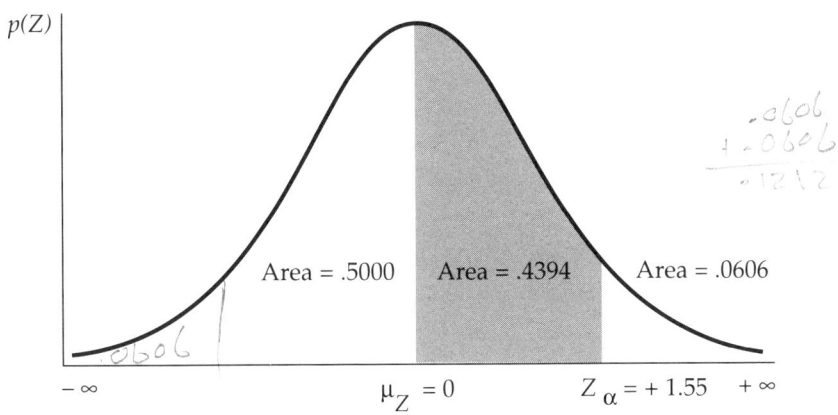

Source: George Bohrnstedt and David Knoke, *Statistics for Social Data Analysis* (Itasca, Ill.: F. E. Peacock Publishers, Inc., 1988), 146.

We have illustrated this in Figure 6.4, where the area between Z_α and ∞ is labeled α. We could also have chosen α to be in the left tail of the distribution. It is for this reason we use **absolute** values of Z and Z_α in the formula.

Sometimes we want to split the probability of a Type I error evenly between the two tails of a distribution. In this case the probability in the upper tail is $\alpha/2$, and the probability in the lower tail is also $\alpha/2$. The two Z scores that cut off these areas in the distribution are labeled $Z_{\alpha/2}$ and $-Z_{\alpha/2}$, respectively. Figure 6.5 should help clarify this discussion, as should the two examples that follow.

Assume we have a problem where the use of the normal curve is appropriate, as will be the case later in this chapter. Suppose further that we choose $\alpha = .05$ and want it to be totally in the upper tail, as is the case in Figure 6.4. The strategy to follow is to ask what value of Z_α will cut off the upper 5% of the normal curve. We look up .4500 in Appendix C, since .5000 − .4500 = .0500. The two values closest to .4500 are .4495 and .4505. They are associated with the outcomes 1.64 and 1.65, respectively. We can simply divide the difference and conclude

FIGURE 6.4   Probability Distribution for a Type I Error in
                             the Right Tail

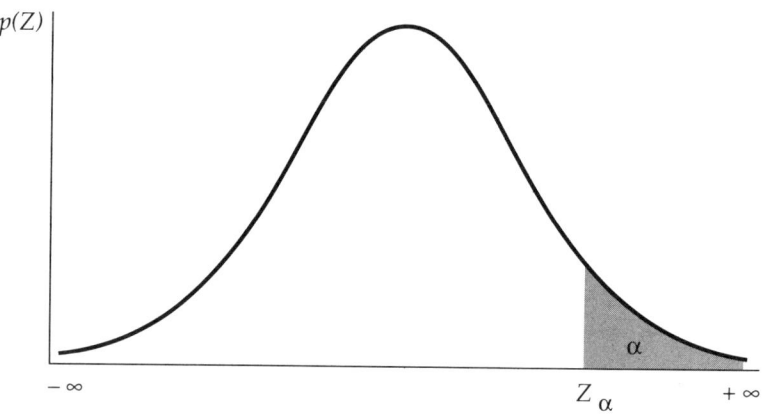

Source: George Bohrnstedt and David Knoke, *Statistics for Social Data Analysis* (Itasca, Ill.: F. E. Peacock Publishers, Inc., 1988), 148.

that a Z_α of 1.645 standard deviations or more above the mean will occur only about 5% of the time in a normal distribution. Therefore $Z_\alpha = 1.645$ for this problem.

If we wish to split the probability of a Type I error between the two tails, as we have done in Figure 6.5, then for $\alpha = .05$, $\alpha/2 = .025$. To determine the Z_αs that place 2.5% of the area under the normal distribution in each tail, we calculate that .5000 − .4750 = .0250, and the Z_α associated with .4750 is 1.96. Since the normal distribution is symmetric, $-Z_\alpha = -1.96$ also.

Another way to think of this is that 95% of the area under a normal curve lies between $-Z_\alpha = -1.96$ and $Z_\alpha = 1.96$. Now, convince yourself that about 68% of the outcomes in a normal distribution fall between standard deviations of -1 and $+1$, about 95% of all outcomes fall between standard deviations of -2 and $+2$, and about 99.7% of all outcomes fall between standard deviations of -3 and $+3$. Assuming a normal distribution, an observation three standard deviations or more from the mean is a rare occurrence indeed. This information is presented graphically in Figure 6.5.

Let's look at another example. The probability of an outcome two standard deviations or more above the mean of a normal

Areas under the Normal Curve for Various
Z Scores

FIGURE 6.5

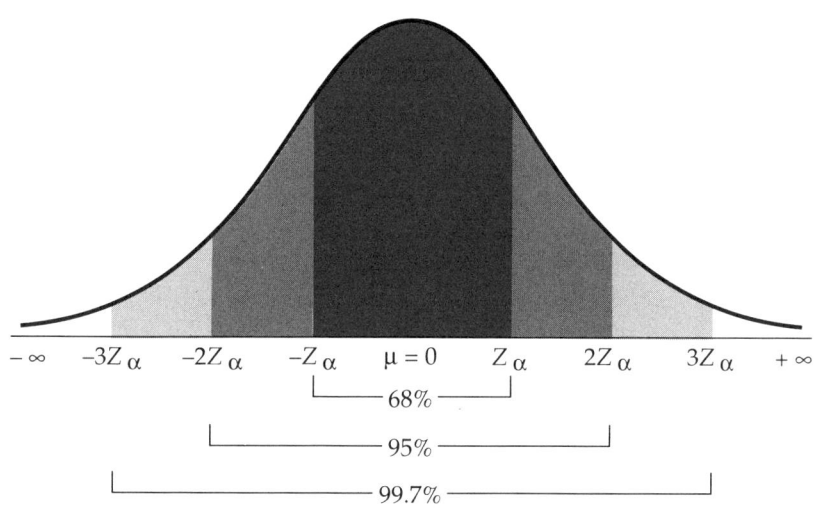

Source: George Bohrnstedt and David Knoke, *Statistics for Social Data Analysis* (Itasca, Ill.: F. E. Peacock Publishers, Inc., 1988), 147.

distribution is $.5000 - .4772 = .0228$ or less. This means that only about 2.3% of the time will an outcome two standard deviations above the mean in a normal distribution be observed. All of this may seem irrelevant right now. However, the use of Z_α and α in using the normal distribution will become clearer when we discuss inference in Section 6.5.

6.4   The Central Limit Theorem

An important application of the normal distribution follows from the **central limit theorem,** which states:

> If all possible random samples of N observations are drawn from a population with mean μ_Y and variance σ_Y^2, then as N grows large, the sample means will be approximately normally distributed with mean μ_Y and variance σ_Y^2/N; this can be stated mathematically as follows:

● **central limit theorem**
a mathematical theorem that states that if repeated random samples of size N are selected from a normally distributed population with mean = μ and variance = σ_Y^2, then the means of the samples will be normally distributed with mean=μ and variance = σ_Y^2/N as N gets large

→ The large N is the closer it will be to population means & variance.

$$\mu_{\bar{Y}} = \mu_{Y}$$

$$\sigma_{\bar{Y}}^2 = \sigma_Y^2/N$$

According to the central limit theorem, the mean of the distribution of all the sample means will equal the mean of the population from which the random samples were drawn as N gets large. The theorem does not make any assumption about the shape of the population from which the samples are drawn.

● sampling distribution of sample means
the population distribution of all possible means for samples of size N selected from a population

The **sampling distribution of sample means** is a theoretical distribution consisting of the sample means that would be obtained by forming all possible samples of size N, drawn from a population. With billions and trillions of unique samples from any large population, no one is actually going to calculate a sampling distribution of means. Nevertheless, since the central limit theorem states the relationship between the population's two parameters (μ_Y and σ_Y^2) and the sampling distribution's mean and variance, we can readily determine the shape of the distribution once we know the values of the mean and variance. The sampling distribution concept will be very useful when we discuss inferences about population means in the next section.

The central limit theorem guarantees that a given sample mean can be made to come close to the population mean in value by simply choosing a very large sample size, N, since the variance of the sampling distribution of means, $\sigma^2_{\bar{Y}}$, becomes smaller as N gets larger.

● standard error
the standard deviation of a sampling distribution

The standard deviation of a sampling distribution has a specific name – the **standard error.** The standard error of the mean is expressed as follows:

$$\sigma_{\bar{Y}} = \frac{\sigma_Y}{\sqrt{N}}$$

Armed with the knowledge that the sampling distribution of sample means is normal, regardless of the shape of the population from which the samples are drawn, and assuming that N is large, we can make some powerful statements.

Suppose a population has a mean of $\mu_Y = 100$ and a standard deviation of $\sigma_Y = 15$ and we draw a random sample of $N = 400$ cases. We can immediately calculate the standard error of the sampling distribution of means for all samples of size 400 which can be drawn from the population. Using the formula, the standard error for this sampling distribution is

$$\sigma_{\bar{Y}} = \frac{15}{\sqrt{400}} = 0.750$$

Based on the information in the preceding section on normal distributions (see Figure 6.5) we expect that 95% of all sample means will fall within $\pm$ 1.96 standard errors of the population mean, or in this example, 95% of all sample means should fall in the interval between 98.53 and 101.47 [100 $\pm$ (1.96)(0.75)]. Therefore, if we draw a random sample of size 400 its mean should be very close to the population mean in value; only 5% of samples drawn at random will lie outside the interval bounded by 98.53 and 101.47. If we increase the sample size from 400 to 1,000, the standard error of the sampling distribution becomes much smaller; specifically, $\sigma_{\bar{Y}} = 15/\sqrt{1,000} = 0.47$. For $N = 1,000$, we would expect 95% of all sample means to lie between 99.08 and 100.92 [100 $\pm$ 1.96(.47)]. This result implies that we can have considerable confidence that any random sample of size 1,000 we choose will give an accurate estimate of the mean of the population from which it was drawn.

While we have said that N must be large for the central limit theorem to apply, we have not addressed the question of how large it must be. Some textbooks say 30; others suggest 100. We do not use any hard-and-fast rule, but we suggest on the basis of experience that when a sample is the size of 50 we can safely assume that the sampling distribution of means closely approximates a normal distribution. Unless the underlying population is extremely odd in shape, we can be relatively confident that the central limit theorem applies for samples as small as 25 or 30.

In Section 6.6 we will introduce the t distributions and some small sample estimation techniques. To make such decisions easier we will recommend that these techniques be used when N is less than 50. You should recognize this as only a rule of thumb, however, not as dogma.

6.5 Sample Point Estimates and Confidence Intervals

● **point estimate**
a sample statistic used to estimate a population parameter

The fact that the mean of the sampling distribution of means equals the mean of the population from which the sample was drawn has an important corollary. Namely, the sample mean for a randomly drawn sample is an unbiased estimator of the population mean from which the sample was drawn. Indeed, when a random sample is drawn, the *best* estimate of the population mean is the sample mean. (A more exact definition of an unbiased estimate will be given in Section 6.7.) Another term for the sample mean is the **point estimate** of the population mean.

● **confidence interval**
a range of values constructed around a point estimate which makes it possible to state the probability that the interval contains the population parameter between its upper and lower confidence limits

Once we choose a sample and compute a mean, we can construct a **confidence interval** around it. For example, we would expect approximately 95% of the intervals constructed in repeated sampling of the same size to contain the population mean, μ_y, when the interval is defined by boundaries approximately two standard errors below and two standard errors above the mean. The **lower confidence limit** (or **LCL**) is $\overline{Y} - 1.96\sigma_{\overline{Y}}$ and the **upper confidence limit** (or **UCL**) is $\overline{Y} + 1.96\sigma_{\overline{Y}}$ for a 95% confidence interval.

● **lower confidence limit (LCL)**
the lowest value of a confidence interval

Based on the information on normal distributions in Section 6.3, we can determine that the LCL and UCL for a 68% confidence interval are $Y - \sigma_{\overline{Y}}$ and $Y + \sigma_{\overline{Y}}$ respectively. And for a 99% confidence interval, the LCL is $Y - 2.58\sigma_{\overline{Y}}$ and the UCL is $Y + 2.58\sigma_{\overline{Y}}$.

● **upper confidence limit (UCL)**
the highest value of a confidence interval

In general, we can construct confidence intervals for any desired level of confidence, say $1 - \alpha$, by this formula.

$$\overline{Y} \pm Z_{\alpha/2}\sigma_{\overline{Y}}$$

We can now define the symbol $Z_{\alpha/2}$ which was introduced in the formula, more precisely. In Appendix C, $Z_{\alpha/2}$ is the value that has an area to the right which is equal to $\alpha/2$. If we want

95% confidence intervals for a given μ_Y, then $\alpha = .05$ by impli-
cation, and $\alpha/2 = .025$. As we saw in Section 6.4, $Z_{\alpha/2} = 1.96$
will give us the correct interval for a given $\sigma_{\bar{Y}}$.

Caution is in order when interpreting confidence intervals.
There is a great temptation to make statements suggesting that
one can be 95% confident that a given interval contains the population mean. In fact, after an interval is constructed, the probability that it contains the true population mean is either one or
zero, depending upon whether it contains the population mean
or not! What we can say is that *in the long run*, 95% of such intervals will contain the population mean.

Figure 6.6 illustrates the concept of a confidence interval.
The solid vertical line represents the true population mean,
which is, of course, a constant. The horizontal lines represent
confidence intervals constructed around 15 different sample
means. Notice that all but one of them (the second from the bottom) contain the population mean, $\mu_Y = 50.5$. The point estimates (i.e., the sample means) are noted beside each interval.
Importantly, it is the *procedure* that guarantees that, in the long
run, 95% of the intervals will contain the true population
parameter.

In general, the larger the sample size, the smaller the
interval around the sample mean for a given confidence interval.
This can be easily shown. Suppose we know that $\sigma_Y = 15$. We
observe $\bar{Y} = 100$ in a random sample of 100. If we want to
construct a 95% confidence interval, the interval is bound by
$100 - (1.96)(15/\sqrt{100})$, or 97.06, and $100 + (1.96)(15/\sqrt{100})$, or
102.94. But now suppose we observe $\bar{Y} = 100$ for a random
sample of 500. In this case, the interval is bound by $100
- (1.96)(15/\sqrt{500})$, or 98.69, and $100 + (1.96)(15/\sqrt{500})$, or 101.31,
for 95% confidence. Thus, for a given α, increasing N decreases
the size of the confidence interval.

This is another way of saying that the larger the N, the better the sample mean, $\bar{Y}$, estimates the population mean, $\mu_{\bar{Y}}$.
This clearly fits our intuition, since we know that the sample
mean equals the population mean as the size of the sample approaches that of the population. You should convince yourself
that even for a sample of $N = 1,500$, confidence intervals around
a given sample mean are quite small relative to the size of the
population standard deviation. This is why public opinion polling is such big business today!

To help you tie things together, here are a few summary statements about assumptions useful for constructing confidence intervals:

1. We assume that the sample for estimating μ_Y is drawn *randomly*.
2. We assume we have chosen $N \geq 50$.
3. We assume we know σ_Y.

To compute the standard error, $\sigma_{\bar{Y}}$, we need knowledge of the population standard deviation, which we do not generally know. When N is "large" (i.e., 50 or more), however, we can be quite confident that the sample standard deviation, s_Y, is a good estimate of σ_Y. A caret (˄) is added to σ_Y to signify that it is an estimated value.

$$\hat{\sigma}_{\bar{Y}} = \frac{s_Y}{\sqrt{N}}$$

In Chapter 3, for example, we estimated average liking scores for China and Russia, using data from Table 3.5. The point estimates on the 10-point scales (where 0 is extreme disliking and 9 is extreme liking) were 4.96 for China and 3.06 for Russia, with standard deviations of 2.24 and 2.50, respectively. The sample sizes on which these statistics were based were 1,404 for China and 1,405 for Russia. Using this information, we can construct a confidence interval. Thus the 95% confidence interval for China is 4.96 $\pm$ (1.96)(2.24/$\sqrt{1,404}$) or a LCL of 4.84 and a UCL of 5.08. For Russia, the confidence interval is 3.06 $\pm$ (1.96)(2.50/$\sqrt{1,405}$), a LCL of 2.93 and a UCL of 3.19. Notice that with these large samples, both confidence intervals are small relative to the size of the standard deviations. This shows the importance of N in making inferences.

We can be even more confident by choosing a larger value for $1 - \alpha$. In these examples, the 99% confidence intervals would be defined by 4.96 $\pm$ (2.58)(2.24/$\sqrt{1,404}$) and 3.06 $\pm$ (2.58)(2.50/$\sqrt{1,405}$). For China the LCL and UCL become 4.81 and 5.11, respectively; for Russia 2.89 and 3.23, respectively.

Example Illustrating the Concept of a
Confidence Interval

FIGURE 6.6

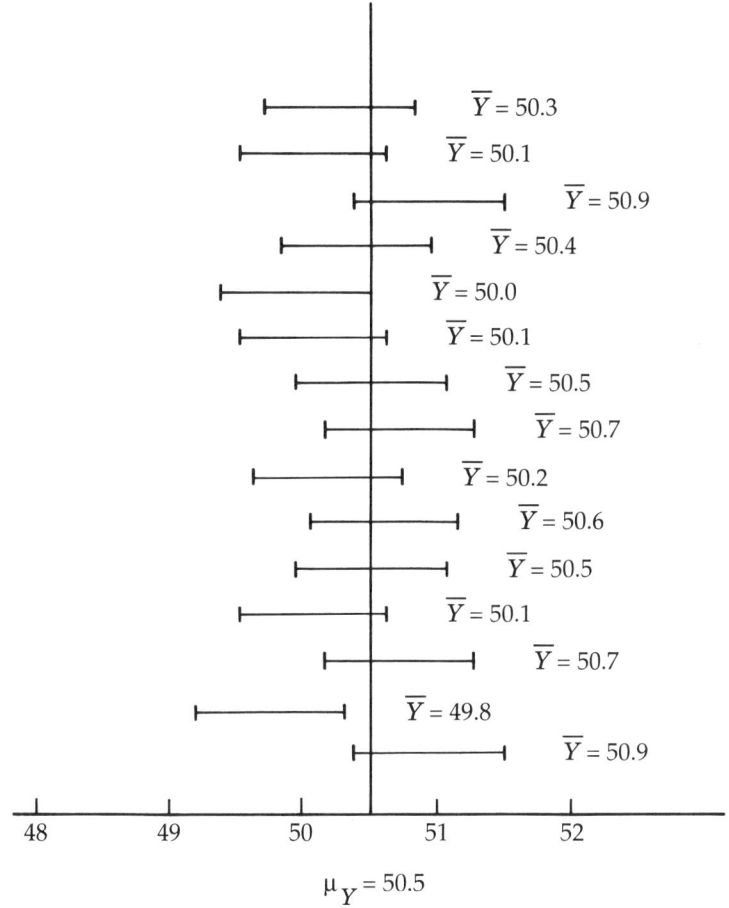

$\mu_Y = 50.5$

Based on all these results, we are virtually certain that
Americans liked China much more than they liked Russia in
1986. What would you guess the results of the 1990 GSS are
considering the momentous events in China and Russia in 1989
and 1990?

6.6   Constructing Confidence Intervals around Estimators When the Standard Error Is Unknown: The *t* Distribution

● **t distributions**
one of a family of
test statistics used
with small samples
selected from
normally distributed
populations or, for
large samples,
drawn from
populations with
any shape

In the preceding examples we have assumed we know the standard error of the sampling distribution of the mean, $\sigma_{\bar{Y}}$. There is another family of distributions that is similar to the family of normal distributions, but for which we do not need to know $\sigma_{\bar{Y}}$. These are referred to as *t* **distributions.**

A *t* **variable,** or *t* **score,** is given as follows:

● **t variable (t
score)**
a transformation of
the scores of a
continuous
frequency
distribution derived
by subtracting the
mean and dividing
by the estimated
standard error

$$t = \frac{\overline{Y} - \mu_Y}{s_Y/\sqrt{N}}$$

The similarity to Z used for drawing inferences is evident. The only difference is that t involves s_Y, whereas Z assumes knowledge of σ_Y. The t statistic was first introduced by W. S. Gossett, who signed his research article "Student." For this reason these sampling distributions are often called Student's t distributions.

There are many t distributions, and their shapes vary with the sample size and the sample standard deviation. All t distributions, like Z-transformed *normal* distributions, are bell-shaped and have a mean of zero. But following are two important differences between a t distribution and a normal distribution:

1.   The use of a t distribution to test hypotheses assumes that the sample is drawn from a normally distributed population.
2.   A t distribution for a given sample size has a larger variance than a normal Z distribution. Therefore, the standard error of a t distribution is larger than that of a normal Z distribution (see Figure 6.7).

Comparing a *t* Distribution with 4 Degrees
of Freedom with the Standardized Normal
Distribution

FIGURE 6.7

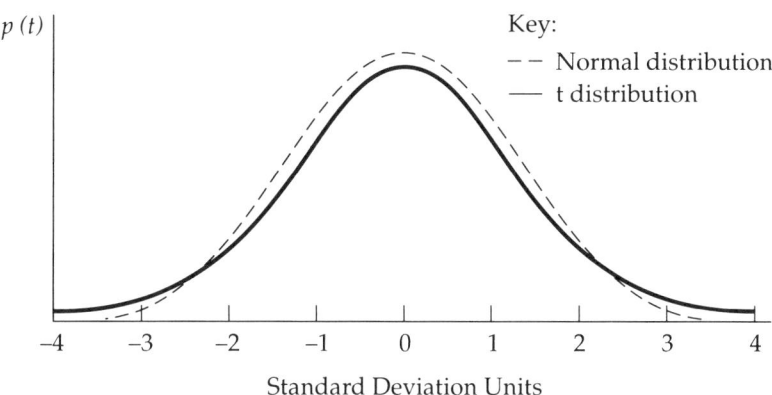

Source: George Bohrnstedt and David Knoke, *Statistics for Social
Data Analysis* (Itasca, Ill.: F. E. Peacock Publishers, Inc., 1988), 159.

The first assumption that a sample is drawn from a normally
distributed population may seem to be restrictive. Research has
shown, however, that violations of this assumption have only
minor effects on the computation of a test statistic. Therefore,
unless we are certain that the underlying population from which
the sample is drawn is grossly non-normal, we can use a *t* distribution even when *N* is small.

The second assumption also needs to be qualified. As *N* gets
large (i.e., in the range of 50), a *t* distribution becomes increas-
ingly similar to a *normal Z* distribution in shape. Therefore, as
N gets large, the standard error of the *t* distribution approaches
that of the normal *Z* distribution. This means that for a large
N, the probabilities associated with outcomes in the two distributions are virtually identical. This can be verified by comparing probabilities for *Z* values in Appendix C with *t* values in

Appendix D for $N = 120$. When N is small, however, as Figure 6.7 makes clear, more cases fall into the extreme sections of the tails of a t compared to a Z distribution. For a given value of α, say .05 (see Section 6.3), t_α will be larger than Z_α (and $t_{\alpha/2}$ will be greater than $Z_{\alpha/2}$). This, too, can be verified by comparing Z values in Appendix C with t values in Appendix D for $N = 30$. For $\alpha = .05$, $t = 1.70$ whereas $Z = 1.65$. But as can be seen even for an N as small as 30, the difference between t and Z is small for a given α level.

As noted in Section 3.2.3, the numerator of the formula for the sample variance, s_Y^2, is divided by $N - 1$ and is called the *degrees of freedom* (see Chapter 4) associated with the t distribution. In a set of N observations with a given mean, $N - 1$ scores can assume any value, but the Nth score is not free to vary for a given mean. For example, if we know the mean of a distribution is 3, $N = 4$, and three observations equal 1, 2, and 4, the fourth value is constrained to be 5. Once we know the mean and $N - 1$ values, the Nth value is constrained. For this reason, we say there are $N - 1$ degrees of freedom (df).

Depending on the population standard deviation and the degrees of freedom, t distributions are bell-shaped, symmetric curves with means of zero and differing standard deviations. The smaller the df, the flatter the curve. This can be seen by examining Figure 6.7 where a t distribution with 4 degrees of freedom is compared to a standard normal distribution.

Since the values of a t distribution are the same as the values of a Z-normal distribution when N is large, we can always use a t distribution to make inferences about means. Because of this, when inferences about means are presented in published research, they are almost always made using a t distribution.

If N is small, however, you need to remember that the t distribution requires random sampling from a normal population, whereas Z does not assume a normal parent population. As suggested above, however, unless the parent population is grossly non-normal, violations of this assumption do not cause serious problems in drawing inferences.

The formula for constructing confidence intervals around a sample mean assuming a Z variable was presented in Section 6.4. It can easily be adapted for use with t variables as follows. A confidence interval can be constructed around the point estimate (i.e., the sample mean) with confidence $1 - \alpha$ by the following formula:

$$\text{Confidence interval} = \overline{Y} \pm t_{a/2} s_Y / \sqrt{N}$$

To use the *t* distribution to build a confidence interval around a sample mean, proceed as follows using Appendix D:

1. Choose the desired degree of confidence by specifying α. For example, for a 95% confidence interval, choose $\alpha = .05$.
2. Move across the row in Appendix D labeled "two-tailed" until you come to the specified α level (.05 for example).
3. Move down this column of numbers until you come to the value associated with the correct degrees of freedom.

For $\alpha = .05$ and $N = 30$, $t = 2.045$ since $N = 30$, the $df = 29$. Hence, the confidence interval would be given by $\overline{Y} \pm 2.045$ $(s_Y / \sqrt{N})$.

6.6.1   An Example Using the *t* Distribution to Construct a Confidence Interval

As is well-known, since World War II, there has been a tremendous increase in the number of women in the labor force in the United States. We can use the 50-States Data Set to estimate the average percentage of women in the labor force and, in addition, to construct a confidence interval around the mean we compute. Using the 50-States Data Set, we find that the mean percentage of women in the labor force across the states is 52.41 and the standard deviation is 4.08. Note that the point estimate suggests that slightly over half of the women in the U.S. work. A 95% confidence interval can now be constructed about this estimate by using Appendix D and the knowledge that for $df = 49$, 2.01 is a good approximation of the true *t* value. Using this value, the point estimate is bound by the following:

$$52.41 \pm 2.01 \left(\frac{4.08}{\sqrt{49}} \right)$$

The LCL and UCL are 51.24 and 53.58, respectively, suggesting that the true mean percent of women working across the states is somewhere between 51.24% and 53.58%. In other words, the point estimate of 52.41 is likely to be very close to the true mean percent of women working.

6.7   Unbiased Estimators

To be useful, sample estimators should have certain desirable characteristics. Since we use sample statistics to make inferences about the parameters, we want them to be "good" estimators. This section identifies one characteristic that makes a good estimator. There are several others as well, but a discussion of these characteristics is beyond the scope of this book.

● **unbiased estimator**
an estimator of a population parameter whose expected value equals the parameter

An **unbiased estimator** is one that, on average, equals the population parameter. If $\hat{\theta}$ is an unbiased estimate of θ, then the mean of the estimator of all possible samples of size N from the same population equals the population parameter, as follows:

$$\mu_{\hat{\theta}} = \theta$$

For example, as we indicated in Section 6.4 on the central limit theorem $\mu_{\bar{Y}} = \mu_Y$, the sample mean, $\bar{Y}$, is an unbiased estimate of μ_Y, the population mean.

In Section 3.2.3, we defined the sample variance as follows:

$$s_{\hat{Y}}^2 = \frac{\sum_{i=1}^{N}(Y_i - \bar{Y})^2}{N - 1}$$

This indicates that the summed and squared deviation is to be divided by $N - 1$ instead of by N, as is done when computing the mean. Suppose we use s_*^2 to symbolize the variance instead of $s_{\hat{Y}}^2$, and define it as follows:

$$s_*^2 = \frac{\sum_{i=1}^{N}(Y_i - \bar{Y})^2}{N}$$

It can also be proven that

$$\mu_{s_*^2} = \left(\frac{N-1}{N} \right) \sigma_Y^2$$

If we take all possible random samples of size N from some population and then we compute s_*^2 for each, the mean of the distribution will be smaller than the population variance by the factor $(N-1)/N$. For s_*^2 to be unbiased, we need to multiply it by the reciprocal of the biasing factor, $N/(N-1)$.

$$\left(\frac{N}{N-1} \right) s_*^2 = \left(\frac{N}{N-1} \right) \sum_{i=1}^{N} \left(\frac{Y_i - \overline{Y}}{N} \right)^2$$

$$= \sum_{i=1}^{N} \frac{(Y_i - \overline{Y})^2}{N-1}$$

$$= s_Y^2$$

Therefore the statistic for the variance of a sample, s_Y^2, is an unbiased estimator of the variance of the population, σ_Y^2. Hopefully, this makes it clear why we divide $\sum_{i=1}^{N} (Y_i - \overline{Y})^2$ by $N-1$ instead of by N; doing so makes s_Y^2 an unbiased estimator of σ_Y^2.

6.8   The Logic of Inferential Statistics

The logic of inferential statistics should now be clear. Every problem involving the drawing of inferences requires the use of three different types of distributions:

1. A population distribution
2. A sampling distribution
3. A distribution of N sample observations (i.e., a sample)

We are always interested in estimating population parameters from sample statistics. We begin by drawing a sample of N observations from the population distribution of interest, and then by calculating the sample mean and standard deviation, $\overline{Y}$ and s_Y. This enables us to make inferences about the value of the population mean and standard deviation, about μ_Y and σ_Y. In order to make these inferences accurately we need a bridge, the sampling distribution. Because the sampling distribution is a normal distribution whose mean and standard deviation are identical to those of the population distribution, when the N drawn is large, we can make probability statements about the accuracy of our sample estimates. Hopefully this discussion clarifies not only the logic of making inferences, but the differences between a sample, a sampling distribution, and a population distribution.

Drawing a random sample and computing sample statistics as estimates of population parameters are, in our judgment, among the most central tasks of the scientist. Estimation is the more important of the two procedures that together constitute the area called statistical inference. The second is called *hypothesis testing* and we now turn to a discussion of it.

6.9   Hypothesis Testing

One of the ways scientists evaluate their scientific propositions is to construct working or operational hypotheses using indicators presumed to measure reliably and validly the concepts contained in the propositions (see Section 1.5). The operational hypotheses can then be converted to statistical hypotheses as a way to evaluate the scientific propositions. An example of this procedure was presented in Chapter 4 where we showed how to test a proposition linking church attendance to marital status using the chi-square test. In that chapter some of the basics of hypothesis testing were outlined. In this section, we expand on the earlier presentation to show how one can test hypotheses about means. **Hypothesis testing** is done to determine whether or not observed sample data could have been generated by chance from a population in which the null hypothesis is true. For now, we restrict our discussion to testing hypotheses about single means. In Chapter 7, however, we discuss inferences about the difference between two means and the rationale for that test.

- **hypothesis testing**
a branch of statistics in which hypotheses are tested to determine whether the observed sample data have been generated by chance from a population in which the null hypothesis is true

- **statistical hypothesis**
a statement about one or more population parameters

6.9.1   Statistical Hypotheses

A **statistical hypothesis** is a statement about one or more population parameters. In this book statistical hypotheses will be limited to statements about a single population parameter, but it need not be. An example of a statistical hypothesis is as follows:

H: The population is normally distributed with $\mu_Y = 20$ and $\sigma_Y = 5$.

As you can see from this example, a statistical hypothesis can be quite different from a substantive scientific proposition, which usually begins with "The greater the . . ." or "If . . . then." Typically, however, statistical hypotheses are developed from scientific propositions. This is done by putting two competing statistical hypotheses together, one will provide support for the scientific, substantive hypotheses if the other can be rejected. Suppose, for example, that a random sample of adult males is drawn in a community to determine average number of years of education completed. Suppose also that the sample mean is 10.4 with a standard deviation of 1.2. Assume a second study is done fewer than six months later, again using a second random sample, and this time the mean equals 9.6 with a standard deviation of 1.4. The survey research organization conducting the research decides to conduct yet a third study a few weeks later to see which of the first two sample means seems to reflect more accurately the true population mean. The researchers use the two sample means to generate two competing hypotheses about the population means, since both are unbiased estimates of the population mean.

$$H_0: \mu_Y = 10.4$$

$$H_1: \mu_Y = 9.6$$

Note that statistical hypotheses are always statements about population parameters. Sample data are used to evaluate which of the two hypotheses is the more plausible. When two *exact hypotheses* are set against one another, it seems likely that neither will be correct. Rather, one is more likely to be closer to the true population parameter than the other. As a result, the researcher is likely to suspend judgment in such a case and instead will be forced to make vague statements about which hypothesis is the more plausible given the sample evidence.

More typically in the social sciences, the null hypothesis is an exact hypothesis and the alternative hypothesis is inexact. For example, drawing on our example using average years of education, we could formulate two hypotheses:

$$H_0: \mu_Y = 10.4$$

$$H_1: \mu_Y < 10.4$$

Or just as plausibly

$$H_0: \mu_Y = 9.6$$

$$H_1: \mu_Y < 9.6$$

Choosing either of the two sets of null and alternative hypotheses undoubtedly assumes more knowledge than we have in the social sciences. Therefore more realistic null and alternative hypotheses might be formulated.

$$H_0: \mu_Y = 10.4$$

$$H_1: \mu_Y \neq 10.4$$

or perhaps

$$H_0: \mu_Y = 9.6$$

$$H_1: \mu_Y \neq 9.6$$

Importantly, note that the null hypothesis is always an exact hypothesis. The alternative may or may not be exact depending upon the certainty with which the scientist believes he or she can state the alternative hypothesis. However, as stated above, the state of knowledge in the social sciences is such that the alternative hypothesis will almost always be an inexact hypothesis.

This discussion should clarify that when testing statistical hypotheses, the scientist's decision about whether a given hypothesis is true or false can never be done with certainty. One always runs a risk of drawing an incorrect inference. However, as we will soon see, there are some ways to assess and to minimize these risks.

Whenever we test statistical hypotheses the assumption is made that the sample is drawn randomly to maximize the likelihood that it is representative of the underlying population from which it is drawn (see Section 4.6). Furthermore, for tests about means when N is small, say 50 or less, we need to assume that the underlying population distribution is normal. This requires using tests with a t variable and the probability values associated with it in Appendix D. If N is large (over 50), however, the central limit theorem (see Section 6.4) allows us to ignore the shape of the distribution of the underlying population, since the sampling distribution will be roughly normal. We could use a Z variable and the probability values associated with it in Appendix C. But as indicated earlier, the probability values for a t variable approach those of a Z variable as N gets "large," so we can usually use a t test (and Appendix D) and forget about using Appendix C. To verify this assertion, recall that 95% of the area lies between -1.96 and $+1.96$ in a normal distribution. (Use Appendix C and Figure 6.5 to verify this.) Now note in Appendix D (the t distribution) that for a two-tailed hypothesis test with $\alpha = .05$, the critical values of t are -1.98 and $+1.98$, only a .02 difference than the comparable values in Appendix C.

6.9.2   Evaluating Statistical Hypotheses Using Sample Data

As we pointed out in Chapter 4, social scientists ordinarily state a null and an alternative hypothesis. And usually the alternative hypothesis represents the substantive hypothesis of interest. And as we further pointed out, support for the alternative hypothesis is provided when the null hypothesis must be rejected. So, for example, in Chapter 4, support for the hypothesis that church attendance and marital status covary (the alternative hypothesis) was provided by rejecting the null hypothesis of no relationship between the two variables. Hypotheses testing about means is done in a similar way. The null hypothesis is typically written to reflect the hypothesis one expects to reject. This can best be seen by considering an example with two exact hypotheses.

6.9.3   An Example of a Hypothesis Test about a Single Mean with Exact Hypotheses

We will use a rather contrived example to show hypothesis testing about a single mean. The example is contrived because social science theory is ordinarily not precise enough to suggest two exact alternatives. However, this example shows some of the important features of hypothesis testing that cannot otherwise easily be shown.

Suppose we have two competing hypotheses based on Theory A indicating that the average percentage of high school graduates in the fifty states in 1980 should have been 68%. Suppose that Theory B indicates that 70% of the citizens of the states have graduated from high school. The null hypothesis and its alternative can then be stated as follows:

$$H_0: \mu_Y = 68\%$$

$$H_1: \mu_Y = 70\%$$

(What is chosen to be the null and the alternative hypothesis is clearly arbitrary in this example.) We used the 50-States Data Set to determine whether H_0 can be rejected or not. We will use a *t* test to evaluate H_0.

● *t* test
a test of significance for continuous variables where the population variance is unknown and the sample is assumed to have been drawn from a normally distributed population

Suppose we set $\alpha = .05$. Using Appendix D and employing a one-tailed test, the observed *t* value must be about 1.67 or larger to reject H_0. We can use this information to see how large the observed mean would have to be to reject H_0. In general, to test a hypothesis about a single mean we use the following formula where μ_{Y0} is the hypothesized mean under H_0:

$$t = \frac{\overline{Y} - \mu_{Y_0}}{s_y/\sqrt{N}}$$

Since $N = 50$, the estimated standard error of the sampling distribution of means is $s_y/\sqrt{N} = 7.57/\sqrt{50} = 1.07$. To determine how large Y would have to be in order to reject H_0 at $\alpha = .05$, we can substitute these numbers in the previous formula as follows:

$$1.67 = \frac{\overline{Y} - 68}{1.07}$$

(Recall that t must be 1.67 or greater to reject H_0.) Solving for $\overline{Y}$ we obtain $\overline{Y}$ = 69.79, which is the critical value (c.v.) for the hypothesis test (see Section 4.5). That is, if $\overline{Y} \geq$ 69.79 we will reject H_0 in favor of H_1. This situation is depicted in Figure 6.8.

Note that there are two separate sampling distributions, the left one under the assumption that H_0 is true and the right one under the assumption that H_1 is true. The shaded area in the tail of the distribution under H_0 is α = .05, or the probability of falsely rejecting the null hypothesis when it is true. We called this a Type I error or a false rejection error in Chapter 4 (see Box 4.1). But there is also a probability of making a Type II, or false acceptance, error that can now be calculated. It is the cross-hatched area in the left tail of the sampling distribution under the assumption that this is the probability of falsely accepting H_0 when H_1 is in fact true. While it is possible to assess β, it is beyond the scope of this book to do so. However, it is important to realize that one can make Type II as well as Type I errors when doing hypothesis testing.

An Example of Testing a Hypothesis about a Single Mean Using the Percent Who Graduated from High School and the 50-States Data Set

FIGURE 6.8

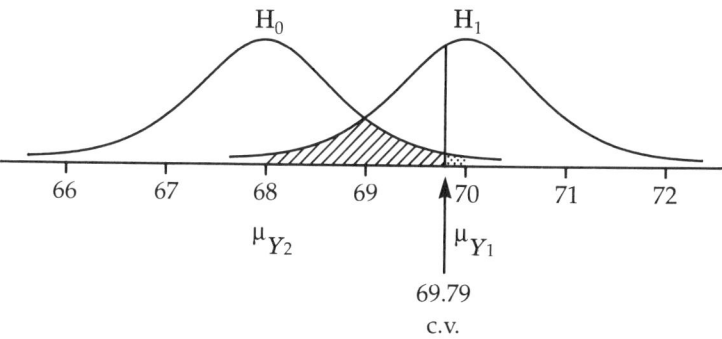

As we stated earlier, this example is highly contrived in that it assumes either H_0 or H_1 is true. In all likelihood neither is true. Indeed, the researcher has the option of **suspending judgment** pending further research instead of accepting either of the exact hypotheses.

● **suspending judgment**
a position taken by a researcher when the results of a statistical test permit neither clear rejection nor clear acceptance of the null or alternative hypotheses

The steps summarizing a test about a single mean with two exact hypotheses are shown in Box 6.2.

6.9.4   An Example of Hypothesis Testing about a Single Mean with Inexact Hypotheses

Considerable research has shown that when people are asked to describe their own physical attractiveness most of them say that their looks are above average.[1] Because physical attractiveness helps determine how others treat and judge them, individuals tend to bias estimates of their own appearance in their favor (in a positive direction). In research done by one of the authors, a sample of 2,013 readers of *Psychology Today* were asked to indicate how physically attractive they considered themselves to be on a 7-point scale of 7 for "much more attractive than others" through 1 for "much less attractive than others." The middle score of the scale, 4, was "about the same as others."[2]

We can test our hypothesis that people tend to bias their ratings of physical attractiveness in the positive direction by positing a null hypothesis (H_0) about a single mean; that is, in the population, the mean score is 4 or lower (i.e., one's physical attractiveness is about the same or less than others).

We choose an inexact alternative (e.g., $\mu_Y > 4.0$). Then the null hypothesis (H_0) and the alternative hypothesis (H_1) can be stated as follows:

$$H_0: \mu_Y = 4.00$$

$$H_1: \mu_Y > 4.00$$

[1] E. Berscheid and E. Walster, "Physical Attractiveness," in *Advances in Experimental Social Psychology*, Vol. 7 (New York: Academic Press, 1974).

[2] E. Berscheid, E. Walster and G. Bohrnstedt, "The Happy American Body: A Survey Report," *Psychology Today* (December 1973): 119–31.

Box 6.2   Testing Two Exact Hypotheses

Step 1. Choose an α level (probability of a Type I or false rejection error) for the null hypothesis.

Step 2. Examine Appendix D to determine how large the t value must be under H_0 in order to reject the null hypothesis.

Step 3. Estimate the standard error of the sampling distribution for the data using $s_y/\sqrt{N}$ and use with μ_0 in the formula for the t statistic to determine the critical value for rejecting H_0.

Step 4. Compare the observed sample mean with the critical value and either reject H_0 or not.

Suppose we choose $\alpha = .01$. Given the large sample size ($N = 2{,}013$), Appendix D can be used to determine the critical value. (What assumption, if any, do we have to make about the shape of the population from which the sample came?) Since α is located entirely in the upper tail of the sampling distribution, the critical value is 2.33. This type of hypothesis test is called a **one-tailed hypothesis test.** Following convention, we evaluate the null hypothesis with a t test. In these data $\overline{Y} = 4.90$ and $s_y = 1.153.$[3] Therefore the t score under H_0 is as follows:

$$t_{2012} = \frac{4.90 - 4.00}{1.153/\sqrt{2{,}013}} = 35.02$$

This is far larger than the c.v. of 2.33. Hence we can confidently reject the null hypothesis that $\mu_y = 4.00$. We conclude that the readership of *Psychology Today* rates itself as above average in physical attractiveness.

● **one-tailed hypothesis test** a hypothesis test in which the alternative is stated in such a way that the probability of making a Type I error is entirely in one tail of a probability

---

[3]Unpublished data from Berscheid, Walster and Bohrnstedt, "The Happy American Body."

When the alternative is inexact, the steps taken to test the hypothesis for statistical significance are identical to those that were given in Box 4.2:

1. Choose an α level.
2. Examine Appendix D to see how large the critical value has to be to reject the null hypothesis.
3. Compute the test statistic under H_0.
4. Compare the test statistic with the critical value. If it is as large or larger, reject the null hypothesis; if not, do not reject the null hypothesis.

Since exact hypotheses can rarely be stated as compelling tests of theory in the social sciences, hypothesis testing is usually a very weak test of any substantive hypotheses. By choosing N very large, we can make the standard error of the sampling distribution very small (recall that $\sigma_{\bar{Y}} = \sigma_Y/\sqrt{N}$) and hence virtually any null hypothesis can be rejected. It is for this reason we stress the importance of *estimation* in addition to hypothesis testing in drawing inferences. In addition to hypothesis testing, our recommendation is to use the sample mean as a point estimate of the population mean and to build a confidence interval around it.

In our example, given $\bar{Y} = 4.90$ and $s_Y = 1.153$ for $N = 2{,}013$, the 99% confidence interval is as follows:

$$4.90 \pm 2.58\ (1.153/\sqrt{2{,}013})$$

This computes to 4.83 and 4.97. This interval does not contain the response "about the same as others" (coded "4"), so we still confidently would conclude that our population of readers does rate itself somewhat above average, but this time with a rather precise numerical estimate of how much above average.

6.10   Two-tailed Test about a Single Mean

Often we are uncertain about what the alternative hypothesis should be; that is, we have a pretty good idea what the null hypothesis is, but if we have to reject the null, we are uncertain whether the true mean is larger or smaller than H_0. When we test hypotheses of this sort, we perform a **two-tailed hypothe-sis test.** In two-tailed hypothesis testing, the null is an exact hypothesis and the alternative is not only inexact, but states that we do not know whether the true population mean is smaller or larger than the mean specified under the null hypothesis.

Perhaps an example will help. Suppose we are uncertain about the number of women in the labor force. As our null hypothesis, we will guess that 50% of women are in the labor force. Since this is just a guess, which may either be too large or too small, our alternative hypothesis is simply that the per-centage is something other than 50. The null and alternative hy-potheses are stated more formally as follows:

$$H_0: \mu_y = 50$$

$$H_1: \mu_y \neq 50$$

This type of hypothesis is called a *two-tailed* hypothesis test be-cause the probability of a Type I error is equally distributed be-tween the upper and lower tails. In this sense, a two-tailed test is like constructing a confidence interval around the mean hypothesized under H_0. (Of course, in fact one only builds confidence intervals around sample statistics and *not* around population parameters.)

As in all hypothesis testing, we first choose an α level, say .05 in this example, then we calculate the c.v. In the case of a two-tailed hypothesis test there are two critical values—one the negative of the other—as shown for the more general case in Figure 6.9. To test our null hypothesis that female labor force participation is 50% we again turn to the 50-States Data Set. With $N = 50$ and $df = 49$, we use Appendix D to ascertain that for $\alpha = .05$ and for a two-tailed test, the c.v. is roughly 2.00. (See Box 6.3 for how to use Appendix D for both one- and two-tailed hypothesis tests.) Since H_0 specifies that $\mu_Y = 50$, the two crit-ical values are $50 - 2.00(4.08/\sqrt{49})$ and $50 + 2.00(4.08/\sqrt{49})$ or 48.83 and 51.17, respectively. H_0 will be rejected if $\overline{Y}$, the ob-served mean, is either less than 48.83 or greater than 51.17. Since the observed value is 52.41, the null hypothesis that the mean labor force participation for women is 50% must be rejected.

Even though hypothesis testing has a long tradition in statis-tics and in the social sciences as well, we strongly believe that estimation is much more useful and important than hypothesis

● **two-tailed hypothesis test**
a hypothesis test in which the region of rejection falls equally within both tails of the sampling distribution

FIGURE 6.9   The *t* Distribution for Two-tailed Hypothesis
                  Tests about a Single Mean

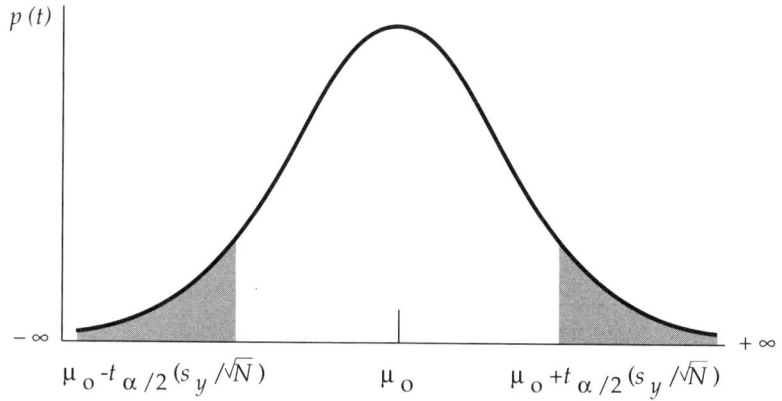

Source: George Bohrnstedt and David Knoke, *Statistics for Social
Data Analysis* (Itasca, Ill.: F. E. Peacock Publishers, Inc., 1988), 176.

testing. Why is this? We can reject virtually any statistical
hypothesis by simply choosing a large enough sample size. It
is for this reason that even though hypothesis testing is very
commonly done, we believe that estimation is far more
important.

As we saw in Section 6.6.1, the 95% confidence interval for
the sample mean for data on the average percentage of women
in the labor force using the 50-States Data Set is bounded by
51.24% and 53.58% and the sample mean is 52.4%. (Recall that
the sample mean is also the best single estimate of the population mean.) Hopefully, you agree with 95% confidence that the
true population mean lies between roughly 51.2 and 53.6% is
much more useful than the information provided by the
hypothesis test, i.e., that the hypothesis that the population
mean is 50% must be rejected.

6.10.1   One-tailed versus Two-tailed Tests

If previous research suggests a clearly stated alternative
hypothesis, then a one-tailed test should be used, although
many researchers and applied statisticians would debate this
point since a one-tailed test requires a smaller c.v. to reject H_0.

Box 6.3   Appendix D for Hypothesis Testing

Appendix D can be used to place the probability of a Type I error (α) all in the upper tail or to divide it between the lower and the upper tails of the t distribution. To place the probability all in the upper tail, look along the row labeled "one-tailed" until you reach the value chosen for α. Then look down the column for the chosen level of α to find the critical value (c.v.). Thus for $\alpha = .05$, the critical value, $t_{.05}$, is found by looking across the row labeled "One-tailed test" until you come to .05; then look down that column. For example, for $\alpha = .05$ and $df = 30$, $t_{.05} = 1.697$. Recall from Section 6.5 that for $\alpha = .05$, $Z = 1.65$. This illustrates that when N is small, a larger critical value is needed to be able to reject the null hypothesis. And the larger the N the smaller the critical value needed to reject the null hypothesis.

Appendix D can also be used to divide the probability of a Type I error into both tails of the distribution. This is especially useful in computing confidence intervals, in addition to computing two-tailed hypothesis tests. For example, for $\alpha = .05$ and $df = 30$, look across the row labeled "Two-tailed test" until you come to .05. Then look down this column until you come to the row labeled 30. In this example you will find that the critical value is 2.042.

On the other hand, if previous research results are mixed, or if one is doing purely exploratory research and does not have a very good idea of what the population mean is compared to that specified under H_0, a two-tailed test is preferred.

As we pointed out, the fact that a one-tailed test allows the researcher to reject a null hypothesis more easily for a given α than a two-tailed test has led many researchers to take the conservative stance of using only two-tailed tests when hypothesis testing. There is nothing wrong with taking this practical stance; indeed there is much to recommend following it. However, technically speaking, the position we have outlined in the previous paragraphs is the correct one.

Again, we must stress that given the relative weakness of hypothesis tests, whether one- or two-tailed, we strongly recommend that estimation of parameters should also always be done whenever one is doing hypothesis testing.

All of the hypothesis tests we have presented in this chapter involve single means. In practice, however, we are rarely interested in hypotheses about a single mean. Instead, we wish to compare two or more means. For example, given equal education and experience for professional men and women, we are interested in whether professional men's salaries are the same or higher than those of professional women in the same occupations. A similar question could be asked comparing the salaries of blacks and whites in the same occupations. Or we might ask whether premarital sexual activity is greater for teenage boys than for teenage girls. All of these questions involve comparing *two* means and asking whether they are significantly different from each other. The evaluation of this type of question is the substance of Chapter 7.

Key Concepts and Symbols

These key concepts and symbols are listed in the order of appearance in the chapter. Combined with the definitions in the margins, these will help you review the material and can serve as a self-test for mastery of the concepts.

discrete probability
    distributions
probability distribution
continuous probability
    distributions
inferential statistics
population parameters
mean of a probability
    distribution
variance of a probability
    distribution
normal distributions
standard normal
    distribution
central limit theorem
sampling distribution of
    sample means
standard error
point estimate
confidence interval
lower confidence limit
    (LCL)
upper confidence limit
    (UCL)

t distributions
t variable (t score)
unbiased estimator
hypothesis testing
statistical hypothesis
t test
suspending judgment
one-tailed hypothesis test
two-tailed hypothesis test
$p(Y)$
μ_Y
σ_Y^2
σ_Y
Z_α
$\mu_{\bar{Y}}$
$\sigma_{\bar{Y}}^2$
$\sigma_{\bar{Y}}$
t
μ_θ
θ
$s_\bullet^2$
μ_{s^2}
H_0
H_1

Problems

General Problems

1. Assuming that birthdays are equally distributed throughout the year, what is the probability of someone chosen at random being born on (a) December 25, (b) in the month of September, or (c) being born on February 29 of leap year?

2. Following is a table of the religion in which persons were raised who participated in the 1987 GSS:

Religion	N
Protestant	969
Catholic	388
Jewish	22
None	43
Other	20
No answer	24
Total	1466

(a) What is the probability of observing someone of the Catholic faith in the 1987 GSS? (b) someone Jewish?

3. Find the areas under the normal distribution between the mean and the following Z scores: (a) 3.00, (b) -2.00, (c) 1.59 and (d) -0.25.

4. Find the Z scores that correspond to the following alphas:

a. $\alpha = .02$, one-tailed   d. $\alpha = .02$, two-tailed
b. $\alpha = .15$, one-tailed   e. $\alpha = .15$, two-tailed
c. $\alpha = .01$, one-tailed   f. $\alpha = .01$, two-tailed

5. Find the areas of the normal distribution between the following Z scores:

a. $-1.00 \leq Z \leq 1.00$ c. $-1.25 \leq Z \leq 2.00$
b. $-2.33 \leq Z \leq 2.33$ d. $-0.25 \leq Z \leq 1.50$

6. According to the central limit theorem, find the means and standard errors of sampling distributions with the following characteristics:

	μ_Y	σ_Y^2	N
a.	10	50	100
b.	20.5	100	500
c.	-5.5	160	100
d.	14	160	80
e.	20	200	200

7. A national study found that the mean number of hours per week that football and basketball players at Division I schools spend on their sport is 30, with a standard deviation of 4. If the sampling distribution of sample means for all samples of size (a) $N = 100$, (b) $N = 400$ and

(c) $N = 4000$ were constructed, what would the means and standard errors of the sampling distributions be?

8. In a population of high school boys, the average number of girls dated over a four year period is 19.6 with a standard deviation of 4.5.

a. Find the standard error for a sampling distribution of sample sizes: (1) $N = 25$, (2) $N = 100$, and (3) $N = 900$. b. What is the probability, in a sample of $N = 100$, that the observed sample mean would be 20.5 or more girls dated?

9. Find the upper and lower confidence limits for the following:

	$\overline{Y}$	$\sigma_{\overline{Y}}$	Confidence level
a.	75	15	90
b.	75	15	99
c.	1.5	0.9	95
d.	15	2.5	95

10. A sample of 25 high schools with a known mean dropout rate of 50% is exposed to a special program designed to reduce the rate of dropping out. At the end of the program the dropout rate for the schools is 40%. If you know the population standard deviation for all schools is known to be 5%, what is the 90% confidence interval for the sample of schools? Can you reject the null hypothesis that the mean dropout rate remains at 50% with $\alpha = .05$?

11. In a sample of 1200 college freshmen, the mean IQ is 112 with a variance of 225. Can you reject the hypothesis that the mean IQ of freshmen is no higher than that for the population of 18 year olds in general in which the mean IQ is 100? Set $\alpha = .01$.

12. Find the approximate areas under the t distribution between the mean and the following values:

	df	t
a.	25	2.06
b.	20	− 1.33
c.	19	2.54
d.	28	3.67
e.	17	− 1.74
f.	300	2.58

13. Find the critical values of t that correspond to the following:

	N	α
a.	20	.05, one-tailed
b.	20	.01, one-tailed
c.	30	.05, one-tailed
d.	30	.05, two-tailed
e.	15	.05, two-tailed
f.	300	.005, one-tailed

14. Find the approximate areas in the tails of the t distribution for the following:

a. $-2.00 \leq t_{20} \leq 2.00$ c. $-1.34 \leq t_{15} \leq 2.13$
b. $-2.75 \leq t_{30} \leq 2.75$ d. $-1.78 \leq t_{12} \leq 3.05$

15. Find the t scores for a test of the null hypothesis that $\mu_Y = 0$ given the following information:

	$\overline{Y}$	s_Y	N
a.	-2.00	1.2	15
b.	3.40	4.5	24
c.	1.15	0.9	9
d.	4.20	1.5	22

16. The standard deviation of a measure of political conservatism in a sample of 25 adults is 3.5 on a 10-point scale. The sample mean is 7.25. Test the null hypothesis that the sample is drawn from a population with a mean of 5.00 on the measure of political conservatism with $\alpha = .01$.

Problems Requiring the 1987 General Social Survey

17. Find the empirical probability distribution of the astrological sign under which the respondents were born (ZODIAC) and determine the probability of being a Libra.

18. With the advent of universal education, the proportion of Americans having only a grade school education has been declining. Using EDUC in the GSS data set, compute the mean and standard deviation for years of formal schooling. Compute the Z score for 8 or fewer years of education. What is the corresponding area under the normal curve (Appendix C) for this Z score?

19. Respondents were asked whether they thought the government ought to do something to reduce the income differences between the rich and the poor, perhaps by raising taxes. Respondents were handed a card where a "1" meant that the government should do something to reduce income differences and a "7" meant that the government should not concern themselves with income differences. A "4" was the mid-point on the card shown them. Test the null hypothesis that the mean in the population for EQWLTH is "4." Set $\alpha = .01$ and test the hypothesis with a two-tailed test.

20. Respondents were asked how happy they are on a three point scale (HAPPY) where "1" = very happy, "2" = pretty happy and "3" = not too happy. Test the hypothesis that the mean in the population is "2" (i.e., respondents are pretty happy) versus the alternative hypothesis that they are happier than "pretty happy." Set $\alpha = .001$.

Problems Requiring the 50-States Data Set

21. Compute the empirical probability that a state has a right to work law (RT2WORK).

22. Find the standard errors of the sampling distributions (taking into account missing data) for (a) the percent of workers who are in unions (UNION), (b) age in years (AGE), and (c) the number of births per 1,000 out of wedlock (WEDLOCK).

23. Test the hypothesis that there has been no change in the population of the states between 1970 and 1980 (POPCHNG). Set $\alpha = .05$. Use a two-tailed test.

24. The growth in the number of persons legally below the poverty line continues to be an important issue for many policy makers. Test the hypothesis that 10% of the population is at the poverty line versus the alternative hypothesis that more than 10% of the population is below the poverty line (POVERTY). Set $\alpha = .05$.

25. The percent graduating from high school remains a concern for educators and policy makers. Test the hypothesis that only two-thirds of states' populations have graduated from high school (HSGRAD) against the alternative that more than two-thirds have graduated from high school. Set $\alpha = .05$.

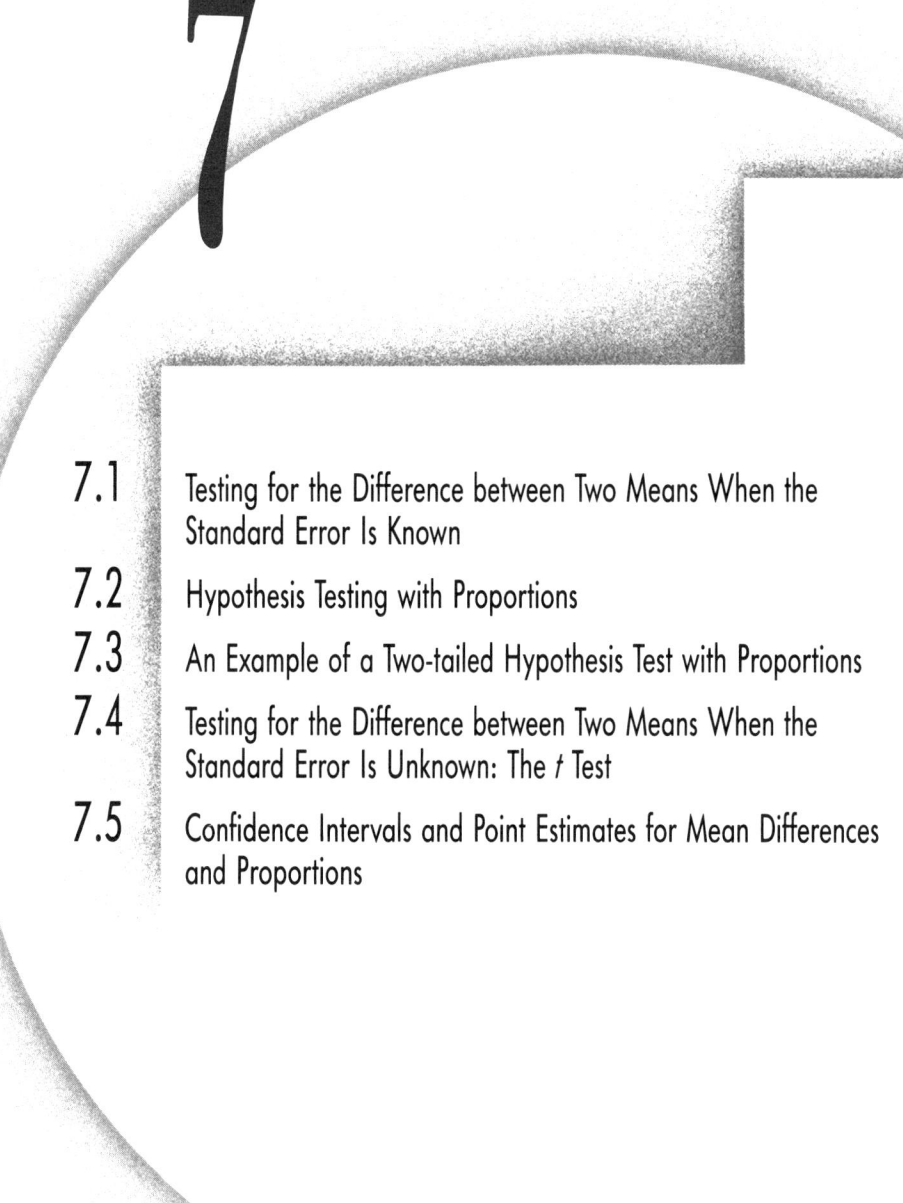

7

Testing for the Difference between Two Means

The information on statistical inference and hypothesis testing presented in Chapter 6 was limited to inferences about a single mean. But social science researchers are interested in relationships and usually want to compare two or more means. Hypotheses identify a relationship to make comparisons, for example, that the average income of high school graduates is higher than that of those who do not reach this level of education, or that people in the South are more religious than those in other parts of the United States, or that college students who attend church or temple regularly engage in premarital sex less than those who do not. All these hypotheses involve comparing two means and then deciding whether one is larger than the other. The statistical procedures presented in this chapter provide ways to test whether two hypothesized population means differ from one another. This procedure is called a **mean difference test.**

● **mean difference test**
a statistical test of whether or not two means differ in the population

7.1 Testing for the Difference between Two Means When the Standard Error Is Known

The research efforts of sociologists have often been directed at improving our understanding of the stratification of society, or social status. Traditionally, studies of social stratification have centered on the prestige conveyed by jobs in the occupational structure, which for years was almost exclusively a male concern. The relation between fathers' and sons' educational and occupational achievements was a popular research topic. Blau and Duncan, for example, suggested two variables that contribute to a man's social status: his own educational achievement and his parents' educations.[1] They argue that the more education the parents have, the more education they were likely to provide for their male offspring. Furthermore, education is seen as an important factor in learning the general and specific skills necessary for occupational achievement.

Because the data to test the hypotheses presented in this section are derived from male respondents in the 1987 GSS, we will use men in our examples. As the boundaries between conventional sex roles for men and women are weakening, however, the conclusions could also apply to women. You might try to examine this hypothesis with the GSS data as an exercise.

We have greatly oversimplified the Blau-Duncan model of occupational achievement, in terms of both the variables in occupational achievement and the level of explanation. The level of detail in the example is sufficient, however, to allow us to state the following general propositions:

> P1: The higher the educational achievement of a man's father, the higher the son's educational achievement.
> P2: The higher a son's educational achievement, the higher his occupational status.

A derivative proposition follows from P1 and P2, namely that men with highly educated fathers should have higher occupational status than those who have less well-educated fathers.

7.1.1   Stating the Operational Hypotheses

We can use the 1987 GSS data set to test these two propositions, since respondent's education, father's education, and the prestige of respondent's occupation were all measured. Our analysis dichotomizes continuous measures, that is, divides them into

---

[1]Peter M. Blau and Otis Dudley Duncan, *The American Occupational Structure* (New York: John Wiley & Sons, 1967).

two groups. To test P1 we recode father's education into two categories—an eighth grade education or less versus at least some high school completed. The respondent's own education is measured by asking how many years of formal schooling he has completed. To test P1 we can use the following hypothesis:

> H1: Men whose fathers completed at least some high school have more years of schooling themselves, on average, than those whose fathers have an eighth grade education or less.

The second proposition (P2) can be tested by recoding the respondent's education into two categories—in this case, a high school degree versus at least some college completed.

The respondent's occupational prestige is measured by an occupational prestige score. Prestige scores were developed at the National Opinion Research Center (NORC) in 1963–65 by asking respondents in a national survey to estimate the social standing of occupations on a nine-step ladder. Occupational titles were printed on small cards and the prestige ratings were collected by requesting respondents to sort the cards into boxes formed by the rungs of the ladder. The prestige scores eventually assigned to occupations were averages, multiplied by ten, computed across all respondents for the three-year period. Using the prestige variables, P2 can be tested with the following:

> H2: Men who have completed at least some college have occupations with higher average prestige scores than those who have a high school education or less.

To evaluate the first research hypothesis, we use the following strategy. As we noted in Chapter 1, hypotheses cannot be proven, only rejected by the data in favor of their opposites. Since we believe the evidence will favor the alternative hypothesis, we need to state a null hypothesis, H_0, that can be tested and, presumably, rejected by the data. Thus, the nature of the alternative or research hypothesis, H_1, gives us the form of the null hypothesis, H_0, that we will test. In this example, H_1 states that the mean years of schooling for the population of men whose fathers had some high school is greater than the mean of the population of those whose fathers did not attend high school. In symbolic form, the hypothesis is expressed as follows:

$$H_1: \mu_2 > \mu_1$$

The mean of the population of men whose father had some high school is μ_2, and μ_1 is the mean of the population of men whose fathers did not attend high school. Here is the contrasting null hypothesis, also expressed in symbolic terms.

$$H_0: \mu_2 = \mu_1$$

Note that in this form, the null hypothesis implies that $\mu_2 - \mu_1 = 0$.

If based on a statistical test of H_0 with data from two **independent random samples** of men we conclude that H_0 can be rejected with a low probability of Type I error, we automatically establish evidence in favor of H_1, the alternative hypothesis. In fact, we do not directly test the hypothesis that $\mu_2 > \mu_1$. Rather, we expect to reject the null hypothesis whose form is given by the way the research hypothesis is formed. Box 7.1 describes these and other forms of null and alternative hypotheses.

● **independent random samples**
a sample drawn according to random selection procedures, in which the choice of one observation from a sample does not affect the probability of another observation being chosen for a different sample

7.1.2   Test Procedures

The central limit theorem (see Section 6.4) guarantees that if the sample size is large enough, the distribution of sample means (i.e., the sample distribution) will be normal, with a mean equal to the mean of the population from which the samples were drawn. A corollary of the central limit theorem that is very useful in testing for the difference between two population means states the following:

> When N_1 and N_2 are large, the distribution of differences between two sample means generated by taking all possible random samples of N_1 and N_2 from populations with mean μ_1 and μ_2 and variance σ_1^2 and σ_2^2, follows a normal distribution, with mean $\mu_2 - \mu_1$ and standard deviation (standard error) $\sqrt{\sigma_1^2/N_1 + \sigma_2^2/N_2}$.

$$\mu_{(\bar{Y}_2 - \bar{Y}_1)} = \mu_2 - \mu_1$$

And

$$\sigma_{(\bar{Y}_2 - \bar{Y}_1)} = \sqrt{\sigma_1^2/N_1 + \sigma_2^2/N_2}$$

Thus, the mean of the sampling distribution of differences between the sample means equals the difference between the two population means, when N_1 and N_2 are large. Note that no assumption has been made about the shape of the original population distributions.

With this corollary, we can use the table of probabilities associated with the normal distribution to perform a **mean difference hypothesis test.** We can test hypotheses about two

● **mean difference hypothesis test**
a statistical test of a hypothesis about the difference between two population means

Box 7.1   Forms of Null and Alternative Hypotheses

Theory and past research generally indicate that one population mean can be expected to be greater than another, although the amount of the difference is unclear. The alternative hypothesis, therefore, can be stated as a general range of values, while any difference in the opposite direction is consistent with the null hypothesis. The examples in this text use the most common form of the null and alternative hypotheses about two population means.

$$H_0: \mu_2 = \mu_1, \text{ or } \mu_2 - \mu_1 = 0$$
$$H_1: \mu_2 > \mu_1, \text{ or } \mu_2 - \mu_1 > 0$$

At times, however, prior knowledge or belief is an insufficient basis for deciding which population mean should be larger, although the researcher expects they will not be equal. Since the substantive hypothesis is that the two means are unequal, the null hypothesis must be that the means are equal. The hypotheses are expressed as follows:

$$H_0: \mu_2 = \mu_1 \text{ or } \mu_2 - \mu_1 = 0$$
$$H_1: \mu_2 \neq \mu_1 \text{ or } \mu_2 - \mu_1 \neq 0$$

Thus, evidence from two samples that the population means are not equal regardless of whether the first mean or the second mean is the larger of the two permits rejection of the null in favor of the alternative hypothesis.

A third form of the test hypothesis is used whenever precise values of the two population means can be stated. For example, if the IQ mean of one group is hypothesized to be 100 and that of a second group is hypothesized to be 115, the researcher can construct null and alternative hypotheses about this precise fifteen-point IQ difference.

$$H_0: \mu_2 - \mu_1 = k$$
$$H_1: \mu_2 - \mu_1 \neq k$$

The hypothesized amount of difference between the two means is k; that is, $k = 15$ in this example. The null hypothesis is rejected if the sample means do not differ significantly from each other by the specified amount, k, because the difference observed in the samples is either greater than k or less than k.

You should recognize, of course, that rejecting the null hypothesis does *not* imply that the alternative hypothesis is true. The results may be consistent with the alternative hypothesis, but as we have noted several times, hypothesis testing never leads to absolute truth.

Most social theory is so imprecise that explicit values for population means can seldom be stated in advance. In their most common form, the null and alternative hypotheses in social research state either a general range of differences or merely that the two groups differ, without indicating which has the larger mean value.

population means, assuming that N_1 and N_2 are large (that is the sum of N_1 and N_2 should be *at least* 50) and estimate the variances of both populations (σ_1^2 and σ_2^2).

7.1.2.1 Estimating the Standard Error.

In social research based on sampled data, we can never know the true values of the population variances. Indeed, if we had population data available to us, there would be no reason to perform significance tests. Instead, we must use information from the two samples to estimate the population standard error for subsequent use in significance tests. When N_1 and N_2 are large (i.e., $N_1 + N_2 \geq$ 50), an appropriate test is the one discussed in this section, although as we indicated in Chapter 6 and will repeat later in this section, even when N_1 and N_2 are large, in practice one always uses a t test. Of course, when N_1 and N_2 are small, the appropriate significance test is always a t test. The use of the t test for the difference between two means will be discussed in Section 7.4.

By substituting for the unknown population variances, σ_1^2 and σ_2^2, with the known sample variances, s_1^2 and s_2^2, we can estimate the standard error of the sampling distribution, $\sigma_{(\bar{Y}_2 - \bar{Y}_1)}$, if $N_1 + N_2$ is large. Our estimated standard error for the sampling distribution of the difference between two means is given by the following:

$$\hat{\sigma}_{(\bar{Y}_2 - \bar{Y}_1)} = \sqrt{s_1^2/N_1 + s_2^2/N_2}$$

7.1.2.2 Testing the Null Hypothesis.

To test the null hypothesis that $\mu_2 = \mu_1$, which implies that $\mu_2 - \mu_1 = 0$, we refer to the summary of steps for testing hypotheses given in Box 4.2. First we need to choose an α level (the probability of making a Type I error). Second, we calculate the test statistic. Third, we calculate the critical value (c.v.). Fourth, we compare the test statistic with the critical value.

In this example we choose $\alpha = .05$. Computing the test statistic requires ascertaining how large the observed difference between the two sample means is against the null hypothesis. Since Appendix C is in standard-score or Z-score form, we compare the observed hypothesized difference as a Z score, which is, in general, $Z_i = (Y_i - \overline{Y})/s_Y$. In generating the difference between two means, $(\overline{Y}_2 - \overline{Y}_1) - (\mu_2 - \mu_1)$ is the numerator of a Z score and $\sigma_{(\overline{Y}_2 - \overline{Y}_1)}$ is the denominator.

Under the null hypothesis, $\mu_2 - \mu_1 = 0$; that is, the mean from the second population equals the mean from the first population. Therefore, when testing the null hypothesis, we need only to determine whether the observed differences in sample means $(\overline{Y}_2 - \overline{Y}_1)$ could have been observed in a sample drawn from populations in which the true difference between the two means is zero.

The Z score actually used to test the null hypothesis will not contain a term involving the population means because the value of their difference under the null hypothesis is zero. Therefore the numerator of Z is $(\overline{Y}_2 - \overline{Y}_1) - 0$, and it follows that

$$
Z_{(\overline{Y}_2 - \overline{Y}_1)} = \frac{\overline{Y}_2 - \overline{Y}_1}{\sigma_{(\overline{Y}_2 - \overline{Y}_1)}}
$$

$$
= \frac{\overline{Y}_2 - \overline{Y}_1}{\sqrt{\sigma_1^2/N_1 + \sigma_2^2/N_2}}
$$

Or, using our large sample estimate for $\sigma_{(\overline{Y}_2 - \overline{Y}_1)}$, which we label $\hat{\sigma}_{(\overline{Y}_2 - \overline{Y}_1)}$, the equation is as follows:

$$
Z_{(\overline{Y}_2 = \overline{Y}_1)} = \frac{\overline{Y}_2 - \overline{Y}_1}{\hat{\sigma}_{(\overline{Y}_2 = \overline{Y}_1)}}
$$

$$
= \frac{\overline{Y}_2 - \overline{Y}_1}{\sqrt{s_1^2/N_1 + s_2^2/N_2}}
$$

7.1.2.3 *Diagraming the Distribution.* To understand what happens when the difference in two sample means is tested, it is useful to diagram the sampling distribution. In Figure 7.1, two situations are depicted for a sampling distribution where the null hypothesis that $\mu_2 - \mu_1 = 0$ is in fact true. In panel A, the difference in observed sample means, $(\overline{Y}_2 - \overline{Y}_1)$, is a small positive value which lies close to the hypothesized population difference of zero. Since this sample difference has a high probability of occurrence in a population where $\mu_2 - \mu_1 = 0$, we would not reject the null hypothesis at conventional levels of α.

In panel B of Figure 7.1, however, the observed sample difference is substantial. It would be found only in a small proportion of all the sample mean differences if the true difference in population means is zero. If the observed means are in fact very different, as they are in panel B of Figure 7.1, we would probably reject the null hypothesis that the two samples came from populations where $\mu_1 = \mu_2$, since the outcome is highly unlikely in the sampling distribution. (Note that it occurs in the far right tail.) Instead we would conclude that the $\overline{Y}_1$ and $\overline{Y}_2$ came from populations where $\mu_2 > \mu_1$.

7.1.2.4 Conclusions.   We rarely specify exactly what μ_2 and μ_1 are in stating the alternative hypothesis. Suppose, however, that we assume our alternative hypothesis is $\mu_2 - \mu_1 = k$, where k is some number derived from previous research. In Figure 7.2, the sampling distribution to the left is the same as it is in Figure 7.1. The sampling distribution to the right, however, is the one associated with the hypothesis that $\mu_2 - \mu_1 = k$. Note that the mean difference $(\overline{Y}_2 - \overline{Y}_1)$ observed in this sample is a highly unlikely outcome if in fact the null hypothesis is true, that is, if $\mu_2 - \mu_1 = 0$. However, the observed $\overline{Y}_2 - \overline{Y}_1$ is a very likely outcome if the alternative hypothesis, $H_1: \mu_2 - \mu_1 = k$, is true.

For this reason we reject the null hypothesis in favor of the alternative. This decision does not imply that the true difference in population means is k, only that this hypothesis is more compatible with the observed sample outcome than the hypothesis that the true difference is zero. In other words, we are quite confident that the true difference is *not* zero, and instead it is some positive number.

7.1.3   Testing the Hypotheses

We can demonstrate these principles by testing the hypotheses about educational achievement and occupational status. Using the GSS data for 1987, we estimate that the mean number of years of education for male respondents is 13.05 for those whose fathers completed at least some college, compared to 12.52 for

FIGURE 7.1   Two Examples of Outcomes When the Null Hypothesis about Mean Differences Is True

A.

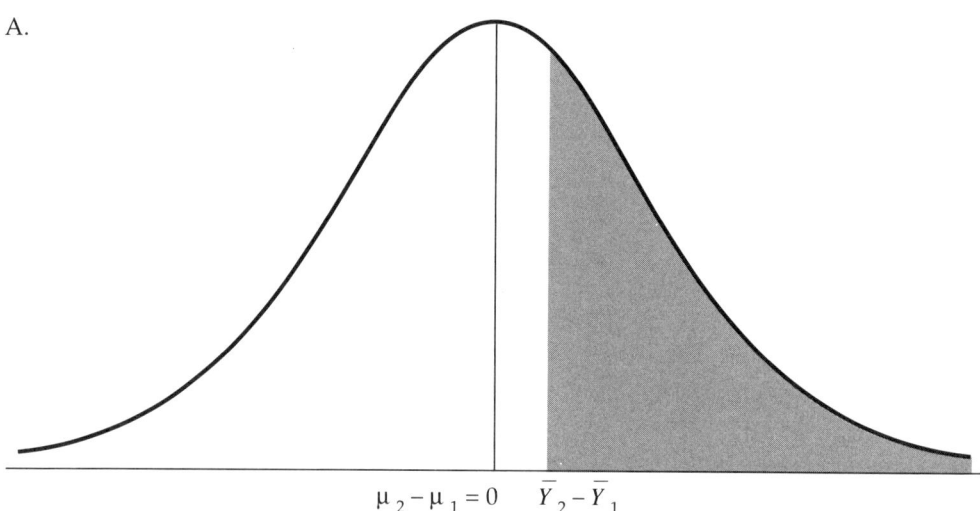

$$\mu_2 - \mu_1 = 0 \quad \overline{Y}_2 - \overline{Y}_1$$

B.

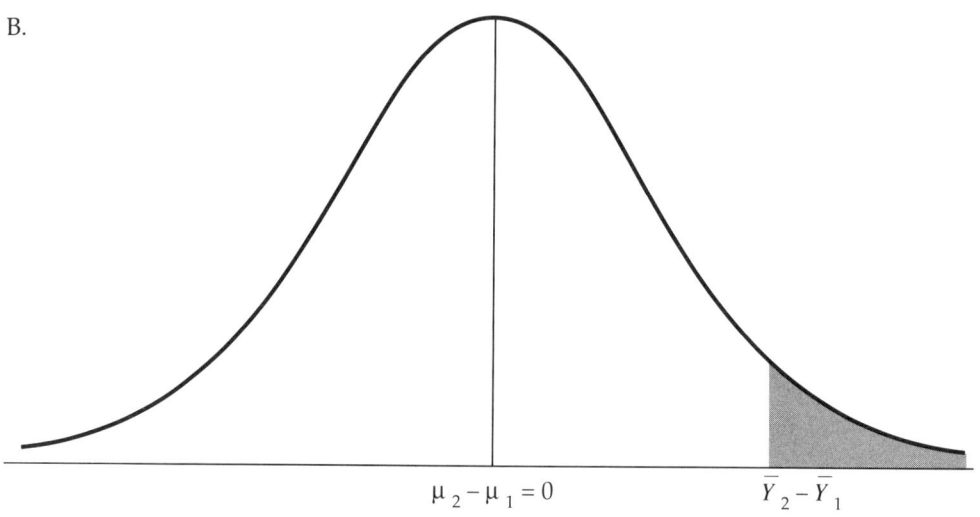

$$\mu_2 - \mu_1 = 0 \qquad \overline{Y}_2 - \overline{Y}_1$$

Source: George Bohrnstedt and David Knoke, *Statistics for Social Data Analysis* (Itasca, Ill.: F. E. Peacock Publishers, Inc., 1988), 195.

Likelihood of the Same Sample Outcome
under Two Different Hypotheses about
Mean Differences

FIGURE 7.2

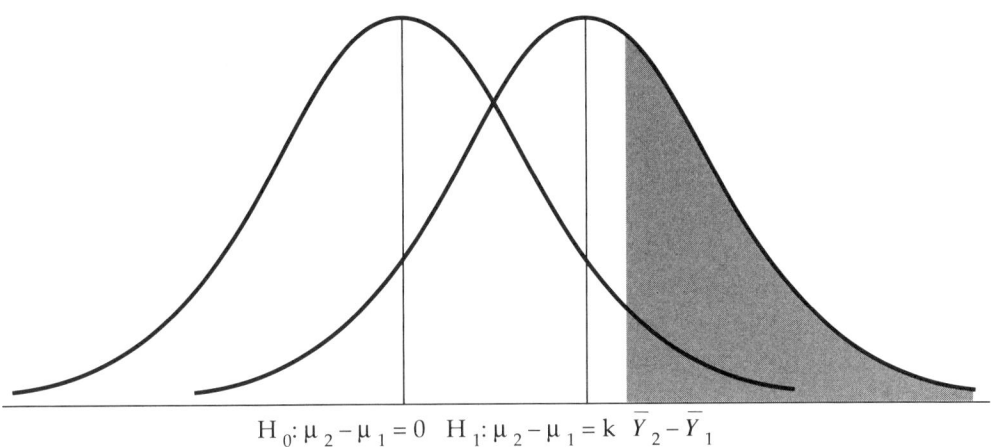

$$H_0: \mu_2 - \mu_1 = 0 \quad H_1: \mu_2 - \mu_1 = k \quad \bar{Y}_2 - \bar{Y}_1$$

Source: George Bohrnstedt and David Knoke, *Statistics for Social Data Analysis* (Itasca, Ill.: F. E. Peacock Publishers, Inc., 1988), 196.

those whose fathers had a high school education or less. The variances for the two groups are 13.78 and 10.24, respectively, based on samples of 265 and 375. The test statistic is computed as follows:

$$Z = \frac{13.05 - 12.52}{\sqrt{\dfrac{13.78}{265} + \dfrac{10.24}{375}}}$$

$$= \frac{0.53}{0.282} = 1.88$$

Now for $\alpha = .05$, the critical value is Z_a which cuts off the upper 5% of the normal distribution. As we found in Section 6.3.1, $Z_{.05} = 1.645$. Finally, we compare the test statistic with the critical value. Since the test statistic is 1.88 and the critical value is 1.645, the null hypothesis can be rejected; that is, the 1987

GSS data provide evidence for the proposition (P1) that fathers' education is positively related to men's own education. However, in spite of the fact that the difference is statistically significant, the small difference between the two means suggests that the relationship is only a weak one. We will return to this point later.

The second hypothesis states that men who have completed at least some college have occupations with more prestige than those who have had a high school education or less. Using the NORC prestige score as the dependent variable, we find that the average prestige score of men who have had at least some college education is 46.61 (with a variance of 201.07), compared to an average score of 35.41 (with a variance of 135.89) for those who have a high school education or less. The sample sizes on which these estimates are based are 288 and 347, respectively. Here we compute the test statistic.

$$Z = \frac{46.62 - 35.41}{\sqrt{\dfrac{201.07}{288} + \dfrac{135.89}{347}}}$$

$$= \frac{11.21}{1.044} = 10.74$$

Since we know from the preceding example that c.v. = 1.645 for $\alpha = .05$, the null hypothesis is rejected. We find strong support for the proposition (P2) that a man's occupational status is positively related to his educational achievement.

Note from these examples that the alternative hypothesis reflects the substantive hypothesis of interest. Remember that we can never prove a hypothesis; we can only offer indirect evidence for it, by rejecting the null hypothesis of no relationship. Hypothesis testing in statistics refers to the practice of deciding whether the null hypothesis can be rejected as a means of garnering support for an alternative or research hypothesis.

By itself, hypothesis testing is obviously not a powerful nor necessarily convincing way to test a hypothesis. For this reason, it is important to replicate the findings with other independently drawn samples. It is also important to estimate the strength of relationships, a concept considered in chapters 8 and 9.

The weakness of only doing hypothesis tests was shown clearly when we tested P1 earlier. The difference in educational achievement of sons who have fathers with at least some college education is statistically significant when compared to the educational achievement of sons whose fathers did not attend college, but the mean difference between the educational achievement of the two groups is a mere 0.53—roughly one-half year.

The role that sample size plays in hypothesis testing should also be emphasized: If we choose N_1 and N_2 large enough virtually any difference between $\overline{Y}_1$ and $\overline{Y}_2$ will be statistically significant. This can be seen clearly by examining the formula for the estimated standard error for the sampling distribution of the difference between two means, $\hat{\sigma}_{(\overline{Y}_2 - \overline{Y}_1)}$ shown in Section 7.1.2. As N_1 and N_2 increase the standard error goes to zero. While this is valuable for making a point estimate of $\mu_2 - \mu_1$ or constructing confidence intervals around $\overline{Y}_2 - \overline{Y}_1$ (as we will do in Section 7.6), in hypothesis testing, the results can be extremely misleading. For this reason more conservative strategies should also be employed.

We might argue, for example, that unless a mean difference of at least one-quarter standard deviation is found, the difference is not substantively important, regardless of whether or not the result is statistically significant. An even better approach, in our opinion, is to use exact methods for estimating the strength of a relationship (as discussed in chapters 8 and 9). The magnitude of a relationship that is considered to be important will vary from research problem to research problem, so general rules are really quite useless. The important point is that you should not be misled by simple statistical significance when testing hypotheses.

7.2   Hypothesis Testing with Proportions

As we defined the term in Chapter 2, a proportion is simply the frequency of cases of a given type, divided by the total number of cases. And as we noted in Chapter 3, the sample mean is given by $\overline{Y} = \sum_{i=1}^{N} Y_i/N$. But if Y_i takes on only the values 1 and 0, the numerator, $\sum_{i=1}^{N} Y_i$ equals f_i. Hence, as we saw in Section 3.1.3, the mean of a dichotomous variable is the proportion of cases with the value of 1, i.e., it is p.

A simple example should make this clear. Assume there are 10 children in a class, 4 of whom are boys. If the boys are coded 1 and the girls 0, the mean is given as follows:

$$\overline{Y} = (1 + 1 + 1 + 1 + 0 + 0 + 0 + 0 + 0 + 0)/10$$

$$= 4/10 = 0.40.$$

Notice that $\sum\limits_{i=1}^{10} Y_i = 4$, which is the number of boys in the class or f_b. But f_b/N equals 4/10, which is exactly equal to the mean of the variable. To use an example from the 1987 GSS, 453 of 1,461 respondents said that they smoke. Hence, the mean number of smokers, 18 and over, is $p = 453/1,461 = 0.31$, or 31%.

● **significance testing with proportions** using statistical tests to determine whether or not the observed difference between sample proportions could occur by chance in the populations from which the samples were selected

Since the proportion of a variable with only two outcomes is the mean of that variable, we can do **significance testing with proportions**, applying the same formulas used in Section 6.1 to test the hypotheses. The variance of a variable with only two outcomes is simply pq, where $q = 1 - p$. Thus in the smoking example, the sample variance is simply $s_Y^2 = (0.310)(1 - 0.310) = (0.310)(0.690) = 0.214$. And the standard error of a sampling distribution of proportions, s_p, is shown by the following:

$$s_p = \sqrt{pq/N}$$

In this example $s_p = \sqrt{0.214/1,461} = 0.012$.

Suppose we hypothesize that Democrats (who are conventionally considered more liberal than Republicans) are more willing to allow a homosexual individual to make a speech in their community than Republicans. Our two hypotheses are symbolized the following way:

$$H_0: p_D = p_R$$

$$H_1: p_D > p_R$$

The proportion of Democrats willing to allow the speech is p_D and the proportion of Republicans willing to allow the speech is p_R. To test whether or not we can reject the null hypothesis, we test whether p_D equals p_R. We again draw on the 1987 GSS data, setting $\alpha = .05$, and find that $p_D = 0.705$ and $p_R = 0.662$. To test whether or not this difference is statistically significant, we calculate the test statistic, using the formula for the difference between two means presented in the preceding section.

$$Z_{(p_D - p_R)} = \frac{p_D - p_R}{\sqrt{\dfrac{p_D\, q_D}{N_D} + \dfrac{p_R\, q_R}{N_R}}}$$

In the example, this would be as follows:

$$Z_{(p_D - p_R)} = \frac{0.705 - 0.662}{\sqrt{\dfrac{(0.705)(0.295)}{566} + \dfrac{(0.662)(0.338)}{391}}}$$

$$= \frac{0.043}{0.031} = 1.403$$

Since the critical value is 1.645, we cannot reject the null hypothesis. We conclude that there is no significant difference between Republicans and Democrats with respect to their willingness to allow a homosexual individual to make a speech in their community.

7.3   An Example of a Two-tailed Hypothesis Test with Proportions

As indicated in Section 6.10, sometimes the researcher does not have a very good guess about the alternative hypothesis. For example, there may be no reason to believe that women are more likely than men to favor allowing a homosexual individual to make a speech in their community. In this case the null and alternative hypothesis can be stated as follows:

$$H_0: p_m = p_f$$

$$H_1: p_m \neq p_f$$

The proportion of men allowing a speech by a homosexual is p_m and the women's proportion is p_f. Note that the alternative hypothesis is simply that the two means (proportions in this case) are not equal; that is, we have no informed guess about which mean is greater if the results direct us to reject the null hypothesis that the two means are equal.

Suppose we set $\alpha = .05$. We want half the area associated with a Type I error to be above the mean and half below. Note that half the area of rejection, or $\alpha/2 = .05/2 = .025$, is in the upper tail, and half is in the lower tail. We look up the $Z_{\alpha/2}$ associated with .5000 = .0250 − .4750 in Appendix C and find it is 1.96. Since the sampling distribution is symmetric, it follows that $-Z_{\alpha/2} = -1.96$. If our test statistic is greater than 1.96 or less than −1.96, we will reject the null hypothesis; otherwise we will not.

We now can use the 1987 GSS data to test the null hypothesis that the proportion of males and females allowing a homosexual person to give a speech is equal. The alternative hypothesis, also stated previously, is that the two proportions are unequal. We choose $\alpha = .01$, compute the two proportions, and find that $p_m = 0.699$ and $p_f = 0.694$, with $N_m = 625$ and $N_f = 801$. These results suggest virtually no difference in the attitudes of males and females about a homosexual individual giving a speech. We can verify this by computing the test statistic used to evaluate the null hypothesis.

$$Z_{(p_m - p_f)} = \frac{0.699 - 0.709}{\sqrt{\dfrac{(0.699)(0.301)}{625} + \dfrac{(0.709)(0.291)}{801}}}$$

$$= \frac{-0.010}{0.0240} = -0.420$$

For $\alpha = .01$ we find that $Z_{\alpha/2} = 2.58$ and $-Z_{\alpha/2} = -2.58$. Since the test statistic is −0.42, as expected, we cannot reject the null hypothesis. We therefore conclude that there is no difference in men's and women's attitudes toward homosexual individuals making a speech in their communities.

7.4   Testing for the Difference between Two Means When the Standard Error Is Unknown: The *t* Test

When we do not know the variances of the variable in each of two populations ($\sigma_{Y_1}^2$ and $\sigma_{Y_2}^2$), as a result we also do not know the standard error of the sampling distribution of mean differences ($\sigma_{(\bar{Y}_2 - \bar{Y}_1)}$). As we showed in Chapter 6, the only statistic necessary to test the difference between two means is the sample variance. The use of the *t* distribution to test the difference between two means is illustrated here with an example involving hypotheses about urban change.

Since the end of World War II, the urban population of the United States has redistributed itself within extended metropolitan areas, as many residents of the central cities have moved to suburbs and to smaller towns surrounding the industrial core areas. At the same time, population shifts across geographic regions have brought the decline of the older Northeastern states and the growth of the Sunbelt states, those in the South and the West. Urbanologists hypothesize that these types of population change have numerous causes: technological developments, such as superhighways, cheap motor fuels, and industrial automation; economic factors, including inexpensive, low-tax suburban industrial parks and nonunion southern plants; the amenities of suburban living, such as low-density housing, quality schools, and a means of escape from blight and crime in the inner city; and the southern climate and life-style.[2]

We will use the 50 states to examine population change in response to two factors. First, the pull of the "Sunbelt" region presumably draws population away from the Northeastern and North Central states (the Frostbelt) as industries and commerce move their operations to the South and West. Second, states located in the Sunbelt should gain population (or at least not lose population) as fast as the Frostbelt during a single period.

---

[2]Thomas M. Guterbock, "The Push Hypothesis: Minority Presence, Crime, and Urban Deconcentration," *The Changing Face of the Suburbs,* ed. Barry Schwartz. (Chicago: University of Chicago Press, 1976).

These considerations lead to the following proposition about urban population change:

> P3: Sunbelt states are gaining population at a faster rate than Frostbelt states.

Changing this proposition into a hypothesis testable with the 50-States Data Set is relatively easy. In our analysis Sunbelt states are Alabama, Alaska, Arkansas, Arizona, California, Colorado, Delaware, Florida, Georgia, Hawaii, Idaho, Kentucky, Louisiana, Maryland, Mississippi, Montana, Nevada, New Mexico, North Carolina, North Dakota, Oklahoma, Oregon, South Carolina, Tennessee, Texas, Utah, Virginia, Washington, West Virginia, and Wyoming.[3] All other states are in the Frostbelt region. To estimate population change in these states we use two populations in 1970 and 1980. The analysis of proposition P1, therefore, will be based on the percentage change in population from 1970 to 1980. The operational or testable hypothesis is as follows:

> H1: Sunbelt states gained population from 1970 to 1980 at a higher rate than did states located in the Frostbelt.

We use the t distribution to test the hypothesis that Frostbelt states gained population at a rate faster than the Sunbelt states between 1970 to 1980. The raw data to test this hypothesis, which show the percentage (to nearest tenth) by which a state's 1970 population grew or declined over the last 10 years appear in Table 7.1. The average for all 50 states was a 16.25% gain (s_y = 14.37). But the means are markedly different for the two regions. The 30 Sunbelt states grew an average of 23.56%, while the 20 Frostbelt states grew by an average of only 5.28% of their 1970 populations. The standard deviations show a substantially greater dispersion in the Sunbelt sample, reflecting in part the extremely high growth of such states as Nevada, Arkansas, and Florida. The smaller value of s_2 = 6.26 for the Frostbelt states compared to s_1 = 13.60 for the Sunbelt states implies that the sample of Frostbelt cities is clustered more closely about the mean.

[3]Obviously we are using the terms "Sunbelt" and "Frostbelt" loosely here. More precisely, we are referring to states in the South and the West.

The null hypothesis is that there is no difference in change in population size between regions. We must perform a significance test to decide whether the observed sample difference in means could have been observed in a population of states where no difference in fact exists. Since the samples are small (30 and 20), the appropriate test of significance is the *t* test. To use the *t* test we assume that independent random samples N_1 and N_2 are drawn from the two normally distributed populations. The null hypothesis states that the Sunbelt states' population gain between 1970 and 1980 is equal to the Frostbelt states' population gain. The alternative hypothesis is that the mean population gain from 1970 to 1980 is greater for Sunbelt than for Frostbelt states.

$$H_0: \mu_1 - \mu_2 = 0$$

$$H_1: \mu_1 - \mu_2 < 0$$

To use the *t* distribution to test hypotheses about means, we need to make the following assumptions:

1. Random samples are drawn from two independent, normally distributed populations.
2. The two population variances are homoscedastic, or equal; that is, $\sigma_1^2 = \sigma_2^2 = \sigma^2$.

With two sample variances, σ_1^2 and σ_2^2, either could be used to estimate σ^2. Since we want the best possible estimate of σ^2, we use a weighted average of σ_1^2 and σ_2^2 rather than arbitrarily choosing one of them as the estimate; that is, we pool the information on variation from both samples into a single estimate, using the following formula:

$$s^2 = \frac{(N_1 - 1)s_1^2 + (N_2 - 1)s_2^2}{N_1 + N_2 - 2}$$

where $N_1 + N_2 - 2$ are degrees of freedom that are associated with s^2.

TABLE 7.1   Percentage of Population Change, 1960–80,
                   for States in the South and West
                   ("Sunbelt") Compared with North and
                   North Central States ("Frostbelt")

	Sunbelt		Frostbelt
State	Change (%)	State	Change (%)
Alabama	12.9	Connecticut	2.5
Alaska	32.4	Illinois	2.8
Arkansas	53.7	Indiana	5.6
Arizona	18.8	Iowa	3.1
California	18.5	Kansas	5.1
Colorado	30.7	Maine	13.2
Delaware	8.6	Massachusetts	0.8
Florida	43.4	Michigan	4.2
Georgia	19.1	Minnesota	7.1
Hawaii	25.3	Missouri	5.1
Idaho	32.4	Nebraska	5.7
Kentucky	13.7	New Hampshire	24.8
Louisiana	15.3	New Jersey	2.7
Maryland	7.5	New York	−3.8
Mississippi	13.7	Ohio	1.3
Montana	13.3	Pennsylvania	0.6
Nevada	63.5	Rhode Island	−0.3
New Mexico	27.8	South Dakota	3.6
North Carolina	15.5	Vermont	15.0
North Dakota	5.6	Wisconsin	6.5
Oklahoma	18.2		
Oregon	25.9		
South Carolina	20.4		
Tennessee	16.9		
Texas	27.1		
Utah	37.9		
Virginia	14.9		
Washington	21.0		
West Virginia	11.8		
Wyoming	41.6		

$N_1 = 30$ $N_2 = 20$
$\overline{Y}_1 = 23.56$ $\overline{Y}_2 = 5.28$
$s_1 = 13.60$ $s_2 = 6.26$

Source: 50-States Data Set.

Note that the degrees of freedom associated with s_1^2 and s_2^2 sum to equal the degrees of freedom associated with s^2. Specifically, $(N_1 - 1) + (N_2 - 1) = N_1 + N_2 - 2$.

The test statistic for the difference between two means under the null hypothesis using small samples is as follows:

$$t_{(N_1 + N_2 - 2)} = \frac{(\overline{Y}_2 - \overline{Y}_1) - (\mu_2 - \mu_1)}{s_{(\overline{Y}_2 - \overline{Y}_1)}}$$

$$= \frac{\overline{Y}_2 - \overline{Y}_1}{\sqrt{s^2/N_1 + s^2/N_2}}$$

And it follows that

$$= \frac{\overline{Y}_2 - \overline{Y}_1}{s\sqrt{1/N_1 + 1/N_2}}$$

To test H_1 in the urban population-change example, we first need to calculate s^2 and then take its square root to obtain s.

$$s^2 = \frac{(30 - 1)13.60^2 + (20 - 1)6.26^2}{30 + 20 - 2}$$

$$= 127.26$$

And then

$$s = 11.28$$

For the *t* test of the null hypothesis we choose $\alpha = .05$, and $df = N_1 + N_2 - 2 = 30 + 20 - 2 = 48$. Then *t* is calculated as follows:

$$t_{48} = \frac{(5.28 - 23.56)}{11.28\sqrt{1/30 + 1/20}}$$

$$= \frac{-18.280}{3.256} = -5.61$$

The critical value is -1.67 for a one-tailed test when $\alpha = .05$ and there are 48 degrees of freedom. Since the test statistic is -5.61, we reject the null hypothesis. Therefore, the alternative hypothesis that Sunbelt states are gaining population faster than Frostbelt states is supported.

As pointed out in Chapter 5, in practice researchers always use t tests rather than Z. They do so for three reasons. First, as N gets large the t and Z distributions converge, so it makes sense to use the t distribution regardless of sample size. You can easily check this assertion by examining Appendix C and Appendix D. In Appendix D (t distribution), look at df equals infinity (∞) for a given α and compare the t value to the Z value in Appendix C for the same α. The two converge. Second, as N gets large (rougly 50 or so) the assumption for using the t distribution that the sample be drawn from a population that is normal becomes less important because of the central limit theorem (see Section 5.5). Third, and finally, for all intents and purposes we never know the standard error of the population, and hence must use a t test. While it is important for technical reasons for you to know the difference between a Z and a t distribution, in practice you will always use a t test.

One final point before moving on to a discussion of confidence intervals and point estimates. Students sometimes ask why it is necessary to use hypothesis testing (and estimation procedures) when the sample is the entire population, as it is when we use the 50-States Data Set. In Section 4.6, we indicated that there are two meanings for statistical inference. The first is the usual one—we are making generalizations from a given sample to a larger population. The second interpretation is that inference is a test of the hypothesis that the process which generated the observed results is random rather than systematic. Thus in our population change example, we are asking whether the process by which population changes are occurring across the states is random or whether something systematic is occurring. If we are unable to reject the null hypothesis we assume that the process is random. If we reject it we assume that something systematic is occurring. In our example, we had to reject the hypothesis that population growth in Frostbelt versus Sunbelt cities is a random process. Instead, for reasons we can only speculate about (e.g., climate, tax incentives), we conclude that the Sunbelt states are growing faster than the Frostbelt states. The important point is this: Even though we are using the entire population of states, we need some method of determining whether differences we observe are "real" or simply occurring by chance. Hypothesis testing can help us make those judgments.

7.5 Confidence Intervals and Point Estimates for Mean Differences and Proportions

7.5.1 Mean Differences

Confidence intervals can be constructed around the difference between two means in much the same way as for a single mean, similar to what we did in Section 5.6. The interpretation also is similar. We can state what the probability is that a randomly chosen **confidence interval for mean differences** will contain the difference between the population means, that is, $\mu_2 - \mu_1$, if we follow the procedure for constructing them outlined next. More formally, we can construct confidence intervals for any desired level of confidence, such as $1 - \alpha$, with this formula.

● **confidence interval for mean differences** a confidence interval constructed around the point estimate of the difference between two population means

$$(\overline{Y}_2 - \overline{Y}_1) \pm t_{\alpha/2}s_{(\overline{Y}_2 - \overline{Y}_1)}$$

Suppose we want to compute a 95% confidence interval around our estimate of difference in percent population change between Sunbelt and Frostbelt states. In Section 7.4 we saw that $\overline{Y}_2 - \overline{Y}_1 = -18.28$, and we calculated $s_{(\overline{Y}_2 - \overline{Y}_1)} = 3.256$. For the 95% confidence level, $t_{\alpha/2}$ is 2.00 with $N_1 + N_2 - 2 = 48$ *df*, as can be verified from Appendix D. Therefore, the lower confidence limit (LCL) is $-18.28 - (2.00)3.256 = -24.79$ and the upper confidence limit (UCL) is $-18.28 + (2.00)3.256 = -11.77$. In other words, the procedure we followed for constructing confidence intervals would result in "capturing" the true mean difference between the Sunbelt and Frostbelt states 95% of the

● **point estimate**
for mean differences
the differences
between the sample
means used to
estimate the
difference between
two population
means

time. And our **point estimate for mean differences,** or our best single estimate of the difference, is simply $\overline{Y}_2 - \overline{Y}_1 = 18.28$.

7.5.2   Differences between Proportions

We can also construct confidence intervals around differences between proportions. In this case the intervals are given by the following:

$$(p_2 - p_1) \pm t_{\alpha/2} s_{(p_2 - p_1)}$$

In the example in Section 7.2 where we examined support for allowing a homosexual to speak in the community, we calculated that $p_D - p_R = 0.043$ and $s_{(p_D p_R)} = 0.031$. Now suppose that we want to construct a 99% confidence interval around the point estimate, 0.043. Since in this sample the number of Democrats was $N_D = 566$ and the number of Republicans was $N_R = 391$, there are $566 + 391 - 2 = 955$ *df*. And we can see from Appendix D that $t_{\alpha/2} = 2.58$.

We can use all of this information to determine that the LCL is $.043 - (2.58)(.031) = -0.037$ and the UCL is $.043 + (2.58)(.031) = 0.123$. Our 99% confidence interval for the true difference between the proportions of Democrats versus Republicans who support free speech for homosexuals is the interval 0.43 ± 0.31 or is between .037 and .123. Furthermore, our best estimate of the true difference is the point estimate, $p_D - p_R = .043$. In other words, on the issue of homosexuals giving speeches in one's community the difference between Republicans and Democrats is essentially zero.

In Chapter 8 we discuss testing the difference between several means.

Key Concepts and Symbols

These key concepts and symbols are listed in the order of appearance in the chapter. Combined with the definitions in the margins, these will help you review the material and can serve as a self-test for mastery of the concepts.

mean difference test	$\mu_{(\bar{Y}_2 - \bar{Y}_1)}$
independent random samples	$\sigma_{(\bar{Y}_2 - \bar{Y}_1)}$
	$\hat{\sigma}_{(\bar{Y}_2 - \bar{Y}_1)}$
mean difference hypothesis test	$Z_{(\bar{Y}_2 - \bar{Y}_1)}$
	$s_{(\bar{Y}_2 - \bar{Y}_1)}$
significance testing with proportions	s_p
	$Z_{(p_D - p_R)}$
confidence interval for mean differences	$s_{(p_D - p_R)}$
	s^2
point estimate for mean differences	$t_{(N_1 + N_2 - 2)}$

Problems

General Problems

1. A theoretical proposition in the sociology of religion states, "If one is conventionally religious one is the less likely one to engage in deviant behaviors than if one is not conventionally religious." Restate this proposition as a pair of null and alternative hypotheses, using symbolic notation. Does the hypothesis require a one- or a two-tailed test of significance?

2. A proposition in the sociology of deviance states, "If one has peers who engage in a deviant behavior, the greater the likelihood that one will engage in that behavior as well." Restate this proposition as a pair of null and alternative hypotheses, using symbolic notation. Does the hypothesis require a one- or a two-tailed test of significance?

3. What are the standard errors for testing for the difference between two means, given the following:

	σ_1^2	σ_2^2	N_1	N_2
a.	15	14	25	64
b.	15	14	100	100
c.	53	58	200	400
d.	0.20	0.50	50	75

4. Find the Z scores for the following and state whether the null hypotheses should be rejected:

	$\overline{Y}_1$	$\overline{Y}_2$	σ_1^2	σ_2^2	N_1	N_2	α
a.	22	20	225	360	80	90	.05, one-tailed
b.	22	20	225	360	800	900	.05, one-tailed
c.	2.4	1.8	6	8	40	80	.05, two-tailed
d.	46	49	60	68	200	250	.01, two-tailed

5. In 1972, the proportion of Americans agreeing that "an admitted communist" should be allowed to make a speech in the community was 0.54. In 1987, the proportion was .55. The two independently drawn samples' sizes are 1,556 and 1,531, respectively. Test the null hypothesis of no change over the 15 year period, using $\alpha = .05$ and a two-tailed test of significance.

6. In 1972, 73.6% of 1,533 respondents interviewed for the GSS said that they would vote for a woman for president if she were qualified for the job. By 1986, this figure had risen to 86.3% based on 1,427 respondents. Test the null hypothesis of no change in the two population percentages using $\alpha = .01$ and a one-tailed test of significance.

7. One sample has 50 respondents and a second has 60. How many degrees of freedom does the sampling distribution of mean differences have associated with it?

8. One sample has 300 respondents and a second has 350. How many degrees of freedom does the sampling distribution of mean differences have associated with it?

9. Give the 95% and 99% confidence intervals for (a) the difference in proportions in Problem 5 and (b) for the difference in proportions in Problem 6.

10. An experimental study of the hypothesis that increased social interaction increases liking for the person with whom one interacts yields the following sample statistics:

$$\text{Control group: } s_1^2 = 36$$

$$\text{Experimental group: } s_2^2 = 64$$

If $\alpha = .01$, should the null hypothesis be rejected?

11. A class of 17 students scored an average of 86 on the statistics midterm examination while a second section of the course with 15 students scored an average of 82. In the first section the standard deviation was 9 and in the second it was 10. Test the null hypothesis that the two classes have the same population means, setting $\alpha = .05$. Use a two-tailed test.

12. A poll at Big State University found that 31% of the 400 freshman randomly sampled were against capital punishment regardless of how serious the crime. A random sample of 400 seniors at the same school showed that 47% were against capital punishment regardless of the crime. Compute the sample point estimate of the difference between the two classes and compute a 95% confidence interval around it. Based on this analysis could you reject the null hypothesis with $\alpha = .05$? Justify your answer.

Problems Requiring the 1987 General Social Survey

13. Test the null hypothesis that religious fundamentalists (FUND) see themselves as no closer to God (NEARGOD) than others. Use a one-tailed test. Set $\alpha = .01$. [Use the following recode, RECODE FUND(3=2).]

14. Test the hypothesis that persons 60 or older are just as happy as those younger than 60. Use a two-tailed test with α = .05. [Use the following recode, RECODE AGE(LO THRU 59=1)(60 thru HI=2).]

15. A fundamental finding in sociology is that education is related to income. Test the hypothesis that those with at least a high school education earn more (INCOME) than those with less than a high school education. Set α = .01. Use a one-tailed test. [Use the following recode, RECODE EDUC(LO THRU 11=1)(12 thru HI=2).]

16. A basic proposition in political sociology holds that voters of different political parties have different political ideologies. Test the hypothesis that Democrats are less conservative than Republicans. Set α = .01. Use a one-tailed test. [Use the following recode, RECODE PARTYID(0, 1=0) (5, 6=1).]

17. Test the hypothesis that smokers rate themselves just as healthy (HEALTHY) as nonsmokers. Set α = .01. Use a two-tailed test.

Problems Requiring the 50-States Data Set

18. Test the hypothesis that as the percentage of births out of wedlock (WEDLOCK) goes up so does the number of single mothers on Aid to Dependent Families (WELFARE). Set α = .05. Use a one-tailed test. [Use the following recode, RECODE WEDLOCK(LO TO 15=1) (16 TO HI= 2).]

19. Test the hypothesis that the turnout in the 1980 election (TURNOUT) is positively related to per capita income (PCINCOME). Set α = .05. Use a one-tailed test. [Use the following recode, RECODE PCINCOME(LO THRU 90 =1)(90.1 THRU HI=2).]

20. Test the hypothesis that as the percentage of drivers driving over 55 MPH increases (SPEED), the number of fatalities per 1,000,000 persons (FATALITY) also increases. Set α = .05. Use a one-tailed test. [Use the following recode, RECODE SPEED(LO THRU 49)(49.1 THRU HI).]

21. Test the hypothesis that change in the size of population from 1970 to 1980 (POPCHNG) is positively related to the divorces per 1,000 persons (DIVORCE). Set α = .05. Use a one-tailed test. [Use the following recode, POPCHNG (LO THRU 16=1)(16.1 THRU HI=20.]

22. Test the hypothesis suggesting that per capita spending on art (ARTFUND) is positively related to per capita income (PCINCOME). Set α = .05. Use a one-tailed test. [Use the following recode, RECODE PCINCOME(LO THRU 90=1)(90.1 THRU HI=2).]

8

Testing for the Difference between Several Means

The procedure for testing the hypothesis that two sample means come from two different populations, rather than being drawn from the same population, was examined in Chapter 7. In this chapter we show how to test the hypothesis that the sample means of two or more, or J, groups come from the same rather than different populations. The technique used is called the **analysis of variance** (ANOVA).

- **analysis of variance**
  a statistical test of the difference of means for two or more groups

8.1 The Logic of Analysis of Variance: An Example

The logic of the analysis of variance is best shown by an example. We were interested in the different reactions to police use of force under varying conditions. Specifically, we were interested in whether or not approval would vary as a function of the act that precipitated the use of force and the gender of the person the policeman was using force against. We formulated this hypothesis.

> H1: College students would be more likely to approve of the use of force if the provoking act was a physical attack as opposed to a verbal assault against the policeman, and they would be more likely to approve of the use of force against a man as opposed to a woman.

To test this hypothesis, we randomly assigned 14 college students to one of four experimental conditions. The four conditions were defined by the situation in which the policeman struck a person. In condition 1 the students were asked whether they would approve or disapprove of a policeman striking a man who was attacking him with his fists. In condition 2 another group of students was asked whether they would approve or disapprove of a policeman striking a man who had said vulgar and obscene things to that policeman. Conditions 3 and 4 were parallel to 1 and 2 except that the policeman was striking a woman instead of a man.

The dependent variable was level of approval of the policeman's behavior on a four point scale where 1=strongly disapprove, 2=mildly disapprove, 3=mildly approve and 4=strongly approve. Our specific hypothesis was that the use of force when the policeman had been himself physically attacked by a man (*pm*) would be more highly approved than if he were physically attacked by a woman (*pw*), which would be more highly approved than if he were verbally assaulted by a man (*vm*), which, in turn, would be more highly approved than if he were verbally assaulted by a woman (*vw*). If the type of precipitating act and the gender of the person involved in the precipitating act are unrelated to the level of approval of the policeman's response, we would expect the four population means (μ_{pm}, μ_{pw}, μ_{vm}, and μ_{vw}) to be equal to one another and hence equal to the overall, or the **grand mean**, of the population (μ). We would also expect that the sample means would be roughly equal to each other if the null hypothesis is true, that is, if there is no relationship between the four conditions and level of approval of the policeman's behavior. However, if the null hypothesis is rejected and the substantive hypothesis holds, then we would expect to find that $\overline{Y}_{pm} > \overline{Y}_{pw} > \overline{Y}_{vm} > \overline{Y}_{vw}$. Before examining the data to see if our substantive hypothesis is supported, we need to describe the analysis of variance more fully.

● **grand mean** in analysis of variance, the mean of all observations

An ANOVA model provides a way to test the null hypothesis that all *J* sample means are drawn from the same population and therefore all population means are equal. Formally, the null hypothesis is expressed as follows:

$$H_0: \mu_1 = \mu_2 = \ldots = \mu_J$$

The alternative hypothesis is that one or more of the sample means are drawn from populations with different population means. The possibility that the null hypothesis can be rejected implies one of several alternative possibilities.

1. All the population means are different from each other, i.e., $\mu_1 \neq \mu_2 \neq \ldots \neq \mu_j$.

2. Some subsets of the population means differ from one another (e.g., μ_1 differs from μ_2 but not from μ_3 and μ_4).

3. Some combination of the population means is different from some single population mean or from some other combination of population means (e.g., μ_2 differs from the average of the means of three other populations).

In other words, if we reject the null hypothesis, we still need to explain how the means differ from one another.

8.2   Effects of Variables

To examine the effects of the variables in an analysis of variance we will consider a population with mean μ. The null hypothesis, as noted above, states that the J group means are all equal, that is, $\mu_1 = \mu_2 = \ldots = \mu_j$. But if they all are equal to each other, clearly they will all equal the overall or grand mean, μ. If, for example, the mean number of hours of television watched is $\mu = 2.80$ per day, and the rate of watching is the same for men and women, then clearly $\mu = \mu_m = \mu_f = 2.80$. To measure the **effect** of an independent variable on a dependent variable, we can take advantage of this fact.

An effect of being in a subgroup or one of a number of groups, labeled j, is defined as follows:

● **effect**
the impact on a dependent variable of being in a certain treatment group

$$\alpha_j = (\mu_j - \mu)$$

Note that if being in group j has no effect on the dependent variable, Y, then $\alpha_j = 0$.[1] But if being in a group does have an effect, α_j will be positive or negative, depending on whether a group's mean is above or below the grand mean, μ.

Suppose young people watch television an average of 5.0 hours per day (μ_Y), middle-aged people watch it 1.5 hours per day (μ_M), and older people watch it 1.9 hours daily (μ_o), and the overall mean equals 2.80. Using the notation for age-group effects, $\alpha_Y = (5.00 - 2.80) = 2.2$, $\alpha_M = (1.50 - 2.80) = -1.3$, and $\alpha_o = (1.90 - 2.80) = -0.9$ hours per day. As the figures show, young people, on average, watch television 2.2 hours more per day than is true in the entire population, middle-aged persons 1.3 hours less than average and older people 0.9 hours less than average.

8.3   The ANOVA Model

The term analysis of variance is not used accidentally. When we do an ANOVA we are asking how much of the total variation in Y can be explained by the "treatment" variable(s) [also called independent variable(s)] and how much is left unexplained. The difference between an observed score and a score predicted by the model is called the **error term,** or residual term. What follows is the general model for ANOVA with one independent variable:

● **error (residual) term**
the difference between an observed score and a score predicted by the model

$$Y_{ij} = \mu + \alpha_j + e_{ij}$$

Where:

$$e_{ij} = \text{the error, or residual, term.}$$

This formula indicates that the score of observation i, which is also a member of group j (hence Y_{ij}), is a function of a group

---

[1] The use of alpha with a subscript (α_j) is not to be confused with α without a subscript, which refers to the probability of a Type I error (see Chapter 4).

effect, α_j, plus the population mean, μ, and random error, e_{ij}. We need the error term to take into account that not every observation in subgroup j has the same Y_{ij}. For example, every young person does not watch exactly 5 hours of TV per day; some watch more and some watch less. The error term, e_{ij}, reflects this fact.

Let's examine how the model would work with the TV watching example used earlier. Here are the three equations "explaining" the TV watching behavior of the young, middle-aged, and older groups.

$$Y_{iy} = 2.8 + 2.2 + e_{iy}$$

$$Y_{im} = 2.8 - 1.3 + e_{im}$$

$$Y_{io} = 2.8 - 0.9 + e_{io}$$

For example, if we were to draw a sample of young persons, we would predict that on average they would watch TV 2.8 + 2.2 = 5.0 hours per day. But the fact that there is an error term, e_{iy}, in the equation allows for the fact that not every young person in the sample will watch TV exactly 5 hours per day. Some will watch more, others less. Similar interpretations can be made of the equations for the middle-aged and older groups.

8.4   Sums of Squares

To be able to estimate the proportion of variance in Y_{ij} due to group effects (the α_j) and due to error, we partition the numerator of the sample variance into two independent additive components. We begin with the following:

$$\sum_{i=1}^{N} (Y_i - \overline{Y})^2$$

Before dividing it into two components, however, we need to reexpress this term to take into account that each of the N observations belongs to one of the J groups.

If the number of cases in the jth group is n_j, then it follows that $n_1 + n_2 + \ldots + n_j = N$; that is, the sum of observations across the J subgroups or treatments equals the total sample size, N. Furthermore

$$\sum_{i=1}^{N} (Y_i - \overline{Y})^2 = \sum_{j=1}^{J} \sum_{i=1}^{n_j} (Y_{ij} - \overline{Y})^2$$

As noted in Appendix A, when there is a double summation operator, the inside one is indexed faster.

Suppose we have $N = 5$ observations. We assign each observation either to group 1 or group 2 (i.e., $J = 2$), and $n_1 = 3$ and $n_2 = 2$. Then if we expand the terms on the right in the equation, we see the following:

$$\sum_{j=1}^{J} \sum_{i=1}^{n_j} (Y_{ij} - \overline{Y})^2 = [(Y_{11} - \overline{Y})^2 + (Y_{21} - \overline{Y})^2 + (Y_{31} - \overline{Y})^2]$$

$$+ [(Y_{12} - \overline{Y})^2 + (Y_{22} - \overline{Y})^2]$$

- **total sum of squares**
  a number obtained by subtracting the scores of a distribution from their mean, squaring, and summing these values

The sum in the first line is for $j = 1$, and in the second for $j = 2$. And the result is the same as if we had used $\sum_{i=1}^{5}(Y_i - \overline{Y})^2$, except that we have tagged the group to which each observation belongs, as well. The term $\sum_{j=1}^{J} \sum_{i=1}^{n_j} (Y_{ij} - \overline{Y})^2$ is called the **total sum of squares,** or SS_{TOTAL}.

- **between sum of squares**
  a value obtained by subtracting the grand mean from each group mean, squaring these differences for all individuals, and summing them

$$SS_{\text{TOTAL}} = \sum_{j=1}^{J} \sum_{i=1}^{n_j} (Y_{ij} - \overline{Y})^2$$

- **within sum of squares**
  a value obtained by subtracting each subgroup mean from each observed score, squaring, and summing

The object of one-way analysis of variance is to divide or partition the total sum of squares into two components: the sum of squares lying between the means of the categories, called the **between sum of squares,** or SS_{BETWEEN}, and the sum of squared deviations about the category means, called the **within sum of squares,** or SS_{WITHIN}.

Box 8.1 defines this algebraically as follows:

$$SS_{TOTAL} = SS_{BETWEEN} + SS_{WITHIN}$$

This partitioning can be easily explained. Whenever observations differ from one another, the variance is greater than zero. Furthermore, some part of this variance is due to the effects of the groups to which the observations belong. In other words, the sum of squares *between* groups captures the effects of the treatment or independent variable under study. However, individuals *within* the same group can still differ from one another, due to the operation of chance factors such as sampling variability or omitted causal variables. The sum of squares within groups reflects the operation of these other, unmeasured factors. Thus the within-group sum of squares (or error sum of squares as the term is used in Chapter 9) implies that by assuming each group member has the same score, we make an error in estimating the individual score.

8.4.1   Sums of Squares in the Example Involving Approval of the Policeman's Behavior

We now return to our example in which we investigate whether the nature of the provoking act and the gender of the person involved in that act are related to approval or disapproval of a policeman striking the provoking person. Suppose the null hypothesis is true and we observe that $\overline{Y}_{pm} = \overline{Y}_{pw} = \overline{Y}_{vm} = \overline{Y}_{vw}$. If the null hypothesis is true, the term $SS_{BETWEEN}$ will equal zero and, hence, $SS_{TOTAL} = SS_{WITHIN}$; that is, all of the observed variance is random error variance. In this case, there are no treatment effects and as a result $\alpha_i = 0$, and the general ANOVA model reduces to this equation.

$$Y_{ij} = \mu + e_{ij}$$

Box 8.1   Partitioning Total Sum of Squares

To partition the total sum of squares into the sum of the between and within sum of squares, we first note that we can take the same value and add it to and subtract it from any deviation without changing that deviation. Suppose, in a sample, we take the mean score of the independent variable category into which observation i falls (denoted $\overline{Y}_j$) and subtract it from and add it to the deviation of that observation from the grand mean.

$$Y_{ij} - \overline{Y} = Y_{ij} + (\overline{Y}_j - \overline{Y}_j) - \overline{Y}$$

Regrouping terms provides the following:

$$Y_{ij} - \overline{Y} = (Y_{ij} - \overline{Y}_j) + (\overline{Y}_j - \overline{Y})$$

Notice that the second term in the previous equation, $(\overline{Y}_j - \overline{Y})$, is the estimate of group effect $\alpha_j = (\mu_j - \mu)$, the effect of being in category j.

Also note that the first term in the same equation, $(Y_{ij} - \overline{Y}_j)$, is an estimate of the error term, e_{ij}. Now if we square both sides of this equation and sum over all scores, after some algebra is applied we obtain the following:

$$\sum_{j=1}^{J} \sum_{i=1}^{n_j} (Y_{ij} - \overline{Y})^2 = \sum_{j=1}^{J} \sum_{i=1}^{n_j} (Y_{ij} - \overline{Y}_j)^2 + \sum_{j=1}^{J} n_j (\overline{Y}_j - \overline{Y})^2$$

This equality shows that the total sum of squares can always be partitioned into the following:

$$SS_{\text{BETWEEN}} = \sum_{j=1}^{J} n_j (\overline{Y}_j - \overline{Y})^2$$

$$SS_{\text{WITHIN}} = \sum_{j=1}^{J} \sum_{i=1}^{n_j} (Y_{ij} - \overline{Y}_j)^2$$

And the total is expressed as follows:

$$SS_{\text{TOTAL}} = SS_{\text{BETWEEN}} + SS_{\text{WITHIN}}$$

Suppose, however, that the nature of the provoking act and the gender of the person involved in that act are related to the approval or disapproval of the policeman's response; that is, in particular, we observe $\overline{Y}_{pm} > \overline{Y}_{pw} > \overline{Y}_{vm} > \overline{Y}_{vw}$. Suppose further that every person within a given experimental condition responds with exactly the same level of approval or disapproval toward the policeman's behavior. The approval scores, i.e., the dependent variable, for the four treatment groups will equal, as follows:

$$Y_{i,pm} = \overline{Y} + \hat{\alpha}_{pm}$$

$$Y_{i,pw} = \overline{Y} + \hat{\alpha}_{pw}$$

$$Y_{i,vm} = \overline{Y} + \hat{\alpha}_{vm}$$

$$Y_{i,vw} = \overline{Y} + \hat{\alpha}_{vw}$$

The caret on α signifies the sample estimate of the population parameter, α. In this case $SS_{TOTAL} = SS_{BETWEEN}$, and hence $SS_{WITHIN} = 0$, meaning that all of the variation in approval ratings is due to the nature of the provoking act and the gender of the person involved in that act. In reality, of course, it is never the case that all of the variation in the dependent variable is explained by the treatment variable. This is true for two reasons. First, *systematic* factors that might influence the dependent variable will not have been measured. Thus, the size of the policeman, or his race or ethnicity, or the sex of the person rating the policeman's behavior all might affect the given approval rating, but were not assessed in the experiment. Second, *random* factors such as respondent fatigue or distractibility might also affect the ratings given. Since we know that variation in the dependent variable is due not only to systematic factors measured in the experiment, but to systematic and random factors not measured as well, the previous equations need an error term added to them.

$$Y_{i,pm} = \overline{Y} + \hat{\alpha}_{pm} + e_{i,pm}$$

$$Y_{i,pw} = \overline{Y} + \hat{\alpha}_{pw} + e_{i,pw}$$

$$Y_{i,vm} = \overline{Y} + \hat{\alpha}_{vm} + e_{i,vm}$$

$$Y_{i,vw} = \overline{Y} + \hat{\alpha}_{vw} + e_{i,vw}$$

TABLE 8.1   Approval Ratings of Policeman's Use of Physical Force as a Function of whether Provoked by Physical or Verbal Assault, by a Male or Female

	Physical assault by				Verbal assault by			
	Male		Female		Male		Female	
	(Obs	Y_{ij})	(Obs	Y_{ij})	(Obs	Y_{ij})	(Obs	Y_{ij})
	1	4	1	4	1	1	1	1
	2	3	2	3	2	1	2	2
	3	4	3	4	3	2	3	1
	4	3	4	2	4	2	4	1
	5	4	5	2	5	2	5	1
	6	4	6	3	6	1	6	1
	7	3	7	4	7	1	7	1
	8	4	8	2	8	1	8	1
	9	3	9	3	9	1	9	1
	10	2	10	2	10	1	10	1
	11	4	11	2	11	4	11	1
	12	2	12	2	12	1	12	1
	13	3	13	2	13	1	13	1
	14	2	14	2	14	1	14	1

$$\Sigma Y_{ij} = 45 \qquad \Sigma Y_{ij} = 37 \qquad \Sigma Y_{ij} = 20 \qquad \Sigma Y_{ij} = 15$$
$$\bar{Y}_{pm} = 3.21 \qquad \bar{Y}_{pf} = 2.64 \qquad \bar{Y}_{vm} = 1.43 \qquad \bar{Y}_{vf} = 1.07$$
$$s_{pm} = 0.81 \qquad s_{pm} = 0.84 \qquad s_{vm} = 0.85 \qquad s_{vf} = 0.27$$

$$\bar{Y} = 2.09$$
$$s_Y = 1.13$$

Let's look at Table 8.1. We see that the mean approval rating for the condition where the policeman was physically struck by a man is 3.21, compared to 2.64 for the condition where the policeman was physically struck by a woman, compared to 1.43 where the policeman was verbally abused by a man, compared to 1.07 where the policeman was verbally abused by a woman. In other words, the results were exactly as predicted. College students appear to be more likely to approve of the policeman striking a man who has physically attacked him than they are to approve of a policeman striking a woman who has physically attacked him. Approval ratings are lower for a policeman striking a man who has verbally abused him and even lower for a policeman striking a woman who has verbally abused him. Importantly, while the results are in the predicted direction in this sample, we do not know whether the observed effect is *statistically significant*. To determine statistical significance requires that we compute several mathematical quantities including the sum of squares, the mean squares, and an F test. We now turn to a discussion of how to compute each of these quantities and how they are used to determine whether or not an observed difference in a given sample is statistically significant.

Notice in Table 8.1 that there is within-group variation (error) in all three groups. And the fact that all four subgroup means differ from one another suggests that there is between-group variation due to treatment effects. The variation in approval ratings scores (SS_{TOTAL}) can be seen in this simple example to be due to both $SS_{BETWEEN}$ and SS_{WITHIN}.

To this point we have not actually computed the three sums-of-squares components in this example. To compute SS_{TOTAL}, we subtract each observation from the grand mean, square them, and add them: $SS_{TOTAL} = (4 - 2.09)^2 + (3 - 2.09)^2 + \ldots + (1 - 2.09)^2 = 70.554$. And $SS_{BETWEEN}$ is directly calculated by this formula.

$$SS_{BETWEEN} = \sum_{j=1}^{J} n_j(\overline{Y}_j - \overline{Y})^2$$

In this case this computes to $14(3.21 - 2.09)^2 + 14(2.64 - 2.09)^2 + 14(1.43 - 2.09)^2 + 14(1.07 - 2.09)^2 = 42.625$.

Now SS_{WITHIN} can be computed in two ways. Here is the direct calculation formula.

$$SS_{WITHIN} = \sum_{j=1}^{J} \sum_{i=1}^{n_j} (Y_{ij} - \overline{Y}_j)^2$$

This directs us to subtract observations from their *subgroup* mean, square them, and sum them. If we do this we find that $SS_{\text{WITHIN}} = (4 - 3.21)^2 + (3 - 3.21)^2 + \ldots + (1 - 1.07)^2 = 27.929$. Since the other formula states that $SS_{\text{TOTAL}} = SS_{\text{BETWEEN}} + SS_{\text{WITHIN}}$, it follows that

---

$$SS_{\text{WITHIN}} = SS_{\text{TOTAL}} - SS_{\text{BETWEEN}}$$

In other words, once we know SS_{TOTAL} and SS_{BETWEEN}, we can simply subtract the latter from the former to obtain SS_{WITHIN}. This checks with the longer method of computation shown earlier. We suggest that you calculate all three components in the example directly, as a check on your understanding and the accuracy of your arithmetic.

8.5   Mean Squares

● **mean squares** estimates of variances used in the analysis of variance

● **mean square between** a value in ANOVA obtained by dividing the between sum of squares by its degrees of freedom

● **mean square within** a value in ANOVA obtained by dividing the within sum of squares by its degrees of freedom

The next step in an analysis of variance is to compute the mean square for SS_{BETWEEN} and SS_{WITHIN}. When we compute **mean squares,** we are computing two variances—one due to treatment effects and one due to error. If treatment effects exist, we expect the between-group variance, which we call **mean square between,** or MS_{BETWEEN}, will be significantly larger than the within-group variance, which we call **mean square within,** or MS_{WITHIN}.

As we noted in Chapter 3, a variance is an average or mean in the sense that it is derived by dividing a sum of squared deviations about the mean by their degrees of freedom. Thus we showed that, in general, the variance of a set of sample scores is as follows:

$$s_Y^2 = \frac{\sum_{i=1}^{N}(Y_i - \overline{Y})^2}{N - 1}$$

The degrees of freedom here are $N - 1$. The degrees of freedom associated with the between-group variance are simply $J - 1$, since once we know the grand mean and $J - 1$ group means, the jth group mean can be determined automatically.

Since there are in general $J - 1$ degrees of freedom in computing the variance due to treatment, to compute MS_{BETWEEN}, we simply divide SS_{BETWEEN} by $J - 1$.

$$MS_{\text{BETWEEN}} = \frac{\sum\limits_{j=1}^{J} n_j(\overline{Y}_j - \overline{Y})^2}{J - 1}$$

$$= \frac{SS_{\text{BETWEEN}}}{J - 1}$$

Therefore, for our experiment on policemen's approval ratings when using force, we compute as follows:

$$MS_{\text{BETWEEN}} = 42.625/(4 - 1) = 14.208$$

The degrees of freedom associated with the mean squares within are $N - J$. Each group has $n_j - 1$ degrees of freedom, so we simply can add them over all J groups.

$$(n_1 - 1) + (n_2 - 1) + \ldots + (n_j - 1)$$

$$= \underbrace{(n_1 + n_2 + \ldots + n_j)}_{N \text{ of these}} - \underbrace{(1 + 1 + \ldots + 1)}_{J \text{ of these}}$$

$$= N - J$$

Therefore, to compute MS_{WITHIN}, we divide SS_{WITHIN} by $N - J$.

$$MS_{\text{WITHIN}} = \frac{SS_{\text{WITHIN}}}{N - J}$$

Using the data from the example, $MS_{\text{WITHIN}} = 27.929/(56 - 4) = .0537$.

The variance due to treatment is considerably larger than that due to error (14.208 versus 0.537), which should be the case if treatment effects exist. We need to examine how hypotheses are tested for statistical significance in ANOVA, however, before drawing any firm conclusions about treatment effects in this example. In particular, the next problem to be considered is how much larger MS_{BETWEEN} must be relative to MS_{WITHIN} before we can reject the hypothesis of no treatment effects.

8.6   The F Distribution

● **F ratio**
a test statistic formed by the ratio of two mean-square estimates of the population error variance

A variable called the **F ratio** is simply the ratio of MS_{BETWEEN} to MS_{WITHIN}.

$$F = \frac{MS_{\text{BETWEEN}}}{MS_{\text{WITHIN}}}$$

Any observed F ratio can be tested against the assumption that it came from a population where the null hypothesis is true, that is, against the hypothesis that none of the observed sum of squares is due to treatment effects. The F ratio has a known sampling distribution under the null hypothesis if two assumptions can be met. Specifically, we must assume that the J samples are independently drawn from a normally distributed population. We must also assume the variance in the population is the same for all J treatment categories. The second assumption is sometimes called **homoscedasticity.** (If the J population variances differ, they are said to be *heteroscedastic.*)

● **homoscedasticity**
a condition in which the variances of two or more population distributions are equal

● **F distribution**
a theoretical probability distribution for one of a family of F ratios having $J - 1$ and $N - J$ df in the numerator and denominator, respectively

If these assumptions are met, and the F ratio is distributed according to the **F distribution,** with $J - 1$ degrees of freedom associated with the numerator and $N - J$ with the denominator. Since the alternative hypothesis in ANOVA implies that the between-group variance is larger than the within-group variance in the population, we usually do a one-tailed test of significance. We choose an α level, and if the observed F ratio is larger than the critical value associated with α, we reject the null hypothesis and instead conclude that there indeed are treatment effects.

We will not show what F distributions look like, since they vary somewhat as a function of the degrees of freedom associated with them. However, we can show the use of the F table with the results of our policeman's response experiment. Suppose we set $\alpha = .05$. Since $J = 4$ and $N = 56$ in our example, there are 3 degrees of freedom associated with the numerator and 52 degrees with the denominator. Appendix E provides tables of the F distribution for $\alpha = .05, .01$, and $.001$. The degrees of freedom for the numerator run across the top rows of the tables and are labeled ν_1 (Greek letter *nu*), and the degrees of freedom associated with the denominator run down the first columns and are labeled ν_2.

To use the first table, for $\alpha = .05$, find the cell where $\nu_1 = 3$ and $\nu_2 = 52$. The value in that cell is the critical value (c.v.) which the observed F ratio must equal or exceed to reject the null hypothesis of no treatment effects. In this case we see that the two closest values are 40 and 60 since there is no printed value for $\nu_2 = 52$. To compute the c.v. we simply add the values for 40 and 60 and divide by 2; that is, $(2.84 + 2.76)/2 = 2.80$. Since $MS_{\text{BETWEEN}} = 14.21$ and $MS_{\text{WITHIN}} = 0.54$, we can compute the following:

$$F_{3,\ 52} = \frac{14.21}{0.54} = 26.45$$

Since the observed F ratio, 26.45, is larger than the c.v., 2.80, we confidently reject the null hypothesis. Furthermore, we conclude that approval ratings of the policeman's behavior were affected by our experimental treatment conditions.

8.7   Reporting an Analysis of Variance

● **ANOVA summary table** a tabular display summarizing the results of an analysis of variance

Procedures have been established for summarizing an analysis of variance in research reports. A common practice is to summarize the results of analysis of variance in an **ANOVA summary table** of the sort shown in Table 8.2. This table is very useful for the reader of the report, since it provides easy access to all the relevant information needed to interpret the research—sums of squares, degrees of freedom, and the F ratio.

8.8   Testing for Differences between Individual Treatment Means

The alternative hypothesis for an ANOVA can take three different forms as noted in Section 8.1: (1) all the population means are different from one another; (2) some subsets of the population means differ from one another; or (3) some combination of means is different from a single mean or from some other combination of means. By itself, the F value is mute on which of these alternatives is true in any given situation. You might think that the thing to do is to test among all possible pairs of means—six in the policeman approval rating example. It can be proven however that for J means, only $J - 1$ of the comparisons among the means (or combinations of means) are independent of each other—three in our example. This lack of independence can be easily seen with a simple example. Suppose that we have three treatment groups all with an equal number of observations in each group. Furthermore, suppose that we observe a grand mean of 5.0. If the mean for group 1 is 4.0 and the mean for group 2 is 5.0, what will the mean of group 3 equal? If the grand mean is 5.0, then the mean for group three must be 6.0. This proves that the means are not independent of one another. In this example, the grand mean and two of the

TABLE 8.2   Summary Table for One-Way Analysis of Variance of Approval Ratings of Policeman's Behavior

Source	SS	df	Mean square	F
Between groups	42.63	3	14.21	26.45*
Within groups (error)	27.93	52	0.54	
Total	70.56	55		

*$p < .05$.

three subgroup means provide sufficient information for determining the third. Similarly, a lack of independence among comparisons among means should make it clear that individual *t* tests are not to be used after one finds a significant *F* value.

There are two standard methods for comparing means. The first is called *a priori*, or **planned comparisons.** When using planned comparisons we state a hypothesis about the differences between and among the population means *before* carrying out the ANOVA. The second method is called *a posteriori*, or **post hoc comparisons.** In this approach one hypothesizes differences between and among the population means *after* the ANOVA is carried out. (Unfortunately, the details of how to do planned and post hoc comparisons are too advanced for an introductory textbook and will not be presented here.)

There is another approach to making comparisons of treatments. Specifically, one can collapse treatment conditions together and rerun the ANOVA. For example, to determine whether there is an effect of type of provocation on a policeman's approval rating we can collapse the data across gender. Similarly, if we want to see if there is a gender effect, we can collapse treatment groups across type of provocation. We will follow this procedure in Section 8.10 to determine the separate effects of type of provocation and gender on policemen's approval ratings.

● **planned comparisons** hypothesis tests of differences between and among population means carried out before doing analysis of variance

● **post hoc comparisons** hypothesis tests of the differences among population means carried out following analysis of variance

8.9 The Relationship of *t* to *F*

You might wonder what the relationship is between the *t* test discussed in Chapter 7 and the *F* test described in this chapter when comparing the means for only two groups, that is, when *J* = 2. Will the *t* test and an ANOVA give the same results, and how do we decide which test to use?

The *t* test and ANOVA yield identical results. Indeed, the square root of an *F* test with 1 and v_2 degrees of freedom equals a *t* test with v_2 degrees of freedom for the same set of data.

$$t_{v_2} = \sqrt{F_{1,\ v_2}}$$

Usually when $J = 2$ the researcher reports a t test, and when $J > 2$, the results of an ANOVA are always reported.

8.10   Determining the Strength of a Relationship: Eta Squared

After the researcher has rejected the null hypothesis in an ANOVA, the question of how strong the relationship is remains to be answered. The problem with hypothesis testing is that almost any difference between and among means will be statistically significant if we choose N to be large enough. For that reason, when the null hypothesis has been rejected we should also assess the strength of the relationship found. This can be done by computing **eta squared**, or η^2 (Greek letter *eta*).

● **eta squared**
a measure of nonlinear covariation between a discrete and a continuous variable; the ratio of SS_{BETWEEN} to SS_{TOTAL}

In Section 8.4 we showed that $SS_{\text{TOTAL}} = SS_{\text{BETWEEN}} + SS_{\text{WITHIN}}$. If we divide both sides of the equation by SS_{TOTAL}, the equation becomes the following:

$$1.00 = \frac{SS_{\text{BETWEEN}}}{SS_{\text{TOTAL}}} + \frac{SS_{\text{WITHIN}}}{SS_{\text{TOTAL}}}$$

$$= \text{"Explained" } SS + \text{"Unexplained" } SS$$

We can think of the ratio of SS_{BETWEEN} to SS_{TOTAL} as the proportion of the total sum of squares explained by the treatment or the independent variable(s) under study. Similarly, the ratio of SS_{WITHIN} to SS_{TOTAL} can be thought of as the proportion of the total sum of squares not explained by the treatment or independent variable(s).

Notice that the two components add to 1.0. Therefore, to determine the proportion of variation in a dependent variable accounted for by a treatment variable, we define as follows:

$$\eta^2 = \frac{SS_{\text{BETWEEN}}}{SS_{\text{TOTAL}}}$$

Eta squared (η^2) is always a positive number ranging between zero and 1.00. It measures the proportion of variance in the dependent variable which is "explained" (in a statistical rather than in a causal sense) by the independent variable. Since η^2 is technically a population parameter, when it is estimated by sample data we place a caret over it (i.e., $\hat{\eta}^2$). The more the sample means differ from each other and the more the sample variances exhibit small dispersions, the higher the $SS_{BETWEEN}$, and hence the larger the value of $\hat{\eta}^2$.

Using the results from the first set of analyses on approval of the policeman's behavior (Table 8.2), we compute as follows:

$$\hat{\eta}^2 = \frac{44.63}{70.55} = 0.633$$

We find here that 63.3% of the variation in approval ratings can be accounted for by the independent variable in the experiment. As social science experiments go, this is a large proportion of variance explained, and therefore it should not be taken as a guideline against which to gauge the strength of findings in general. Typically, a single independent variable in the social sciences will account for no more than 25 to 30% of the variance in a dependent variable, and often as little as 5% or 10%.

We can examine the effects of the type of provocation from panel A in Table 8.3. In this case we have the following:

$$\hat{\eta}^2 = \frac{39.45}{70.56} = 0.559$$

The type of provocation without reference to the gender of the person provoking the policeman accounts for 55.9% of the variance in approval ratings of his response.

The same analyses for gender of the provoking person (calculated from panel B of Table 8.3) yields:

$$\hat{\eta}^2 = \frac{3.02}{70.56} = 0.043$$

Only 4.3% of the variance in the ratings can be explained by gender.

TABLE 8.3

Analyses of Variance for Approval Ratings of a Policeman's Behavior as a Function of the Type of Provoking Act and the Gender of the Provoking Person

A. When the provoking act is physical versus verbal

	Physical	Verbal
Mean	2.93	1.25
Standard deviation	0.86	0.65
N	28	28

Analysis of variance summary

Source	SS	df	Mean Square	F
Between groups	39.45	1	39.45	68.48*
Within groups	31.11	54	0.58	
Total	70.56	55		

*$p < .05$.

B. When the provoking person is male versus female

	Male	Female
Mean	2.32	1.86
Standard deviation	1.22	1.01
N	28	28

Analysis of variance summary

Source	SS	df	Mean Square	F
Between groups	3.02	1	3.02	2.41*
Within groups	67.54	54	1.25	
Total	70.56	55		

*n.s. (not significant).

These results, along with those reported earlier, make it clear that it is primarily the type of provocation rather than the gender of the provoking person that is affecting college students' decisions to approve of the policeman's behavior.

When one is able to reject the null hypothesis it is useful either to table the numerical results or to put them in a graph. Graphs are especially useful tools for displaying data. We have displayed the results of the analysis reported in Table 8.2 in Figure 8.1. The graph suggests clearly that approval of the policeman's behavior is highest if he is physically attacked rather than verbally assaulted. While the gender of the provoking person also appears to have an effect, it does not appear to be as large as that associated with the type of provocation (physical versus verbal).

To determine if the type of provocation and the gender of the provoking person have independent effects, we will undertake two additional analyses. In the first analysis, we will confirm that the effect of type of provocation indeed is statistically significant. We do this by taking the observations in columns

Effects of Provocation and Gender on Approval of Policeman's Behavior

FIGURE 8.1

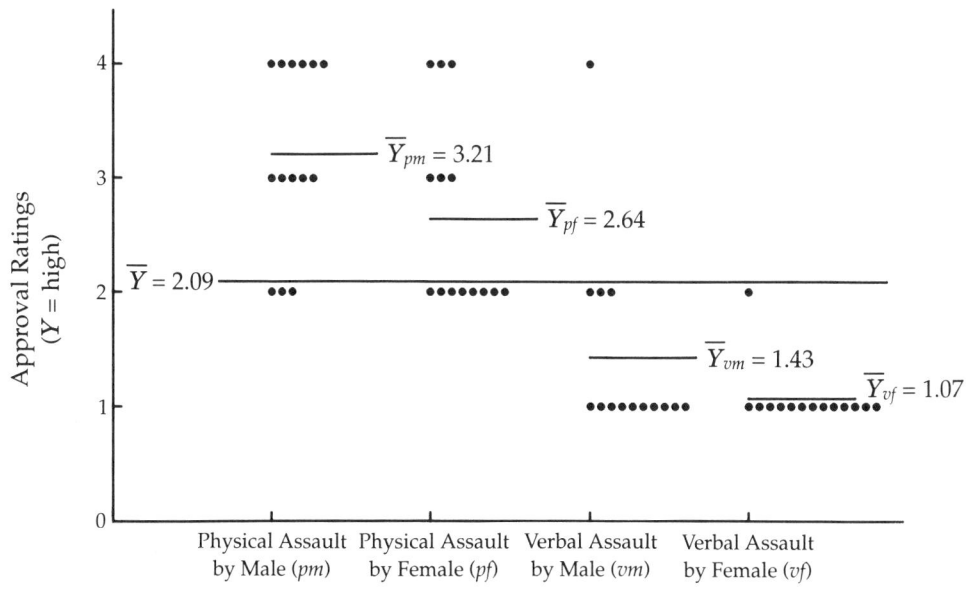

1 and 2 in Table 8.1 and combining them into one group—a group of approval ratings under the condition that the policeman was physically assaulted. In this new group $N_p = 28$. We also combine the two groups of observations in the third and fourth columns into a new group who was told that the policeman had been verbally assaulted. In this group $N = 28$ as well. The results of the analysis of variance are shown in part A of Table 8.3. Notice first that the mean approval rating for the policeman's behavior is 2.93 when the subjects were told that he had been physically assaulted compared to a mean of 1.25 when he had been verbally assaulted. As the results of the ANOVA shown in panel A of Table 8.3 indicate, these differences are highly significant at the $\alpha = .05$ level.

In the second analysis, we examine the gender of the provoking person to see if it has an impact on the ratings of the subjects, regardless of whether the policeman was physically or verbally assaulted. The results are shown in part B of Table 8.3. Notice that the mean approval rating of the policeman's behavior if the provoking person is male is 2.32 compared to a mean approval rating of 1.86 if the provoking person is female. However, this difference is not statistically significant for $\alpha = .05$. Therefore we conclude that college students' approval of a policeman using physical force against a person who has provoked him is a function of the type of provocation and not of the gender of the person who provoked the response.

Importantly, these results derive from a single study done with a set of college students in one course on one university campus. To substantiate our findings would require that we replicate this study with a random sample of college students drawn from a random sample of colleges. It is only with the replication of results that our confidence in a set of findings grows.

8.11   The Use of ANOVA in Nonexperimental Research

The term *treatment* has a long history in discussions of the analysis of variance. In fact, ANOVA was designed originally for the analysis of data generated by experiments and the treatments used in them. But the technique is very useful for the analysis of nonexperimental data as well.

The term *independent variable* can be freely substituted for treatment when the analysis involves nonexperimental data. This will often be the case in social sciences such as sociology and political science. The term *effect* can be substituted for *treatment effect* in the same way. However, it is much more difficult to draw causal inferences from nonexperimental research designs. An example in which some actual nonexperimental data are examined is presented in the next section.

8.11.1   An Example Using ANOVA with Nonexperimental Data

Recall in Chapter 7, we tested the proposition and supported the hypothesis that the Frostbelt gained in population at a slower rate than the Sunbelt between 1970 and 1980. Now we will examine the relationship between geographic area and population growth in a slightly different way. The U.S. Census Bureau classifies states by region. One such classification has four regions—Northeast, North Central, South, and West. If one thinks of the South and the West as corresponding roughly to the notion of Sunbelt, one might expect those two areas of the country to have experienced greater population growth between 1970 and 1980 than the states in the Northeast and North Central parts of the country, states that correspond roughly to the notion of the Frostbelt.

To test the hypothesis we first posit the null hypothesis of no difference between the regions.

$$H_0: \mu_{Yne} = \mu_{Ync} = \mu_{Ys} = \mu_{Yw}$$

Again, our alternative hypothesis is that the states in the South and the West will have shown more population growth than the states in the other two regions.

We will use the 50-States Data Set to test the hypothesis. We set $\alpha = .05$. With 3 and 46 *df* the c.v. is roughly 2.80 as can be verified from Appendix E. The raw data are shown in Table 8.4.

To compute SS_{TOTAL}, we subtract the observations in Table 8.4 from the grand mean, 16.25, square each of the differences, and then sum them.

TABLE 8.4　　　Percentage Distribution for Population Change from 1970–80 by Census Region

Population change			
Northeast	North Central	South	West
2.5	2.8	12.9	32.4
13.2	5.6	18.8	53.1
0.8	3.1	8.6	18.5
24.8	5.1	43.4	30.7
2.7	4.2	19.1	25.3
−3.8	7.1	13.7	32.4
0.6	5.1	15.3	13.3
−0.3	5.7	7.5	63.5
15.0	1.3	13.7	27.8
	3.6	15.5	25.9
	6.5	5.6	37.9
		18.2	21.0
		20.4	41.6
		16.9	
		27.1	
		14.9	
		11.8	

$\overline{Y}_n = 6.17 \quad \overline{Y}_{nc} = 4.55 \quad \overline{Y}_s = 16.67 \quad \overline{Y}_w = 32.57$
$s_n = 9.36 \quad s_{nc} = 1.73 \quad s_s = 8.60 \quad s_w = 13.89$
$n_n = 9 \quad n_{nc} = 11 \quad n_s = 17 \quad n_w = 13$

$$\overline{Y} = 16.25$$
$$s = 14.37$$
$$N = 50$$

Source: 50-States Data Set.

$SS_{TOTAL} = [(2.5 - 16.25)^2 + (13.2 - 16.25)^2 + \ldots +$

$(41.6 - 16.25)^2]$

$= 10,114.64$

Now SS_{BETWEEN} is computed using the formula given in Section 8.4.1.

$$SS_{\text{BETWEEN}} = 9(6.17 - 16.25)^2 + 11(4.55 - 16.25)^2 +$$

$$17(16.67 - 16.25)^2 + 13(32.57 - 16.25)^2$$

$$= 5,884.81$$

We can now compute SS_{WITHIN} as the difference between SS_{TOTAL} and SS_{BETWEEN}.

$$SS_{\text{WITHIN}} = 10,114.64 - 5,884.81 = 4,229.83$$

As an exercise you should calculate SS_{WITHIN} directly from the data as well.

To compute the mean squares, we need to calculate the degrees of freedom. For SS_{BETWEEN} there are $4 - 1 = 3$ df, while for SS_{WITHIN} there are $50 - 4 = 46$ df.

$$MS_{\text{BETWEEN}} = 5,884.81/3 = 1,961.60$$

$$MS_{\text{WITHIN}} = 4,229.83/46 = 91.95$$

With this information we can calculate the test statistic.

$$F_{3,\,46} = 1,961.60/91.95 = 21.33$$

Note that the F ratio of 21.33 is far greater in value than the c.v of 2.80 needed to reject the null hypothesis. The results of the ANOVA are summarized in Table 8.5.

Finally, to determine the strength of the relationship, we calculate eta squared.

$$\hat{\eta}^2 = \frac{5,884.81}{10,114.64} = 0.582$$

These results taken together clearly confirm our substantive hypothesis. While the Northeast and the North Central had, respectively, 6.2% and 4.6% growth rates between 1970 and 1980, the South and West had growth rates of 40.9% and 32.6%,

TABLE 8.5   Summary Table for One-Way Analysis of Variance of Population Change from 1970–80.

Source	SS	df	Mean Square	F
Between groups	5,884.81	3	1,961.60	21.33*
Within groups (error)	4,229.83	46	91.95	
Total	10,114.64	49		

*$p < .05$.

respectively. Furthermore, region has a substantial effect, explaining over 58% of the variance in population growth. In summary, this analysis further corroborates that it is the Sunbelt states that are growing faster than the Frostbelt states.

This concludes our introduction of how to test for the difference between several means. In the next and final chapter we turn to the estimation of the linear effects of one variable on a second, a topic called *bivariate regression analysis*.

Key Concepts and Symbols

These key concepts and symbols are listed in the order of appearance in the text. Combined with the definitions in the margins, these will help you review the material and can serve as a self-test for mastery of the concepts.

analysis of variance	planned comparisons
grand mean	post hoc comparisons
effect	eta squared
error (residual) term	α_j
total sum of squares	SS_{TOTAL}
between sum of squares	SS_{BETWEEN}
within sum of squares	SS_{WITHIN}
mean squares	MS_{BETWEEN}
mean square between	MS_{WITHIN}
mean square within	F
F ratio	ν_1
homoscedasticity	ν_2
F distribution	η^2
ANOVA summary table	$\hat{\eta}^2$

Problems

General Problems

1. A social psychologist hypothesizes that persons whose work is closely monitored make fewer errors than those whose work is not closely monitored. Write the null and alternative forms in symbolic form.

2. A political scientist hypothesizes that voters in the western states are more favorable toward legislation limiting off-shore drilling than voters are in other parts of the country. Write the null and alternative forms in symbolic form.

3. On a measure of support for right to life legislation, a sociologist finds that the overall mean is 10.6. The mean for Catholics is 13.7, for Protestants 11.1, for Jews 10.1, and for those with no religious identification, 8.2. What are the effects on support for right to life legislation for being a member of each of the religious groups (α_j)?

4. A psychologist administers differing doses of an amphetamine to college students to observe the effect of the drug on a recall ability task. The means were 12.1 for the controls, 11.9 for those given a low dose and 6.0 for those given a high dose. The overall mean for the three groups is 10.0. What are the effects (α_j) for the three dosage levels?

5. What are the assumptions for an analysis of variance testing the equality of J population means?

6. Distinguish between MS_{BETWEEN} and MS_{WITHIN} when computing an ANOVA.

7. Find the degrees of freedom and the critical values of F for the following:

   a $\alpha = .01$, 3 groups, 30 subjects.
   b. $\alpha = .01$, 4 groups, 20 subjects.
   c. $\alpha = .05$, 2 groups, 60 subjects.
   d. $\alpha = .05$, 2 groups, 30 subjects.

8. Find the degrees of freedom and the critical values of F for the following:

   a. $\alpha = .05$, $n_1 = 8$, $n_2 = 12$, $n_3 = 10$.
   b. $\alpha = .01$, $n_1 = 20$, $n_2 = 9$, $n_3 = 11$.
   c. $\alpha = .001$, $n_1 = 28$, $n_2 = 12$, $n_3 = 30$.
   d. $\alpha = .05$, $n_1 = 20$, $n_2 = 20$, $n_3 = 20$.

9. If three groups are of equal size and two of the groups have means of 4.0 and 7.0, respectively, what must the mean of the third group be if the grand mean is 5.0?

10. If four groups are of equal size and three of the groups have means of 3.2, 4.7, and 4.1 respectively, what must the mean of the fourth group be if the grand mean is 4.6?

11. Listed below are gains on the Scholastic Aptitude Test (SAT) for three groups, those who did nothing special to prepare for the test (controls), those who prepared by using a set of print materials designed to improve SAT scores

(Print), and those who used a computer-assisted (Computer) set of materials designed to improve the scores:

Control	Print	Computer
4	5	7
2	7	9
2	7	10
3	8	10
5	5	11

Compute the effect parameter (α_j) for each treatment condition. Then calculate the total sum of squares, the between sum of squares, and the within sum of squares. Determine the mean square between and the mean square within. Find the F ratio and evaluate it against the null hypothesis that the three population means are equal. Display these results in an ANOVA summary table. Finally, compute $\hat{\eta}^2$ and interpret the results.

12. An educational psychologist is interested in whether four types of reinforcers improve the degree to which 5-year-olds pay attention to the completion of a puzzle. Following are the results for the four methods:

A	B	C	D
20	15	22	19
22	18	21	23
21	20	24	20
20	18	25	18
20	18	25	18
19	19	24	15

Compute the effect parameter (α_j) for each treatment condition. Then perform an ANOVA, testing the hypothesis of no difference in means with $\alpha = .05$, and present the results in a summary table. Finally, compute $\hat{\eta}^2$ and interpret the results.

Problems Requiring the 1987 General Social Survey

13. Test the hypothesis that marital status (MARITAL) is related to happiness (HAPPY) by doing an ANOVA. Set $\alpha = .01$. Interpret the results.

14. Test the hypothesis that there is no relationship between the astrological sign under which one was born (ZODIAC) and one's health (HEALTH). Set $\alpha = .001$. Compute $\hat{\eta}^2$ and interpret the results.

15. Test the hypothesis that one vice begets another by doing an ANOVA with smoking behavior (SMOKE) the independent variable and whether one ever drinks too much (DRUNK) as the dependent variable. Set $\alpha = .01$. Compute $\hat{\eta}^2$ and interpret the results.

16. A hypothesis in the sociology of work argues that span of authority on the job is related to one's work satisfaction. Test this hypothesis by examining satisfaction with one's job (SATJOB) as a function of whether one supervises others on the job or not (WKSUP). Set $\alpha = .01$. Interpret the results.

17. Sociologists hypothesize that one's income is at least partially determined by one's level of education. Test this hypothesis by doing an ANOVA using current income (INCOME) as the dependent variable and one's years of education (EDUC) as the independent variable. Set $\alpha = .01$. Compute $\hat{\eta}^2$ and interpret the results.

Problems Requiring the 50-States Data Set

18. Determine if the divorce rates (DIVORCE) in the Pacific coast states are higher than those in the rest of the country (REGION9). Set $\alpha = .05$. Compute $\hat{\eta}^2$ and interpret the results. [Recode REGION9 as follows: RECODE REGION9(1,8=1)(9=2).]

19. Determine whether the abortion rates (ABORTION) in the Pacific coast states differ from those in the rest of the country (REGION9). Set $\alpha = .05$. Compute $\hat{\eta}^2$ and interpret the results. [Recode REGION9 as follows: RECODE REGION9(1,8=1)(9=2).]

20. Examine whether the percentage of women in the labor force (WRKWMN) varies as a function of whether a state has a right-to-work law or not (RT2WORK). Set $\alpha = .05$. Compute $\hat{\eta}^2$ and interpret the results.

21. Determine whether the percentage of nonagricultural workers in states who are unionized (UNION) varies as a function of whether a state has a right to work law or not (RT2WORK). Set $\alpha = .05$. Compute $\hat{\eta}^2$ and interpret the results.

22. Test the hypothesis that voter turnout (TURNOUT) is related to having at least a high school degree (HSGRAD). Set $\alpha = .05$. Compute η^2 and interpret the results. [Recode HSGRAD as follows: RECODE HSGRAD(LO thru 68=1)(68.1 thru HI=2).]

9

Estimating Relations between Two Continuous Variables: Bivariate Regression and Correlation

Continuous measures, with their assumption of a meaningful distance between numbers along the measurement scale, place at the researcher's disposal a powerful set of tools for evaluating relationships between the measures. In particular, to be able to apply the methods detailed in this chapter, you need to assume the following: (1) the form of relationship is a linear one (as opposed to a curvilinear one, for example), and (2) the distribution of the dependent variable follows a normal curve for every possible outcome of the independent variable. Even when these assumptions are not met and the method is applied, however, the results of the analyses are often quite robust. If one or both of the assumptions are violated, we will not often find that a finding which is observed as statistically significant is in fact not statistically significant, and vice versa.

9.1 An Example Using Bivariate Regression and Correlation: Support for Educational Expenditures and Personal Income

It is reasonable to hypothesize that states' investment of tax dollars in educational expenditures will vary as a function of the educational level of its citizenry. In particular, the higher the average level of education by state, the greater we would expect that state's average investment in education to be. Furthermore, it seems reasonable to assume that the higher the per capita income in a state, all other things being equal, the more money per capita the state will spend on education. All other things being equal, the more money a state collects per capita in income taxes the more we would expect it to invest in education.

The two inferences that we briefly outlined can be thought of as two propositions we have about determinants of states' expenditures for education.

> P1: The more highly educated a state, the higher its investment in education.
> P2: The wealthier a state, the higher its investment in education.

By substituting two operational hypotheses for these concepts, we arrive at two testable hypotheses using the 50-States Data Set.

> H1: The higher the percent of citizens with at least a high school degree, the higher the per capita expenditure on education.
> H2: The higher the per capita income of a state, the higher its per capita expenditure on education.

9.1.1   New Notational Convention for Bivariate Regression and Correlation

A new notational convention for designating variables is now necessary. The dependent variable in an analysis, such as per capita expenditures on schools, is usually designated with a Y, while the independent variable is usually labeled X. The reason will become apparent in the next section, where joint frequency plots on Cartesian coordinates are discussed.

When we estimate the relationship between the dependent variable, Y, and an independent variable, X, we speak of regressing Y on X (i.e., we regress the dependent variable on the independent variable).

9.2   Scatterplots and Regression Lines

When both variables are continuous measures, displaying their relationship requires different techniques than those that have already been described. Combining outcomes on the independent variable to create broader categories for display purposes is one possible solution, but in many cases following this procedure can distort the true relationship between the measures.

An alternative way to present the data visually is with a **scatterplot**. To construct a scatterplot, a set of Cartesian axes is drawn with the independent variable on the horizontal axis (X) and the dependent variable (Y) on the vertical axis. Then the position of each observation in this two-dimensional space is designated by a point corresponding to its X and Y values. If a strong relationship is present between the pair of variables, it should be evident from the scatter of points on the figure.

● **scatterplot**
a type of diagram that displays the covariation of two continuous variables as a set of points on a Cartesian coordinate system

Figure 9.1 displays six different scatterplots. Panels A and B, respectively, show positive and negative relationships in the plots. Panel C displays a null or zero relationship. The other three panels show more complex nonlinear relations. For example, panel D suggests a logarithmic relationship between X and Y, panel E a reciprocal relationship between the two variables, and panel F an exponential relationship. Obviously, all of these scatterplots are highly idealized.

Figure 9.2 is more typical of what one observes with actual data sets. It displays the scatterplot of the joint distribution of the outcomes for per capita school expenditures and the percent with at least a high school diploma (data for this figure are presented in Table 9.1 in the next section). A clear trend is evident from tracing the points from the lower left hand corner of the scatterplot to the upper right hand corner, suggesting that low values on one of the variable cluster with low values on the second variable and high values on the one variable cluster with high values on the second. This scatterplot thus provides visual indication that per capita school expenditures and percent with at least a high school diploma covary positively.

● **linear relationship**
covariation in which the value of the dependent variable is proportional to the value of the independent variable

As useful as a scatterplot is, we need a more precise expression of the relationship between the variables. One possibility is to measure the degree to which the data approximate a **linear relationship.** If the relationship between per capita school

FIGURE 9.1 Examples of Types of Scatterplots

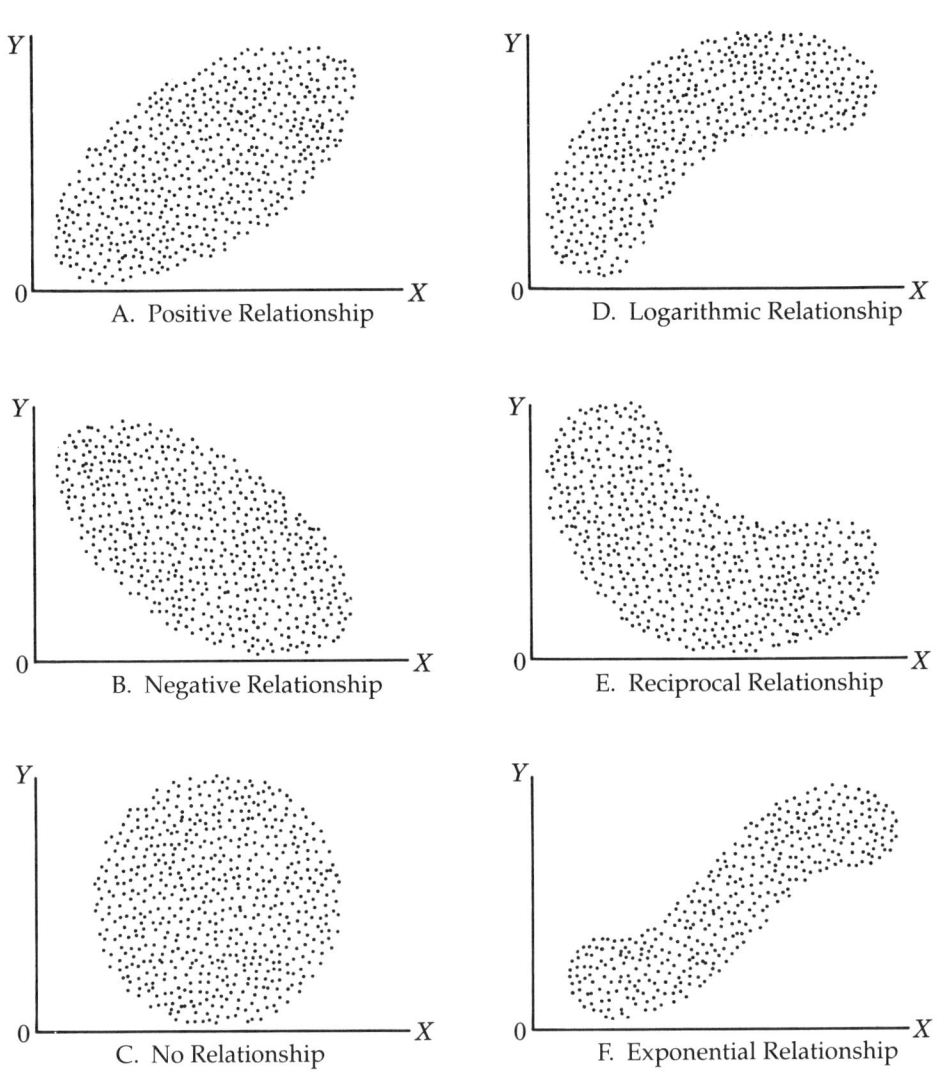

A. Positive Relationship

B. Negative Relationship

C. No Relationship

D. Logarithmic Relationship

E. Reciprocal Relationship

F. Exponential Relationship

expenditures and percent with at least a high school diploma is perfectly linear, all of the data points would fall along a straight line with the slope of the line representing the strength of the relationship. We generally assume that, in the social sciences,

Scatterplot of Educational Expenditures by Percentage with H.S. Diplomas

FIGURE 9.2

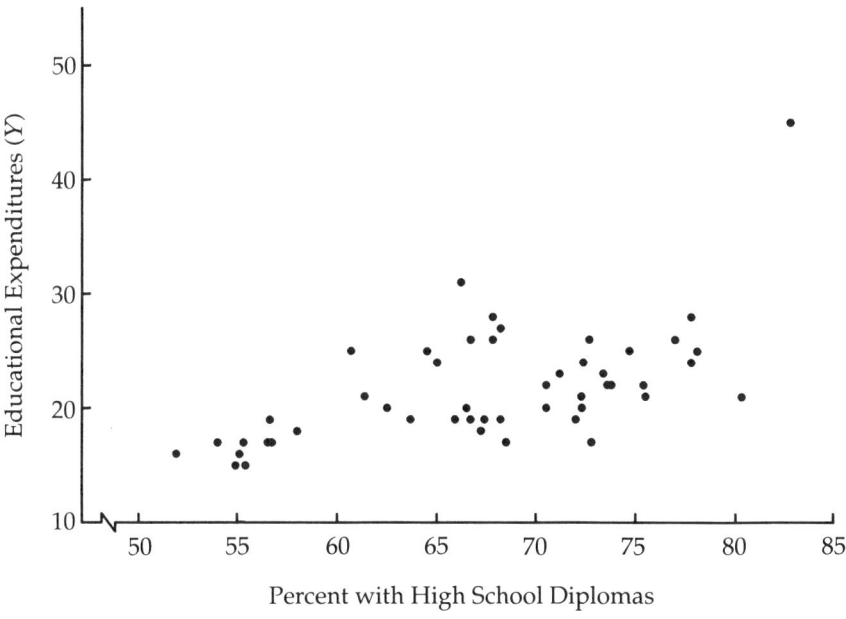

Source: 50-States Data Set.

variables are linearly rather than exponentially related; that rather than following a more general polynomial function they follow a linear one, simply because a linear relationship is the most elemental. Since *parsimony*, or economy in describing relationships between variables, is one of the major goals of science, asking whether a linear function can account for the relationship makes sense as a first step. If a straight line does not adequately describe the form of the relationship, then more complex functional forms, forms that are beyond the scope of this book, will need to be used. (Panels D, E, and F in Figure 9.1 show scatterplots best described by nonlinear mathematical functions.)

In our example, the empirical relationship falls considerably short of perfect linearity, but it does not depart so far from it as to form a random scatter pattern. The scatterplot does *not* suggest that a conventional curvilinear function would better fit the data. We will now describe a technique for measuring how well a straight line describes the tendency for the two continuous variables to covary.

In high school algebra you learned how to write the equation for a straight line for Cartesian coordinates.

$$Y = a + bX$$

The ordinate, or the Y value, is the sum of a constant, a, which is the point at which the line crosses the Y-axis, plus the product of the slope of the line, b, times the X value. For a line to be drawn through the scatter of points, the line must come closer on average to all points in a scatterplot than to any other line that could be drawn.

The equation $Y = a + bX$ assumes that the Ys are exact functions of the Xs. But the model should allow for errors in the prediction of Y from X since empirical relations are almost never perfect. Hence the **regression model** employed is as follows (for the ith observation):

● **regression model**
an equation for the linear relationship between a continuous dependent variable and one or more independent variables, plus an error term

$$Y_i = a + bX_i + e_i$$

The term e_i takes into account that the ith observation is not accounted for perfectly by the following **prediction equation:**

● **prediction equation**
a regression equation without the error term, useful for predicting the score on the dependent variable from the independent variable(s)

$$\hat{Y}_i = a + bX_i$$

For this reason, e_i is called the *error (or residual) term*, a concept introduced in Chapter 8 in our discussion of the analysis of variance model.

● **regression line**
a line that is the best fit to the points in a scatterplot, computed by ordinary least squares regression

This equation, in which the values of a and b are estimated from the scores on Y and X for all observations, is also called the **regression line.** It has the unique property that given any value for X–whether or not such a value occurs for any actual outcome of X—we can predict Y_i, on the assumption that the relationship between X and Y is linear. The predicted scores of Y_i, written $\hat{Y}_i$, can be compared to the actual score, Y_i, for any individual i to see how well the relationship holds and to determine the error term.

$$e_i = Y_i - \hat{Y}_i$$

In the next section we develop the necessary tools to construct a regression equation for fitting a line through the scatterplot.

9.3   The Bivariate Linear Regression Equation

In the per capita educational expenditures example, the procedure for estimating the regression line must make use of all of the information on both variables for each state (the Y for the X value for each state). The estimates of a and b should have the property that the sum of the squared differences between the observed Y and the score predicted by the regression equation, $\hat{Y}_i$, is a minimum sum compared to the quantity obtained using any other straight line.

$$\sum_{i=1}^{N}(Y_i - \hat{Y}_i)^2 = \sum_{i=1}^{N} e_i^2$$

This estimation criterion is called the *least squares* error sum, or more simply, a and b are said to be estimated using **ordinary least squares (OLS)**. Note the similarity between the OLS regression and the variance. As indicated in Chapter 3, the variance has the desirable property of minimizing the sum of all the squared differences for a set of scores. Similarly, the equation for the regression line minimizes the sum of squared errors in prediction.

One useful interpretation of linear regression is that it estimates a **conditional mean** for Y. Regression analysis provides an estimate of the expected value of Y (see Section 6.2.1) for

● **ordinary least squares**
a method for obtaining estimates of regression equation coefficients that minimizes the error sum of squares

● **conditional mean**
the expected average score on the dependent variable, Y, for a given value of the independent variable, X

a given value of the independent variable X_i, on the assumption that the relationship between the variables is linear. If no linear relationship exists between the variables, the regression slope, b, will equal zero, and the expected value, $\hat{Y}_i$, for any value of X_i will simply equal the intercept, a. And the value of a will be the mean score of $\overline{Y}$ for all of the observations (i.e., will equal $\overline{Y}$). Furthermore, if Y and X are linearly related to each other, we will find that the conditional mean of Y is dependent on the outcome of X. Finally, the conditional means will fall on a straight line when plotted.

A visual method that is useful in helping to decide what kind of mathematical function (e.g., linear or nonlinear) best fits a bivariate scatterplot is the examination of the **path of conditional means**. One constructs the path of conditional means by plotting the observed conditional means of the dependent variable, Y, for the various outcomes of the independent variable, X, and connecting the means by straight line segments.

Figure 9.3 displays two examples of paths of conditional means. The data in the upper panel suggest that a straight line will fit the scatterplot quite well. By contrast, a straight line would fit the scatterplot in the lower panel very poorly. Instead an inverted U-shaped function is needed to describe it.

Assuming a linear relationship is the appropriate one for a given scatterplot of data, an empirical estimate of b, the **bivariate regression coefficient**, or the slope of the regression line, is obtained from the observed X and Y scores applying the following formula:

$$b = \frac{\Sigma(X_i - \overline{X})(Y_i - \overline{Y})}{\Sigma(X_i - \overline{X})^2}$$

The numerator is the sum of the product of the deviations of the Xs and the Ys about their respective means. When divided by $N - 1$ in the sample (or N in the population), this term is the **covariance**, and is labeled s_{XY}.

● **path of conditional means** a visual method used to help determine what kind of mathematical function best fits a bivariate scatterplot

● **bivariate regression coefficient** a parameter estimate of a bivariate regression equation that measures the amount of increase or decrease in the dependent variable for a one-unit difference in the independent variable

● **covariance** the sum of the product of deviations of the Xs and Ys about their respective means, divided by N-1 in the sample and N in the population

Two Examples of Paths of Conditional Means

FIGURE 9.3

A. An Approximate Linear Relationship

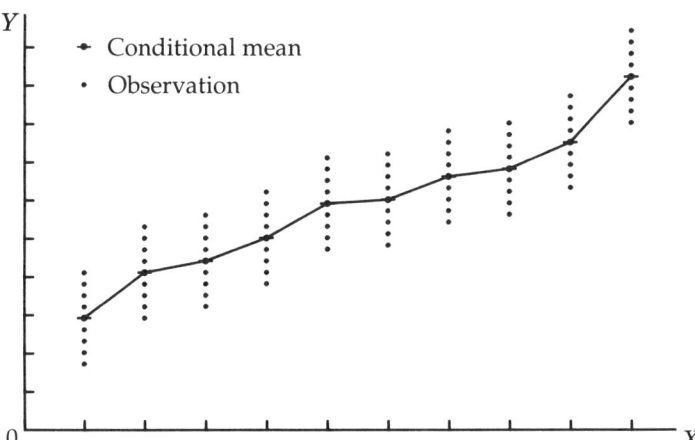

B. An Approximate Inverted U-Shaped Relationship

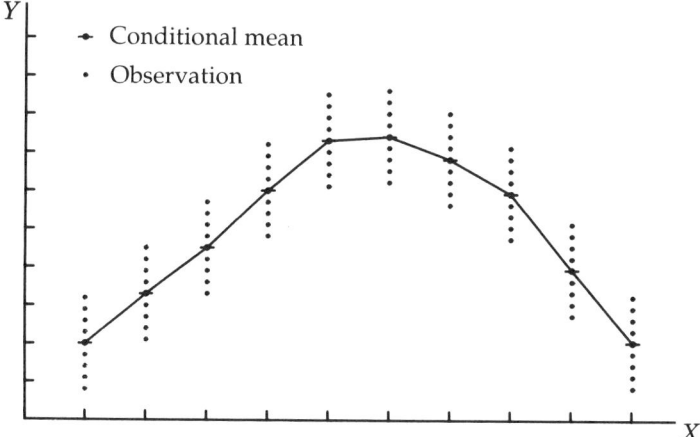

$$s_{XY} = \frac{\Sigma(X_i - \overline{X})(Y_i - \overline{Y})}{N - 1}$$

The denominator of the regression coefficient is the sum of the squared deviations of the independent variable, X, about its mean. If divided by $N - 1$, the term would be the *variance*, a statistic you first encountered in Chapter 3.

$$s_Y^2 = \frac{\sum\limits_{i=1}^{N}(Y_i - \overline{Y})^2}{N - 1}$$

Note that in the formula for b, the $N - 1$ in the numerator has canceled with the $N - 1$ in the denominator. Hence, the slope of the regression line (i.e. the regression coefficient) is estimated by the ratio of the covariance between Y and X to the variance of X.

$$b = \frac{s_{XY}}{s^2_X}$$

● **intercept**
a constant value in a regression equation showing the point at which the regression line crosses the Y axis when values of X equal zero

Although the **intercept** (a) is not derived here, it can be easily estimated by the following:

$$a = \overline{Y} - b\overline{X}$$

Note that if the regression slope, b, is zero, the second term drops out. Then our estimate of the intercept is simply the mean of Y. Thus when Y and X are unrelated, the best fitting regression line will be parallel to the X-axis, passing through the Y-

axis at the sample mean. Knowing a specific value of X will not yield a predicted value of Y different from the mean.

While the two formulas for b just presented are conceptually straightforward, they are unwieldy to use without a computer. If one has a good hand calculator, the following computing formula for b can be used:

$$b = \frac{N\Sigma Y_i X_i - \Sigma Y_i \Sigma X_i}{N\Sigma X^2_i - (\Sigma X_i)^2}$$

We now move to our educational example on per capita expenditures to show how the computing formula for b can be used with actual data.

9.3.1   Linear Regression Applied to Educational Expenditures

To show how the formulas for b and a associated with linear regression are applied to data, Table 9.1 displays the sums, sums of squares and sums of cross products for the educational expenditures and educational achievement data by state. Column 2 displays the sum of the Ys (ΣY), column 3 the sum of the Xs (ΣX), column 4 the sum of the X^2s (ΣX^2), column 5 the sum of the cross products (ΣYX), and column 6 the sum of the Y^2s (ΣY^2). At the bottom of the table all of the relevant summary statistics have been calculated as well, i.e., the means, variances, and the covariance. Following is the general form of the computing formula for the covariance employed in Table 9.1:

$$s_{XY} = \frac{N\Sigma Y_i X_i - \Sigma Y_i \Sigma X_i}{N(N - 1)}$$

TABLE 9.1   Calculation of Means, Variances, Correlation and Regression Coefficients for Educational Expenditures (*Y*) and Percentage with High School Diplomas (*X$_1$*)

(1) Obs No.	(2) Y	(3) X	(4) X^2	(5) YX	(6) Y^2
1	17	56.7	3214.89	963.9	289
2	45	82.8	6855.84	3726.0	2025
3	20	72.3	5227.29	1446.0	400
4	15	54.9	3140.01	823.5	225
5	22	73.6	5416.96	1619.2	484
6	25	78.1	6099.61	1952.5	625
7	22	70.5	4970.25	1551.0	484
8	26	67.8	4596.84	1762.8	676
9	18	67.2	4515.84	1209.6	324
10	17	56.5	3192.25	960.5	289
11	23	73.4	5387.56	1688.2	529
12	17	72.8	5299.84	1237.6	289
13	24	65.0	4225.00	1560.0	576
14	19	65.9	4342.81	1252.1	361
15	23	71.2	5069.44	1637.6	529
16	21	72.3	5227.29	1518.3	441
17	16	51.9	2693.61	830.4	256
18	18	58.0	3364.00	1044.0	324
19	17	68.5	4692.25	1164.5	289
20	26	66.7	4448.89	1890.2	676
21	26	72.7	5285.29	1890.2	676
22	27	68.2	4651.24	1841.4	729
23	24	72.4	5241.76	1737.6	576
24	16	55.1	3036.01	881.6	256
25	19	63.7	4057.69	1210.3	361
26	22	75.4	5685.16	1658.8	484
27	22	73.8	5446.44	1623.6	484
28	21	75.5	5700.25	1585.5	441
29	19	72.0	5184.00	1368.0	361
30	28	67.8	4596.04	1898.4	784
31	19	68.2	4651.24	1295.8	361
32	31	66.2	4382.44	2052.2	961
33	17	55.3	3058.09	940.1	289
34	20	66.5	4422.25	1330.0	400
35	19	67.4	4542.76	1280.6	361
36	19	66.7	4448.89	1267.3	361

Table 9.1 (continued)

(1) Obs No.	(2) Y	(3) X	(4) X²	(5) YX	(6) Y²
37	25	74.7	5580.09	1867.5	625
38	25	64.5	4160.25	1612.5	625
39	25	60.7	3684.49	1517.5	625
40	17	54.0	2916.00	918.0	289
41	17	68.5	4692.25	1164.5	289
42	15	55.4	3069.16	831.0	225
43	21	61.4	3769.96	1289.4	441
44	21	80.3	6448.09	1686.3	441
45	20	70.5	4970.25	1410.0	400
46	20	62.5	3906.25	1250.0	400
47	26	77.0	5929.00	2002.0	676
48	19	56.6	3203.56	1075.4	361
49	24	77.8	6052.84	2178.4	784
50	28	77.8	6052.84	2178.4	784
SUMS(Σs)	1083	3366.9	229527.01	74025.8	24733

$$\overline{Y} = 1083/50 = 21.6$$

$$\overline{X} = 3366.9/50 = 67.338$$

$$s_Y^2 = \frac{50(24,733) - (1083)^2}{50(49)} = 26.025$$

$$s_X^2 = \frac{50(229,527.01) - (3366.9)^2}{50(49)} = 57.280$$

$$s_{XY} = \frac{50(74,025.8) - (1083)(3366.9)}{50(49)} = 22.423$$

Using these values, it is easy to compute as follows:

$$b = \frac{50(74,025.8) - (1083)(3366.9)}{50(229,527.01) - (3366.9)^2}$$

$$= 0.391$$

Or alternatively,

$$b = s_{XY}/s_X^2 = 22.423/57.280 = 0.391$$

The b coefficient has a simple interpretation. The bivariate regression coefficient measures the average amount of increase or decrease in the dependent variable for a one-unit change in the independent variable. In this example, therefore, every percent increase in the citizenry with a high school diploma is associated with an average increase in educational expenditures of $391 ($0.391 \times 1000$).

To complete the calculation of the bivariate OLS regression equation, we also need to calculate our estimate of the intercept term, a. Since $\overline{X} = 67.338$, $\overline{Y} = 21.660$, and $b = 0.391$, we can compute that

$$a = 21.660 - (0.391)67.338 = -4.70$$

Thus the prediction equation may be written as follows:

$$\hat{Y}_i = -4.70 + 0.391X_i$$

In a later section we will show how to test for whether this relationship is statistically different from zero. First, however, we show the regression line graphed onto its scatterplot, as has been done in Figure 9.4.

In this figure, the regression line through the scatterplot intercepts the Y-axis at -4.70 and it has a positive slope of 0.391. While the line passes through or close to several data points, most observations fall off the line, about as many above as below. Note that the regression line passes exactly through the point which is the mean of both Y and X. This relationship follows from the formula for the calculation of the intercept, a.

Figure 9.4 can also be used to illustrate the concept of *residuals*, or *errors in prediction*. As noted in Section 9.2, a residual, or error, is simply the difference between an observed value and the value predicted using the regression equation, that is, $e_i = Y_i - \hat{Y}_i$. We have shown two such residuals, or errors in prediction, for observations 32 and 44 in Figure 9.4. Our ability to calculate the errors of prediction provides a measure of the degree of linear association between continuous variables, as will be explained in the next section.

Scatterplot of Educational Expenditures by Percentage with H.S. Diplomas, with Regression Line

FIGURE 9.4

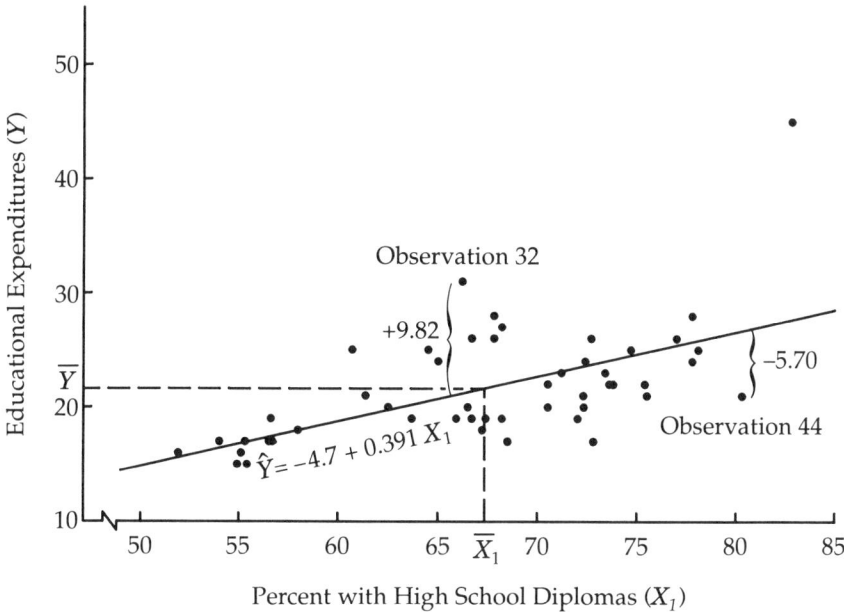

Source: 50-States Data Set.

9.4   Measuring Association: The Coefficient of Determination and the Correlation Coefficient

Linear regression analysis is not limited to estimating an equation showing the precise quantitative relationship between two variables. It can also be used to determine the strength of association between the pair of variables. One way to determine the strength of association is to ascertain how close the observed values are to the regression line. As pointed out several times earlier, in the ideal case all of the observations would fall exactly on the regression line. In this case we would be able to predict the Y scores without error simply based on our knowledge about outcomes on the X variable. But when using actual data, perfect prediction simply is not observed. Instead, the observed scores are thought of as due to a systematic component due to X and to a random error component. We can partition the total sum of squares into a systematic and a random component, just as we did in the previous chapter on ANOVA.

If we begin with the observation Y_i, which has been centered about its mean (i.e., $Y_i - \overline{Y}$), the following identity can be constructed:

$$(Y_i - \overline{Y}) = (Y_i - \hat{Y}_i) + (\hat{Y}_i - \overline{Y})$$

Thus an observation can be seen to be a function of two components. The first component, $Y_i - \hat{Y}_i$, indicates the discrepancy between an observation and the predicted value for that observation. Recall that this discrepancy is simply e_i. The second component, $\hat{Y}_i - \overline{Y}$ is that part of the observed score that can be accounted for by the regression line. You can see this clearer by examining Figure 9.5 where a single observation deviated from the mean is shown as a function of both a regression component and an error component.

● **regression sum of squares**
a number obtained in linear regression by subtracting the mean of a set of scores from the value predicted by linear regression, squaring, and summing these values

If we square and sum the components shown above, they are called the **regression sum of squares** and the **error sum of squares**. If we rearrange the terms, we observe the following:

$$\Sigma(Y_i - \overline{Y})^2 = \Sigma(\hat{Y}_i - \overline{Y})^2 + \Sigma(Y_i - \hat{Y}_i)^2$$

Or

$$SS_{\text{TOTAL}} = SS_{\text{REGRESSION}} + SS_{\text{ERROR}}$$

● **error sum of squares**
a numerical value obtained in linear regression by subtracting the regression sum of squares from the total sum of squares

Method of Accounting for an Observation by the Regression Line and an Error Component

FIGURE 9.5

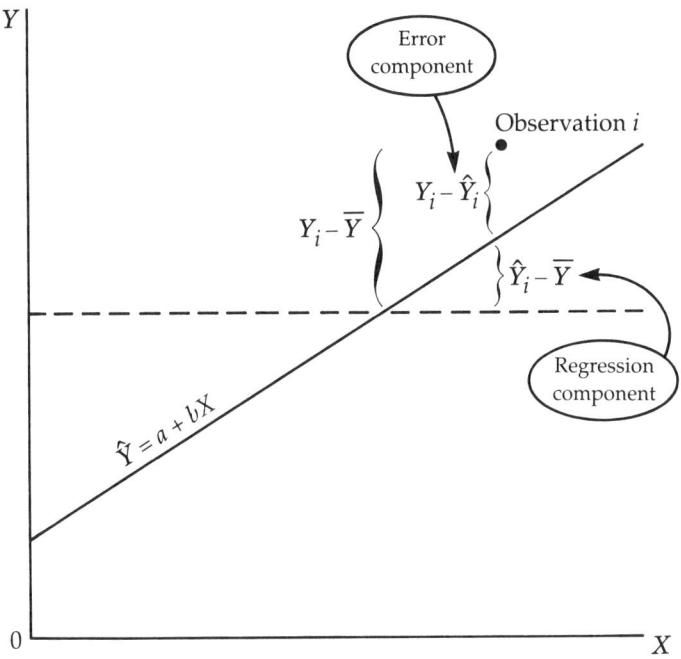

This formulation is obviously very similar to that used in ANOVA, in which, as described in Chapter 8, $SS_{TOTAL} = SS_{BETWEEN} + SS_{WITHIN}$. (The term SS_{ERROR} used in regression is analogous to SS_{WITHIN} used in ANOVA.) The difference, however, is an important one. In ANOVA we make no assumption about the form of the relationship between the independent and the dependent variable. We only seek to know how much variation in SS_{TOTAL} can be explained as a function of the various outcomes of the independent variable. In ANOVA we have a very general statement of the functional form between Y and X, symbolized by $Y = f(X)$, which merely means that Y is *some* function of X although we don't know the form of that function. But in regression analysis we assume that the relationship between the independent and the dependent variable can be described by the equation for a straight line, i.e., $Y = f(X)$ where $f(X) = a + bX$. Therefore, ANOVA can be thought of as a more general model than regression (not better, just more general).

What is the *maximum possible error of prediction* we might make using a regression model in predicting Y from X? As we saw earlier in the chapter, if we have no information at all about the relationship between the two variables, the best single prediction we could make for Y, is the sample mean, $\overline{Y}$, for every value of X observed. In the absence of any knowledge about the functional form linking Y to X the sum of squared errors, $\Sigma(Y_i - \hat{Y}_i)^2$ becomes $\Sigma(Y_i - \overline{Y})^2$ when substituting the mean for Y_i. As we noted in Section 3.2.5 in Chapter 3, $\sum_{i=1}^{N}(Y_i - \overline{Y})^2$ is the numerator of the variance of Y or s_Y^2. These two terms, the sum of the squared errors for regression ($SS_{REGRESSION}$) and the sum of the squared errors about the mean (SS_{TOTAL}), give us all the information we need to construct a **proportional reduction in error**, or **PRE** measure of association for linear regression. As shown in Chapter 5, all PRE measures take on this general form:

● proportional reduction in error (PRE)
a characteristic of some measures of association that allows the calculation of reduction in errors in predicting the dependent variable, given knowledge of its relationship to an independent variable

$$PRE\ statistic = \frac{\text{Error without decision rule} - \text{Error with decision rule}}{\text{Error without decision rule}}$$

The linear regression equation can be considered to be one rule for making decisions (predictions) about expected Y values (i.e., means conditional on the X values). If any relationship exists between Y and X, the linear prediction will result in a smaller error of prediction than relying only on guessing the mean. Therefore, as the degree of predictability from X to Y increases, the size of prediction errors that result is reduced.

● coefficient of determination
a PRE statistic for linear regression that expresses the amount of variation in the dependent variable explained or accounted for by the independent variable(s) in a regression equation.

9.4.1   The Coefficient of Determination

The PRE statistic used with linear regression is called the **coefficient of determination**, because it indicates the proportion of total variation in Y "determined" by X. Its symbol is

R_{YX}^2 (read "R squared"). Substituting the two prediction components into the general PRE formula yields the following:

$$R_{YX}^2 = \frac{\Sigma(Y_i - \overline{Y})^2 - \Sigma(Y_i - \hat{Y}_i)^2}{\Sigma(Y_i - \overline{Y})^2}$$

Or

$$R_{YX}^2 = \frac{SS_{TOTAL} - SS_{ERROR}}{SS_{TOTAL}}$$

$$= 1 - \frac{SS_{ERROR}}{SS_{TOTAL}}$$

The coefficient of determination, R_{YX}^2, is 1 minus the ratio of error sum of squares to the total sum of squares. Note that when SS_{ERROR} is zero, $R_{YX}^2 = 1.0$. But when $SS_{ERROR} = SS_{TOTAL}$ (i.e., all the variation is error variance), $R_{YX}^2 = 0.0$. Also note that since $SS_{REGRESSION} = SS_{TOTAL} - SS_{ERROR}$, this must follow:

$$R_{YX}^2 = \frac{SS_{REGRESSION}}{SS_{TOTAL}}$$

(Section 8.9 established that $\eta^2 = SS_{BETWEEN}/SS_{TOTAL}$.) The coefficient of determination, therefore, equals the proportion of total sum of squares accounted for fitting a least squares regression line to the data.

An alternative approach to computing the coefficient of determination involves using the covariance and the variances. In particular the coefficient of determination equals the ratio of the square of the covariance between X and Y to the product of the variances of each variable.

$$R^2_{YX} = \frac{s^2_{XY}}{s^2_X s^2_Y}$$

To be able to calculate the coefficient of determination using the formula above, we use the calculating formula for the covariance introduced in Section 9.3.

$$s_{XY} = \frac{N \sum_{i=1}^{N} Y_i X_i - \sum_{i=1}^{N} Y_i \sum_{i=1}^{N} X_i}{N(N-1)}$$

Using the data in Table 9.1, we compute the following:

$$s_{XY} = \frac{50(74{,}025.8) - (1083)(3366.9)}{50(49)}$$

$$= 22.423$$

We can use the sums of columns in Table 9.1 to compute $s^2_X = 57.280$ and $s^2_Y = 26.025$, as well. Using all of this information in the formula for the coefficient of determination, we now calculate.

$$R^2_{YX} = \frac{22.423^2}{(26.025)(57.280)} = 0.337$$

Since the largest value the coefficient of determination can reach is 1.00 and the minimum value is zero, it can be interpreted as the proportion or percentage of total variation in Y which can be attributed to its linear relationship with X. In the example, 33.8% of the variation in educational expenditures can be "explained" (in a statistical sense rather than in a causal sense) by the percentage of the state's citizens with at least a high school diploma. A bivariate association of this magnitude is quite large by nonexperimental social science standards.

The quantity $1 - R^2_{YX}$ is the amount of variance in the variable Y that cannot be explained by X. This quantity is called the **coefficient of nondetermination.** In our example this coefficient is $1 - 0.337 = 0.663$; that is, 66.3% of the variance in Y is *not* explained by X.

9.4.2   The Correlation Coefficient

In social science research the linear relationship between two continuous measures often is presented, not as R^2_{YX}, but as its square root. The square root, called the Pearson product-moment **correlation coefficient** after the famous statistician, Karl Pearson, is shown here.

$$r_{XY} = \sqrt{R^2_{YX}}$$

Since, as we saw above, R^2_{YX} is defined as $R^2_{YX} = s^2_{XY}/(s^2_X s^2_Y)$, the following is also true:

$$r_{XY} = \frac{s_{XY}}{s_X s_Y}$$

Pearson's r_{XY} has a positive or a negative sign attached to it to indicate the direction of the covariation. This sign must agree with the sign of the regression coefficient (b). In the educational expenditure example, the correlation between educational expenditures and the percentage in the state with at least a high school diploma was found to be 0.581. Unlike R^2_{YX}, r_{XY} can range between -1.00 for a perfect inverse association to $+1.00$ for a perfect direct association, with $r_{XY} = 0$ indicating no relationship between X and Y. The usefulness of the correlation coefficient lies in its communication of directionality. By contrast, R^2_{YX} conceals whether the variables are directly or inversely related.

● **coefficient of nondetermination**
a statistic that expresses the amount of variation in a dependent variable that is left *un*explained by the independent variable(s) in a regression equation

● **correlation coefficient**
a measure of association between two continuous variables that estimates the direction and strength of a linear relationship

The correlation coefficient is *symmetric*, in particular $r_{XY} = r_{YX}$. This means that the correlation between X and Y is the same as the correlation between Y and X. By contrast, you should convince yourself that b_{YX} does *not* equal b_{XY}. Regressing X on Y does *not*, in general, yield the same regression coefficient as the regression of Y on X.

9.4.3   Correlating Z Scores

When we correlate two variables that have been converted to Z scores, some interesting results emerge. The standard deviation of a Z score is always 1.0 as we noted in Section 3.3 in Chapter 3. Since, in general $r_{XY} = s_{XY}/(s_X s_Y)$, for two Z scores, it follows that

$$r_{Z_X Z_Y} = \frac{s_{Z_X Z_Y}}{s_{Z_X} s_{Z_Y}} = \frac{s_{Z_X Z_Y}}{(1)(1)} = s_{Z_X Z_Y}$$

The correlation between two Z scores, then, equals the covariance of two Z scores!

Furthermore, since $s_{Z_X Z_Y} = \Sigma(Z_X - \overline{Z}_X)(Z_Y - \overline{Z}_Y)/(N - 1)$ and $\overline{Z}_X = \overline{Z}_Y = 0$ (i.e., the mean of a Z score is zero), it follows that

$$r_{Z_X Z_Y} = s_{Z_X Z_Y} = \frac{\Sigma Z_X Z_Y}{N - 1}$$

The correlation between two standardized variables, Z_X and Z_Y, is the sum of the product of the two variables divided by $N - 1$. (In the population, this correlation is the sum of products divided by N instead of $N - 1$.)

Since $Z_X = (X - \overline{X})/s_X$ and $Z_Y = (Y - \overline{Y})/s_Y$, it follows that

$$r_{Z_X Z_Y} = \frac{\Sigma Z_X Z_Y}{N - 1}$$

$$= \frac{\Sigma[(X - \overline{X})/s_X][(Y - \overline{Y})/s_Y]}{N - 1}$$

$$= \frac{\Sigma(X - \overline{X})(Y - \overline{Y})/(N-1)}{s_X s_Y}$$

$$= \frac{s_{XY}}{s_X s_Y}$$

$$= r_{XY}$$

The correlation between two Z-transformed variables, Z_X and Z_Y, is the same as the correlation between the original variables X and Y. The correlation coefficient is unaffected by whether the variables are in raw form or have been Z-transformed.

9.4.4   The Relation of Regression and Correlation Coefficients

The relationship between a regression coefficient and a correlation coefficient is easy to show in the bivariate case. First, we recall that the regression coefficient (b) can be expressed as follows:

$$b = \frac{s_{XY}}{s_X^2}$$

Solving for s_{XY}, we get

$$s_{XY} = bs_X^2$$

Next, we substitute bs_X^2 for s_{XY} in the expression, $r_{XY} = \dfrac{s_{XY}}{s_X s_Y}$, which gives us $r_{XY} = bs_X^2 (s_x s_Y)$.

Simplifying gives us an expression for r_{XY} in terms of b.

$$r_{XY} = b \frac{s_X}{s_Y}$$

And conversely,

$$b = r_{XY} \frac{s_Y}{s_X}$$

Therefore if we know b, s_x and s_y we can easily determine r_{XY}. Or if we know r_{XY}, s_X, and s_y we can easily determine b.

9.5   Standardized Regression or Beta Coefficients

Regression coefficients provide a clear interpretation of the linear relationship between two variables with unambiguous units of measurement. However, they can be difficult to interpret when the unit of the variables is not clear. Many variables in the social sciences that researchers regard as continuous have no natural or universal unit of measure. Examples of such variables include industrialization, religiosity, alienation, and socioeconomic status. Because of this lack of a natural unit of measurement, many researchers prefer to standardize their variables, i.e., convert them to Z scores prior to carrying out their analyses.

Z scores always have a mean of zero and a standard deviation of 1, and, as we showed in the preceding section $r_{XY} = b(s_X/s_Y)$. But we standardize both X and Y by converting them to Z scores, s_X and s_Y both equal unity (1.0), and the regression coefficient for the standardized scores equals the correlation coefficient, r_{XY}.

The regression coefficient for standardized variables is commonly called the **beta coefficient**, or **beta weight**, for which β^* is the symbol.[1] As the preceding section suggests, for bivariate regression analysis the following applies:

● **beta coefficient (beta weight)** a standardized regression coefficient indicating the amount of net change, in standard deviation units, of the dependent variable for an independent variable change of one standard deviation.

$$\beta^* = r_{XY}$$

Since Z scores convert variables to standard deviation units, the interpretation of β^* is as follows: For a standard deviation difference in X, the predicted difference in Y is β^* standard deviations. In the educational expenditures example, the correlation coefficient of 0.581 between per capita educational expenditures and percent with at least a high school diploma indicates that each standard deviation increase in the percent with at least a high school diploma produces an expected 0.581 standard deviation change in per capita educational expenditures, i.e., $(0.581)(5.101) \times 1000 = \$2970$ in educational expenditures, where, as you might recall, 5.101 is the standard deviation of Y.

Since $a = \overline{Y} - b\overline{X}$ for raw, unstandardized data, and since the mean of a standardized variable is zero, the intercept of the regression coefficient when both X and Y are converted to Z

---

[1] We have starred (∗) the beta coefficient (β) to differentiate it from the population parameter β, to be introduced in the next section.

scores is zero. This is true because $a = 0 - b(0) = 0$. The prediction equation for two standardized variables Z_X and Z_Y is as follows:

$$\hat{Z}_Y = \beta * Z_X$$

$$= r_{XY}Z_X$$

9.6   Significance Tests for Bivariate Regression and Correlation

Like other descriptive statistics, regression and correlation coefficients are estimated on data sampled from a larger population of potential observations. The important question to be answered is as follows: What is the probability, given the observed sample correlation and regression coefficients, that the population parameters being estimated are zero? In other words, we need to investigate what inferential statistics can be calculated to test the statistical significance of the regression and correlation coefficients.

The t test introduced in Chapter 6 and Chapter 7, and the F test, introduced in Chapter 8, are the basic inferential statistics for testing the significance of relationships among continuous data. In this section we will show how these tests can be applied to R_{YX}^2, b, a, and r_{XY}.

9.6.1   Testing the Significance of the Coefficient of Determination

To test R_{YX}^2 for statistical significance, we will use an F test very similar to that used in the analysis of variance in Chapter 8.

We know from Section 8.5 that SS_{TOTAL} has $N - 1$ degrees of freedom associated with it. And we know that $SS_{\text{REGRESSION}}$, defined in Section 9.4, is estimated from a single function of the

$X_i s$, namely b, and it has 1 degree of freedom associated with it. Since $df_{\text{TOTAL}} = df_{\text{REGRESSION}} + df_{\text{ERROR}}$ and $N - 1 = 1 + df_{\text{ERROR}}$, it follows that $df_{\text{ERROR}} = N - 2$.

We can construct the **mean square regression** and **mean square error** by dividing the appropriate sums of squares by their associated degrees of freedom, in much the same way as we did for mean square within and mean square between for ANOVA in Chapter 8.

● **mean square regression**
a value in linear regression obtained by dividing the regression sum of squares by its degrees of freedom

● **mean square error**
a value in linear regression obtained by dividing the error sum of squares by its degrees of freedom

$$MS_{\text{REGRESSION}} = \frac{SS_{\text{REGRESSION}}}{1}$$

$$MS_{\text{ERROR}} = \frac{SS_{\text{ERROR}}}{N - 2}$$

Where ρ^2_{YX} (Greek letter *rho*) refers to the population coefficient of determination, it can be proven that if the null hypothesis, H_0: $\rho^2_{YX} = 0$, is true, then both $MS_{\text{REGRESSION}}$ and MS_{ERROR} are unbiased estimates of σ^2_e, the variances of prediction errors (i.e., the e_i). If, however, $\sigma^2_e > 0$ *in the population, we would also expect that* $MS_{\text{REGRESSION}} > MS_{\text{ERROR}}$ in the sample.

Since the F ratio is simply the ratio of two estimates of the same variance, σ^2_e in this case, it follows that we can test the null hypothesis that $\rho^2_{YX} = 0$ in the population by choosing an α level and calculating.

$$F_{1, N-2} = \frac{MS_{\text{REGRESSION}}}{MS_{\text{ERROR}}}$$

If the obtained value of F is as large or larger than the critical value for a given α level, the obtained value of R^2_{YX} is significantly greater than zero. If the obtained F is not larger, we cannot reject the hypothesis that $\rho^2_{YX} = 0$ in the population.

There are several ways to compute $SS_{\text{REGRESSION}}$. The most straightforward one follows from the knowledge that $R^2_{YX} = SS_{\text{REGRESSION}}/SS_{\text{TOTAL}}$, as we showed in Section 9.4.1. From this it follows directly that

$$SS_{\text{REGRESSION}} = R^2_{YX}SS_{\text{TOTAL}}$$

Recall the definition for the variance given in Chapter 3.

$$s^2_Y = \frac{\sum_{i=1}^{N}(Y_i - \overline{Y})^2}{N - 1}$$

And further recall the expression in Section 8.4.

$$SS_{\text{TOTAL}} = \Sigma(Y_i - \overline{Y})^2$$

From these two facts, we can state the following:

$$SS_{\text{TOTAL}} = s^2_Y (N - 1)$$

We can easily use this information to deduce SS_{ERROR}, and since $SS_{\text{TOTAL}} = SS_{\text{REGRESSION}} + SS_{\text{ERROR}}$, we deduce the following:

$$SS_{\text{ERROR}} = SS_{\text{TOTAL}} - SS_{\text{REGRESSION}}$$

In the per capita educational expenditures example (see Table 9.1), $s^2_Y = 26.025$. We also know that $R^2_{YX} = 0.337$ and $N = 50$. Therefore, using the formulas in the three boxes immediately above, we can compute that

$$SS_{TOTAL} = (26.025)(49) = 1765.225$$

$$SS_{REGRESSION} = (0.337)(1765.225) = 594.881$$

And

$$SS_{ERROR} = 1765.225 - 594.881 = 1170.334$$

Furthermore,

$$MS_{REGRESSION} = 594.881/1 = 594.881$$

And

$$MS_{ERROR} = 1170.344/(50 - 2) = 24.382$$

If we fix $\alpha = .05$, we see from Appendix E that the critical value for an F with 1 and 60 degrees of freedom is 4.00. But our test statistic is $F_{1, 48} = 594.801/24.382 = 24.395$. Hence we can easily reject the null hypothesis that $\rho_{YX}^2 = 0$ in the population.

Once we have finished these computations we can summarize them in an ANOVA table, such as Table 9.2.

9.6.2   Testing the Significance of b and a

The conventional representation of a sample statistic is to use italic English letters, while Greek letters stand for population parameters. Hence the bivariate regression equation for sample data can be expressed as follows:

$$\hat{Y} = a + bX$$

And we can write the **population regression equation.**

● **population regression equation** a regression equation for a population rather than a sample

$$\hat{Y} = \alpha + \beta X$$

The population parameters, α and β, are to be estimated by a and b in the sample data.

TABLE 9.2   ANOVA Summary Table for Per Capita Educational Expenditures Example

Source	df	SS	MS	F
Regression	1	594.881	594.881	24.395*
Error	48	1170.334	24.382	
Total	49	1765.225		

* Significant at α = .05.

Do not confuse β with the beta coefficient (β^*) described earlier. Also do not confuse this alpha with the same symbol used to designate probability levels. This need for many symbols to play double and triple duty is an unfortunate aspect of the field of statistics. You will have to learn to accommodate this confusing practice by keeping alert to the context in which the symbols are used. Doing so should make it relatively easy for you to keep their uses straight.

The null hypothesis asserts that the population parameter is zero: H_0: β = 0. As with many other statistics drawn from large populations, a sample regression coefficient, b, has a known sampling distribution. To determine whether b is significantly different from zero, we will construct a t test to determine significance, just as we have done to determine the statistical significance of several other statistics (e.g., to determine whether the difference between two means is different than zero). We construct the t test for the null hypothesis in bivariate regression as follows:

$$t = \frac{b - \beta}{s_b}$$

$$= \frac{b - 0}{s_b}$$

Where s_b equals the sample estimate of σ_b.

To be able to construct this ratio we need the sample estimate of β, namely b and an estimate of the standard error of b or s_b. The *standard error*, a concept introduced in Chapter 6, is the standard deviation of the sampling distribution of b.

If we assume that, in the population being sampled, Y is normally distributed for every outcome of X, and we further assume that the variance of the errors of prediction is the same for every outcome of X (i.e., the variance exhibits *homoscedasticity*), then the sampling distribution of b will be normally distributed as N gets large. The mean of the sampling distribution will equal β, the true population regression coefficient and

$$\sigma_b^2 = \frac{\sigma_e^2}{\Sigma(X_i - \overline{X})^2}$$

It may not be obvious, but these results are due to the central limit theorem, which was used in Chapter 6 to derive the sampling distribution for the mean.

As an estimate of the variance of errors in prediction, σ_e^2, we can simply use MS_{ERROR} from the significance test for R_{YX}^2.

$$\hat{\sigma}_e = \sqrt{MS_{ERROR}}$$

There are $N - 2$ degrees of freedom associated with this t test since those are the df associated with MS_{ERROR}. With these facts established we can now construct a t ratio.

$$t_{N-2} = \frac{b - \beta}{\sqrt{\dfrac{MS_{\text{ERROR}}}{\Sigma(X_i - \overline{X})^2}}}$$

$$= \frac{b - 0}{\sqrt{\dfrac{MS_{\text{ERROR}}}{s_X^2(N - 1)}}}$$

Using the per capita educational expenditures example, we can compute.

$$t_{(50 - 2)} = \frac{0.391}{\sqrt{\dfrac{24.382}{(57.280)(49)}}}$$

$$= \frac{0.391}{0.0932} = 4.20$$

For $\alpha = .05$ and $df = 48$, the critical value in Appendix D is estimated to be approximately 2.01. Since $t_{48} = 4.20$ we reject the hypothesis that $\beta = 0$ in the population. We can conclude with little chance of being wrong in our population of states, that per capita educational expenditures and the percent with at least a high school diploma covary in a positive direction.

The intercept, a, can also be tested for statistical significance with a t test.

$$t_{N-2} = \frac{a - \alpha}{\sqrt{\dfrac{MS_{\text{ERROR}}}{N}}}$$

In the example, for $\alpha = .05$, $a = -4.70$, and $df = 48$, we can test the hypothesis that $\alpha = 0$ in the population as follows:

$$t_{48} = \frac{-4.70 - 0}{\sqrt{\dfrac{24.382}{50}}}$$

$$= -11.246$$

This result is highly significant, since the critical value is -2.01, the negative of the value used in testing for the statistical significance for b.

9.6.3   Confidence Intervals

The standard error of b, s_b, can be used to construct a confindence interval around the sample estimate, in a fashion similar to the confidence interval constructed around the sample mean in chapters 6 and 7. Again, we decide on a probability level, this time selecting a corresponding t value for a two-tailed test (since the interval will be symmetrical around the observed value). If we pick $\alpha = .05$, the critical value for $df = 48$ rounds to ± 2.01. The upper and lower 95% confidence intervals are $b + s_b(2.01)$ and $b - s_b(2.01)$.

In the per capita educational expenditures example, the confidence interval is bounded by $0.391 + 0.0932(2.01) = 0.578$ and $0.391 - 0.0932(2.01) = 0.204$. Therefore the confidence interval ranges from 0.204 to 0.578. Remember that the correct interpretation of a confidence interval is as follows: In repeated samples of size N, the confidence intervals computed will contain the population parameter, β, 95% of the time. It is *incorrect* to state that the population parameter has a 95% chance of being inside the interval (either it is in the interval or it is not!).

If we had a much larger sample of cases, the t ratio for the $\alpha = .05$ interval would be 1.96 (i.e., the Z score for a two-tailed test using the normal distribution). Since this value is very close to 2.00, a statistical rule of thumb has been developed which asserts that if a regression coefficient is twice its standard error in size, the b is significant at the .05 level. In general, the upper and lower confidence intervals for a given α level are $b \pm s_b$ (c.v.).

9.6.4   Testing the Significance of the Correlation Coefficient

Since the correlation coefficient, r_{XY}, is the square root of the coefficient of determination, R_{YX}^2, and since we determined above that its value of 0.337 for our example of per capita educational expenditures is statistically significant, it must also logically be true that the observed correlation $r_{XY} = 0.581$ is statistically significant.

There is a separate statistic to test for the significance of the correlation coefficient, however, and we present it here. To test the null hypothesis, H_0: $\rho_{XY} = 0$, where ρ_{XY} is the symbol for the population correlation coefficient, we will use the Z-score table in Appendix C to determine the probability of observing a given r_{XY} under H_0. The **r-to-Z transformation**, which was developed by the celebrated English statistician, R.A. Fisher, is a function of the natural logarithm.

● **r-to-Z transformation** a natural logarithm transformation in the value of the correlation coefficient to a Z score, to test the probability of observing r under the null hypothesis

$$ Z = \left(\frac{1}{2}\right) \ln \left(\frac{1 + r_{XY}}{1 - r_{XY}}\right) $$

Modern pocket calculators with a natural logarithm key make such a calculation effortless. In case you do not have this function on your calculator, an r-to-Z table in Appendix F gives values for virtually all possible correlation coefficients.

The variance of Z is a function of the sample size.

$$ \hat{\sigma}_Z^2 = \frac{1}{N - 3} $$

And the test statistic is as follows:

$$ Z = \frac{Z_r - Z_{\rho_0}}{\hat{\sigma}_Z} $$

If the hypothesized population value of the correlation is zero, then $Z\rho_0 = 0$. Since we already know that $r_{XY} = 0.581$ is significantly different from zero, we can test a different hypothesis. For example, what is the probability that $\rho_{XY} = .60$, given that the sample correlation is 0.581 and $N = 50$? The r-to-Z transformations are 0.662 and 0.693, respectively, while $\hat{\sigma}_Z^2$ is 0.0213. Hence the ratio, distributed approximately as a Z score following the normal distribution, is computed as follows:

$$\frac{0.693 - 0.662}{\sqrt{0.0213}} = 0.212$$

This Z value falls considerably short of the critical value necessary to reject the hypothesis, even at $\alpha = .05$ using a one-tailed test. Therefore, we conclude that we cannot reject the hypothesis that population correlation is 0.60.

This chapter concludes our treatment of topics related to bivariate regression and correlation. Our treatment is merely an introduction. In more advanced courses you will learn more about how to do regression analyses with more than a single independent variable. You will also learn how to use functional forms other than a straight line to fit the relationship between a dependent and one or more independent variables.

Key Concepts and Symbols

These key concepts and symbols are listed in the order of appearance in the chapter. Combined with the definitions in the margins, these will help you review the material and can serve as a self-test for mastery of the concepts.

scatterplot
linear relationship
regression model
prediction equation
regression line
ordinary least squares
  (OLS)
conditional mean
path of conditional means
bivariate regression
  coefficient
covariance
intercept
regression sum of squares
error sum of squares
proportional reduction in
  error (PRE)
coefficient of determination
coefficient of
  nondetermination
correlation coefficient
beta coefficient (beta
  weight)
mean square regression
mean square error

population regression
  equation
r-to-Z transformation
$\hat{Y}_i$
e_i
b
s_{XY}
SS_{TOTAL}
$SS_{\text{REGRESSION}}$
SS_{ERROR}
R^2_{YX}
r_{XY}
$r_{Z_X Z_Y}$
$s_{Z_X Z_Y}$
$\beta*$
$\hat{Z}_Y$
$MS_{\text{REGRESSION}}$
MS_{ERROR}
ρ^2_{YX}
σ^2_e
σ^2_b
$\hat{\sigma}_e$
ρ_{XY}
$\hat{\sigma}^2_Z$
Z_{ρ_0}

Problems

General Problems

1. Construct a scatterplot for the following data on ten persons, showing the relationship between fathers' education and high school freshmen's estimate of the probability that they will go to college, and provide a verbal description of the relationship:

Person (i)	Probability of attending college (Y)	Fathers' years of schooling (X_1)
1	.3	12
2	.2	10
3	.6	14
4	.1	8
5	.7	16
6	.5	12
7	.4	12
8	.8	16
9	.9	18
10	.4	17

2. For the data in Problem 1 solve the following:

    a. Show the predicted regression equation.
    b. Calculate the expressed probability of going to college given one's father has 16 years of college.
    c. Calculate the covariance between the probability of attending college and the number of years one's father went to school.
    d. Report the residuals for each of the ten persons.
    e. What is the least squares error sum?

3. In a study of adolescent drug use, a social psychologist regresses the number of times marijuana has been smoked in the past month (Y) on the number of one's best friends who use marijuana at least once per week (X). The analysis yields the following regression equation: $\hat{Y}_i = 1.5 + 0.6X_i$.

    a. For every friend who uses marijuana at least weekly, how many more times is one predicted to use marijuana each month?

b. If one has five friends who use marijuana at least weekly, how many times is one predicted to use marijuana each month?

4. A college admissions office uses the following regression equation for predicting freshman grades in college (Y) from Scholastic Aptitude Test (SAT) scores (X): $\hat{Y}_i = 1.40 + 0.0002X_i$. If the college has a rule against admitting students likely to average C− or lower (1.5 GPA), what is the minimum SAT score a prospective student must have to gain admittance?

5. Given that $\overline{X} = 30$, $\overline{Y} = 25$, $N = 100$, $s_{XY} = 1,400$, $s_X = 40$ and $s_Y = 60$, what is the regression equation for predicting Y from X?

6. Fill in the missing values in the table below:

	SS_{TOTAL}	$SS_{REGRESSION}$	SS_{ERROR}
a.	−	210	120
b.	14.23	−	10.21
c.	123.73	90.12	−

7. For the data in problem 1, find (a) SS_{ERROR}, (b) $SS_{REGRESSION}$, (c) SS_{TOTAL} and (d) compute the coefficient of determination (R^2_{YX}).

8. A political scientist examining the relationship between the probability that one votes as a function of one's knowledge of key issues in the election finds that the coefficient of determination is 0.340. Given that the total sum of squares is 10,267, find (a) $SS_{REGRESSION}$ and (b) SS_{ERROR}.

9. Fill in the missing blanks in the table below:

	b	s_X	s_Y	r_{XY}
a.	−	20	30	0.20
b.	−2.3	4	22	−
c.	0.8	−	20	0.40
d.	1.4	30	−	0.60

10. Find β^* for the following:

	b	s_Y	s_X
a.	1.2	30	20
b.	−2.3	14.8	2.2
c.	0.43	0.94	0.42
d.	−2.44	12.6	2.5

11. In Problem 1, test for the significance of R_{YX}^2. Give the F ratio and state whether the null hypothesis that $\rho_{YX}^2 = 0$ may be rejected with $\alpha = .01$.

12. Test the following for significance at $\alpha = .05$:

	R_{YX}^2	N	SS_{TOTAL}
a.	0.20	15	450.50
b.	0.20	400	450.50
c.	0.10	20	240.60
d.	0.10	200	240.60

13. Test whether $\beta = 0$ in for the data in Problem 1. Set $\alpha = .05$.

14. Where $H_0: \beta = 0$, calculate t ratios and test hypotheses for the following:

	b	MS_{ERROR}	s_X^2	N	α
a.	1.6	2.20	6	24	.05
b.	−0.50	40.45	2.5	140	.01
c.	4.0	240.12	22.0	650	.005
d.	0.60	305.60	12.4	24	.05

15. Construct 95% confidence intervals around the b's given in Problem 14.

16. For the following data, using a two-tailed test, calculate the test statistics for the hypothesis that $\rho = 0$:

	r	N	α
a.	0.10	20	.05
b.	0.10	300	.05
c.	−0.45	25	.01
d.	0.30	350	.001
e.	−0.05	750	.05

Problems Requiring the 1987 General Social Survey

17. Some sociologists argue that the amount of education one has is related to the development of more liberal political and economic values. Test this argument by regressing one's self-rated political conservatism versus liberalism (POLVIEWS) on years of education (EDUC). Set $\alpha = .01$ to examine the significance of the regression coefficient. Use a one-tailed test. Interpret the results.

18. Many social scientists argue that the more contact one has with members of other races the more tolerant they are of having members of those races living close by. Test this hypothesis for whites only by examining the regression of belief in the right to a segregated neighborhood (RACSEG) on how close one lives to members of another race (RACDIS). Set $\alpha = .01$ to examine the significance of the regression coefficient. Use a one-tailed test. Interpret the results. [Recode RACSEG and RACDIS as follows: RECODE RACSEG RACDIS(1=4)(2=3)(3=2)(4=1).]

19. Some sociologists have argued that, counter to the perception provided by the mass media, the older one is, the happier one is. Test this hypothesis by regressing HAPPY on AGE. Set $\alpha = .01$ to examine the significance of the regression coefficient. Use a one-tailed test. Interpret the results. [Recode HAPPY as follows: RECODE HAPPY(1=3)(3=1)]

20. One might guess that those who earn less would be more in favor of government intervention to reduce income differences. Test this hypothesis by regressing EQWLTH on INCOME. Set $\alpha = .01$ to examine the significance of the regression coefficient. Use a one-tailed test. Interpret the results. [Recode EQWLTH as follows: RECODE EQWLTH (1=7)(2=6)(3=5)(5=3)(6=2)(7=1)]

21. Attitudes toward sexuality are usually hypothesized as varying as a function of one's religious beliefs. Test the hypothesis that attitudes against extramarital sexual behavior are positively related to religiosity by regressing XMARSEX on ATTEND. Set $\alpha = .005$ to examine the significance of the regression coefficient. Interpret the results. [NOTE: Recode XMARSEX as follows: RECODE XMARSEX (1=4)(2=3)(3=2)(4=1)]

Problems Requiring the 50-States Data Set

22. Construct a scatterplot of the relationship between the percentage of vehicles driven over 55 miles per hour (SPEED) and the death rate per million miles driven (FATALITY). What does the scattergram suggest about the relationship between speeding and fatalities on the highway?

23. What is the regression equation for the prediction of the death rate per million miles driven (FATALITY) from the percentage of vehicles driven over 55 miles per hour (SPEED)? Is the relationship significant at the $\alpha = .05$ level using an F test? How much of the variance in the death rate on the highways can be explained by speeding?

24. Some social scientists have argued that poverty and the amount of education go hand in hand, i.e. the less education the more poverty. Test this hypothesis by regressing POVERTY on HSGRAD using the $\alpha = .05$ level of significance using an F test.

25. Criminologists have several hypotheses for why urban areas have more murders than rural areas including the amount of education, the degree of overcrowding and anonymity in cities compared to rural areas, and so on. Test the hypothesis that the number of murders is dependent on degree of urbanization by regressing MURDER on URBAN using the $\alpha = .05$ level of significance using an F test.

26. Some policy makers have argued that one way to keep the number of children born out of wedlock down is to allow for a liberalization of abortion laws. Examine whether states with a higher proportion of abortions (ABORTION) have a lower proportion of out of wedlock births (WEDLOCK) using the $\alpha = .05$ level of significance using an F test.

Appendix A

The Use of Summations

1. Variables and Subscripts

In this text we use the letters X, Y, and Z to stand for *variables*. Variables have outcomes that can be kept track of through the use of *subscripts*. If we have N individuals in our sample, then X_i denotes the particular value or outcome observed for individuals, i. For example, if we have four persons in a sample, then the four outcomes associated with them are represented by X_1, X_2, X_3, and X_4.

2. Sums

Many of the statistical techniques used in this text depend on the *sum* of observations across the N individuals in the sample. The Greek symbol sigma (Σ) is used to stand for the sum of the values that immediately follow the summation sign. An index value below Σ indicates the lowest value the summation will take, and an index value above Σ indicates the highest value the summation will take. Therefore

$$\sum_{i=1}^{N} X_i$$

is read as "the sum of the N outcomes of X_i from X_1 to X_N," or

$$\sum_{i=1}^{N} X_i = X_1 + X_2 + X_3 + \ldots + X_N$$

Suppose we observe four individuals (i.e., $N = 4$), and the four outcomes are $X_1 = 2$, $X_2 = 6$, $X_3 = 0$, and $X_4 = 3$. Then we insert them:

$$\sum_{i=1}^{4} X_i = 2 + 6 + 0 + 3 = 11$$

The simplest use of the summation is in computing the *mean*, which is simply the average value across a set of observations. As you probably know, an average of this sort is computed by adding up all the outcomes and then dividing the sum by the number of observations.

$$\frac{\sum_{i=1}^{N} X_i}{N}$$

Or, in the example, the mean is computed as follows:

$$\frac{\sum_{i=1}^{4} X_i}{4} = \frac{11}{4} = 2.75$$

After you become familiar with the use of Σ and it becomes clear from the context that we are summing across all observations, we may use either $\sum_i X_i$ or ΣX_i instead of the longer $\sum_{i=1}^{N} X_i$ notation.

Sometimes variables are represented by more than a single subscript. This will be done for two reasons. The first is that we sometimes wish to represent not only an individual, i, but also a group, j, to which the person belongs (e.g., sex or religious identification). In this case the notation is X_{ij}. If the last observation in group j is notated by n_j, then the sum across the n_j individuals in group j is the following:

$$\sum_{i=1}^{n_j} X_{ij}$$

Written out, this is

$$\sum_{i=1}^{n_j} X_{ij} = X_{1j} + X_{2j} + X_{3j} + \ldots + X_{n_j j}$$

If we wish to sum across all J groups of n_j individuals, this is symbolized by

$$\sum_{j=1}^{J} \sum_{i=1}^{n_j} X_{ij}$$

And when written out, it is

$$\sum_{j=1}^{J} \sum_{i=1}^{n_j} X_{ij} = (X_{11} + X_{21} + \ldots + X_{n_{11}}) +$$

$$(X_{12} + X_{22} + \ldots + X_{n_{22}}) +$$

$$(X_{1J} + X_{2J} + \ldots + X_{n_{jJ}})$$

As an example, suppose we have three political groups where 1 = Republican, 2 = Democrat, and 3 = other, and there are four Republicans, three Democrats, and two others in the groups. We observe the following outcomes:

$i =$

		1	2	3	4
	1	3	4	2	3
$j = 2$		2	0	1	
	3	2	4		

Now if we want to sum the values of the Republicans (where $j = 1$), we have

$$\sum_{i=1}^{4} X_{i1} = 3 + 4 + 2 + 3 = 12$$

The sum of the "others" is

$$\sum_{i=1}^{2} X_{i3} = 2 + 4 = 6$$

Or, summing *all* observations across groups

$$\sum_{j=1}^{3} \sum_{i=1}^{n_j} X_{ij} = (3 + 4 + 2 + 3) + (2 + 0 + 1) + (2 + 4)$$

$$= 12 + 3 + 6 = 21$$

Where there is no ambiguity about the groups and individuals being summed across, we will also use $\Sigma\Sigma X_{ij}$ or $\Sigma\Sigma X_{ij}$, instead of the more cumbersome $\sum\limits_{j=1}^{J} \sum\limits_{i=1}^{n_j} X_{ij}$.

3. Rules of Summation

There are a few simple rules of summation that you should learn. If you do, you should have no difficulty with the few derivations presented in this book.

> *Rule 1:* The sum over a constant for N observations equals N times the constant. That is, if a is a constant, then

$$\sum_{i=1}^{N} a = Na$$

This may not seem intuitively obvious, but an example should make the rule clear. Suppose we have $N = 4$ observations, and each observation equals 5. Then $a = 5$ and

$$\sum_{i=1}^{4} a = (5 + 5 + 5 + 5) = (4)(5) = 20$$

We can also extend this rule, as shown by the following:

> *Rule 2:* If each observation is multiplied by a constant, the sum of the constant times the observations equals the constant times the sum of the observations.

$$\sum_{i=1}^{N} aX_i = a \sum_{i=1}^{N} X_i$$

For example, consider $a = 4$ and $X_1 = 2$, $X_2 = 6$, and $X_3 = 1$. Then

$$\sum_{i=1}^{3} 4X_i = 4 \cdot 2 + 4 \cdot 6 + 4 \cdot 1 = 4(2 + 6 + 1)$$

$$= 4 \sum_{i=1}^{3} X_i = 36$$

This rule can also be applied to double sums.

$$\sum_{j=1}^{J} \sum_{i=1}^{n_j} aX_{ij} = a \sum_{j=1}^{J} \sum_{i=1}^{n_j} X_{ij}$$

Rule 3: If the only operation to be carried out before a summation is itself a sum, the summation can be distributed.

This rule sounds more complex than it is. Consider the following example:

$$\sum_{i=1}^{3} (X_i + 2) = (X_1 + 2) + (X_2 + 2) + (X_3 + 2)$$

$$= (X_1 + X_2 + X_3) + (2 + 2 + 2)$$

$$= \sum_{i=1}^{3} X_i + \sum_{i=1}^{3} 2$$

$$= \sum_{i=1}^{3} X_i + (3)(2)$$

$$= \sum_{i=1}^{3} X_i + 6$$

A more general expression of this rule is

$$\sum_{i=1}^{N} (X_i \pm a) = \sum_{i=1}^{N} X_i \pm \sum_{i=1}^{N} a$$

$$= \sum_{i=1}^{N} X_i \pm Na$$

This last step, that $\sum_{i=1}^{N} a = Na$, follows from Rule 1. Note, however, that

$$\sum_{i=1}^{N} (X_i + a)^2 \neq \sum_{i=1}^{N} X_i^2 + \Sigma a^2$$

We can only distribute the summation sign when the term within the parentheses is itself a simple sum or difference.

If we expand the term $(X + a)^2$, we can then distribute the sum, as follows:

$$\Sigma(X_i + a)^2 = \Sigma(X_i^2 + 2aX_i + a^2)$$

$$= \Sigma X_i^2 + \Sigma 2aX_i + \Sigma a^2$$

Now it follows from Rules 1 and 2 that we can simplify this expression even further, to

$$\Sigma X_i^2 + 2a\Sigma X_i + Na^2$$

4. Sums of Two or More Variables

Sometimes we will want to examine sums of two or more variables at once. Suppose we ask what the sum of a product of two variables across N observations is.

> *Rule 4:* If each observation has a score on two variables, X_i and Y_i, then

$$\sum_{i=1}^{N} X_i Y_i = X_1 Y_1 + X_2 Y_2 + \ldots + X_N Y_N$$

Suppose there are three persons for whom we have observations on two variables, X and Y. The observations are

i	X_i	Y_j
1	2	1
2	4	-2
3	2	-3

Then

$$\sum_{i=1}^{3} X_i Y_i = (2)(1) + (4)(-2) + (2)(-3) = -12$$

Convince yourself, using this last example, that in general

$$\sum_{i=1}^{N} X_i Y_i \neq \Sigma X_i \Sigma Y_i$$

Thus, we *cannot* distribute a summation sign across products. But Rule 2 *does* apply to products.

$$\Sigma a X_i Y_i = a \Sigma X_i Y_i$$

This can be seen using the data from the example immediately above. Let $a = 3$; then

$$\sum_{i=1}^{3} 3 X_i Y_i = 3(2)(1) + 3(4)(-2) + 3(2)(-3)$$

$$= 3((2)(1) + (4)(-2) + (2)(-3)) = (3)(-12) = -36$$

$$= 3 \sum_{i=1}^{3} X_i Y_i$$

Rule 5: The sum of two or more variables equals
the sum of the sums of the variables.

$$\sum_i (X_{1i} + X_{2i} + \ldots + X_{ki}) = \sum_i X_{1i} + \sum_i X_{2i} + \ldots + \sum_i X_{ki}$$

Where

$X_1, X_2, \ldots X_k$ refers to k different variables.

A special case of this rule is

$$\sum_i (X_i + Y_i) = \sum_i X_i + \sum_i Y_i$$

Again using the data from the example above, we can show
this rule as follows:

$$\sum_{i=1}^{3} (X_i + Y_i) = (2 + 1) + (4 + (-2)) + (2 + (-3))$$

$$= (2 + 4 + 2) + (1 + (-2) + (-3)) = 4$$

$$= \sum_{i=1}^{3} X_i + \sum_{i=1}^{3} Y_i$$

Rule 6: For constants a and b,

$$\sum_i (aX_i + bY_i) = a\sum_i X_i + b\sum_i Y_i$$

Rule 6 is really derived from Rules 2 and 5. Rule 5 states
that we can distribute the summation sign across sums of variables, and Rule 2 states that we can pull a constant out in front
of a sum.

Again using the example data above, let $a = 2$ and $b = 4$.
Then

$$\sum_{i=1}^{3} (2X_i + 4Y_i) = ((2)(2) + (4)(1)) + ((2)(4) + (4)(-2))$$

$$+ ((2)(2) + (4)(-3))$$

$$= 2(2 + 4 + 2) + 4(1 - 2 - 3)$$

$$= 0$$

$$= 2\sum_{i=1}^{3} X_i + 4\sum_{i=1}^{3} Y_i$$

With this set of rules you should be able to follow the algebra used in this text. Our one piece of advice is not to be overwhelmed by sums. When in doubt about an equivalence, for example, try writing out the sums. They usually are not as complex as they seem.

Appendix B

Critical Values of Chi-Square

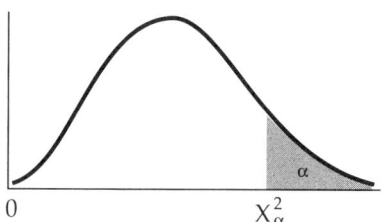

	Level of Significance (α)					
df	.100	.050	.025	.010	.005	0.001
1	2.7055	3.8414	5.0238	6.6349	7.8794	10.828
2	4.6051	5.9914	7.3777	9.2103	10.5966	13.816
3	6.2513	7.8147	9.3484	11.3449	12.8381	16.266
4	7.7794	9.4877	11.1433	13.2767	14.8602	18.467
5	9.2363	11.0705	12.8325	15.0863	16.7496	20.515
6	10.6446	12.5916	14.4494	16.8119	18.5476	22.458
7	12.0170	14.0671	16.0128	18.4753	20.2777	24.322
8	13.3616	15.5073	17.5346	20.0902	21.9550	26.125
9	14.6837	16.9190	19.0228	21.6660	23.5893	27.877
10	15.9871	18.3070	20.4831	23.2093	25.1882	29.588
11	17.2750	19.6751	21.9200	24.7250	26.7569	31.264
12	18.5494	21.0261	23.3367	26.2170	28.2995	32.909
13	19.8119	22.3621	24.7356	27.6883	29.8194	34.528
14	21.0642	23.6848	26.1190	29.1413	31.3193	36.123
15	22.3072	24.9958	27.4884	30.5779	32.8013	37.697
16	23.5418	26.2962	28.8454	31.9999	34.2672	39.252
17	24.7690	27.5871	30.1910	33.4087	35.7185	40.790
18	25.9894	28.8693	31.5264	34.8058	37.1564	42.312
19	27.2036	30.1435	32.8523	36.1908	38.5822	43.820
20	28.4120	31.4104	34.1696	37.5662	39.9968	45.315
21	29.6151	32.6705	35.4789	38.9321	41.4010	46.797
22	30.8133	33.9244	36.7807	40.2894	42.7956	48.268
23	32.0069	35.1725	38.0757	41.6384	44.1813	49.728
24	33.1963	36.4151	39.3641	42.9798	45.5585	51.179

continued

Source: Abridged from Table IV of Fisher and Yates: *Statistical Tables for Biological, Agricultural and Medical Research,* published by Longman Group Ltd. London (1974) 6th edition. (Previously published by Oliver & Boyd Ltd. Edinburgh) and by permission of the authors and publishers.

Critical Values of Chi-Square (Cont.)

df	.100	.050	.025	.010	.005	0.001
			Level of Significance (α)			
25	34.3816	37.6525	40.6465	44.3141	46.9278	52.620
26	35.5631	38.8852	41.9232	45.6417	48.2899	54.052
27	36.7412	40.1133	43.1944	46.9680	49.6449	55.476
28	37.9159	41.3372	44.4607	48.2782	50.9933	56.892
29	39.0875	42.5569	45.7222	49.5879	52.3356	58.302
30	40.2560	43.7729	46.9792	50.8922	53.6720	59.703
40	51.8050	55.7585	59.3417	63.6907	66.7659	73.402
50	63.1671	67.5048	71.4202	76.1539	79.4900	86.661
60	74.3970	79.0819	83.2976	88.3794	91.9517	99.607
70	85.5271	90.5312	95.0231	100.425	104.215	112.317
80	96.5782	101.879	106.629	112.329	116.321	124.839
90	107.565	113.145	118.136	124.116	128.299	137.208
100	118.498	124.342	129.561	135.807	140.169	149.449

Appendix C

Area under the Normal Curve

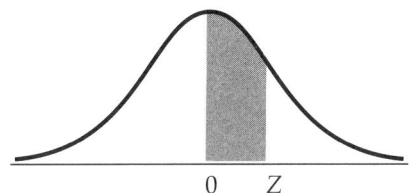

0   Z

z	.00	.01	.02	.03	.04	.05	.06	.07	.08	.09
0.0	.0000	.0040	.0080	.0120	.0160	.0199	.0239	.0279	.0319	.0359
0.1	.0398	.0438	.0478	.0517	.0557	.0596	.0636	.0675	.0714	.0753
0.2	.0793	.0832	.0871	.0910	.0948	.0987	.1026	.1064	.1103	.1141
0.3	.1179	.1217	.1255	.1293	.1331	.1368	.1406	.1443	.1480	.1517
0.4	.1554	.1591	.1628	.1664	.1700	.1736	.1772	.1808	.1844	.1879
0.5	.1915	.1950	.1985	.2019	.2054	.2088	.2123	.2157	.2190	.2224
0.6	.2257	.2291	.2324	.2357	.2389	.2422	.2454	.2486	.2517	.2549
0.7	.2580	.2611	.2642	.2673	.2704	.2734	.2764	.2794	.2823	.2852
0.8	.2881	.2910	.2939	.2967	.2995	.3023	.3051	.3078	.3106	.3133
0.9	.3159	.3186	.3212	.3238	.3264	.3289	.3315	.3340	.3365	.3389
1.0	.3413	.3438	.3461	.3485	.3508	.3531	.3554	.3577	.3599	.3621
1.1	.3643	.3665	.3686	.3708	.3729	.3749	.3770	.3790	.3810	.3830
1.2	.3849	.3869	.3888	.3907	.3925	.3944	.3962	.3980	.3997	.4015
1.3	.4032	.4049	.4066	.4082	.4099	.4115	.4131	.4147	.4162	.4177
1.4	.4192	.4207	.4222	.4236	.4251	.4265	.4279	.4292	.4306	.4319
1.5	.4332	.4345	.4357	.4370	.4382	.4394	.4406	.4418	.4429	.4441
1.6	.4452	.4463	.4474	.4484	.4495	.4505	.4515	.4525	.4535	.4545
1.7	.4554	.4564	.4573	.4582	.4591	.4599	.4608	.4616	.4625	.4633
1.8	.4641	.4649	.4656	.4664	.4671	.4678	.4686	.4693	.4699	.4706
1.9	.4713	.4719	.4726	.4732	.4738	.4744	.4750	.4756	.4761	.4767
2.0	.4773	.4778	.4783	.4788	.4793	.4798	.4803	.4808	.4812	.4817
2.1	.4821	.4826	.4830	.4834	.4838	.4842	.4846	.4850	.4854	.4857
2.2	.4861	.4864	.4868	.4871	.4875	.4878	.4881	.4884	.4887	.4890
2.3	.4893	.4896	.4898	.4901	.4904	.4906	.4909	.4911	.4913	.4916
2.4	.4918	.4920	.4922	.4925	.4927	.4929	.4931	.4932	.4934	.4936
2.5	.4938	.4940	.4941	.4943	.4945	.4946	.4948	.4949	.4951	.4952
2.6	.4953	.4955	.4956	.4957	.4959	.4960	.4961	.4962	.4963	.4964
2.7	.4965	.4966	.4967	.4968	.4969	.4970	.4971	.4972	.4973	.4974
2.8	.4974	.4975	.4976	.4977	.4977	.4978	.4979	.4979	.4980	.4981
2.9	.4981	.4982	.4982	.4983	.4984	.4984	.4985	.4985	.4986	.4986
3.0	.4987	.4987	.4987	.4988	.4988	.4989	.4989	.4989	.4990	.4990

Source: Abridged from Table I of *Statistical Tables and Formulas,* by A. Hald (New York: John Wiley & Sons, Inc., 1952). Reproduced by permission of A. Hald and the publishers, John Wiley & Sons, Inc.

Appendix D

Student's *t* Distribution

A. Two-tailed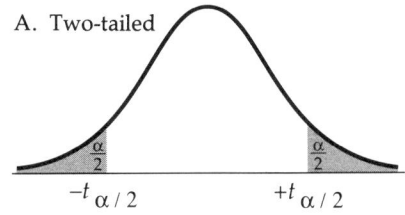

$-t_{\alpha/2}$ $+t_{\alpha/2}$

B. One-tailed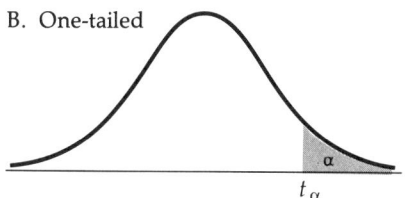

t_α

		Level of Significance for					
Two-tailed test	df	.20	.10	.05	.02	.01	.001
One-tailed test		.10	.05	.025	.01	.005	.0005
	1	3.078	6.314	12.706	31.821	63.657	636.619
	2	1.886	2.920	4.303	6.965	9.925	31.598
	3	1.638	2.353	3.182	4.541	5.841	12.941
	4	1.533	2.132	2.776	3.747	4.604	8.610
	5	1.476	2.015	2.571	3.365	4.032	6.859
	6	1.440	1.943	2.447	3.143	3.707	5.959
	7	1.415	1.895	2.365	2.998	3.499	5.405
	8	1.397	1.860	2.306	2.896	3.355	5.041
	9	1.383	1.833	2.262	2.821	3.250	4.781
	10	1.372	1.812	2.228	2.764	3.169	4.587
	11	1.363	1.796	2.201	2.718	3.106	4.437
	12	1.356	1.782	2.179	2.681	3.055	4.318
	13	1.350	1.771	2.160	2.650	3.012	4.221
	14	1.345	1.761	2.145	2.624	2.977	4.140
	15	1.341	1.753	2.131	2.602	2.947	4.073
	16	1.337	1.746	2.120	2.583	2.921	4.015
	17	1.333	1.740	2.110	2.567	2.898	3.965
	18	1.330	1.734	2.101	2.552	2.878	3.922
	19	1.328	1.729	2.093	2.539	2.861	3.883
	20	1.325	1.725	2.086	2.528	2.845	3.850
	21	1.323	1.721	2.080	2.518	2.831	3.819
	22	1.321	1.717	2.074	2.508	2.819	3.792
	23	1.319	1.714	2.069	2.500	2.807	3.767
	24	1.318	1.711	2.064	2.492	2.797	3.745
	25	1.316	1.708	2.060	2.485	2.787	3.725
	26	1.315	1.706	2.056	2.479	2.779	3.707
	27	1.314	1.703	2.052	2.473	2.771	3.690
	28	1.313	1.701	2.048	2.467	2.763	3.674
	29	1.311	1.699	2.045	2.462	2.756	3.659
	30	1.310	1.697	2.042	2.457	2.750	3.646
	40	1.303	1.684	2.021	2.423	2.704	3.551
	60	1.296	1.671	2.000	2.390	2.660	3.460
	120	1.289	1.658	1.980	2.358	2.617	3.373
	∞	1.282	1.645	1.960	2.326	2.576	3.291

Source: Abridged from Table III of Fisher and Yates: *Statistical Tables for Biological, Agricultural and Medical Research,* published by Longman Group Ltd. London (1974) 6th edition. (Previously published by Oliver & Boyd Ltd. Edinburgh) and by permission of the authors and publishers.

Appendix E
F Distribution

The *F* distribution table consists of three parts, for $\alpha = .05$, $\alpha = .01$, and $\alpha = .001$. These tables appear on the next three pages.

$\alpha = .05$

v_2 \ v_1	1	2	3	4	5	6	7	8	9	10	12	15	20	24	30	40	60	120	∞
1	161.4	199.5	215.7	224.6	230.2	234.0	236.8	238.9	240.5	241.9	243.9	245.9	248.0	249.1	250.1	251.1	252.2	253.3	254.3
2	18.51	19.00	19.16	19.25	19.30	19.33	19.35	19.37	19.38	19.40	19.41	19.43	19.45	19.45	19.46	19.47	19.48	19.49	19.50
3	10.13	9.55	9.28	9.12	9.01	8.94	8.89	8.85	8.81	8.79	8.74	8.70	8.66	8.64	8.62	8.59	8.57	8.55	8.53
4	7.71	6.94	6.59	6.39	6.26	6.16	6.09	6.04	6.00	5.96	5.91	5.86	5.80	5.77	5.75	5.72	5.69	5.66	5.63
5	6.61	5.79	5.41	5.19	5.05	4.95	4.88	4.82	4.77	4.74	4.68	4.62	4.56	4.53	4.50	4.46	4.43	4.40	4.36
6	5.99	5.14	4.76	4.53	4.39	4.28	4.21	4.15	4.10	4.06	4.00	3.94	3.87	3.84	3.81	3.77	3.74	3.70	3.67
7	5.59	4.74	4.35	4.12	3.97	3.87	3.79	3.73	3.68	3.64	3.57	3.51	3.44	3.41	3.38	3.34	3.30	3.27	3.23
8	5.32	4.46	4.07	3.84	3.69	3.58	3.50	3.44	3.39	3.35	3.28	3.22	3.15	3.12	3.08	3.04	3.01	2.97	2.93
9	5.12	4.26	3.86	3.63	3.48	3.37	3.29	3.23	3.18	3.14	3.07	3.01	2.94	2.90	2.86	2.83	2.79	2.75	2.71
10	4.96	4.10	3.71	3.48	3.33	3.22	3.14	3.07	3.02	2.98	2.91	2.85	2.77	2.74	2.70	2.66	2.62	2.58	2.54
11	4.84	3.98	3.59	3.36	3.20	3.09	3.01	2.95	2.90	2.85	2.79	2.72	2.65	2.61	2.57	2.53	2.49	2.45	2.40
12	4.75	3.89	3.49	3.26	3.11	3.00	2.91	2.85	2.80	2.75	2.69	2.62	2.54	2.51	2.47	2.43	2.38	2.34	2.30
13	4.67	3.81	3.41	3.18	3.03	2.92	2.83	2.77	2.71	2.67	2.60	2.53	2.46	2.42	2.38	2.34	2.30	2.25	2.21
14	4.60	3.74	3.34	3.11	2.96	2.85	2.76	2.70	2.65	2.60	2.53	2.46	2.39	2.35	2.31	2.27	2.22	2.18	2.13
15	4.54	3.68	3.29	3.06	2.90	2.79	2.71	2.64	2.59	2.54	2.48	2.40	2.33	2.29	2.25	2.20	2.16	2.11	2.07
16	4.49	3.63	3.24	3.01	2.85	2.74	2.66	2.59	2.54	2.49	2.42	2.35	2.28	2.24	2.19	2.15	2.11	2.06	2.01
17	4.45	3.59	3.20	2.96	2.81	2.70	2.61	2.55	2.49	2.45	2.38	2.31	2.23	2.19	2.15	2.10	2.06	2.01	1.96
18	4.41	3.55	3.16	2.93	2.77	2.66	2.58	2.51	2.46	2.41	2.34	2.27	2.19	2.15	2.11	2.06	2.02	1.97	1.92
19	4.38	3.52	3.13	2.90	2.74	2.63	2.54	2.48	2.42	2.38	2.31	2.23	2.16	2.11	2.07	2.03	1.98	1.93	1.88
20	4.35	3.49	3.10	2.87	2.71	2.60	2.51	2.45	2.39	2.35	2.28	2.20	2.12	2.08	2.04	1.99	1.95	1.90	1.84
21	4.32	3.47	3.07	2.84	2.68	2.57	2.49	2.42	2.37	2.32	2.25	2.18	2.10	2.05	2.01	1.96	1.92	1.87	1.81
22	4.30	3.44	3.05	2.82	2.66	2.55	2.46	2.40	2.34	2.30	2.23	2.15	2.07	2.03	1.98	1.94	1.89	1.84	1.78
23	4.28	3.42	3.03	2.80	2.64	2.53	2.44	2.37	2.32	2.27	2.20	2.13	2.05	2.01	1.96	1.91	1.86	1.81	1.76
24	4.26	3.40	3.01	2.78	2.62	2.51	2.42	2.36	2.30	2.25	2.18	2.11	2.03	1.98	1.94	1.89	1.84	1.79	1.73
25	4.24	3.39	2.99	2.76	2.60	2.49	2.40	2.34	2.28	2.24	2.16	2.09	2.01	1.96	1.92	1.87	1.82	1.77	1.71
26	4.23	3.37	2.98	2.74	2.59	2.47	2.39	2.32	2.27	2.22	2.15	2.07	1.99	1.95	1.90	1.85	1.80	1.75	1.69
27	4.21	3.35	2.96	2.73	2.57	2.46	2.37	2.31	2.25	2.20	2.13	2.06	1.97	1.93	1.88	1.84	1.79	1.73	1.67
28	4.20	3.34	2.95	2.71	2.56	2.45	2.36	2.29	2.24	2.19	2.12	2.04	1.96	1.91	1.87	1.82	1.77	1.71	1.65
29	4.18	3.33	2.93	2.70	2.55	2.43	2.35	2.28	2.22	2.18	2.10	2.03	1.94	1.90	1.85	1.81	1.75	1.70	1.64
30	4.17	3.32	2.92	2.69	2.53	2.42	2.33	2.27	2.21	2.16	2.09	2.01	1.93	1.89	1.84	1.79	1.74	1.68	1.62
40	4.08	3.23	2.84	2.61	2.45	2.34	2.25	2.18	2.12	2.08	2.00	1.92	1.84	1.79	1.74	1.69	1.64	1.58	1.51
60	4.00	3.15	2.76	2.53	2.37	2.25	2.17	2.10	2.04	1.99	1.92	1.84	1.75	1.70	1.65	1.59	1.53	1.47	1.39
120	3.92	3.07	2.68	2.45	2.29	2.17	2.09	2.02	1.96	1.91	1.83	1.75	1.66	1.61	1.55	1.50	1.43	1.35	1.25
∞	3.84	3.00	2.60	2.37	2.21	2.10	2.01	1.94	1.88	1.83	1.75	1.67	1.57	1.52	1.46	1.39	1.32	1.22	1.00

Source: Adapted from E. S. Pearson and H. O. Hartley, *Biometrika Tables for Statisticians*, 2nd ed. (Cambridge: Cambridge University Press, 1962).

$$\alpha = .01$$

ν_2 \ ν_1	1	2	3	4	5	6	7	8	9	10	12	15	20	24	30	40	60	120	∞
1	4052	4999.5	5403	5625	5764	5859	5928	5982	6022	6056	6106	6157	6209	6235	6261	6287	6313	6339	6366
2	98.50	99.00	99.17	99.25	99.30	99.33	99.36	99.37	99.39	99.40	99.42	99.43	99.45	99.46	99.47	99.47	99.48	99.49	99.50
3	34.12	30.82	29.46	28.71	28.24	27.91	27.67	27.49	27.35	27.23	27.05	26.87	26.69	26.60	26.50	26.41	26.32	26.22	26.13
4	21.20	18.00	16.69	15.98	15.52	15.21	14.98	14.80	14.66	14.55	14.37	14.20	14.02	13.93	13.84	13.75	13.65	13.56	13.46
5	16.26	13.27	12.06	11.39	10.97	10.67	10.46	10.29	10.16	10.05	9.89	9.72	9.55	9.47	9.38	9.29	9.20	9.11	9.02
6	13.75	10.92	9.78	9.15	8.75	8.47	8.26	8.10	7.98	7.87	7.72	7.56	7.40	7.31	7.23	7.14	7.06	6.97	6.88
7	12.25	9.55	8.45	7.85	7.46	7.19	6.99	6.84	6.72	6.62	6.47	6.31	6.16	6.07	5.99	5.91	5.82	5.74	5.65
8	11.26	8.65	7.59	7.01	6.63	6.37	6.18	6.03	5.91	5.81	5.67	5.52	5.36	5.28	5.20	5.12	5.03	4.95	4.86
9	10.56	8.02	6.99	6.42	6.06	5.80	5.61	5.47	5.35	5.26	5.11	4.96	4.81	4.73	4.65	4.57	4.48	4.40	4.31
10	10.04	7.56	6.55	5.99	5.64	5.39	5.20	5.06	4.94	4.85	4.71	4.56	4.41	4.33	4.25	4.17	4.08	4.00	3.91
11	9.65	7.21	6.22	5.67	5.32	5.07	4.89	4.74	4.63	4.54	4.40	4.25	4.10	4.02	3.94	3.86	3.78	3.69	3.60
12	9.33	6.93	5.95	5.41	5.06	4.82	4.64	4.50	4.39	4.30	4.16	4.01	3.86	3.78	3.70	3.62	3.54	3.45	3.36
13	9.07	6.70	5.74	5.21	4.86	4.62	4.44	4.30	4.19	4.10	3.96	3.82	3.66	3.59	3.51	3.43	3.34	3.25	3.17
14	8.86	6.51	5.56	5.04	4.69	4.46	4.28	4.14	4.03	3.94	3.80	3.66	3.51	3.43	3.35	3.27	3.18	3.09	3.00
15	8.68	6.36	5.42	4.89	4.56	4.32	4.14	4.00	3.89	3.80	3.67	3.52	3.37	3.29	3.21	3.13	3.05	2.96	2.87
16	8.53	6.23	5.29	4.77	4.44	4.20	4.03	3.89	3.78	3.69	3.55	3.41	3.26	3.18	3.10	3.02	2.93	2.84	2.75
17	8.40	6.11	5.18	4.67	4.34	4.10	3.93	3.79	3.68	3.59	3.46	3.31	3.16	3.08	3.00	2.92	2.83	2.75	2.65
18	8.29	6.01	5.09	4.58	4.25	4.01	3.84	3.71	3.60	3.51	3.37	3.23	3.08	3.00	2.92	2.84	2.75	2.66	2.57
19	8.18	5.93	5.01	4.50	4.17	3.94	3.77	3.63	3.52	3.43	3.30	3.15	3.00	2.92	2.84	2.76	2.67	2.58	2.49
20	8.10	5.85	4.94	4.43	4.10	3.87	3.70	3.56	3.46	3.37	3.23	3.09	2.94	2.86	2.78	2.69	2.61	2.52	2.42
21	8.02	5.78	4.87	4.37	4.04	3.81	3.64	3.51	3.40	3.31	3.17	3.03	2.88	2.80	2.72	2.64	2.55	2.46	2.36
22	7.95	5.72	4.82	4.31	3.99	3.76	3.59	3.45	3.35	3.26	3.12	2.98	2.83	2.75	2.67	2.58	2.50	2.40	2.31
23	7.88	5.66	4.76	4.26	3.94	3.71	3.54	3.41	3.30	3.21	3.07	2.93	2.78	2.70	2.62	2.54	2.45	2.35	2.26
24	7.82	5.61	4.72	4.22	3.90	3.67	3.50	3.36	3.26	3.17	3.03	2.89	2.74	2.66	2.58	2.49	2.40	2.31	2.21
25	7.77	5.57	4.68	4.18	3.85	3.63	3.46	3.32	3.22	3.13	2.99	2.85	2.70	2.62	2.54	2.45	2.36	2.27	2.17
26	7.72	5.53	4.64	4.14	3.82	3.59	3.42	3.29	3.18	3.09	2.96	2.81	2.66	2.58	2.50	2.42	2.33	2.23	2.13
27	7.68	5.49	4.60	4.11	3.78	3.56	3.39	3.26	3.15	3.06	2.93	2.78	2.63	2.55	2.47	2.38	2.29	2.20	2.10
28	7.64	5.45	4.57	4.07	3.75	3.53	3.36	3.23	3.12	3.03	2.90	2.75	2.60	2.52	2.44	2.35	2.26	2.17	2.06
29	7.60	5.42	4.54	4.04	3.73	3.50	3.33	3.20	3.09	3.00	2.87	2.73	2.57	2.49	2.41	2.33	2.23	2.14	2.03
30	7.56	5.39	4.51	4.02	3.70	3.47	3.30	3.17	3.07	2.98	2.84	2.70	2.55	2.47	2.39	2.30	2.21	2.11	2.01
40	7.31	5.18	4.31	3.83	3.51	3.29	3.12	2.99	2.89	2.80	2.66	2.52	2.37	2.29	2.20	2.11	2.02	1.92	1.80
60	7.08	4.98	4.13	3.65	3.34	3.12	2.95	2.82	2.72	2.63	2.50	2.35	2.20	2.12	2.03	1.94	1.84	1.73	1.60
120	6.85	4.79	3.95	3.48	3.17	2.96	2.79	2.66	2.56	2.47	2.34	2.19	2.03	1.95	1.86	1.76	1.66	1.53	1.38
∞	6.63	4.61	3.78	3.32	3.02	2.80	2.64	2.51	2.41	2.32	2.18	2.04	1.88	1.79	1.70	1.59	1.47	1.32	1.00

F Distribution (Cont.)

$\alpha = .001$

ν_2＼ν_1	1	2	3	4	5	6	7	8	9	10	12	15	20	24	30	40	60	120	∞
1	4053*	5000*	5404*	5625*	5764*	5859*	5929*	5981*	6023*	6056*	6107*	6158*	6209*	6235*	6261*	6287*	6313*	6340*	6366*
2	998.5	999.0	999.2	999.2	999.3	999.3	999.4	999.4	999.4	999.4	999.4	999.4	999.4	999.5	999.5	999.5	999.5	999.5	999.5
3	167.0	148.5	141.1	137.1	134.6	132.8	131.6	130.6	129.9	129.2	128.3	127.4	126.4	125.9	125.4	125.0	124.5	124.0	123.5
4	74.14	61.25	56.18	53.44	51.71	50.53	49.66	49.00	48.47	48.05	47.41	46.76	46.10	45.77	45.43	45.09	44.75	44.40	44.05
5	47.18	37.12	33.20	31.09	29.75	28.84	28.16	27.64	27.24	26.92	26.42	25.91	25.39	25.14	24.87	24.60	24.33	24.06	23.79
6	35.51	27.00	23.70	21.92	20.81	20.03	19.46	19.03	18.69	18.41	17.99	17.56	17.12	16.89	16.67	16.44	16.21	15.99	15.75
7	29.25	21.69	18.77	17.19	16.21	15.52	15.02	14.63	14.33	14.08	13.71	13.32	12.93	12.73	12.53	12.33	12.12	11.91	11.70
8	25.42	18.49	15.83	14.39	13.49	12.86	12.40	12.04	11.77	11.54	11.19	10.84	10.48	10.30	10.11	9.92	9.73	9.53	9.33
9	22.86	16.39	13.90	12.56	11.71	11.13	10.70	10.37	10.11	9.89	9.57	9.24	8.90	8.72	8.55	8.37	8.19	8.00	7.81
10	21.04	14.91	12.55	11.28	10.48	9.92	9.52	9.20	8.96	8.75	8.45	8.13	7.80	7.64	7.47	7.30	7.12	6.94	6.76
11	19.69	13.81	11.56	10.35	9.58	9.05	8.66	8.35	8.12	7.92	7.63	7.32	7.01	6.85	6.68	6.52	6.35	6.17	6.00
12	18.64	12.97	10.80	9.63	8.89	8.38	8.00	7.71	7.48	7.29	7.00	6.71	6.40	6.25	6.09	5.93	5.76	5.59	5.42
13	17.81	12.31	10.21	9.07	8.35	7.86	7.49	7.21	6.98	6.80	6.52	6.23	5.93	5.78	5.63	5.47	5.30	5.14	4.97
14	17.14	11.78	9.73	8.62	7.92	7.43	7.08	6.80	6.58	6.40	6.13	5.85	5.56	5.41	5.25	5.10	4.94	4.77	4.60
15	16.59	11.34	9.34	8.25	7.57	7.09	6.74	6.47	6.26	6.08	5.81	5.54	5.25	5.10	4.95	4.80	4.64	4.47	4.31
16	16.12	10.97	9.00	7.94	7.27	6.81	6.46	6.19	5.98	5.81	5.55	5.27	4.99	4.85	4.70	4.54	4.39	4.23	4.06
17	15.72	10.66	8.73	7.68	7.02	6.56	6.22	5.96	5.75	5.58	5.32	5.05	4.78	4.63	4.48	4.33	4.18	4.02	3.85
18	15.38	10.39	8.49	7.46	6.81	6.35	6.02	5.76	5.56	5.39	5.13	4.87	4.59	4.45	4.30	4.15	4.00	3.84	3.67
19	15.08	10.16	8.28	7.26	6.62	6.18	5.85	5.59	5.39	5.22	4.97	4.70	4.43	4.29	4.14	3.99	3.84	3.68	3.51
20	14.82	9.95	8.10	7.10	6.46	6.02	5.69	5.44	5.24	5.08	4.82	4.56	4.29	4.15	4.00	3.86	3.70	3.54	3.38
21	14.59	9.77	7.94	6.95	6.32	5.88	5.56	5.31	5.11	4.95	4.70	4.44	4.17	4.03	3.88	3.74	3.58	3.42	3.26
22	14.38	9.61	7.80	6.81	6.19	5.76	5.44	5.19	4.99	4.83	4.58	4.33	4.06	3.92	3.78	3.63	3.48	3.32	3.15
23	14.19	9.47	7.67	6.69	6.08	5.65	5.33	5.09	4.89	4.73	4.48	4.23	3.96	3.82	3.68	3.53	3.38	3.22	3.05
24	14.03	9.34	7.55	6.59	5.98	5.55	5.23	4.99	4.80	4.64	4.39	4.14	3.87	3.74	3.59	3.45	3.29	3.14	2.97
25	13.88	9.22	7.45	6.49	5.88	5.46	5.15	4.91	4.71	4.56	4.31	4.06	3.79	3.66	3.52	3.37	3.22	3.06	2.89
26	13.74	9.12	7.36	6.41	5.80	5.38	5.07	4.83	4.64	4.48	4.24	3.99	3.72	3.59	3.44	3.30	3.15	2.99	2.82
27	13.61	9.02	7.27	6.33	5.73	5.31	5.00	4.76	4.57	4.41	4.17	3.92	3.66	3.52	3.38	3.23	3.08	2.92	2.75
28	13.50	8.93	7.19	6.25	5.66	5.24	4.93	4.69	4.50	4.35	4.11	3.86	3.60	3.46	3.32	3.18	3.02	2.86	2.69
29	13.39	8.85	7.12	6.19	5.59	5.18	4.87	4.64	4.45	4.29	4.05	3.80	3.54	3.41	3.27	3.12	2.97	2.81	2.64
30	13.29	8.77	7.05	6.12	5.53	5.12	4.82	4.58	4.39	4.24	4.00	3.75	3.49	3.36	3.22	3.07	2.92	2.76	2.59
40	12.61	8.25	6.60	5.70	5.13	4.73	4.44	4.21	4.02	3.87	3.64	3.40	3.15	3.01	2.87	2.73	2.57	2.41	2.23
60	11.97	7.76	6.17	5.31	4.76	4.37	4.09	3.87	3.69	3.54	3.31	3.08	2.83	2.69	2.55	2.41	2.25	2.08	1.89
120	11.38	7.32	5.79	4.95	4.42	4.04	3.77	3.55	3.38	3.24	3.02	2.78	2.53	2.40	2.26	2.11	1.95	1.76	1.54
∞	10.83	6.91	5.42	4.62	4.10	3.74	3.47	3.27	3.10	2.96	2.74	2.51	2.27	2.13	1.99	1.84	1.66	1.45	1.00

*Multiply these entries by 100.

Appendix F
Fisher's r-to-Z Transformation

r	Z	r	Z	r	Z	r	Z	r	Z
.000	.000	.200	.203	.400	.424	.600	.693	.800	1.099
.005	.005	.205	.208	.405	.430	.605	.701	.805	1.113
.010	.010	.210	.213	.410	.436	.610	.709	.810	1.127
.015	.015	.215	.218	.415	.442	.615	.717	.815	1.142
.020	.020	.220	.224	.420	.448	.620	.725	.820	1.157
.025	.025	.225	.229	.425	.454	.625	.733	.825	1.172
.030	.030	.230	.234	.430	.460	.630	.741	.830	1.188
.035	.035	.235	.239	.435	.466	.635	.750	.835	1.204
.040	.040	.240	.245	.440	.472	.640	.758	.840	1.221
.045	.045	.245	.250	.445	.478	.645	.767	.845	1.238
.050	.050	.250	.255	.450	.485	.650	.775	.850	1.256
.055	.055	.255	.261	.455	.491	.655	.784	.855	1.274
.060	.060	.260	.266	.460	.497	.660	.793	.860	1.293
.065	.065	.265	.271	.465	.504	.665	.802	.865	1.313
.070	.070	.270	.277	.470	.510	.670	.811	.870	1.333
.075	.075	.275	.282	.475	.517	.675	.820	.875	1.354
.080	.080	.280	.288	.480	.523	.680	.829	.880	1.376
.085	.085	.285	.293	.485	.530	.685	.838	.885	1.398
.090	.090	.290	.299	.490	.536	.690	.848	.890	1.422
.095	.095	.295	.304	.495	.543	.695	.858	.895	1.447
.100	.100	.300	.310	.500	.549	.700	.867	.900	1.472
.105	.105	.305	.315	.505	.556	.705	.877	.905	1.499
.110	.110	.310	.321	.510	.563	.710	.887	.910	1.528
.115	.116	.315	.326	.515	.570	.715	.897	.915	1.557
.120	.121	.320	.332	.520	.576	.720	.908	.920	1.589
.125	.126	.325	.337	.525	.583	.725	.918	.925	1.623
.130	.131	.330	.343	.530	.590	.730	.929	.930	1.658
.135	.136	.335	.348	.535	.597	.735	.940	.935	1.697
.140	.141	.340	.354	.540	.604	.740	.950	.940	1.738
.145	.146	.345	.360	.545	.611	.745	.962	.945	1.783
.150	.151	.350	.365	.550	.618	.750	.973	.950	1.832
.155	.156	.355	.371	.555	.626	.755	.984	.955	1.886
.160	.161	.360	.377	.560	.633	.760	.996	.960	1.946
.165	.167	.365	.383	.565	.640	.765	1.008	.965	2.014
.170	.172	.370	.388	.570	.648	.770	1.020	.970	2.092
.175	.177	.375	.394	.575	.655	.775	1.033	.975	2.185
.180	.182	.380	.400	.580	.662	.780	1.045	.980	2.298
.185	.187	.385	.406	.585	.670	.785	1.058	.985	2.443
.190	.192	.390	.412	.590	.678	.790	1.071	.990	2.647
.195	.198	.395	.418	.595	.685	.795	1.085	.995	2.994

Appendix G

SPSS/PC+™ File for the 50-States Data Set

```
TITLE 'CREATE AN SPSS PC+ FILE FOR 50 STATES'.
DATA LIST FIXED/
IDNUMBER 1-2 DECK1 4 NAME 6-7(A) POPULAT 9-11 POPCHNG  13-16(1)
URBAN 18-21(1) BLACK 23-26(1) PCINCOME 28-30 AGE 32-35(1)
DIVORCE 37-39 HSGRAD 41-44(1) SCHOLEXP 46-47 MURDER 49-51
ROBBERY 53-56 BIRTHS 58-61 WEDLOCK 63-66(1) ABORTION 68-70
WELFARE 72-75(1) TURNOUT 77-80(1)/
IDNO 1-2 NAME2 4-5(A) SPEED 7-10(1) FATALITY 12-15(2)
VOTE 17-20(1) UNEMPLOY 22-25(1) WRKWMN 27-30(1) UNION 32-35(1)
RT2WORK 37 POVERTY 39-42(1) NEWS 44-46 ARTFUND 48-51(2)
PRISONER 53-55 POLICE 57-59 MFGING 61-64(1) GOVTL 66-69(1)
SERVICE 71-74(1) REGION9 76 REGION4 78.
MISSING VALUE DIVORCE(999) WEDLOCK (99.9) FATALITY (9.99).
VAR LABELS IDNUMBER 'STATE IDENTIFICATION NUMBER'/
           DECK1     'DECK 1'/
           NAME      'TWO-LETTER STATE NAME '/
           POPULAT   'POPULATION IN 100,000S'/
           POPCHNG   'POP CHANGE 1970-80 PER CENT '/
           URBAN     'LIVING IN URBAN AREAS PER CENT'/
           BLACK     'BLACK RESIDENTS PER CENT'/
           PCINCOME  'INCOME PER CAPITA $100'/
           AGE       'MEDIAN AGE IN YEARS'/
           DIVORCE   'DIVORCES PER 1,000 MARRIAGES'/
           HSGRAD    'HIGH SCHOOL GRADUATES PER CENT'/
           SCHOLEXP  'EXPENDITURES PER PUPIL $100'/
           MURDER    'MURDERS PER MILLION RESIDENTS'/
           ROBBERY   'ROBBERIES PER MILLION RESIDENTS'/
           BIRTHS    'CHILDREN PER 1,000 WOMEN 15-44 YRS'/
           WEDLOCK   'BIRTHS OUT OF WEDLOCK PER CENT'/
           ABORTION  'ABORTIONS PER 1,000 BIRTHS'/
           WELFARE   'SINGLE MOTHERS ON AFDC PER CENT'/
           TURNOUT   'VOTING IN 1980 ELECTION PER CENT'/
           IDNO      'STATE ID NO.'/
           NAME2     'STATE NAME'/
           SPEED     'VEHICLES OVER 55-M.P.H. PER CENT'/
           FATALITY  'DEATHS PER 100 MILLION MILES'/
           VOTE      'VOTES FOR REAGAN 1980 PER CENT'/
           UNEMPLOY  'LABOR FORCE UNEMPLOYED PER CENT'/
           WRKWMN    'WOMEN IN PAID LABOR FORCE PER CENT'/
           UNION     'NON-AGRIC. WORKERS UNIONIZED PER CENT'/
           RT2WORK   'STATE HAS RIGHT TO WORK LAW'/
           POVERTY   'PERSONS BELOW POVERTY LINE PER CENT'/
```

SPSS/PC+™ File for the 50-States Data Set (Cont.)

```
            NEWS      'DAILY NEWSPAPER CIRCULATION PER 1,000'/
            ARTFUND   'STATE FUNDS FOR ARTS AGENCIES $ PER CAPITA'/
            PRISONER  'FED + STATE PRISONERS PER 100,000 RESIDENTS'/
            POLICE    'POLICE EMPLOYEES PER 100,000'/
            MFGING    'EMPLOYED IN MANUFACTURING, NON-AGRIC PERCENT'/
            GOVTL     'EMPLOYED GOVERNMENT, NON-AGRIC PER CENT'/
            SERVICE   'EMP. SERVICE + FINANCE, ETC. PER CENT'/
            REGION9   'STATE LOCATED IN ONE OF NINE REGIONS'/
            REGION4   'STATE LOCATED IN ONE OF FOUR REGIONS'.
VALUE LABELS RT2WORK 0 'NONE' 1 'HAS RT2WORK LAW'/
    REGION9 1 'NEW ENGLAND' 2 'MID ATLANTIC' 3 'E.N. CENTRAL'
    4 'W.N. CENTRAL' 5 'S. ATLANTIC' 6 'E.S. CENTRAL'
    7 'W.S. CENTRAL' 8 'MOUNTAIN' 9 'PACIFIC'/
    REGION4 1 'NORTH EAST' 2 'NORTH CENTRAL' 3 'SOUTH' 4 'WEST'.
BEGIN DATA
01 1 AL  39 12.9 60.0 25.6   75 29.3 548 56.7 17 132 1321 1417 21.8 252 30.9 56.4
01 AL 53.7 3.28 48.8   8.8 47.2 21.8 1 18.9 192 0.14 149 230 26.7 22.1 19.4 6 3
02 1 AS   4 32.4 64.5   3.4 128 26.1 677 82.8 45  97  900 1346 13.9 292 55.8 56.8
02 AS 30.3 3.30 54.3   9.5 60.6 33.7 0 12.6 266 4.76 143 350  7.7 32.5 22.5 9 4
03 1 AZ  27 53.1 83.8   2.8  88 29.2 659 72.3 20 103 1936 1338 17.1 171 26.4 53.5
03 AZ 63.2 5.03 60.6   6.6 49.8 15.8 1 13.2 228  .11 160 310 15.3 20.1 26.1 8 4
04 1 AK  23 18.8 51.6  16.3  73 30.6 864 54.9 15  92  809 1514 19.6 173 36.5 57.2
04 AK 45.9 3.62 48.1   7.6 49.0 16.0 1 19.0 210  .39 128 190 28.2 18.9 19.6 7 3
05 1 CA 237 18.5 91.3   7.7 109 29.9 615 73.6 22 143 3842 1229 99.9 515 66.0 53.8
05 CA 61.7 3.52 52.7   6.8 53.8 27.0 0 11.1 254  .48  98 270 20.3 18.0 28.3 9 4
06 1 CO  29 30.7 80.6   3.5 100 28.6 533 78.1 25  69 1601 1195 12.3 345 35.0 63.4
06 CO 35.9 3.16 55.1   5.6 59.5 18.1 0 10.1 312  .25  96 270 14.5 19.4 26.4 8 4
07 1 CT  31  2.5 78.8   7.0 117 32.0 444 70.5 22  47 2180 1183 99.9 385 57.3 67.6
07 CT 48.8 2.87 48.2   5.9 56.0 22.9 0  8.0 292  .40  68 260 31.0 12.9 27.5 1 1
08 1 DL   6  8.6 70.7  16.1 103 29.7 523 67.8 26  69 1370 1264 22.9 399 50.0 60.4
08 DL 57.9 3.61 47.2   7.7 52.1 25.1 0 11.8 262  .29 183 280 27.5 17.4 23.3 5 3
09 1 FL  98 43.4 84.3  13.8  90 34.7 646 67.2 18 145 3555 1261 22.4 465 27.2 55.5
09 FL 57.6 9.99 55.5   6.0 45.8 11.7 1 13.4 270  .28 208 300 12.8 17.3 29.9 5 3
10 1 GA  55 19.1 62.3  26.8  81 28.7 485 56.5 17 138 1976 1389 99.9 409 27.3 53.5
10 GA 37.6 3.48 41.0   6.4 53.1 15.0 1 16.6 190  .24 219 240 24.0 20.1 21.2 5 3
11 1 HW  10 25.3 86.5   1.8 101 28.4 376 73.4 23  87 1902 1186 16.3 351 90.8 55.9
11 HW 38.7 3.29 42.9   5.0 56.7 27.9 0  9.3 247 2.04  65 290  5.9 22.0 32.9 9 4
12 1 ID   9 32.4 54.0   0.3  81 27.6 508 72.8 17  31  468 1561  7.0 124 38.9 70.1
12 ID 39.0 4.77 66.5   7.9 51.8 18.5 0 12.6 221  .12  87 240 16.6 20.8 25.6 8 4
13 1 IL 114  2.8 83.0  14.7 105 29.9 456 65.0 24 106 2170 1327 21.9 376 59.9 66.4
13 IL 45.0 3.08 49.6   8.3 52.6 30.6 0 11.0 249  .28  94 320 25.0 15.6 25.7 3 2
14 1 IN  55  5.6 64.2   7.6  89 29.2 999 65.9 19  89 1414 1388 14.6 168 34.5 61.6
14 IN 56.6 3.17 56.0   9.6 53.2 30.4 0  9.7 297  .23 114 210 30.8 16.6 20.5 3 2
15 1 IO  29  3.1 58.6   1.4  94 30.0 427 71.2 23  22  549 1369  9.4 111 64.6 67.7
15 IO 48.6 3.30 51.3   5.7 52.9 22.0 1 10.1 303  .11  86 200 22.2 18.8 24.2 4 2
16 1 KS  24  5.1 66.7   5.3 100 30.1 537 72.3 21  69 1131 1360 11.8 332 44.8 63.6
16 KS 58.1 3.44 57.9   4.4 56.1 15.4 1 10.1 253  .15 106 230 20.0 19.9 23.1 4 2
17 1 KY  37 13.7 50.8   7.1  76 29.1 495 51.9 16  88  952 1400 14.0 188 42.0 56.9
17 KY 43.1 3.25 49.1   8.1 50.0 24.0 0 17.6 207  .28  99 200 22.8 19.3 21.6 6 3
18 1 LA  42 15.3 68.6  29.4  85 27.4 999 58.0 18 157 1970 1483 22.8 170 40.4 63.9
18 LA 41.3 4.86 51.2   6.7 46.6 16.3 0 18.6 193  .48 211 290 13.5 19.5 21.6 7 3
19 1 ME  11 13.2 47.5   0.3  79 30.4 435 68.5 17  28  308 1356 12.7 252 71.7 68.2
19 ME 46.0 3.50 45.6   7.7 50.3 24.2 0 13.0 258  .19  61 200 27.0 19.8 22.9 1 1
20 1 MD  42  7.5 80.3  22.7 105 30.3 354 66.7 26  95 3927 1221 99.9 510 54.8 58.6
20 MD 27.0 2.71 44.2   6.4 57.1 22.6 1  9.8 167  .37 183 310 14.0 24.0 26.7 5 3
21 1 MA  57  0.8 83.8   3.9 101 31.2 336 72.7 26  41 2355 1110 14.8 602 79.4 65.6
21 MA 48.3 2.49 41.9   5.6 54.1 24.9 0  9.6 353  .70  56 290 25.4 15.5 30.1 1 1
22 1 MI  93  4.2 70.7  12.9 100 28.9 456 68.2 27 102 2440 1342 99.9 313 78.3 64.1
22 MI 47.9 2.86 49.0  12.6 50.4 37.4 0 10.4 264  .55 163 250 29.2 18.2 23.2 3 2
```

SPSS/PC+™ File for the 50-States Data Set (Cont.)

```
23 1 MN  41  7.1 66.8  1.3  97 29.2 400 72.4 24  26  991 1284 10.5 288 64.4 73.3
23 MN 55.2 3.03 42.6  5.7 59.1 26.2 0  9.5 250 .75  49 190 21.1 17.0 26.2 4 2
24 1 MS  25 13.7 47.3 35.2  66 27.4 480 55.1 16 145 810 1514 27.2  96 38.4 67.3
24 MS 52.6 4.22 49.4  7.5 48.5 16.3 1 23.9 158 .15 132 200 26.6 23.5 18.5 6 3
25 1 MO  49  5.1 68.1 10.5  90 30.9 500 63.7 19 111 2236 1334 16.9 220 50.6 67.3
25 MO 50.1 3.45 51.2  7.0 50.6 27.6 0 12.2 315 .51 112 280 22.1 17.2 25.6 4 2
26 1 MT   8 13.3 52.9  0.2  85 29.0 593 75.4 22  40 340 1416 99.9 250 31.4 67.6
26 MT 57.8 4.91 56.8  6.0 51.9 29.3 0 12.3 250 .12  94 240  8.5 25.3 24.6 8 4
27 1 NB  16  5.7 62.7  3.1  94 29.7 457 73.8 22  44 822 1309 10.8 177 44.3 63.3
27 NB 53.1 3.52 65.5  4.0 54.5 18.2 1 10.7 310 .28  89 220 15.2 20.8 25.5 4 2
28 1 NV   8 63.5 85.3  6.4 107 30.3 118 75.5 21  20 4606 1291 99.9 539 18.2 49.3
28 NV 56.0 5.67 62.5  6.2 59.1 23.8 1  8.7 278 .11 230 360  4.8 14.3 46.8 8 4
29 1 NH   9 24.8 52.2  0.4  91 30.1 562 72.0 19  25 420 1241 10.1 243 46.2 68.2
29 NH 35.1 3.02 57.7  4.7 57.3 15.8 0  8.5 213 .18  35 240 30.4 14.8 24.2 1 1
30 1 NJ  74  2.7 89.0 12.6 109 32.2 470 67.8 28  69 3037 1213 20.2 269 78.4 59.6
30 NJ 45.9 2.23 52.0  7.2 52.3 25.6 0  9.5 230 .41  76 350 25.6 17.2 25.0 2 1
31 1 NM  13 27.8 72.2  1.8  78 27.4 640 68.2 19 131 1279 1464 99.9 203 46.1 58.8
31 NM 67.4 5.42 54.9  7.4 46.9 18.9 0 17.6 210 .17 106 280  7.4 27.1 26.2 8 4
32 1 NY 176 -3.8 84.6 13.7 103 31.9 384 66.2 31 127 6413 1193 99.9 666 64.2 54.8
32 NY 45.4 3.35 46.7  7.5 47.7 38.7 0 13.4 449 1.90 123 370 20.1 18.2 32.3 2 1
33 1 NC  59 15.5 48.0 22.4  78 29.6 349 55.3 17 106 823 1288 18.5 349 30.1 52.2
33 NC 44.7 3.63 49.3  6.5 55.6  9.6 1 14.8 235 .24 244 220 34.5 17.2 18.3 5 3
34 1 ND   7  5.6 48.8  0.4  87 28.3 349 66.5 20  12  77 1338  8.3 168 41.8 71.9
34 ND 58.3 2.86 64.2  4.9 51.7 17.1 1 12.6 300 .15  28 180  6.5 24.8 24.4 4 2
35 1 OH 108  1.3 73.3 10.0  95 29.9 585 67.4 19  81 2237 1330 99.9 255 54.2 60.7
35 OH 55.2 2.82 51.5  8.4 50.5 31.5 0 10.3 305 .43 125 210 28.8 15.7 23.6 3 2
36 1 OK  30 18.2 67.3  6.8  91 30.1 521 66.7 19  51 1049 1392 14.0 227 35.6 59.4
36 OK 47.9 3.55 60.5  4.8 48.7 15.3 0 13.4 277 .29 151 230 16.7 19.8 22.4 7 3
37 1 OR  26 25.9 67.9  1.4  93 30.2 775 74.7 25  51 1524 1310 13.4 337 39.2 65.9
37 OR 38.1 3.38 48.3  8.2 53.8 26.0 0 10.7 267 .13 120 240 20.6 19.4 25.0 9 4
38 1 PA 119  0.6 69.3  8.8  94 32.1 365 64.5 25  68 1779 1230 17.2 407 80.3 54.9
38 PA 46.0 2.92 49.6  7.8 46.6 34.6 0 10.5 325 .24  68 240 27.9 15.3 26.0 2 1
39 1 RI   9 -0.3 87.0  2.9  94 31.8 503 60.7 25  44 1186 1140 14.3 440 66.6 64.7
39 RI 52.4 2.38 37.2  7.2 54.7 28.4 0 10.3 334 .43  65 280 32.1 15.0 26.1 1 1
40 1 SC  31 20.4 54.1 30.4  73 28.2 256 54.0 17 114 1181 1364 12.9 220 37.6 51.4
40 SC 45.5 3.78 49.4  6.9 51.2  7.8 1 16.6 193 .33 238 240 33.0 20.0 17.4 5 3
41 1 SD   7  3.6 46.4  0.3  78 28.9 316 68.5 17   7 201 1364 11.8 111 44.1 74.5
41 SD 50.0 3.68 60.5  4.7 55.3 14.7 1 16.9 252 .23  88 200 11.0 24.5 25.7 4 2
42 1 TN  46 16.9 60.4 15.8  77 20.1 512 55.4 15 108 1806 1358 19.0 324 33.8 56.7
42 TN 49.7 3.29 48.7  7.2 49.5 19.1 1 16.4 235 .11 153 210 29.1 18.2 21.1 6 3
43 1 TX 142 27.1 79.6 12.0  95 28.2 519 61.4 21 169 2085 1405 99.9 290 20.2 51.1
43 TX 64.7 4.01 55.3  5.2 52.3 11.4 1 14.7 242 .09 210 240 17.9 17.0 23.1 7 3
44 1 UT  15 37.9 84.4  0.6  76 24.2 466 80.3 21  38 802 1638  5.5  87 34.0 72.2
44 UT 61.9 3.09 72.8  6.2 51.6 17.8 1 10.3 190 .80  64 240 16.1 22.7 22.7 8 4
45 1 VT   5 15.0 33.8  0.2  78 29.4 486 70.5 20  22 389 1234 11.5 395 58.7 61.3
45 VT 54.9 3.73 44.4  6.4 54.8 18.0 0 12.1 231 .27  67 200 25.5 18.5 26.0 1 1
46 1 VA  53 14.9 66.0 18.9  94 29.8 392 62.5 20  86 1201 1236 18.4 426 32.7 55.2
46 VA 39.9 2.71 53.0  5.1 54.5 14.7 1 11.8 204 .24 161 230 19.4 24.0 23.2 5 3
47 1 WA  41 21.0 73.6  2.6 103 29.8 610 77.0 26  55 1351 1284 12.6 539 53.8 61.2
47 WA 48.9 3.34 49.7  7.5 52.3 34.4 0  9.8 287 .16 106 210 19.1 20.5 24.9 9 4
48 1 WV  19 11.8 36.2  3.3  78 30.4 568 56.6 19  71 485 1388 11.9  98 45.5 58.4
48 WV 48.4 5.03 45.3  9.4 39.1 34.4 0 15.0 242 .85  64 180 18.1 20.6 18.6 5 3
49 1 WI  47  6.5 64.2  3.9  93 29.4 436 70.0 24  29 707 1297 12.8 244 71.7 74.5
49 WI 50.2 3.11 47.9  7.0 56.3 28.6 0  8.7 260 .15  85 240 28.8 16.5 23.6 3 2
50 1 WY   5 41.6 62.8  0.7 109 27.1 582 77.8 28  62 444 1464  7.8  84 27.5 59.4
50 WY 57.5 4.89 62.6  3.9 55.5 18.6 1  7.9 206 .19 113 310  5.3 20.4 17.5 8 4
END DATA.
FREQUENCIES VARIABLES=ALL.
FINISH.
```

Glossary of Terms

A

ANOVA. See **analysis of variance.**

ANOVA summary table. A tabular display summarizing the results of an analysis of variance.

A posteriori comparisons. See **post hoc comparisons.**

A priori comparisons. See **planned comparisons.**

Alpha. The probability level for rejection of a null hypothesis when it is true, conventionally set at .05 or lower. Symbolized α.

Alpha error. See **Type I error (false rejection error).**

Alternative hypothesis. A secondary hypothesis about the value of a population parameter that often mirrors the research or operational hypothesis. Symbolized H_1.

Analysis of variance. A statistical test of the difference of means for two or more groups. Symbolized ANOVA.

Association. See **covariation; measures of association.**

Asymmetric measure of association. A measure of covariation where a conceptual and computational distinction between the independent and dependent variable is required, such as Somers's d_{yx}.

Asymmetry. A property of a distribution that exhibits skewness.

B

Bar chart. A type of diagram for discrete variables in which the numbers or percentages of cases in each outcome are displayed.

Beta. The probability level for failing to reject a null hypothesis when it is false. Symbolized β.

Beta coefficient. A standardized regression coefficient indicating the amount of net change, in standard deviation units, of the dependent variable for an independent variable change of one standard deviation. Symbolized β^*.

Beta error. See **Type II error (false acceptance error).**

Beta weight. See **beta coefficient.**

Between sum of squares. A value obtained by subtracting the grand mean from each group mean, squaring these differences for all individuals, and summing them. Symbolized SS_{BETWEEN}.

Bias. An inaccurate estimate of a population parameter as represented by a sample statistic.

Average

Average. See **mean; central tendency.**

Average deviation. The mean of the absolute values of the difference between a set of continuous measures and their mean. Symbolized AD.

Bivariate association. Covariation between two variables; measures of bivariate association include gamma, Yule's Q, tau c, phi, eta, the correlation coefficient, the odds ratio, and the bivariate regression coefficient.

Bivariate linear relationship. Covariation between two variables which can be represented by a straight line.

Bivariate regression coefficient. A parameter estimate of a bivariate regression equation that measures the amount of increase or decrease in the dependent variable for a one-unit difference in the independent variable.

C

Cells. Intersections of rows and columns in crosstabulations of two or more variables. Numerical values contained within cells may be cell frequencies, cell proportions, or cell percentages.

Central limit theorem. A mathematical theorem that states that if repeated random samples of size N are selected from a normally distributed population with mean = μ and standard deviation = σ, then the means of the samples will be normally distributed with mean = μ and variance = σ_Y^2/N as N gets large.

Central tendency. A value that describes the typical outcome of a distribution of scores.

Chi-square distribution. A family of distributions, each of which has different degrees of freedom, on which the chi-square test statistic is based.

Chi-square test. A test of statistical significance based on a comparison of the observed cell frequencies of a joint contingency table with frequencies that would be expected under the null hypothesis of no relationship. Symbolized χ^2.

Coefficient of determination. A PRE statistic for linear regression that expresses the amount of variation in the dependent variable explained or accounted for by the independent variable(s) in a regression equation. Symbolized R_{YX}^2.

Coefficient of nondetermination. A statistic that expresses the amount of variation in a dependent variable that is left *un*explained by the independent variable(s) in a regression equation. Symbolized $1 - R_{YX}^2$.

Column marginals. The frequency distribution of the variable shown across the columns of a crosstabulation.

Concept. A precise definition of an object, behavior, perception (self or other), or phenomenon that is theoretically relevant.

Concordant pairs. In a crosstabulation of two orderable discrete variables, the number of pairs having the same rank order of inequality on both variables. Symbolized n_s.

Conditional mean. The expected average score on the dependent variable, Y, for a given value of the independent variable, X.

Conditional odds. The frequency of an outcome occurring divided by the frequency of that outcome not occurring within a given category of a second variable.

Confidence interval. A range of values constructed around a point estimate that makes it possible to state the probability that the interval contains the population parameter between its upper and lower confidence limits.

Confidence intervals for mean differences. A confidence interval constructed around the point estimate of the difference between two population means.

Confidence limits. The extreme upper and lower values of a confidence interval.

Constant. A value that does not change.

Constructs. Unobserved concepts social scientists may use to explain observations.

Contingency table. See **crosstabulation.**

Continuous probability distributions. Probability distributions for continuous variables with no interruptions or spaces between the outcomes of the variables.

Continuous variables. Variables that, in theory, can take on all possible numerical values in a given interval.

Correlation coefficient. A measure of association between two continuous variables that estimates the direction and strength of a linear relationship.

Covariance. The sum of the product of deviations of the Xs and Ys about their respective means, divided by $N - 1$ in the sample or N in the population. Symbolized s_{XY} in the sample.

Covariation. Joint variation, or association, between a pair of variables.

Critical region. See **region of rejection.**

Critical value. The minimum value of a test statistic that is necessary to reject the null hypothesis at a given probability level. Symbolized c.v.

Cross classification. See **crosstabulation.**

Crosstabulation (joint contingency table). A tabular display of the joint frequency distribution of two discrete variables which has r rows and c columns.

Cumulative frequency. For a given score or outcome of a variable, the total number of cases in a distribution at or below that value.

Cumulative frequency distribution. A distribution of scores showing the number of cases at or below each outcome of the variable being displayed in the distribution.

Cumulative percentage. For a given score or outcome of a variable, the percentage of cases in a distribution at or below that value.

Cumulative percentage distribution. A distribution of scores showing the percentage of cases at or below each outcome of the variable being displayed in the distribution.

Curvilinear relationship. Covariation between two variables that is best fit by a curved rather than a straight line.

D

Data. The numbers or scores assigned to outcomes of variables in a given sample or population of observations.

Deduction. The process of deriving a conclusion about relationships among concepts by logical reasoning about their connections to common concepts.

Degrees of freedom. The number of values free to vary when computing a statistic. Symbolized df.

Dependent variable. A variable that has a consequent, or affected, role in relation to an independent variable.

Descriptive statistics. Numbers that describe features of a set of observations; examples are percentages, modes, variances, and correlations.

Diagrams. Visual representations of sets of data.

Dichotomous variables (dichotomies). Variables consisting of only two categories.

Direction of association. For continuous or orderable discrete variables, a pattern of association in which variables either positively covary (high scores coincide with the high scores on both measures and low scores coincide with the low scores on both measures) or negatively covary (high scores on one variable coincide with low scores on another variable, and vice versa).

Discordant pairs. In a crosstabulation of two orderable discrete variables, the number of pairs having reverse rank order of inequality on both variables. Symbolized n_d.

Discrete probability distributions. Probability distributions for discrete variables.

Discrete variables. Variables that classify persons, objects, or events according to the kind or quality of their attributes.

Dispersion. See **variation.**

E

Effect. The impact on a dependent variable of being in a certain treatment group. Symbolized α_j.

Equiprobable distribution. A probability distribution in which each outcome has an equal chance of occurrence.

Error sum of squares. A numerical value obtained in linear regression by subtracting the regression sum of squares from the total sum of squares. Symbolized SS_{ERROR}. See **within sum of squares**.

Error (residual) term. The difference between an observed score and a score predicted by the model.

Eta squared. A measure of nonlinear covariation between a discrete and a continuous variable; the ratio of $SS_{BETWEEN}$ to SS_{TOTAL}. Symbolized η^2.

Exhaustiveness. A property of a classification system that provides sufficient categories so that *all* observations can be located in some category.

Expected frequencies. In chi-square tests, the values that cell frequencies are expected to take, given the hypothesis under study (ordinarily, the null hypothesis).

F

F **distribution.** A theoretical probability distribution for one of a family of *F* ratios, having $J - 1$ and $N - J\,df$ in the numerator and denominator, respectively.

F **ratio.** A test statistic formed by the ratio of two mean-square estimates of the population error variance. Symbolized *F*.

False acceptance error. See **Type II error**.

False rejection error. See **Type I error**.

Frequency. The number of cases in a given outcome of a variable. Symbolized *f*.

Frequency distribution. A table of the outcomes of a variable and the number of times each outcome is observed in a sample.

G

Gamma. A symmetric measure of association for orderable discrete variables that takes into account only the number of untied pairs. Symbolized γ.

Goodness-of-fit test. The chi-square statistic applied to a single discrete variable, with $K - 1$ degree of freedom, where expected frequencies are generated on some theoretical basis.

Grand mean. In the analysis of variance, the mean of all observations. Symbolized μ.

Graph. See **diagrams**.

Grouped data. Data that have been collapsed into a smaller number of categories.

Grouping error. Error that arises from use of the midpoint of grouped frequency distributions to represent all scores in the measurement class.

H

Histogram. A type of diagram that uses bars to represent the frequency, proportion, or percentage of cases associated with each outcome or interval of outcomes of an ordered discrete variable.

Homoscedasticity. A condition in which the variances of two or more population distributions are equal.

Horizontal axis. In graphing, the horizontal line along which values of an independent variable, usually labeled X, are located; also called the *abscissa*.

Hypothesis. See **operational hypothesis**.

Hypothesis testing. A branch of statistics in which hypotheses are tested to determine whether the observed sample data have been generated by chance from a population in which the null hypothesis is true.

I

Independent random samples. Samples drawn according to random selection procedures, in which the choice of one observation for a sample does not affect the probability of another observation being chosen for a different sample.

Independent variable. A variable that has an antecedent, or causal, role in relation to a dependent variable.

Inference. The process of making generalizations or drawing conclusions about the attributes of a population from evidence contained in a sample.

Inferential statistics. Numbers that represent generalizations, or inferences, drawn about some characteristic of a population, based on evidence from a sample of observations from the population.

Intercept. A constant value in a regression equation that shows the point at which the regression line crosses the Y axis when values of X equal zero. Symbolized a.

J

Joint contingency table. See **crosstabulation.**

Joint frequency distribution. See **crosstabulation.**

L

Least squares. The sum of squared deviations of a set of scores about the mean that is a minimum.

Level of significance. See **probability level.**

Linear relationship. Covariation in which the value of the dependent variable is proportional to the value of the independent variable.

Lower confidence limit. The lowest value of a confidence interval.

M

Marginal distributions. The frequency distributions of each of two crosstabulated variables.

Mean. A measure of central tendency for continuous variables calculated as the sum of all scores in a distribution, divided by the number of scores; the arithmetic average. Symbolized $\overline{Y}$ in the sample.

Mean difference hypothesis test. A statistical test of a hypothesis about the difference between two population means.

Mean difference test. A statistical test of whether or not two means differ in the population.

Mean of a probability distribution. The expected value of a population of scores. Symbolized μ_Y.

Mean square. Estimate of variance used in the analysis of variance.

Mean square between. A value in ANOVA obtained by dividing the between sum of squares by its degrees of freedom. Symbolized MS_{BETWEEN}.

Mean square error. A value in linear regression obtained by dividing the error sum of squares by its degrees of freedom. Symbolized MS_{ERROR} or MS_{WITHIN}.

Mean square regression. A value in linear regression obtained by dividing the regression sum of squares by its degrees of freedom. Symbolized $MS_{\text{REGRESSION}}$.

Mean square within. A value in ANOVA obtained by dividing the within sum of squares by its degrees of freedom.

Measurement. The assignment of numbers to observations according to a set of rules.

Measurement classes (measurement intervals). Ranges of scores on variables into which observations are grouped.

Measurement intervals. See **measurement classes.**

Measures of association. Statistics that show the direction and/or magnitude of a relationship between variables.

Median. The value or score that exactly divides an ordered frequency distribution into equal halves; the value of the category of which the cumulative percentage equals 50%. Symbolized M.

Mode. The value of the category in a frequency distribution that has the largest number, or percentage, of cases.

Mutual exclusiveness. A property of a classification system that places each observation in one and only one category of a variable.

N

Negative relationships. A pattern of covariation in which high values of one variable are associated with low values of another variable, and vice versa.

Negative skew. A property of a frequency distribution whereby larger frequencies are found toward the positive end and smaller frequencies toward the negative end.

Nonorderable discrete variables. Discrete measures in which the sequence of categories cannot be meaningfully ordered.

Normal curves. See **normal distributions.**

Normal distributions. Smooth, bell-shaped theoretical probability distributions for continuous variables that can be generated from formulas.

Null hypothesis. A statistical hypothesis that one usually expects to reject. Symbolized H_0.

Null hypothesis about a single mean. A null hypothesis that the population mean is equal to or unequal to a specific value.

Number of cases. See **sample size.**

O

Observations. The outcomes of specific empirical cases under investigation.

Observed frequencies. The frequencies actually observed in the data in the chi-square test of independence and goodness-of-fit test.

Odds. The frequency of an outcome occurring divided by the frequency of that outcome not occurring.

Odds ratio (cross-product ratio). The ratio formed by dividing one conditional odds by another conditional odds.

One-tailed hypothesis test. A hypothesis test in which the alternative is stated in such a way that the probability of making a Type I error is entirely in one tail of a probability distribution.

Operation. Any method for observing and recording those aspects of persons, objects, or events that are relevant to testing a hypothesis.

Operational hypothesis. A proposition restated with observable, concrete referents or terms replacing abstract concepts.

Orderable discrete variable. Discrete measure in which the categories are arranged from smallest to largest, or vice versa.

Ordinary least squares. A method for obtaining estimates of regression equation coefficients that minimizes the error sum of squares. Symbolized OLS.

Outcomes. Response categories of a variable.

P

PRE measure of association. See **proportional reduction in error.**

p value. The probability of observing a test statistic under the assumption that the null hypothesis is true.

Pairs. The set of all possible pairs of observations in a sample, used in several measures of association for discrete orderable variables. See **tied cases; untied cases; concordant pairs; discordant pairs.**

Parameters. See **population parameters.**

Path of conditional means. A visual method used to help determine what kind of mathematical function best fits a bivariate scatterplot.

Pearson product-moment correlation coefficient. See **correlation coefficient.**

Percentage distribution. A distribution of relative frequencies or proportions in which each entry has been multiplied by 100.

Percentages. Numbers created by multiplying proportions by 100.

Percentaging rule. A rule that provides that in crosstabulation, percentages should be computed within categories of the independent variable.

Percentile. The outcome or score below which a given percentage of the observations in a distribution fall.

Phi. A symmetric measure of association for 2×2 crosstabulations, equivalent to the correlation coefficient. Symbolized ϕ.

Phi adjusted. A symmetric measure of association for 2×2 crosstabulations, in which phi is divided by phi maximum to take into account the largest covariation possible, given the marginals. Symbolized ϕ_{adj}.

Phi coefficient. See **phi.**

Phi maximum. The largest value that phi can attain for a given 2×2 crosstabulation; used in adjusting phi for its marginals. Symbolized ϕ_{max}.

Planned comparisons. Hypothesis tests of differences between and among population means carried out before doing an analysis of variance.

Point estimate. A sample statistic used to estimate a population parameter.

Point estimate for mean differences. The difference between the sample means used to estimate the difference between two population means.

Polygon. A diagram constructed by connecting the midpoints of a histogram with a straight line.

Population. A set of persons, objects, or events having at least one common attribute allowing a researcher to generalize on the basis of a representative sample of observations.

Population parameters. Descriptive characteristics of populations, such as means, variances, or correlations; usually designated by Greek letters.

Population regression equation. A regression equation for a population rather than a sample.

Positive relationship. A pattern of covariation in which high values of one variable are associated with high values of another variable, and low values of both variables are associated.

Positive skew. An asymmetrical frequency distribution characteristic whereby, in a graphic display, larger frequencies are found toward the negative end and smaller frequencies toward the positive end.

Post hoc comparisons. Hypothesis tests of the differences among population means carried out following analysis of variance.

Prediction equation. A regression equation without the error term, useful for predicting the score on the dependent variable from the independent variable(s).

Probability distribution. A set of outcomes, each of which has an associated probabil-

ity of occurrence.

Probability level. The probability selected for rejection of a null hypothesis, which is the likelihood of making a Type I error. Symbolized α.

Proportional reduction in error. A characteristic of some measures of association that allows the calculation of reduction in errors in predicting the dependent variable, given knowledge of its relationship to an independent variable. Symbolized PRE.

Proportions. Numbers formed by dividing the cases associated with an outcome of a variable by the total number of cases. Symbolized p. See **relative frequencies.**

Proposition. A statement about the causal connection between abstract concepts.

Q

Q. See **Yule's Q.**

R

R **squared.** See **coefficient of determination.**

r-to-*Z* **transformation.** A natural logarithm transformation in the value of the correlation coefficient to a Z score, to test the probability of observing r under the null hypothesis.

Random sample. A sample whose cases or elements are selected at random from a population.

Random sampling. A procedure for selecting a set of representative observations from a population, in which each observation has an equal chance of being selected for the sample.

Range. A measure of dispersion based on the difference between the largest and smallest outcomes in a distribution.

Ranked data. Orderable discrete measures in which each observation is assigned a number from 1 to N, to reflect its standing relative to the other observations.

Ranks. Positions occupied by observations in distributions when scores on some variable have been ordered from smallest to largest (or vice versa).

Recoding. Changing a range of codes or scores of a variable to have equal values.

Region of rejection. An area in the tail(s) of a sampling distribution for a test statistic determined by the probability level chosen for rejection of the null hypothesis.

Regression equation. See **regression model.**

Regression line. A line that is the best fit to the points in a scatterplot, computed by ordinary least squares regression.

Regression model. An equation for the linear relationship between a continuous dependent variable and one or more independent variables, plus an error term.

Regression sum of squares. A number obtained in linear regression by subtracting the mean of a set of scores from the value predicted by linear regression, squaring, and summing these values. Symbolized $SS_{\text{REGRESSION}}$.

Relationship. A connection between two concepts or variables that is the focus of social research.

Relative frequencies. Numbers formed by dividing the cases associated with an outcome of a variable by the total number of cases. See **proportions.**

Representativeness. The degree to which characteristics of a sample accurately stand for the population from which observations were selected.

Research hypothesis. See **operational hypothesis.**

Residual term. See **error term.**

Rounding. Expressing digits in more convenient and interpretable units, such as tens, hundreds, or thousands, by applying an explicit rule.

Row marginals. The frequency distribution of the variable shown across the rows of a crosstabulation.

S

Sample. A subset of cases or elements selected from a population.

Sample size. The number of cases or observations selected from a population for a specific sample. Symbolized N.

Sample statistics. See **statistics.**

Sampling distribution. A theoretical frequency distribution of a test statistic under the assumption that all possible random samples of a given size have been drawn from some population.

Sampling distribution of sample means. The population distribution of all possible means for samples of size N selected from a population.

Scatterplot. A type of diagram that displays the covariation of two continuous variables as a set of points on a Cartesian coordinate system.

Scope conditions. The times, places, or units of analysis for which a proposition is expected to be valid.

Scores. Numerical values assigned to empirical observations.

Significance. See **probability level.**

Significance testing with proportions. Using statistical tests to determine whether or not the observed difference between sample proportions could occur by chance in the populations from which the samples were selected.

Simple random sampling. A procedure for selecting cases from a population in which each observation has an equal chance of being selected.

Skewed distribution. A frequency distribution that is asymmetric with regard to its dispersion. See **positive skew; negative skew.**

Skewness. A property of a frequency distribution that refers to the degree of asymmetry. See **positive skew; negative skew.**

Social theory. A set of two or more propositions in which concepts referring to certain social phenomena are assumed to be causally related.

Somer's d_{yx}. An asymmetric measure of association for two orderable discrete variables that takes into account the numbers of untied pairs and of pairs tied only on the dependent variable. Symbolized d_{yx}.

Standard deviation. The square root of the variance. Symbolized s_Y for a sample.

Standard error. The standard deviation of a sampling distribution. Symbolized $\sigma_{\bar{Y}}$.

Standard normal distribution. The normal distribution of a Z variable (score).

Standard scores. See **Z scores.**

Standardized regression coefficient. See **beta coefficient.**

Statistics. Numerical characteristics of samples, usually designated by italic English letters.

Statistical hypothesis. A statement about one or more population parameters.

Statistical independence. A condition of no relationship between variables in a population.

Statistical significance. Significance of a relationship in a statistical sense, as indicated by rejection of a null hypothesis at a particular level. Because results can be due to a large sample size, statistical significance does not necessarily reveal practical importance. See **substantive significance.**

Statistical significance tests. Tests of inference that conclusions based on samples of observations also hold true for the populations from which the samples were selected.

Statistical tables. Numerical displays which either summarize data or present the results of data analyses.

Substantive significance. The practical importance of a research finding for theory, policy, or explanation, apart from its statistical significance. See **statistical significance.**

Sum of squares. See **between sum of squares; error sum of squares; regression sum of squares; total sum of squares; within sum of squares.**

Suspending judgment. A position taken by a researcher when the results of a statistical test permit neither clear rejection nor clear acceptance of the null or alternative hypotheses.

Symmetric measure of association. A measure of covariation where the distinction between independent and dependent variables is not required.

Symmetry. A property of a distribution that exhibits no skewness.

T

t distributions. One of a family of test statistics used with small samples selected from normally distributed populations or, for large samples, drawn from populations with any shape.

t scores. See **t variable.**

t test. A test of significance for continuous variables where the population variance is unknown and the sample is assumed to have been drawn from a normally distributed population.

t variable (t score). A transformation of the scores of a continuous frequency distribution derived by subtracting the mean and dividing by the estimated standard error.

Tally. A count of the frequency of outcomes observed for a variable or the frequency of joint outcomes of several variables.

Tau c. A symmetric measure of association for two orderable discrete variables with unequal numbers of categories that takes into account only the number of untied pairs. Symbolized τ_c.

Test of significance. A statistical method to determine the probability of an observed finding in a sample, given a null hypothesis about a population parameter.

Test statistic. A number used to evaluate a statistical hypothesis about a population, calculated from data on a sample selected from a population.

Theoretical probability distribution. A probability distribution for a set of theoretical observations.

Theory. See **social theory.**

Tied cases. In a crosstabulation of two orderable discrete variables, the number of pairs of cases with at least one row or column in common. Symbolized n_s and n_d.

Total sum of squares. A number obtained by subtracting the scores of a distribution from their mean, squaring, and summing these values. Symbolized SS_{TOTAL}.

Treatment level. A term in experimental research to indicate the experimental group to which a subject has been assigned.

True limits. The exact upper and lower limits of a measurement class or interval into which rounded values are grouped.

Two-tailed hypothesis test. A hypothesis test in which the region of rejection falls equally within both tails of the sampling distribution.

Type I error (false rejection error). A statistical decision error that occurs when a true null hypothesis is rejected; its probability is alpha.

Type II error (false acceptance error). A statistical decision error that occurs when a false null hypothesis is not rejected; its probability is beta.

U

Unbiased estimator. An estimator of a population parameter whose expected value equals the parameter.

Units of analysis. The general levels of social phenomena that are the objects of observations (e.g., individuals, nations).

Universe. See **population**.

Untied cases. In a crosstabulation of two orderable discrete variables, the sum of the number of concordant and discordant pairs. Symbolized $n_s + n_d$.

Upper confidence limit. The highest value of a confidence interval.

V

Variable. A characteristic or attribute of persons, objects, or events that differs in value across persons, objects, or events.

Variance. A measure of dispersion for continuous variables indicating an average of squared deviations of scores about the mean. Symbolized s_Y^2 in a sample.

Variance of a probability distribution. The expected spread or dispersion of a population of scores. Symbolized σ_Y^2.

Variation. The spread or dispersion of a set of scores around some central value.

Vertical axis. In graphing, the vertical line along which values of a dependent variable, usually labeled Y, are located; also called the *ordinate*.

W

Within sum of squares. A value obtained by subtracting each subgroup mean from each observed score, squaring, and summing. Symbolized SS_{WITHIN}.

Working hypothesis. See **operational hypothesis**.

Y

Y intercept. See **intercept**.

Yule's Q. A symmetric measure of association for 2 × 2 crosstabulations, equivalent to gamma. Symbolized Q.

Z

Z scores. A transformation of the scores of a continuous frequency distribution by subtracting the mean from each outcome and dividing by the standard deviation. Symbolized Z.

Z test. A test of significance for continuous variables where the sampling distribution is normally distributed and population variance is known.

List of Mathematical and Statistical Symbols

a	1. Frequency in the upper-left cell of a 2×2 crosstabulation.
	2. Intercept term in a regression equation for sample data.
$a < b$	a is less than b.
$a > b$	a is greater than b.
$a \leq b$	a is less than or equal to b.
$a \geq b$	a is greater than or equal to b.
AD	Average deviation.
α	1. Greek letter, lowercase *alpha*.
	2. Probability level for Type I error (false rejection error).
α_j	The effect of being in group j.
b	1. Frequency in the upper-right cell of a 2×2 crosstabulation.
	2. Regression coefficient for sample data.
β	1. Greek letter, lowercase *beta*.
	2. Probability of Type II error (false acceptance error).
	3. Regression coefficient in a population.
β^*	Beta coefficient, beta weight; standardized regression coefficient for a sample.
c	Frequency in the lower-left cell of a 2×2 crosstabulation.
c_p	Cumulative frequency up to but not including the interval containing P_i.
$c\%$	Cumulative percentage.

331

cf	Cumulative frequency.
C	1. Number of columns in a crosstabulation.
χ^2	Chi square (Greek letter, lowercase *chi*, squared).
χ^2_ν	Chi square with ν degrees of freedom.
c.v.	Critical value.
$\wedge$	Caret; estimated value of a parameter or variable.
d	Frequency in the lower-right cell of a 2×2 crosstabulation.
d_i	Deviation of ith observation from the mean.
d_{yx}	Somers's d, a measure of association.
df	Degrees of freedom.
e_i	Error term for the ith case in regression equation.
e_{ij}	Error term for ith case in jth group in the analysis of variance.
η	Greek letter, lowercase *eta*.
η^2	Eta squared, the correlation ratio.
f	Frequency, count, or tally.
f_i	Frequency of cases of type Y_i.
f_p	Frequency in the interval containing the ith percentile.
$\hat{f}_{ij}$	Expected frequency in row i and column j under null hypothesis of independence in a crosstabulation.
F	F ratio.
F_{ν_1,ν_2}	F ratio with ν_1 and ν_2 degrees of freedom.
G	Value of gamma in a sample.
GSS	General Social Survey.
γ	1. Greek letter, lowercase *gamma*. 2. A measure of association in a population.
H_0	Null hypothesis.
H_1	Alternative hypothesis.
H1	A numbered hypothesis.
i	A generic subscript value that may be replaced by actual numeric values.
$\neq$	Inequality sign ("does not equal").
∞	Infinity.
j	A generic subscript value that may be replaced by actual numeric values.
J	Number of subgroups or treatment groups in the analysis of variance.

K	Number of outcomes or categories in the distribution of a variable.
L_p	True lower limit of the interval containing the ith percentile.
M	Median.
m	The smaller of the number of rows or columns in a crosstabulation.
$Min(i,j)$	The lower of two numbers, i or j.
μ	Greek letter, lowercase mu.
μ_Y	Population mean of variable Y.
$\mu_{\bar{Y}}$	Mean of the sampling distribution of means for variable Y.
μ_{Y_0}	Population mean for variable Y under the null hypothesis.
μ_{Y_1}	Population mean for variable Y under the alternative hypothesis.
$\mu_{(\bar{Y}_2 - \bar{Y}_1)}$	Difference between the means of variables Y_1 and Y_2 in a population.
n_j	Number of observations in jth group.
n_d	Number of discordant untied pairs in computing association with discrete variables.
n_s	Number of concordant untied pairs in computing association with discrete variables.
N	Total number of observations in a sample.
N_i	Number of cases in subsample i.
$N \rightarrow \infty$	N (sample size) goes to infinity.
ν	1. Greek letter, lowercase nu. 2. Degrees of freedom for a χ^2 or t test of significance.
ν_1, ν_2	Number of degrees of freedom in an F test.
p	1. Proportion. 2. Probability of an event.
p_i	1. Proportion of cases in the ith category. 2. ith percentile written as a proportion.
$p(Y_i)$	Probability of outcome i for variable Y.
$p(|Z| \geq k)$	Probability that the absolute value of Z is equal to or greater than some number, k.
$p(a \leq Y_i \leq b)$	Probability that outcome i of variable Y lies between values a and b, inclusive.
P_i	Score of the ith percentile.
$P1$	A numbered proposition.

ϕ	1. Greek letter, lowercase *phi*.
	2. Phi, a measure of association in a 2×2 crosstabulation that equals the correlation coefficient.
ϕ_{adj}	Phi adjusted for marginal distributions.
ϕ_{max}	Maximum value of ϕ, given marginal distributions.
π	1. Greek letter, lowercase *pi*.
	2. A mathematical constant approximately equal to 3.14159.
%	Percent.
%ile	Percentile.
q	Probability of events not defined by p; $q = 1 - p$.
Q	Yule's Q, a measure of association in a 2×2 crosstabulation.
r	Correlation coefficient in a sample.
r_{XY}	Correlation coefficient between variables X and Y in a sample.
$r_{Z_X Z_Y}$	Correlation coefficient between standardized scores of variables X and Y.
R	Number of rows in a crosstabulation.
R^2	R squared, the sample coefficient of determination in a regression analysis.
R^2_{YX}	Coefficient of determination for the sample regression of variable Y on variable X.
$1 - R^2_{YX}$	Coefficient of nondetermination.
ρ	Greek letter, lowercase *rho*.
ρ_{XY}	Correlation coefficient between variables X and Y in the population.
ρ^2_{YX}	Coefficient of determination for the regression of variable Y on X in the population.
s_b	Estimated standard error for a regression coefficient.
s_p	Estimated standard error of sampling distribution of proportions.
$s_{(p_2 - p_1)}$	Estimated standard error of sampling distribution of the difference between two proportions.
s_Y	Sample standard deviation of variable Y.
s_{YX}	Covariance between variables X and Y.
s^2_Y	Variance of variable Y in a sample.
$s^2_{Z_Y}$	Variance of Y in standard-score (Z-score) form in a sample.

σ	Greek letter, lowercase *sigma*.
σ_b	Standard error for the regression coefficient, *b*.
σ_Q	Standard error for the sampling distribution of Yule's *Q*.
σ_Y	Standard deviation of variable *Y* in the population.
$\sigma_{\bar{Y}}$	Standard error of the sampling distribution of sample means for variable *Y*.
$\sigma_{(\bar{Y}_2 - \bar{Y}_1)}$	Standard error of the sampling distribution for difference between two means, Y_2 and Y_1.
$\sigma_{d_{yx}}$	Standard error for Somers's d_{yx}.
σ_e^2	Error variance in a population.
σ_Y^2	Variance of variable *Y* in a population.
$\sigma_{\bar{Y}}^2$	Variance of the sampling distribution of sample means for variable *Y*.
σ_Z^2	Variance of a *Z* score.
$\sigma_{\chi^2}^2$	Variance of a chi-square variable.
Σ	1. Greek letter, uppercase *sigma*. 2. Summation sign.
$\displaystyle\sum_{i=1}^{N} Y_i$	Sum of all scores on variable *Y* for observations from $i = 1$ to *N*.
$\displaystyle\sum_{j=1}^{J}\sum_{i=1}^{N} Y_{ij}$	Sum of all scores on variable *Y* for observations from $i = 1$ to *N*, for groups from $j = 1$ to *J*.
$\sqrt{}$	Square root, or radical sign.
t	Student's *t*.
t_c	Tau *c* for a sample.
t_{N-2}	*t* test with $N-2$ degrees of freedom.
t_α	Critical value of *t* for probability level α, one-tailed test.
$t_{\alpha/2}$	Critical value of *t* for probability level α, two-tailed test.
t_ν	*t* score with ν degrees of freedom.
T_c	Number of ties for the column variable in computing measures of association for discrete variables.
T_r	Number of ties for the row variable in computing measures of association for discrete variables.
τ	Greek letter, lowercase *tau*.
τ_c	Tau *c*, a measure of association in an R $\times$ C cross-tabulation when $R = C$.
θ	1. Greek letter, lowercase *theta*. 2. A general notation to designate any population parameter.

2×2	Crosstabulation of two dichotomous variables, creating a table with four cells, a, b, c, and d.
W_i	Width of the interval containing P_i, the ith percentile score.
X_i	Score or value of ith observation on variable X.
X_{1i}	Score or value of ith observation on variable X_1.
Y_i	Score of the ith observation on variable Y.
$\hat{Y}_i$	Expected score at the ith observation on variable Y; used in regression analysis.
$\overline{Y}$	Mean of variable Y in a sample.
$\overline{Y}_j$	Mean of the jth group on variable Y in a sample.
$\lvert Y \rvert$	Absolute value of variable Y.
Z_i	Standard score or Z score of the ith observation.
$Z_{(p_2 - p_1)}$	Z score of the difference between two populations, p_2 and p_1.
Z_r	Correlation coefficient r transformed to a Z score.
Z_α	Critical value of Z score for probability level α, one-tailed test.
$Z_{\alpha/2}$	Critical value of Z score for probability level α, two-tailed test.
Z_0	Z score for the null hypothesis test statistic.
Z_1	Z score for the alternative hypothesis test statistic.

Answers to Problems

1. The first and third statements are propositions because each gives an implied causal relation between two concepts. The second statement is not a proposition, but an operational definition of study time.

2. a. Concepts are study time and course grade; relationship is direct.
   b. Concept is study time; no relationship.
   c. Concepts are average course grade and starting salary; relationship is direct.

3. The more violent television programs a person watches, the more he or she supports capital punishment.

4. Some possible operational definitions of social power are (1) the amount of wealth controlled by a group; (2) the number of votes controlled by the group; and (3) the quantity of coverage of the group's demands in the mass media. There are many other possible operational definitions.

5. a. constant.   e. variable.
   b. variable.   f. constant.
   c. variable.   g. variable.
   d. constant.   h. variable.

6. a. independent—illegal drug profits; dependent—smuggling and dealing.
   b. independent—electoral competition; dependent—turnout.
   c. independent—age (generation); dependent—church attendance.

337

7. a. continuous.
   b. nonorderable discrete.
   c. orderable discrete.
   d. nonorderable discrete.
   e. continuous.
   f. orderable discrete.
   g. orderable discrete.
   h. continuous.

8. a. violates both mutually exclusive (European and English, Italian), and exhaustive (no categories for Latin American, Australian, etc.) criteria.
   b. Suggest using a list of some 100 nations from which Americans' ancestors came.

9. a. samples, populations.
   b. false.
   c. measures of association.
   d. statistical inference.

10. If the test results do not reject the research hypothesis, confidence in the proposition's truth value increases. If the hypothesis is rejected, the proposition may be modified or replaced by an alternative.

Answers to Chapter 2 Problems

1. a. Tally of fifth-grade pupils' recess activities:

Activity	Tally	Frequency
Marbles (M)	|||| |	6
Hopscotch (H)	||||	5
Jump rope (J)	|||| |	6
Talking (T)	||||	5
Other (O)	||	2
(N = 24)		

b. and c. Relative frequencies and percentages of recess activities:

Activity	f	p	%
M	6	.250	25.0
H	5	.208	20.8
J	6	.250	25.0
T	5	.208	20.8
O	2	.083	8.3
Total		1.000	100.0
(N = 24)			

d. Graph not shown.

2. American states classified by region:

Region	f	p	%
Northeast	9	.180	18.0
South	11	.220	22.0
North Central	17	.340	34.0
West	13	.260	26.0
Total		1.000	100.0
(N = 50)			

Graph not shown.

3. Statistics students classified by class rank:

Class	f	p	%
Senior	14	.424	42.4
Junior	12	.364	36.4
Sophomore	3	.091	9.1
Special	4	.121	12.1
Total	33	1.000	100.0

Histogram not shown.

4. Graphs not shown. The percentage of single adult households more than doubled, while dual adult households and households with three or more adults fell.

5. 507; 544; 367; and 48.

6. Graph not shown.

7. Cumulative distribution of contacts with the dead:

Frequency of contact	f	$c\%$
Never	834	57.7
Once or twice	337	81.0
Several times	200	94.9
Often	74	100.0
Total		100.0
(N = 1,445)		

Source: 1984 General Social Survey.

Graph not shown.

8. a. 1983, p = .344; 1984, p = .394; 1985, p = .416; 1986, p = .425; 1987, p = .423.
   b. Graph not shown. The proportion saying too much is spent on the military increased from 1983 to 1986 before levelling off.

9. 4 feet; 14 feet; 13 inches; 12 inches; 11 miles; 6 miles.

10. Cumulative distribution of being threatened or shot at by a gun:

Category	cf	$c\%$
Never	1,180	.806
Once	1,350	.922
Two or three	1,412	.964
Four or more	1,464	1.000
Total		1.000
(N = 1,464)		

Source: 1984 General Social Survey.

A large majority of adult Americans have never been threatened or shot at; fewer than 8% have been threatened or shot at more than once.

11. Types of organizations to which people belong:

Category	f_i	%
None	470	32.3
One	386	26.5
Two	254	17.4
Three	137	9.4
Four	85	5.8
Five	59	4.1
Six	27	1.9
Seven	18	1.2
Eight	11	.8
Nine	5	.3
Ten	2	.1
Sixteen	2	.1
Total		100.0
(N = 1,456)		

Source: 1987 General Social Survey.
Missing data = 10.

12. Support for freedom of speech:

	SPKRAC	SPKMIL	SPKHOMO
Allowed	61.8%	58.0%	69.6%
Not allowed	38.2	42.0	30.4
Total	100.0%	100.0%	100.0%
(N)	1,434	1,420	1,426
(Missing data)	(32)	(46)	(40)

Source: 1987 General Social Survey.

Speeches by homosexuals are the most tolerated, and those by militarists are the least tolerated.

13. Frequency of prayer by gender:

Prayer Frequency	Male	Female
Several times a day	17.8%	30.6%
Once a day	26.7	35.0
Several times a week	14.4	13.9
Once a week	11.6	6.8
Less than weekly	28.6	13.5
Never	1.0	.2
Total	100.0%	100.0%
(N)	(630)	(808)
(Missing cases)	(11)	(17)

Source: 1987 General Social Survey.

Women still pray more frequently than men.

14. Region of residence at age 16 and today:

REGION	REG16	REGION
Foreign	3.8%	0.0%
New England	5.0	5.3
Middle Atlantic	15.3	14.1
East North Central	20.3	18.9
West North Central	10.3	8.5
South Atlantic	14.9	18.3
East South Central	9.9	8.0
West South Central	7.4	8.0
Mountain	4.7	7.1
Pacific	8.4	12.1
Total	100.0%	100.0%
(N)	(1,466)	(1,466)

Source: 1987 General Social Survey.

The most noticeable changes involve movements away from the Midwestern regions toward the Southern and Western regions.

15. Voting in the 1984 presidential election by race:

PRES84	White	Black
Mondale	22.8%	46.6%
Reagan	42.7	7.3
Other	.4	.5
Refused	.2	1.0
Didn't vote	33.8	44.5
Total	100.0%	100.0%
(N)	(1,222)	(191)

Source: 1987 General Social Survey.

Whites voted for Reagan almost six times more often than did blacks.

16. There are 11 states below a million; 33 states between 1 and 10 million; and 6 states with 10 million or more.

17. State murder rates:

Murder rate per million	%
0–50	32.0
51–100	36.0
101–150	28.0
151–200	4.0
Total	100.0
(N)	(50)

Source: 50-States Data Set.

18. 1984 Reagan vote by states:

Vote percentage	c%
30.0–39.9	2.0
40.0–49.9	50.0
50.0–59.9	82.0
60.0–69.9	98.0
70.0–79.9	100.0
(N)	(50)

Source: 50-States Data Set.

Answers to Chapter 3 Problems

1. (a) The mode = 94, 95, and 109; median = 95; mean = 95.93; range = 31.
   (b) The mode = none; median = 26.3; mean = 24.5; range = 29.1.
   (c) The mode = none; median = 124.0; mean = 139.9; range = 188.

2. Firearms were the modal method for both sexes, although the distribution for women is almost bimodal, with solid or liquid poison close to firearms in frequency.

3. The mode = 2; median = 2; mean = 2.71; skew = positive; range = 9.

4. Average deviation = 8.58; variance = 113.90; standard deviation = 10.67.

5. (a) 9.42; (b) 10.16; (c) 59.13.

6. (a) 0; (b) 2; (c) 1.93; (d) 8; (e) 3.37; (f) 1.84; (g) +0.58.

7. (a) +5.00; (b) −1.67; (c) −2.67; (d) −1.54; (e) +2.00.

8. (a) 28.9; (b) 20.7; (c) 35.0; (d) 22.2.

9. (a) Y_{72} = .574; s_{72} = .495; Y_{80} = .716; s_{80} = .451; $\overline{Y}_{87}$ = .741; s_{80} = .438. The trend is for increasing favor of capital punishment.
   (b) p_{72} = .574; p_{80} = .716; p_{87} = .741. When a dichotomy is coded 0 and 1, then the mean equals the proportion of cases coded 1.

10. The mean tuition is higher at the private colleges ($10.83) than at the public schools ($6.17), but the dispersion is also greater (standard deviations are 2.32 and 1.47, respectively), suggesting that public school tuitions are less variable than private school tuitions.

11. The mean is 40.48; the median 40; the mode 50; the standard deviation 13.83; the variance 191.32; and the range 70.

12. (a) 12; (b) 12; (c) 20; (d) 12.53; (e) 10.12; (f) 3.18; (g) +0.46.

13. The mean for family is lower (2.10) than for friends (2.18), but the family variance (1.82) is larger than for friends (1.47), suggesting somewhat more satisfaction with one's family (since higher scores mean less satisfaction) although more variation in those ratings.

14. Democrats are the least conservative (mean = 3.69), followed by Independents (3.94), and Republicans (4.66).

15. Men express more happiness with marriage (mean = 1.33) than women (1.40), but less general happiness (1.73) than do women (1.67).

16. The mode = 64.2%; median = 67.1%; mean = 66.9%; range = 57.5; standard deviation = 14.4; variance = 207.4.

17. The mean = 3.54; standard deviation = .79. Z scores for Wyoming = +1.71; Texas = +.59; Connecticut = −.85; Rhode Island = −1.47. There appears to be some support for the hypothesis, but other states must also be examined.

18. The following results show higher levels of population increase in the South and West:

REGION4	Mean	s.d.	(N)
North East	6.17	9.36	(9)
North Central	4.64	1.68	(12)
South	17.36	8.38	(16)
West	32.57	13.89	(13)

Answers to Chapter 4 Problems

1. Frequency crosstabulation of vote by region:

Vote	Region		Total
	Sunbelt	Frostbelt	
Bush	80	90	170
Dukakis	50	120	170
Nonvoter	40	90	130
Total	170	300	470

Percentage crosstabulation of vote by region:

	Region		
Vote	Sunbelt	Frostbelt	Total
Bush	47.1%	30.0%	36.2%
Dukakis	29.4	40.0	36.2
Nonvoter	23.5	30.0	27.7
Total	100.0%	100.0%	100.1%*
(N)	(170)	(300)	(470)

*Does not equal 100.0 due to rounding.

Although Bush and Dukakis tied in the national totals, Sunbelt voters supported Bush and Frostbelt voters went for Dukakis. Nonvoters were more than a quarter of the sample—slightly higher in the Frostbelt than in the Sunbelt.

2. Expected frequencies for problem 1 under statistical independence:

	Region	
Vote	Sunbelt	Frostbelt
Bush	61.5	108.5
Dukakis	61.5	108.5
Nonvoter	47.0	83.0

3. a. Women and men work the same number of hours at home and on the job.
   b. Lower-class people drink as many alcoholic beverages as upper-class people.
   c. Homeowners in dry climates consume as much water as those in wet climates.
   d. Intensity of law enforcement effort is unrelated to illegal drug supply.

4.

	df	c.v.
a.	6	12.59
b.	12	21.03
c.	21	38.93
d.	12	32.91
e.	11	24.73
f.	120	>149.45
g.	12	32.91

5. a. 24.99.
   b. 30.58.
   c. 37.70.

6. $x^2 = 13.72$ for $df = 2$; reject H_0 at .005.

7. With a probability level set at traditional α levels (e.g., .05 or .01), one could not reject a null hypothesis of no difference in birth defects between children whose mothers did or did not take the drug. However, the critical factor is the probability of a Type II error, because failure to reject a false null hypothesis may allow a harmful substance to become available. Usually, public health officials would err on the side of caution by not permitting the drug to become available. In the case of Accutane, which was already on the market, and for which no equivalent substitutes were available, the government decided not to remove it from use but to increase warnings and raise awareness of potential harm among women users.

8. $x^2 = 117.71$, $df = 4$, reject H_0 at $\alpha = .001$.

9. $x^2 = 0.83$, $df = 1$. You can reject H_0 only at $\alpha > .10$.

10. Because the goodness-of-fit x^2 is 1.58 for $df = 5$, the null hypothesis that each face comes up with equiprobability (1/6, or 8.33 times out of 50 tosses) cannot be rejected at the $\alpha = .05$ level.

11. $x^2 = 15.85$, $df = 3$; reject the null hypothesis. Non-smokers are more likely to rate their health as excellent.

12. $x^2 = 2.39$, $df = 3$; do not reject the null hypothesis. Drunks and non-drunks are not significantly different in reported health.

13. $x^2 = 109.94$, $df = 6$; reject the null hypothesis. More-educated respondents disagree with racial segregation more than do the less-educated.

14. $x^2 = 4.36$, $df = 1$; reject the null hypothesis. Men are 5% more likely to favor capital punishment.

15. $x^2 = 91.87$, $df = 4$; reject the null hypothesis. While Protestants, Catholics, and others have similarly high levels of belief in a life after death, Jewish and nonreligious people have much lower levels of belief.

16. $x^2 = 8.19$, $df = 1$; reject the null hypothesis. States with fewer high school graduates have higher poverty rates.

17. χ^2 = 15.90, df = 1; reject the null hypothesis. States without right to work laws are more likely to have high levels of unionization compared to states with such laws.

18. χ^2 = 0.72, df = 1; do not reject the null hypothesis. Although higher death rates occur in states where more vehicles exceed the speed limit, the relationship is not statistically significant.

Answers to Chapter 5 Problems

1. Yule's Q = +.06. After converting to percentages, the table suggests that women were actually slightly more likely to vote for Reagan (60.4%) than were men (57.3%).

2. Yule's Q = +.43. This is a weak relationship, with persons having interracial contact more opposed to housing discrimination than persons without such contacts.

3. ϕ = +.190. ϕ_{adj} = +.247. Pro-choice attitudes are stronger among those with some college or more than among those having only a high school or less education.

4. ϕ = -.085. ϕ_{adj} = -.011. Almost no relationship exists between having been beaten and opposing a gun permit.

5. The odds in favor = 1.06, odds opposed = .36, odds neither = .28.

6. The odds in favor for better educated = 5.17, odds in favor for less educated = 1.44, odds ratio = 3.58.

7. The gamma = .62, t_c = .30. Excitement and happiness weakly covary.

8. The gamma = .19, t_c = .10. Almost no relation of nearness to God and happiness.

9. With health as dependent, Somer's d = .26, with life as dependent, Somer's d = .21.

10. Somer's d with job satisfaction as dependent = .15.

11. χ^2 = 11.50, df = 1; ϕ = .09. Men are more likely to smoke (35.7%) than women (27.3%).

12. χ^2 = 6.32, df = 2, gamma = .17; not significant at α = .01.

13. χ^2 = 108.7, df = 16; gamma = −.22, t_c = −.19.
Fundamentalists attend church more frequently than religious moderates or liberals.

14. χ^2 = 6.31, df = 2, not significant at α = .01. Somer's d = .07 with GETAHEAD dependent.

15. χ^2 = 122.77, df = 6. Somer's d = .20 with HOMOSEX dependent.

16. χ^2 = 20.48, df = 1, ϕ = .68, gamma = .93, t_c = .68, and Somer's d = .68 with ROBBERY dependent. This is a strong relationship.

17. χ^2 = 2.93, df = 1, ϕ = −.28, gamma = −.52, t_c = −.28, and Somer's d = −.28 with MFGING dependent. This is a moderate relationship.

18. χ^2 = 6.49, df = 1, ϕ = .40, gamma = .69, t_c = .40, and Somer's d = .40 with MURDER dependent. This is a moderate relationship.

Answers to Chapter 6 Problems

1. (a) 1/365; (b) 1/12; (c) 1/1461.

2. (a) 388/1466 = .265; (b) 22/1466 = .015.

3. (a) .4987; (b) .4773; (c) .4441; (d) .0987.

4. (a) 2.05; (b) 1.04; (c) 2.33; (d) −2.33, 2.33; (e) −1.42, 1.42; (f) −2.57, 2.57.

5. (a) .6826; (b) .9802; (c) .8716; (d) .5319.

6. (a) 10, .707; (b) 20.5, .447; (c) −5.5, 1.265; (d) 14, 1.414; (e) 20, 1.0.

7. (a) 30, .40; (b) 30, .20; (c) 30, .063.

8. (a) .90, .45, .15; (b) ≤ .0228.

9. (a) 50.25, 99.75; (b) 36.30, 113.70; (c) −0.26, 3.26; (d) 10.1, 19.9.

10. 38.35, 41.65, $t = -10.0$, c.v. = 1.71. Therefore reject the hypothesis that the dropout rate is 50%.

11. $t = 27.7$ and the c.v. = 2.33. Therefore reject the hypothesis that the mean IQ of freshmen is no higher than that for the population of all 18-year-olds.

12. (a) .475; (b) .400; (c) .490; (d) .4995; (e) .450; (f) .495.

13. (a) 1.725; (b) 2.528; (c) 1.697; (d) 2.042; (e) 2.131; (f) 2.576.

14. (a) .05; (b) .01; (c) .125; (d) .055.

15. (a) -6.45; (b) 3.70; (c) 3.83; (d) 13.13.

16. $t = 3.21$, but the c.v. = 2.797. Therefore reject the null hypothesis that the population mean is 5.00.

17. Aries = .096, Taurus = .070, Gemini = .090, Cancer = .083, Leo = .084, Virgo = .096, Libra = .091, Scorpio = .077, Sagittarius = .079, Capricorn = .078, Aquarius = .076 and Pisces = .080. The probability of observing a Libra is .091.

18. 12.528, 3.181, -1.42, 0.078.

19. $t = -4.73$. The c.v. = -2.58. Therefore reject the hypothesis that the mean is 4.00.

20. $t = -11.56$. The c.v. = -11.67. Therefore we reject the null hypothesis that people are "pretty happy" in favor of the alternative that they are happier than that.

21. No right-to-work law, .6; right to work law, .4.

22. 1.064, 0.305, 0.798.

23. $t = 8.00$. The c.v. is 2.01. Reject the hypothesis of no population change.

24. $t = 5.13$. The c.v. is 2.01. Reject the hypothesis that the poverty rate is 10% or less in favor of the alternative that over 10% of the population falls below the poverty line.

25. $t = 0.63$. The c.v. is 2.01. Cannot reject the null hypothesis that the high school graduation rate is two-thirds of the population.

Answers to Chapter 7 Problems

1. $H_0: \mu_R - \mu_N = 0$ and $H_1: \mu_R - \mu_N < 0$, where R = conventionally religious and N = not conventionally religious groups. A one-tailed test is required.

2. $H_0: \mu_P - \mu_N = 0$ and $H_1: \mu_P - \mu_N > 0$, where P = the group that has peers who engage in a given deviant behavior and N = the group that doesn't have peers who engage in it. A one-tailed test is required.

3. (a) .90; (b) .54; (c) .64; (d) .10.

4. (a) $-.77$, do not reject H_0; (b) -2.42, reject H_0; (c) -1.20, do not reject H_0; (d) 3.97, reject H_0.

5. $Z = .56$. Do not reject H_0.

6. $Z = 8.77$. Reject H_0.

7. 108.

8. 648.

9. (a) $LCD_{.95} = -0.025$ and $UCL_{95} = 0.045$; $LCD_{.99} = -0.036$ and $UCL_{99} = 0.056$; (b) $LCD_{.95} = .098$ and $UCL_{95} = .156$; $LCD_{.99} = .089$ and $UCL_{99} = .165$.

10. Since $t_{23} = -2.82$ and the c.v. $= -2.51$ for $df = 23$, reject H_0.

11. $t_{30} = 1.19$. Since the c.v. for 30 $df = 2.04$, do not reject H_0.

12. The point estimate of the difference is 0.16. The $LCL_{95} = .093$ and the $UCL_{95} = .227$. Reject the null hypothesis, because zero is not included in the confidence interval.

13. Reject the null hypothesis since $t = -4.88$. Those who are fundamentalists state that they feel closer to God than others.

14. Since $t = 1.76$ the null hypothesis cannot be rejected.

15. Reject the null hypothesis since $t = -13.83$. Those who have 16 years or more of education earn more income than those with under 16 years of education.

16. Since $t = -11.19$ the null hypothesis must be rejected. Democrats see themselves as less conservative than Republicans.

17. The null hypothesis cannot be rejected since $t = 2.50$. Interestingly, smokers see themselves as just as healthy as nonsmokers.

18. Since $t = -0.32$, one cannot reject the null hypothesis that there is no difference in the number of single mothers on welfare as a function of the number of babies born out of wedlock.

19. Since $t = -0.21$, one cannot reject the null hypothesis that there is no difference in voter turnout as a function of per capita income.

20. Must reject the null hypothesis since $t = -1.71$ thereby offering support to the hypothesis that speed is related to the number of fatalities.

21. Must reject the null hypothesis since $t = -2.64$ thereby offering support to the hypothesis that population change is related to the divorce rate.

22. Since $t = -1.43$, one cannot reject the null hypothesis that there is no difference between the amount of money for art as a function of per capita income.

Answers to Chapter 8 Problems

1. $H_0: \mu_{Ym} = \mu_{Yn}; H_1: \mu_{Ym} < \mu_{Yn}$.

2. $H_0: \mu_{Yw} = \mu_{Yo}; H_1: \mu_{Yw} > \mu_{Yo}$.

3. $\alpha_{cath} = 3.1; \alpha_{prot} = 0.5; \alpha_{jew} = -0.5; \alpha_{nri} = -2.4$.

4. $\alpha_{control} = 2.1; \alpha_{lo\ dose} = 1.9$ and $\alpha_{hi\ dose} = -4.0$.

5. (a) J random samples are independently drawn from normal distributions and (b) the variances are homoscedastic, i.e., the variance in the population is the same for all J treatment categories.

6. $MS_{BETWEEN}$ is a measure of the variance due to the treatment effects and MS_{WITHIN} is a measure of the error variance.

7. (a) $F_2 = 5.49$; (b) $F_3 = 5.29$; (c) $F_{1,\ 58} = 4.00$; (d) $F_{1,\ 28} = 4.20$.

8. (a) $F_{2, 27} = 3.35$; (b) $F_{2, 37} = 5.33$; (c) $F_{2, 67} = 7.76$; (d) $F_{2, 58} = 3.17$.

9. 4.0.

10. 6.4.

11. $\alpha_1 = -3.13$, $\alpha_2 = 0.07$ and $\alpha_3 = 3.07$. Since the c.v. = 3.89 for $\alpha = .05$, reject the null hypothesis. The ANOVA summary table is as follows:

Source	SS	df	MS	F
Between	96.133	2	48.067	24.9
Within	23.200	12	1.933	
Total	119.333	14		

$\hat{\eta}^2 = 0.806$. That is, 80.6% of the variance in SAT scores can be explained by the method of studying. (Obviously, this is a fictitious example!)

12. $\alpha_A = 0.17$, $\alpha_B = -2.17$, $\alpha_C = 3.33$ and $\alpha_D = -1.33$. Since the c.v. for 3 and 20 df is 3.10 and $F = 10.41$, reject the null hypothesis. The ANOVA summary table is as follows:

Source	SS	df	MS	F
Between	105.667	3	35.222	10.41
Within	67.667	20	3.383	
Total	173.333	23		

$\hat{\eta}^2 = 0.610$. That is, 61% of the variance in performance on the puzzle task can be explained by the type of reinforcer used.

13. $F_{4,1436} = 15.43$. Reject H_0 since the c.v. is 3.32. The results strongly suggest that those who are currently married are significantly happier than those who are widowed, divorced, separated, or those who have never married.

14. $F_{11,1441} = 2.60$. Do not reject H_0 since the c.v. is 2.85. Does not make sense to compute η^2 since the null hypothesis cannot be rejected.

15. $F_{1,1053} = 36.12$. Reject H_0 since the c.v. is 6.63. Vices do seem to be at least weakly related to each other since those who smoke also report having drunk too much as well. $\hat{\eta}^2 = 0.033$ indicating that only a small amount of the variance in drinking to excess can be explained by one's smoking behavior.

16. $F_{1,987} = 6.47$. Do not reject H_0 since the c.v. is 6.63. Though nearly significant, we cannot reject the null hypothesis that supervising someone else on one's job is unrelated to job satisfaction.

17. $F_{20,1373} = 13.55$. Reject H_0, since the c.v. is 1.88. The data suggest a modest relationship between education and income. $\hat{\eta}^2 = 0.165$ indicating that 16.5% of the variance in income can be explained by one's education.

18. $F_{1, 46} = 5.16$. Reject H_0 since the c.v. is 4.04. And $\hat{\eta}^2 = 0.101$ indicating that 10.1% of the variance in divorces by state can be explained by knowing whether a state is on the Pacific coast or not.

19. $F_{1,48} = 3.41$. Cannot reject H_0 since the c.v. is 4.04. Does not make sense to compute $\hat{\eta}^2$ since the test is not statistically significant. One cannot reject the hypothesis that abortions are distributed the same in Pacific coast states as in other states.

20. $F_{1,48} = 0.02$. Cannot reject H_0 since the c.v. is 4.04. Does not make sense to compute $\hat{\eta}^2$ since the test is not statistically significant. One cannot reject the hypothesis that the percentage of women in the work force is the same in both states that have and those that do not have right to work laws.

21. $F_{1,48} = 36.67$. Reject H_0 since the c.v. is 4.04. Furthermore, $\hat{\eta}^2 = 0.433$ indicating that 43.3% of the variance in the percentage of nonagricultural workers who are unionized can be explained by whether a state has right to work law or not.

22. $F_{1,48} = 0.04$. Cannot reject H_0 since the c.v. is 4.04. Does not make sense to compute $\hat{\eta}^2$ since the test of is not statistically significant. One cannot reject the null hypothesis that the percentage who voted in 1980 is unrelated to the percentage who graduated from high school.

Answers to Chapter 9 Problems

1. Scatterplot not shown. The more years of education one's father has, the higher one's estimated probability of attending college.

2. (a) $Y_i = -0.428 + 0.068\ X_i$; (b) 0.66; (c) 0.717; (d) -0.088, -0.052, 0.076, -0.016, 0.040, 0.112, 0.012, 0.140, 0.104, -0.328; (e) 0.1688.

3. (a) 0.6 times; (b) 4.5.

4. 500.

5. $Y_i = -1.25 + 0.875X_i$.

6. (a) 330; (b) 4.02; (c) 33.61.

7. (a) 0.1688; (b) 0.4402; (c) 0.6090; (d) 0.7228.

8. (a) 3,490.78; (b) 6,776.22.

9. (a) 0.30; (b) -0.418; (c)10; (d) $S_Y = 70$.

10. (a) 0.8; (b) -0.3419; (c) 0.1921; (d) -0.4841.

11. $F_{1,8} = 20.86$. Since c.v. = 11.26, reject H_0.

12. (a) $F_{1,13} = 3.25$. Since c.v. = 4.67, cannot reject H_0; (b) $F_{1,398} = 99.5$. Since c.v. = 3.84, reject H_0; (c) $F_{1,18} = 2.00$. Since c.v. = 4.41, cannot reject H_0; (d) $F_{1,198} = 22.0$. Since c.v. = 3.84, reject H_0.

13. $t_8 = 4.57$. Since c.v. = 2.31, reject H_0.

14. (a) $t_{22} = 12.67$. Since c.v. = 2.07, reject H_0; (b) $t_{138} = -1.47$. Since c.v. = 2.576, do not reject H_0; (c) $t_{648} = 30.84$. Since c.v. = 3.29, reject H_0; (d) $t_{22} = 0.58$. Since c.v. = 2.07, reject H_0.

15. (a) $LCL_{95} = 1.34$, $UCL_{95} = 1.86$; (b) $LCL_{95} = -1.17$, $UCL_{95} = 0.17$; (c) $LCL_{95} = 3.75$, $UCL_{95} = 4.25$; (d) $LCL_{95} = -1.55$, $UCL_{95} = 2.75$.

16. (a) $Z = 0.41$, do not reject H_0 since c.v. is 1.96; (b) $Z = 1.72$, do not reject H_0 since c.v. is 1.96; (c) $Z = -2.28$, do not reject H_0 since c.v. is -2.58; (d) $Z = 5.77$, reject H_0 since c.v. is 3.29; (e) $Z = -1.37$, do not reject H_0 since c.v. is -1.96.

17. $t_{1,1373} = -0.29$. The hypothesis is not supported since the c.v. is 2.33. There is no relationship between one's political liberalism and years of education.

18. $t_{1,1128} = -6.26$. The null hypothesis must be rejected since the c.v. is -2.33. The closer whites live to a member of the opposite race the less likely they are to think that they (whites) have a right to a segregated neighborhood.

19. $t_{1,1433}$ = 1.91. The hypothesis is not supported since the c.v. is 2.33. There appears to be no relationship between age and happiness.

20. $t_{1,1378}$ = 6.26. Reject the null hypothesis since the c.v. is 2.33. Those who earn less are more likely to favor government intervention to reduce income differences compared to those who earn more.

21. $t_{1,1432}$ = 10.8. The hypothesis is supported since the c.v. is 2.58. The more religious one is the more one is likely to believe that extramarital sex is wrong.

22. Scatterplot not shown. The scatterplot suggests that those states with a high percentage of speeders have more highway fatalities per capita than those states with a lower percentage of drivers who speed.

23. Y_i = 2.03 + 0.03X_i. Since $t_{1,47}$ = 3.38 and the c.v. is 2.01, the relationship is statistically significant. Speed can explain about 11% of the variance in deaths on the highway.

24. $F_{1,48}$ = 47.05. The hypothesis that poverty and education covary in a positive fashion is supported since the c.v. is 4.04.

25. $F_{1,48}$ = 3.11. The null hypothesis of no relationship between murder and urbanization cannot be rejected since the c.v. is 4.04.

26. $F_{1,48}$ = 3.90. The null hypothesis of no relationship between the number of abortions a state has and the number of births out of wedlock cannot be rejected since the c.v. is 4.04.

Index

BASIC SOCIAL STATISTICS

Typeset by Pam Frye Typesetting, Inc.,
Des Plaines, Illinois.

The typefaces are Palatino,
Futura Regular and Condensed.

Printing and binding by Arcata Graphics,
Kingsport, Tennessee.

Cover and internal design by Michael Welch,
Proof Positive/Farrowlyne Associates, Inc.,
Evanston, Illinois.